RED STRANGERS

Red Strangers

The White Tribe of Kenya

C. S. NICHOLLS

TIMEWELL
PRESS

First published in Great Britain in 2005 by
Timewell Press Limited
10 Porchester Terrace, London w2 3TL

ISBN 1 85725 206 3

Typeset by Antony Gray
Printed and bound in Great Britain by
Biddles Ltd, King's Lynn

Contents

For Isabel and Ian,
with love and admiration

Acknowledgements

This book could not have been written without the generous assistance of many people. Several of them kindly gave me interviews, others provided photographs, some gave me items of useful information, and yet others commented on the text or allowed me to read papers in their possession. Andreas Campomar, Joan Considine and Stephen North need special mention, and to all the following I am also profoundly grateful: Peter Ayre, Veronica Bellers, Juanita Carberry, David and Joan Christie-Miller, J. P. Cooper, Kathy Cuthbert, Anna Czyzewska, Peter and Elizabeth Fullerton, E. T. Funnell, John Golds, Kathini Graham, Zoe and Robin Horsfall, Lotte Hughes, Sir John Johnson, Tommy Joseph, Nick Klaprott, David Lichtenstein, Virginia Llewellyn Smith, Mary Lovell, Andrew Lownie, Ralph Lownie, Valerie McCabe, Fergus MacCartney, Mervyn Maciel, Neil McCormick, Hazel Macgregor, Geraldine Macoun, Elfrida Murray, Dorothy Myers, Elisabeth Richmond, Leontia Stephen, Willoughby Thompson, Elizabeth Tonkin and Henry Wright.

Rhodes House Library in Oxford (now the Bodleian Library of Commonwealth and African Studies) was a pleasure to work in and its librarians, John Pinfold and Alan Lodge, went out of their way to be helpful.

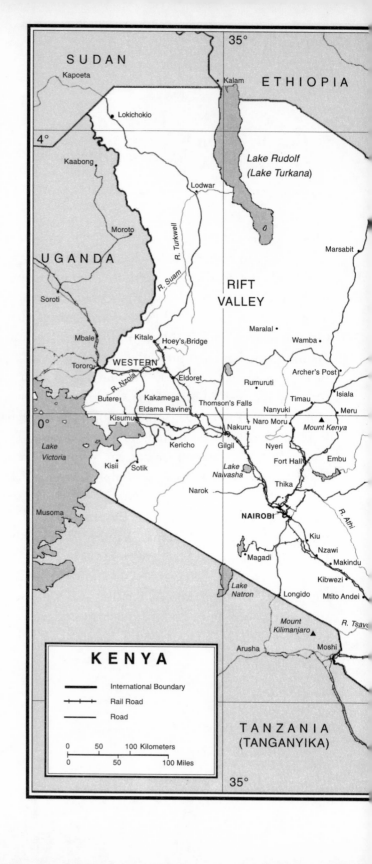

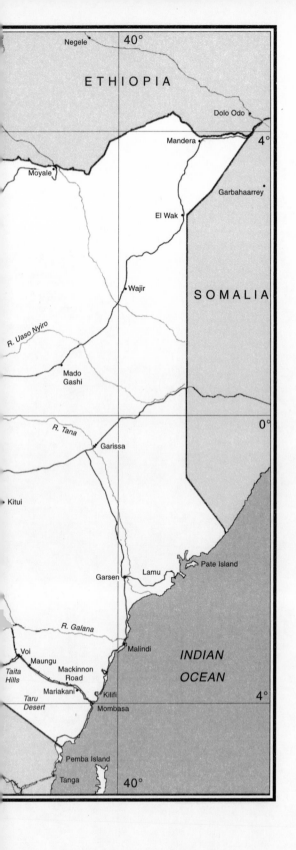

Introduction

Forty-two years ago, at the age of nineteen, I watched the stately lowering of the red, white and blue British union flag in Kenya, and the raising, to ecstatic applause, of the red, black, white and green standard of the new, independent Kenya. Ever since that chilly night in Nairobi, I have wanted to find out what had brought the whites to Kenya in the first place and why they stayed there for seventy years. I must declare an interest – I grew up and went to school in Kenya, and the colour of my skin is white. Can I therefore be impartial? I think I can, particularly as I was a child and young adult in Kenya and one's ideas are not fully formed then.

Now it is fashionable piously to disavow the colonial years. But, rather than condemn the whites, as has been the fashion, as an alien elite and the cause of every historical ill, I want to evaluate their real contribution to the development of Kenya. Their way of life is intrinsically interesting and important, and ought to be chronicled before the demise of all its witnesses.

What people forget today is that before 1950 the British empire was considered something we should be proud of. But after African countries became independent in the 1950s and 1960s the Western incursion into Africa was censured. There is indeed much to condemn. But the truth remains that there was a great deal of good, and too few people are prepared to stress this. I try to do so, while keeping in mind that the immigrants were as fallible as human beings everywhere.

I describe an adventurous, if often amateurish, attempt to transplant the British way of life into a wonderfully attractive region whose indigenous peoples themselves had a culture very difficult for the incomers to comprehend. The pioneers suffered immense danger and well nigh impossible conditions as they secured British control over the main trade route through what is now Kenya to the rich region of what became Uganda, the land round Lake Victoria.

These years involved terrible privations for the whites and for the hapless Africans who worked for them on walking caravans to Uganda. After the British Government took over responsibility for the region in 1895, there followed the most important stimulus to external settlement in Kenya: the building of a railway from Mombasa on the coast to Lake Victoria in the interior, to replace the inefficient walking caravans. The railway led to an influx of Indian labour and European engineers, overseers and administrators.

From then onwards, there arrived in increasing numbers administrative and military officers, missionaries, farmers who came to tame the harsh environment and had poverty as their constant companion, independent professionals (doctors, lawyers and teachers), businessmen and technical staff such as road and railway engineers. A white class system developed as people from different social strata formed friendships with those of their own kind. The coming of a few British aristocrats, some of them paid an allowance by their families to keep them out of their home country, led to an informal grouping called the 'Happy Valley' crowd, who caught the attention of a wider world. The antics of this wealthy and un-representative coterie, notorious for its licentious and irresponsible behaviour, have attracted all too much attention, whereas the real creators of what became the flourishing British colony of Kenya have languished in relative obscurity. It is one of my purposes to redress that balance.

Though white settlement in Kenya became a social organism, there were certainly contradictions and tensions within it. But at the same time the European inhabitants clung together when faced by threats from the indigenous African population and the ever-growing number of immigrants from India. I ask how the white population met these challenges, using interviews, letters, journals, and unpublished reminiscences and memoirs to illuminate the whites' everyday concerns and way of life. Oral evidence is evanescent, but I have been able to catch its last breaths. Many of the sources I use, such as letters and diaries, were written at the time, which gives them a freshness and immediacy lacking in later recollections.

Eventually Kenya's whites had to face up to the heart-breaking necessity of leaving their country and the impossibility of return, when Kenya became independent in 1963. Only a very few people failed to hear the clock strike. There was a large exodus of whites, but they had cast indelible shadows, and their influence echoes and reverberates even today. All of them left something of themselves in the land that had nurtured them.

The new exiles, particularly those born in Kenya, struggled with a loss of identity and culture. They tried to retain something of the latter by creating groups and societies in their adopted countries. Their reunions were always well attended. Yet, as members die, so the societies become ever smaller. Soon the culture may wither away, but here it is recorded for posterity so that it is not forgotten. No graves exist in Kenya for those who had to leave, but their footprints remain. As for the whites who died and are buried in Kenya, some of their graves are overgrown, some have disappeared entirely under the bush, and others are tended in cemeteries by young Africans born well after the white exodus who know nothing of colonial times. Perhaps this book will go some distance towards helping Africans to judge the contribution of the graves' occupants to the country now wholly theirs, towards understanding how and why Kenya was a corner of the British empire for over half a century. During the colonial period the voices of Africans were too little heard, or if noticed at all, too often ignored. There were reasons for this, though the subject is so vast it requires books of its own. Many have been written already, so the pieces of the jigsaw can be slotted into place and the colonial period in Kenya can be viewed as a whole. It is far too simplistic to see one side as villains and the other as heroes. Everyone made contributions, whether greater or lesser, to the story, one aspect of which – the story of the whites – is told here.

The Kikuyu people described the white men who came to their lands in the late nineteenth century as 'red strangers': hence the title of this book.

I

High Hopes and Valiant Hearts

One part of Africa was uncommonly resistant to penetration by European explorers and missionaries: the land which was to become Kenya. Yet the whites eventually entered this region in the 1890s, settled there, and developed a particular way of life which intrigued the rest of the world with its romanticism. Seventy years later they were ousted by the local Africans. How did this happen?

Whites came to Kenya because the area to the south, later called Tanganyika, was relatively easy of access, and in the 1850s white explorers marched 600 miles through it to find the sources of the Nile in a vast inland sea they named Lake Victoria, in honour of their queen. There they found several fertile and settled kingdoms straddling the headwaters of the Nile. One of the kings asked for British missionaries to be sent to him, to counter the Muslim influence infiltrating from the Sudanese region to the north. Christian missionaries, quick to seize an opportunity, hurried to the lake kingdoms to forestall rival Christian groups. So it was not long before both British and French missionaries settled in what later became Uganda.

Then in the 1880s Africa became the focus of European imperial ambitions. Many nations were staking claims in the continent, parcelling it out and drawing borders blind to tribal groupings. The British also wanted their share. Missionaries by Lake Victoria were already pressing for more support from home, and politicians, too, were casting glances lakewards. Now occupying Egypt, the British saw the River Nile as crucial to their strategy to control the Suez Canal. But unhappily for them, the Germans, in the person of Carl Peters, were showing far too conspicuous a curiosity in the little kingdoms around Lake Victoria. Yet further interest in Uganda came from imperialists dreaming of a Cape–Cairo railway, and humanitarians anxious to suppress the Indian Ocean slave trade at its source.

Already there were some European traders settled on the coast of East Africa, on the island of Zanzibar. Compared with the interior, the East African coast was a relatively sophisticated trading society that had been in contact with lands across the sea for centuries. There the enemy was not man but the mosquito.

From the 1840s onwards there were also two white missionaries, Johann Ludwig Krapf and Johann Rebmann, living on the coast a little to the north of Zanzibar, near the island of Mombasa. They failed singularly to convert the coastal people, Muslims in the towns and animists in the hinterland, to Christianity. So they turned to other interests. Their scholarly and enquiring minds wondered what existed in the African interior to their west. But they were wary of exploring this area because travellers brought back terrifying tales of the fearsome Wakwafi there, a pugnacious branch of the Maasai otherwise known as Oloikop, the scourge of all who tried to pass through their territory. Arab merchants on the coast told similar stories of murder and mayhem in Wakwafi country. Krapf and Rebmann took a risk and trekked inland. To their astonishment they saw two lofty mountains topped with snow – Mts Kenya and Kilimanjaro. Before that, though, their journeys passed through miles of waterless scrub, an even more effective barrier to the interior than the Wakwafi. It was these two factors – the desert and the hostility of Africans – which made Kenya one of the last of the lands to be penetrated by Europeans.

After missionaries settled in Uganda, trade was expected to follow, reversing the usual pattern of religion following trade. The white entrepreneurs in Zanzibar were already trying to exploit the coastal region of East Africa – the Germans the mainland opposite Zanzibar, and the British the area north of the River Umba. From 1887 a commercial venture known as the British East Africa Association was granted a concession by the Sultan of Zanzibar, giving it full judicial and political authority over his mainland possessions from the Umba river in the south to Kipini in the north, in return for paying him a proportion of the customs dues they were allowed to collect. Within a year of its inauguration the Association was claiming sovereign rights for 200 miles inland, and in 1888 it formed itself into the Imperial British East Africa Company (IBEAC).

Though the mainly Scottish IBEAC had capital of only £250,000, its grandiose ambition was to develop commercial opportunities in Uganda and along the East African coast. Unfortunately the distance between the two was 600 miles, and the only way to get to Uganda was to walk there through Tanganyika, carrying everything that was needed. But the Germans had signed a similar treaty as IBEAC with the Sultan of Zanzibar, giving them the coast from the Umba river southwards, so it would have been imprudent of the British Company to reach Uganda via the Tanganyika region. It therefore became imperative to map more direct routes further to the north, through what became Kenya.

After Krapf's and Rebmann's journeys inland, a few isolated Europeans had explored parts of the region, but no one found it suitable for trade. Frederic Holmwood, the British vice-consul at Zanzibar, had penetrated the interior from Mombasa to Taveta and Gustav Fischer was the first white man to reach the Rift Valley, in 1882. Joseph Thomson had travelled through Maasailand, the Rift Valley and the Uasin Gishu plateau on behalf of the Royal Geographical Society in 1883–84, while Harry Johnston had explored Kilimanjaro in 1884 for the Royal Society. Bishop James Hannington had undertaken a most hazardous journey through Kenya on his way to a Uganda mission, only to be murdered when he got there, in 1885. Helpful though the information from these men's writings was, IBEAC decided there was no alternative to sending an expedition to look for a feasible, safe route to Uganda as soon as possible.

The expedition was led by Frederick Jackson, a keen birdwatcher and ivory-hunter, a Cambridge man who had been travelling in East Africa since 1884, initially at the prompting of the writer Rider Haggard, brother of the British official stationed at Lamu, an island north of Mombasa. Several of Jackson's exploits were fictionalised in Rider Haggard's *She*. Jackson agreed to go to Uganda to make treaties with local potentates and bring back Emin Pasha, the pro-British governor of part of southern Sudan, now isolated after General Gordon's defeat in Khartoum.

In 1888 Jackson reached Mombasa, a tumbledown and somewhat decayed Swahili port on an offshore island, visited annually by about 400 dhows trading from Arabia and India on the monsoon winds. The Imperial British East Africa Company had already established itself in a small way there, despite the hostility of local Arab and Swahili traders. It had acquired offices and living quarters for its personnel in a stone building called Leven House overlooking the harbour, and had begun to build its own offices and port works in the town, where houses were all jumbled together in a maze of narrow streets, and piles of rotting rubbish exuded evil smells. The whitewashed buildings were of coral rag and lime. Behind the town, narrow footpaths straggled over the rest of the small island through baobabs, coconut palms and mango trees, and scrub struggling for life in the parched coral ground. There was also an African village of mud-and-wattle huts on the island. On the main-land beside Mombasa lay missionary settlements, one at Rabai, a few miles inland, and one at Freretown, or Kisauni, a place of refuge for freed and runaway slaves, on the northern mainland overlooking the island. The missionaries did not mix with Company officials, who could get cold lunches at M. R. de Souza's store, which thus became a meeting place for all non-missionary whites on the island of Mombasa.

Jackson was supposed to leave for Uganda in the last quarter of 1888 but did not start properly until 23 May 1889, due to difficulties with providing equipment, food and porters. Meanwhile he was stuck at Nzawi, 200 miles from the coast, awaiting supplies. After returning to the coast to sort things out, Jackson set off again, this time with Ernest Gedge, a former tea-planter in Assam and now an IBEAC employee, the son of the Revd Augustus Gedge of Ludborough, Lincolnshire. The other two white men on the trip were C. S. Latrobe Bateman, another IBEAC employee, and James Martin, whose real name was Antonio Martini, an illiterate Maltese sail-maker born in 1857. He had gone to Zanzibar on an American ship and now earned a living as a guide for explorers and the occasional sportsman. Everyone loved 'little Martin', a superb organiser of caravans and the most affable of men. 'To the day of his death in September 1924,' said Jackson, 'I doubt if anyone had a more devoted and loyal friend than I had in that little man.'[1] Jackson tried, but failed, to teach Martin to read and write. Martin was a good choice for this trek because he had escorted Joseph Thomson on his journey to the interior.[2]

There already existed a caravan route to the interior through the Kenya region, regularly used by Arab and Swahili expeditions in search of slaves and ivory. It was a single, winding track, over 700 miles long and full of peril. As the prevalence of the tsetse fly prohibited animal transport, everything was carried along the track by slave porters. Jackson and Gedge, owning no slaves of course, had to recruit porters on the coast, but few coastal Africans wanted to hazard their lives and health on a gruelling trek of 700 miles and the same distance back, a journey which lasted five months. A solution was found when Arab and Swahili residents of Mombasa and Zanzibar hired out their slaves to Jackson as porters for the expedition. Each man carried a load of sixty pounds in weight for ten to fifteen miles a day. The first fifteen miles from Mombasa were easy, through hilly, well-watered country thick with vegetation – mangoes, coconuts, oranges and bananas all flourishing in the annual rainfall of forty-five inches.

After caravans reached Mariakani there was a pronounced change in terrain. The profuse vegetation and coconut palms came to an abrupt end: the waterless Taru desert stretched ahead, with its penetrating dust, acacia scrub and stark baobab trees which looked as if they had been planted upside down. It took two days to cross the fifty-five miles to Maungu on the other side of the desert, and you had to carry all your water with you. Accidents and evaporation, leakage and theft, and the absence of shade trees made the journey a torment. Some inadequate waterholes did exist at Ziwa Matatu and Buchuma, but they were more often than not dry and invariably putrid if wet. It was in this stretch of hostile territory that most desertions occurred, to a fate which could only be death by thirst. Indeed, James Martin always chained his porters together until they were well into the desert, to try to prevent desertion.

The only way to cross the wilderness was by the system of *terekeza*, or two marches a day. Up by dawn and carrying water, and food prepared at Taru, the caravan marched to Buchuma, where it halted to eat and drink. The men then carried on till dark, when no food was cooked or water drunk. Just before daylight the men pressed on again, their eyes fixed on Maungu hill, which they had to reach by night without food and water or they would perish.[3] Even when Maungu was reached the torture continued – there was a stiff climb up Maungu hill to reach the lifegiving liquid collected in a depression.

Many men sickened and died on these dreadful journeys. On J. R. L. Macdonald's caravan in 1892 forty-five men died, most of smallpox and one by hyena attack, and many were left ill at camps along the way. Sickness caused delay. It was a common occurrence after two miles or so of a day's journey for a porter to break down. When this happened, the line of men was ordered to halt, a litter constructed, and five men's loads distributed among other porters, an action likely to produce near rebellion (though the sick man's pay was distributed among them to prevent malingering). If the porter was desperately ill and water was far away, the caravan was split into two and the advance party and invalid travelled at full speed to the source with the white man in attendance. After water was reached, the invalid and a few porters would stay beside it while the European and the other men returned to the rest of the caravan with water for those left behind.

Each night the camps were surrounded with thorn fences to deter lion, elephant and rhino. Even so, many porters were taken by lions. After the day's march of ten to fifteen miles was over, a meal would be cooked and the fence built, which took the rest of the day. Night fell at 7 p.m. On every caravan there were armed headmen and trusted porters who kept the others in order and, it was hoped, deterred raiding from refractory locals. In general, though, *hongo*, or tribute, was paid to inhabitants of the lands the caravan traversed, and this kept trouble at bay. What often caused local hostility was any theft of crops or interference with women by members of the caravan. If this occurred, the *kilangozi*, or head porter, would punish the culprits by flogging or docking of pay, or putting the men in the chain gang.

At length, six days and 100 miles from Mombasa, the Taita hills and Voi river were reached, and the worst part of the journey was over. Now water could be found at regular intervals for the rest of the way to Uganda. The next camping places were Ndi, Tsavo (with its wonderfully cool water from Kilimanjaro), Kenani, Mtito Andei, Masongoleni, where the stream was often dry and you had to dig for water in the riverbed, and Kibwezi. It took eight days to travel from Taita to Kibwezi, at which point caravans were 200 miles and fourteen days from the coast. Thence they proceeded via Mbwinzau to Makindu, where drinking water had to be drawn from a series of pools covered in duckweed, and on to Kiboko river, Wakufukoa river and Nzawi, whose peak was a prominent landmark.

The men marched onwards through Kilungu and up the sandy watercourse of the Keite river to the village where there lived the friendly leader Machako until his death in about 1887. The ninety-five miles from Kibwezi to Machako's (or Machakos as it became known) took eight days, so caravans had now been marching for twenty-six days. They then descended into the vast Athi plains, infested with infamous and insatiable tiny red ticks, with on one side the smooth, round, white peak of Kilimanjaro and on the other the mystical, craggy and elusive Mt Kenya, usually veiled in cloud throughout the day. There was a halt at Athi River, a torrent difficult to negotiate in the rainy season. Once across the water, caravans made for Ngongo Bagas (now Ngong), a few miles from the edge of the Kikuyu forest, near the present site of Nairobi. They had now been on the road for thirty days.

At this stage it was obligatory to stock up with food, because there was none to be had until Mumia's village was reached, in three weeks' time. Happily the Kikuyu people of the area were willing to sell provisions to caravans. The journey through well-cultivated Kikuyuland's rich red soil took two days, with halts at first swamp and second swamp, or Mianzini and Kinangop. The caravans were now in the highlands, with their cold, frosty nights, before they came to an almost sheer drop of 1,500 feet, into the Kedong valley, part of the Rift Valley. Two nights were spent in the Kedong before the floor of the Rift Valley was reached, on the way to Lake Naivasha. Caravans were now 400 miles and thirty-four days from the coast, and still had 220 more miles to go before Mumia's was attained. The line of men skirted the beautiful Lake Naivasha to the south west if the river was too high to cross on the east side, and proceeded onwards to Lake Nakuru.

There was a three-day climb up the other side of the Rift Valley, into the cool Mau hills and their forests, which took another seven days to traverse. Caravans would then proceed to Kwa Sundu or Mumia's village near the foot of Mt Elgon, before reaching Lake Victoria, though there was also a more southerly route to the lake, through Sotik and Kisii country. By now the men were fifty-one days from the coast. Usually a quarter of the porters had died, others were ill, and the Europeans, if not already ill, soon became so on the malarial shores of the lake. But for caravans travelling on to Uganda via Mumias (the apostrophe was soon dropped), there was another 185 miles or twenty days' march to Mengo and Fort Kampala. When they reached their journey's end, the men had been walking for seventy-one days or ten weeks.[4] And it would take another two and a half months to return to the coast – altogether five months of very hard labour before white men reached what they regarded as civilisation again and porters and askaris (African policemen, men recruited on the coast and given guns) saw their families once more. It is little wonder that Kenya was not among the first of Africa's lands to be colonised, and that the idea of building a railway soon took root in the minds of whites.

*   *   *

Jackson reached Machakos, where the Kamba people lived, without serious incident. There he made a treaty with the local chief, who clearly failed to understand the implications or he would have never put his mark to it. Latrobe Bateman was left in the village, with orders to build a stockade for IBEAC. As a lone white man unable to summon assistance, he must have been very frightened.

Jackson and Martin pushed on across the Athi plains to the edge of the Kikuyu forest, where they camped near the site of the present Muthaiga Club. Again they met with no hostility. The local Kikuyu people were used to Arab and Swahili caravans trading provisions for beads, cloth and wire highly prized by the Africans, and going on their way to ivory country in the north west. They had no way of telling that Jackson's caravan heralded a far more sinister development: the white colonisation of their lands. To them, the caravan seemed no different from its Arab predecessors. Jackson then crossed the Rift Valley, explored Mt Elgon and the Uasin Gishu plateau, and discovered Emin Pasha had left Uganda with Henry M. Stanley, the leader of an expedition sent from the other side of Africa to relieve him. Jackson also found that the ubiquitous German Carl Peters was signing treaties with Uganda chiefs. He hurried coastwards with the news, leaving Gedge in charge in Uganda.

Meanwhile IBEAC had not been idle. Still searching for routes to the interior, the Company sent Frederick Lugard to the Sabaki river and John R. W. Pigott, 'a strict and zealous English Churchman'[5] who married a devout missionary lady, to the Tana river, to see whether either of those watercourses would be a suitable way inland. Lugard and Pigott both established stockaded stations, though they found neither river appropriate as a route to Uganda, because both were too shallow in the dry season. Moreover, the Tana river could not be used for transport because its higher reaches featured cascades, narrows, islands and reefs; and its lower, bends, narrows and shoals.

Eventually IBEAC reluctantly accepted that there was no way of avoiding the depressing and waterless Taru desert on the route to Uganda. At this point the struggling Company received excellent news. Four strands – the missionary, humanitarian, commercial and diplomatic – had combined in 1890 to compel the British and

German governments to sign a treaty delimiting their spheres of influence in East Africa. Germany was to have the area from the coast to Lake Victoria south of the River Umba, and Britain was to have Uganda and the land between it and the coast. This was, however, only a sphere of influence – the British Government had no intention of directly ruling the region, which would be far too expensive. It was happy that its area be run by a commercial company, as British India had been in its early days, and IBEAC admirably fitted the bill.

The Company now sent Frederick Lugard through the Kenya region to Uganda to undo the damage to British interests inflicted by the German Carl Peters. Lugard's brief was to build stations along the way and sign treaties with local chiefs. The son of a senior chaplain on the Madras establishment and his missionary wife, Lugard was an ambitious young man and lately the leader of a small force of the African Lakes Company sent to defend a fort in the Nyasa region, a brave exploit that caught the attention of Cecil Rhodes. He had subsequently joined IBEAC. Recently crossed in love, he was touchy and highly strung, but he possessed initiative and resolution. He pushed inland to Machakos, where he found Bateman despised as a drunkard by the local people, who refused to sell food to the caravan. Lugard settled the disputes and pushed on across the Athi plains. He by-passed Ngongo Bagas, the camping place for Swahili caravans on the edge of Maasai country and only a few miles from the rich food-producing Kikuyu country. Rather than build a fort there, as he had been instructed, he chose a site at Dagoretti, a few miles away, on the advice of two Kikuyu leaders. After a stockade was built, Lugard pressed onwards to Uganda in November 1990, leaving George Wilson, an Australian he had found teaching freed slaves in Mombasa, in charge at Dagoretti, with thirty Africans to support him. Wilson was visited in January 1891 by Captain Eric Smith, of the 1st Life Guards, a man sent inland by IBEAC to explore a route for a possible railway. It may have been the behaviour of some of the men in Smith's caravan which poisoned relations with the local Kikuyu, for on 30 March Wilson felt it prudent to retire from Dagoretti fort, a wise move as the Kikuyu then overran and burnt it.[6] When new supplies arrived with a caravan led by George Leith, who took over Machakos from Bateman, Wilson reoccupied Dagoretti but soon left it and joined Smith on the way back to the coast. There he was dismissed from the Company – according to Ernest Gedge, for 'seduction, and flogging a man to death' on the evil report of the blackguards Leith and Bateman.[7] Things were not going well for the whites trying to set up forts in the interior as a prelude to developing commerce with Uganda. There is no doubt that the behaviour of these pioneer whites was frequently shocking, and certainly so to the twenty-first-century mind. Generally of a middle-class background and often the sons of clergymen, they must have been anxious, if not terrified, when alone in the interior, far from the coast, among people they regarded as savages. To keep order they relied on provoking dread – of flogging, chain gangs and imprisonment – because they were in fear for their lives and the treaties they signed with local potentates were no protection. These treaties are extraordinary. One of them, complete with important-looking Company crest and seal, is tucked in Edward Russell's 1896 diary, now in an Oxford library. Printed on thick paper of the highest quality, it reads: 'Let it be known to all whom it may concern that —— [space for a name to be inserted] has placed Himself and all his Territories, Countries, Peoples and Subjects under the protection, rule and government of the IMPERIAL BRITISH EAST AFRICA COMPANY, and has ceded to the said Company all his sovereign rights and rights of government over all his Territories.'[8] Quite how the Company intended to protect and govern the Africans of the interior, with one Company white man and his few motley askaris, is a puzzle. It was nothing but wishful thinking.

*   *   *

By the time IBEAC came to Mombasa, missionaries were already established in the area. Krapf and Rebmann, who though German belonged to the Church of England Church Missionary Society (CMS), had settled at Rabai behind Mombasa in the 1840s. In 1860 Krapf was invited to England by the Methodist Missionary

Congress and his tales inspired the Methodists to establish missions
of their own in East Africa. 'At which point in this almost
unknown land,' they asked Krapf, 'was the start to be made in
blazing the trail that was to become the highway of the Lord?' In
the 1860s and 1870s they settled at Ribe, a few miles from Rabai,
and neighbouring Ganjoni (Mazeras), Chonyi and Jomvu.[9] Then
in 1884 they built a mission at Golbanti on the Tana river, but its
occupants, the Houghtons, were murdered by the Galla people. As
for the CMS, it continued at Rabai and in 1882 established another
mission 100 miles inland, at Sagalla in the Taita hills. The CMS
missionaries branched out in 1875 to build Freretown, a colony for
freed slaves, on the mainland opposite Mombasa, thus making
themselves grossly unpopular with local slave-owning Swahilis and
Arabs. They became culturally isolated and personally lonely. One
of them, Harry Kerr Binns, valued the ringing of the bell hourly at
Rabai as it helped to keep away his feelings of solitariness in a
foreign land. Those missionaries who sought relief from isolation
in sexual companionship with Africans paradoxically found that
they were more lonely than ever, for their white colleagues
ostracised them.

Most CMS missionaries came from the petit bourgeoisie.
Among their former occupations were clerk, carpenter, shipwright,
mechanic, printer and tailor. There is no doubt that becoming a lay
missionary from one of these trades was a quick way to become
ordained, which happened locally in East Africa without the usual
tough examinations required in the home country. Britain sent
most of its better-educated missionary recruits to India and China,
countries regarded as more 'civilised' than Africa. Missionaries
around Mombasa developed as a rather status-conscious group of
people jealous to preserve their personal spheres of influence.

One would have expected the missionaries to welcome the
advent of IBEAC and their fellow whites in Mombasa, but this was
far from the case. The missionaries refused to mix with the
newcomers, many of whom, it is true, drank more than was good
for them. IBEAC men in their turn despised the missionaries, on
the grounds that they enjoyed an inappropriately self-indulgent

lifestyle – 'These infernal missionaries do more to bring religion into ridicule than all the atheists and sinners that ever lived – poor, deluded people at home support them in a luxury that I for one could not afford.'[10] The implication was that donations collected in the mother country were being put to improper use. Yet it should be remembered that for the men of the cloth (and some women, though these were never considered the equal of their male counterparts), the missions were their homes, the missionaries were not monks, and they were doing what they could to make their lives tolerable in a land far from home.

The missionary death-rate was always high – about a third of the whites died *in situ* and another third had to be invalided back to Europe. Indeed, a large part of a book setting down the history of the early Methodist missions is a record of the lives of thirteen of them who died in post, or, as the author put it, were 'called to pass the veil, whose brighter colours are all upon the other side'.[11] One of them, John Henry Martin (died 1879) wrote home to his family most pertinently: 'In Africa you can do nothing in a hurry, except it be to die. All kinds of business and locomotion are performed leisurely [*sic*]. But in sickness you travel at railway speed to the last goal.'[12] Malaria and dysentery were the usual causes of misery, though sheer discomfort ranked a close second. 'It is a strange land this,' said the missionary Willis Hotchkiss, 'where extremes meet in confusing proximity. Elephants and jiggers, hippos and fleas, rhinos and tick birds, giraffes and ants – they bulk here as in no other country on earth. The big things are talked about most, but it is the little things that creep into the crevices of your life and make you miserable.'[13]

The CMS missionaries expended much of their energy on helping freed slaves. In this period the British maintained a squadron of ships in the Indian Ocean to intercept vessels bearing slaves to Arabia and India, and any slaves they liberated they delivered into missionary hands. To enable these unfortunates to read the Bible, the CMS taught them to read and write; sometimes they also taught them a trade. This put the missionaries in a quandary. They disapproved of nakedness or scanty clothing (African children at the coast generally went naked and African women only covered themselves below the waist), and yet they disliked Africans 'aping' whites with European clothing. While they taught African children to read the Bible, they despised their pupils' 'uppishness' in considering themselves superior to their unlettered brethren. The missionaries' attitudes were full of contradictions, for they wanted to remain paternal while offering Africans the way to equality, and they wished to retain the psychological and social differences between Africans and themselves while at the same time the Bible taught them that all men were of equivalent merit.

After the coming of IBEAC to Mombasa, it was not long before the Roman Catholics, in the person of the Holy Ghost Fathers, arrived and set up a station in 1889, at Ndera on the Tana river, the year before the CMS began a mission at Jilore, on the Sabaki river. But the Catholics had to leave after being flooded out by heavy rains and forced to take refuge up a tree. Undeterred, Father Alexandre le Roy went to Mombasa, disguised as an Arab in order to avoid religious rivalry. A Goan merchant in Ndia Kuu put him up and made a little chapel in his house. In 1891 le Roy bought the present site of Mombasa's Roman Catholic cathedral for £30 an acre and cleared the bush from it. A mission was opened there in 1892, and a church, convent and presbytery were built on the site from coral blocks quarried in the immediate vicinity, a grotto being created in the excavated hollow.

The family of Sir William Mackinnon, the chairman of IBEAC, subscribed £10,000 to build a Scottish Industrial Mission in the interior. On its behalf, on 19 September 1891 James Stewart and seven other white missionaries went inland, hoping to establish a mission in Kikuyu country. The turbulence following the evacuation of Dagoretti fort persuaded them to stop far short of their goal, and they settled instead at Kibwezi, in Kamba country. This group's great contribution to the future of Kenya was to introduce Arabian coffee in 1893, on the advice of John Patterson, a missionary agriculturalist,[14] and to provide a haven for caravans, where supplies were replenished and the sick could be left for treatment.

With Dagoretti evacuated, it was essential to have another way station nearby for caravans going to Uganda. Captain (later Major) Eric Smith chose a site a few miles away, on a flat-topped spur in the middle of the Kikuyu leader Waiyaki's territory. Born in 1857, Smith had to leave the Royal Life Guards after he lost an eye and his left arm. Somewhat curmudgeonly, he was inclined to squabble with colleagues and never became popular. He joined IBEAC in 1890 from the British army, and became expert in organising and participating in caravans to Uganda (though he refused to serve with Lugard on a march to Uganda because he was militarily senior to Lugard). Waiyaki had no option but to accede to Smith's decision, because the white man's caravan was large and well equipped with men and guns.

For months Smith and his young assistant W. P. Purkiss, a former sailor lately in South Africa, toiled to build a well-defended fort, oblong in shape and surrounded by a ditch outside of which was a barbed-wire fence supported by strong wooden posts. An acre in area, the fort was entered by two drawbridges raised at night. Since Purkiss was a talented brickmaker there were burnt brick sleeping quarters for the whites, neatly plastered and thatched with grass, and mud-and-wattle barracks for the African askaris. Stores for grain and wood, a bastion and two caponiers completed the structure, and the Company's flag flew from a tall flagstaff in the centre. There was a small stream within easy reach and all the land around was cultivated, mainly with sweet potatoes. After the fort's completion Smith left it in the charge of Purkiss, pending the arrival of Captain R. H. Nelson, 'a fine fellow', formerly of Methuen's Horse and one of Henry M. Stanley's companions on his Emin Pasha expedition.[15]

All these activities in the interior, the antechamber to Uganda and as yet untouched by Company commerce, were extremely expensive. IBEAC's rapidly dwindling assets were further depleted by the infrastructure necessary in Mombasa. In order to house increasing numbers of IBEAC men, wood and iron bungalows were built, and an office and store rooms in the main street, Ndia Kuu. Rubbish in the streets was cleared, sanitary regulations enforced and a twelve-bed hospital for whites built facing the sea on a breezy promontory. An iron pier with a steam crane was erected in the harbour, now boasting permanent moorings for vessels and iron lighters to load and discharge cargo. A Public Works Department operated on the mainland, from English Point, with a stone wharf and another steam crane. Two and a half miles across the island, at Kilindini, a house was built for the IBEAC boss, known as the Administrator; it overlooked a harbour deeper and more promising than that on the other side of the island. Some specially imported rails, intended mainly for a railway line inland, were laid around the island and on them ran trolleys with canvas roofs, pushed by Africans, to transport whites wherever they wished to go.

The expansion of the Company's activities and the need to collect customs dues along the coast caused IBEAC's white staff to swell to twenty-five, most of them Scottish as was the chairman, Sir William Mackinnon. By the end of 1891 they manned eight departments: finance, customs, shipping, transport, public works, post office, general store and medical.[16] Order was maintained by the Company's troops, two companies of Sudanese recruited in Cairo. At the end of 1889 these troops took over Fort Jesus from the Sultan of Zanzibar's men. Fort Jesus was a huge fort in Mombasa, dating from the sixteenth century when the Portuguese ruled the island. For further security, the Company also imported 200 trained police from India, under the charge of a white man, Captain A. S. Rogers. They were soon put to use. The people of Witu, 100 miles north of Mombasa, murdered eleven German traders in October 1890. This was regarded as setting a dangerous precedent. A punitive expedition, led by Admiral Sir Edmund Fremantle, was formed from the Company's Indian police, Zanzibari troops and 700 seamen and marines from the anti-slavery ships stationed on the East African coast by the British Government. This over-mighty force easily quelled the hapless Sultan of Witu. The fact that the anti-slavery squadron, whose ships regularly put in to Mombasa, was present on the coast was always beneficial to the Company, though of course it was useless for operations any distance inland.

Thus the Company was able to control the coast, but not the interior. The naval squadron also brought peripheral benefits because its personnel socialised with IBEAC men. Rowing and yacht races round the island of Mombasa were popular with both sides.

The lives of the Company men were improved by the arrival early in 1890 of their own 1,800-ton steamer, *Juba*. This eased trade and communications along the coast. And by 1891 the ports of Mombasa, Malindi and Lamu were all connected by a telegraph built by the Eastern Telegraph Company. IBEAC's most ambitious and ill-fated scheme was to build a railway to the interior, with a two-foot gauge, right to Lake Victoria. It was begun in 1890 but only the first eight miles were completed. Then a small steamer was ordered in pieces from England, to be carried to Lake Victoria, where it was to be reassembled and launched. Another steamer, the *Kenya*, was assembled at Mombasa and taken to the Tana river to make a survey, under the charge of C. W. Hobley, a recent IBEAC employee. Despite all this activity, IBEAC's shareholders became restless as they continued to derive no return from their investments. It looked as if white enterprise in the Kenya region might have to come to a premature end.

Throughout these early years, Sir William Mackinnon, IBEAC's chairman, had been urging the British Government to assist him in East Africa. It was, he thought, too much to expect a commercial company to undertake the entire expense of developing such an extensive area. He maintained that it was vital to have a railway financed by the British Government from the coast to Lake Victoria, to continue what he had begun. At first the British Government was reluctant to get involved, but eventually at the end of 1891 unwillingly agreed to send a survey party. Led by Captain J. R. L. Macdonald of the Royal Engineers in India, the Survey started work in December 1891, taking with it into the interior Frederick Jackson. But poor Jackson had to be left behind at Kibwezi suffering from inflamed piles. He was a great loss to the members of the party, who found him 'such a cheery, amusing fellow and always good-tempered'.[17]

It took a year to complete the work. The Survey found that
IBEAC had been right in believing routes inland along the Sabaki
river were non-starters, and it came to the same conclusion as
the Company, that the railway should follow the caravan route to
the Rift Valley, and then find the easiest gradient over the Mau hills
until it dropped to the shores of Lake Victoria. Macdonald and his
second-in-command, John Wallace Pringle, favoured the building
of the railway, particularly as very little land would have to be
bought since most of the territory seemed empty, except in the
well-cultivated Kikuyu area. They suggested Kikuyuland as a place
of residence suitable for whites, for 'the subsequent traffic on the
railway depends entirely on the development of the country'. The
railway would, they added with some cunning, bring civilisation
and commerce, for 'civilisation alone will have an enormous
deterrent effect on slavery, and civilisation can only reach such a
distance in the wake of a railway'.[18] They rejected the Company's
two-foot gauge and suggested one of three feet six inches. This was
welcome news to the cash-strapped IBEAC, which abandoned its
own, differently gauged railway with considerable relief. But when
Parliament received the report of the Survey there was considerable
opposition to a railway paid for by the British Government or even
to one financed jointly with IBEAC. There matters rested for the
time being.

Some other, more immediate, solution to the problems of
transporting supplies to Uganda would have to be found. To speed
up communications, a start was made on constructing a road
suitable for oxcart transport to the interior. C. W. Hobley began to
build a road inland from Mombasa and when money for this ran
out, Sir William Mackinnon used his own funds to pay George
Wilson, formerly of Dagoretti fort, to drive it onwards through the
appalling Taru desert. His missionaries inland at Kibwezi also
pushed a road south-eastwards to meet up with the one Wilson
was making. And in 1893 Francis George Hall, stationed at Fort
Smith, was ordered to construct 150 miles of road to go coastwards
from Fort Smith to Kibwezi, in order to complete the 300 miles
from Mombasa to Kikuyuland. Many Kikuyu took quickly to the

idea of paid labour, so Hall recruited fifty of them, made a cart and began to thrust the road through the forest. To do this, he had to cut through several Kikuyu plantations of standing crops, to the dismay of the farmers, but he pressed on and soon four miles of road were completed. He then reached the Nairobi river, ten miles from the fort, and by the month of August was at the Athi River, twenty-four miles from the start, when circumstances forced him back to Fort Smith to take charge there.

In 1895 and 1896 Captain B. L. Sclater and some Royal Engineers from India completed the missing section from Kibwezi to Athi River and also continued the road north-westwards from Fort Smith to Uganda. At various places along the way, such as Naivasha, Sclater built bomas and depots which later developed as towns. He also brought the first bullock wagons into the interior – they arrived at Fort Smith on 8 January 1896.[19] With a road built, settlers could surely not be far behind.

The road eased the caravan journey from the coast, though the high death-rate of donkeys and oxen from tsetse fly bites meant that human porterage was still the most common method of carriage. Fort Smith was made responsible for acquiring 120 loads of provisions each month for a regular run of supplies to Eldama Ravine, another Company station beyond the Rift Valley. The fort at Eldama Ravine was built in 1894 overlooking a ravine 400-feet deep. It became a vital supply depot because there was no food available for purchase on the twenty-five-day journey between Fort Smith and the ravine. Fort Smith and Eldama Ravine swelled in importance as the amount of traffic to the interior increased rapidly in 1894, and on one occasion in 1895 there were more than 1,000 porters staying at the former.[20] Francis Hall estimated that between 1,500 and 2,000 men were expected to pass through Kikuyuland between September and November 1894, en route for Uganda, and all would have to be fed.[21] Non-whites living permanently at Fort Smith also rose in number. By mid-1893 their numbers had increased from ninety to 150 and by mid-1894 to about 400; the food requirement for each man was between one and a half and three pounds of flour daily.

How did the fort commanders manage to acquire so much food from the surrounding countryside? Just as formerly they had bartered with the Swahili caravans, so some of the Kikuyu and Kamba were not unwilling to trade with the Company new-comers. They quickly expanded their planting to produce a surplus of crops for sale. Though Hall at Fort Smith persistently complained about the volume of food he had to procure, he seems to have had little difficulty in increasing stocks upon demand. The practice was for fifty or sixty well-armed men from the fort to travel to market areas specifically set up for them, and buy supplies. Not all the Kikuyu were willing to trade and some resented their fellow entrepreneurs.[22] This meant that occasionally force had to be used – for example, in January 1894 Hall attacked a village when he could not get provisions, and killed ninety people.[23] The Kikuyu had no overall leader or unified political structure: rather, they were an agglomeration of small societies living side by side, with a common language and culture. The behaviour of one group was not necessarily condoned by another. Because the leader of one party had no power over another, there was no question of negotiating peace with 'all the Kikuyu'. The occupants of the Company forts were therefore in constant danger of attack from parties of Kikuyu who resented others trading with the fort. 'I think,' said Hall, 'the continual strain and anxiety about the natives tells on one pretty heavily.'[24]

African attacks on caravans, forts or Company employees were met with a degree of violence that seems excessive today. The European fort commanders ordered punitive retaliatory raids in which many Kikuyu were shot, and had their animals seized and huts burned. After Nelson died at Fort Smith in December 1892 Purkiss took over. He soon found himself besieged for six days. Fortunately a caravan turned up on its way to the coast from Uganda and relieved him, though with the loss of ten killed and two wounded.[25] On another occasion Purkiss again nearly lost his life, at the hands of one of the Kikuyu leaders, Waiyaki, but he managed to wound and capture his assailant. Waiyaki died on the way to exile at the coast, at Kibwezi. Ironically, Purkiss also died at

Kibwezi a year later, and the two men's graves lay close together in the mission cemetery.[26] When Purkiss died Frank Hall had to interrupt his construction of the road to Athi River, and take over the command of Fort Smith.

Hall was a young man admirably suited to Victorian imperial life. Born in India of military parents, and educated at Sherborne and Tonbridge schools, he had served with the Bechuana Field Force and worked in the South African goldfields before joining IBEAC. His experiences had taught him how to deal forcibly with dissentient Africans while inviting their trust. He faced plenty of discord – by October 1892 the Kikuyu had attacked a caravan transporting to Lake Victoria a steel boat in sections and wrecked the lot. They had furthermore murdered three mailmen and destroyed the mails, and also killed another Company man. To crush behaviour of this sort, armed raids were made from Fort Smith. Then the advent of the railway survey caravan so strengthened the fort's garrison that a much stronger force, consisting of 200 African riflemen, was able to go out and burn several huts, and raze ripening crops.

Hall undertook a similar raid shortly afterwards, with 150 men. They burned and destroyed everything their quarry owned, took all their goats and cattle and shot five of their men. The maxim gun, that great bolster of Victorian imperialism, was also fired from the fort, killing one man and wounding two.[27] On another occasion a year later Hall swooped upon some Kikuyu found guilty of murdering some Maasai, killed nine of them and wounded five, and took 1,000 goats and six cattle.[28] By such methods he paraded his power and discouraged dissent. Gradually he built up relationships with Kikuyu groups whom he called 'friendlies', using the co-operative ones, such as Kinanjui, to counter hostility from other Kikuyu leaders.[29] Thus trade and white patronage spread from Fort Smith as some of the Africans gravitated towards the protection Hall could offer them. Gradually, therefore, African animosity to whites diminished, though it was always a threat in these early years.

It was not only people from Kikuyu groups who intimidated whites in Company caravans and forts. The Maasai were trouble-

some at times, though not to the extent that earlier travellers' tales
had led the newcomers to anticipate. This was because Maasai
society had suffered severely in the latter part of the nineteenth
century. What had happened to the turbulent Wakwafi and their
warriors, the scourge of previous caravans? By 1890 they were a
spent force. Whereas earlier in the century they had dominated the
hinterland, now they were broken by a succession of disasters.
Rinderpest, which spread down from the Red Sea in 1889, had
killed their cattle, and smallpox and famine reduced their numbers.
Reduced from their former position of power to one of internal
conflict, disease, poverty and hunger, they were no longer a threat
to intruders.[30] Maasai warriors now began fairly regular raiding
and it is they who were responsible for some of the murders of
IBEAC's lone mailmen, who ran along the route from coast to
interior and back again once a month. Matters improved somewhat in February 1894 when several hundred Maasai came to Hall
in Fort Smith and asked if they could live near the fort for safety's
sake, because they were being harassed by the Kilimanjaro Maasai.
Since there would be many advantages to such an arrangement,
Hall acceded to the request.

By April Hall had enough authority over these Maasai to enable
him to give some of their men 100 strokes for selling their children
for goats.[31] He also made use of the Maasai in his retaliatory raids
on the Kikuyu – in May 1895 he raided Guru Guru (Liguru) with
eighty guns and 300 Maasai and friendly Kikuyu in warpaint.[32]
Whereas Hall had written in wildly exaggerated manner to his
father in 1892, 'It is almost impossible to get at them [the Maasai]
to exterminate the lot, though they get some pretty hot lessons
occasionally for they are always shot like dogs when seen',[33] now
matters were more tranquil. It was the experiences of men like
Hall that filled the books of Victorian children with stories and
pictures of deeds of valour as lone white men in Africa knelt down
and shot at hordes of nearly naked 'savages', a word constantly used
at the time to describe Africans.

Hall was now in a strong enough position to build another fort,
at Ngong (Ngongo Bagas), to prevent incursions of the Kamba and

to control the Maasai. At the beginning of October 1895 he ordered his second-in-command, Edward Russell, to build a fort at Ngong to maintain peace and order among the Maasai, and encourage them to abandon their pastoral ways, which provoked livestock stealing, and settle down to a life of cultivating crops. The arrogance of a man of one culture taking it upon himself to change the age-old way of life of the people of another was typically Victorian. Missionaries did it all the time. Ngong fort was opened in September 1896 by James Martin's wife, who hoisted the flag to the sound of two bugles frightfully out of tune, and was named Fort Elvira in her honour.[34]

It was not always easy for the older Maasai to control the activities of their young warriors, or moran. Probably a group of these men killed Francis Colquhoun and Dr David Charters, of the Scottish Industrial Mission at Kibwezi, who went out shooting near Makindu and were never seen again.[35] The moran also made a particularly bloodthirsty raid in 1896, killing over 600 African porters and askaris of an official caravan in the Kedong valley. The few survivors fell in with a caravan led by Andrew Dick shortly after it had left Fort Smith. Dick was a thirty-four-year-old Scotsman well known in his youth as an athlete – he had been one of the founders of the Clydesdale Harriers and a leading spirit in the formation of the Scottish Harriers' Union. He had been seen off at Glasgow railway station in 1889 by 600 people waving him farewell as he departed for a new job with IBEAC in Mombasa. After a period as an accountant in the Company's service he resigned and began trading in the interior on his own account. When he came across the Kedong massacre survivors he sent back to Fort Smith for reinforcements. Two French travellers who happened to be at Fort Smith went out to advise him to return to the fort, but he refused and sat down to write a letter to the fort commander before setting off to determine the strength and position of the Maasai. 'If I am killed,' he wrote, 'think kindly of me and forgive my little ways hasty temper impatience etc etc we all have our faults I'll do my best anyway.'[36] He was surrounded and killed by the Maasai, while the Frenchmen retreated to Fort Smith. A huge war party marched out from the fort to fight the warriors, only to discover they had fled. Dick's body was, however, recovered and buried. The Maasai were inclined to revere Dick because he shot about a hundred of them before he was overcome. A later inquiry concluded that the official caravan party had provoked the Maasai.

In 1897 Fort Elvira at Ngong was reinforced by Sudanese soldiers under the command of the eccentric Captain F. S. Dugmore, RNR, on retired pay of the 64th Regiment. Dugmore came to East Africa in 1896 with an organ and a party of people called Freelanders, an association of Europeans of various nationalities intending to set up a socialist colony on the mainland behind Lamu, north of Mombasa. Their leader, an Austrian chemist, Dr Julius Wilhelm, had no real control over the group, which included Pier Scavenius, the son of a member of the Danish cabinet, and 'several ladies of advanced political and social ideas'.[37] They took a large house on the Lamu seafront and proceeded to scandalise the pious Muslim inhabitants by being frequently drunk and taking liberties with native women. Soon their funds ran short, and some of them died in Lamu, others went to Mombasa and the rest returned to Europe.

Dugmore was one of those who went to Mombasa. As a retired British military officer he was put in charge of a detachment of Sudanese troops and sent upcountry to help garrison the forts. Hall and Russell did not take to him at all, for he was decidedly strange. Instead of walking a few paces to discuss matters face to face with his white colleagues, Dugmore would type them lengthy letters signed 'Mugdore ye Looniac' or 'The Bloody Old Shit'. He sent Mrs Martin an elephant foot as a delicacy for her table. To counter fleas, he soaked his pyjamas in paraffin before going to bed, which brought him out in boils all over his body. And when his pet monkey got into some of his belongings he gave it a sound flogging – 'What the natives can think of him I don't know,' said a despairing Edward Russell.[38] He was seconded to Uganda, and when he returned to Fort Elvira he found he had been replaced by Captain William Cooke. After displaying signs of insanity he was sent to Machakos under the escort of Cooke, whom he shot dead at Athi River. Arrested and sent to Mombasa for trial, he committed suicide by means of a bootlace.[39] Dugmore was an example of the less than satisfactory personnel sometimes employed to guard the British empire overseas – men whose behaviour would not be tolerated at home.

Dangers to white men from the indigenous human inhabitants and the likes of Dugmore were matched by perils posed by wild animals. Unlike Australia, which had no large predators, East Africa was very hazardous in this respect. High grass or thick forests obscured walkers' views, and a traveller could suddenly come across an elephant, lion, buffalo or rhino, all of them highly dangerous creatures, particularly when guarding young. Europeans also brought trouble upon themselves, for young men away from home found the lure of pitting their wits against such animals irresistible, and many shooting expeditions were undertaken, for sport rather than to procure meat for the table.

Wounds inflicted by wild animals were frequently fatal in this pre-antibiotic age. Just before Christmas 1894 Frank Hall was tossed by a rhino, which badly damaged his leg. Then a few months later a leopard he was grappling with sank its teeth into his knee. The first his colleague Russell knew of this was to be handed a pencilled note reading: 'Dear Russell, Send a few men out to help my fellows in. A leopard is responsible this time but nothing very serious.'[40] He found Hall approaching Fort Smith on a litter, having been carried by his men for three whole days. He was in a very bad way, and Russell immediately plied him with half a bottle of champagne before applying forty leeches to his hugely swollen leg. Russell sent a runner to Felice Scheibler, who was shooting game with his wife on the Athi plains, requesting more champagne. He sent another messenger to Machakos, asking for a prayer book, for he did not think that Hall would live. The Scheiblers and an IBEAC official at Machakos, Thomas Gilkison, hurried to Fort Smith, to find that Hall had now developed bedsores. Although Mrs Scheibler made him a round cushion to relieve the pressure, by 6 April Hall's bed was a pool of pus. Happily at this point the very unpopular Dr William John Ansorge arrived on his way to Uganda as medical officer, and operated under chloroform to excise dead flesh from the leg. On 20 June Russell took Hall to the coast on a stretcher, arriving on 9 July. After a sojourn in Mombasa hospital Hall was sent home to England; it was a close-run thing but he survived his ordeal to return to his post in Fort Smith, with one leg permanently straight.[41]

With his charismatic personality, Hall had the strength of character to work in highly difficult circumstances in the East African interior, with all its attendant risks. John Ainsworth, his colleague at Machakos forty miles from Fort Smith, was equally strong-willed. These two men were crucial to the establishment of British hegemony in what became Kenya. The fort Ainsworth ran at Machakos had had an inauspicious inception because George C. Leith, Latrobe Bateman's replacement, was as much of a drunkard as his predecessor, and the Kamba hated him, not least because he took supplies from them by force and without payment. He also cut down an ithembo tree, where the Kamba made offerings to the spirits, to use it as a flagpole. Leith scattered the men who came to protest with rifle fire and burned several Kamba huts. Ainsworth took over from Leith in 1892.[42]

Born in 1864 at Urmston near Manchester, the son of a Manchester trader of the same name, John Ainsworth had gone to the Congo to trade and then joined IBEAC in 1889. After his posting to Machakos, he immediately spent twenty months building a stone fort with residences, offices, stores and barracks. Known to the Kamba as Nzuenzi, he was highly efficient, setting up excellent food stores for caravans and offering them in addition fresh milk, butter, and vegetables which he grew himself. Machakos eventually provided 400,000 pounds of food a year for caravans. As a personal touch Ainsworth planted a flower garden in the fort, with mignonettes, nasturtiums and sunflowers, the first such garden in Kenya. His isolation came to an end in October 1894 when he was sent a European assistant, C. R. W. Lane, and his loneliness on 3 November 1897 when he married at Machakos Annie ('Ina') Cameron Scott, sister of Peter Cameron Scott and youngest daughter of Mr and Mrs John Scott, American missionaries from the recently arrived Seventh Day Adventist Africa Inland Mission.[43]

He was wise to make his claim early: there were twelve white missionaries at the Adventists' mission at Nzawi in 1897, but by 1899 only one remained. Peter Scott had died of blackwater fever on 4 December 1896. However, according to Hall, who disliked him, Ainsworth had not been entirely without female companionship because he kept Kamba women in the fort.

Ainsworth managed to keep order in the Kamba region with a garrison of fifty Africans provided by IBEAC and employed as police, despatch runners and porters as occasion demanded. 'Generally speaking,' said Ainsworth, 'I liked the Wakamba and we got on very well. Naturally now and again there arose occasions when corrective measures became necessary.'[44] These were the usual flogging and hut burning, but Ainsworth had more sympathy with Africans than his fellow administrators and his softer methods had pleasing results. One traveller described his administration as 'tactful' and his fort as 'homely'.[45] Soon the Kamba were using money rather than barter in their exchanges with him, reducing the quantities of heavy cloth and iron to be carried from the coast. However, it was not all plain sailing and when trouble arose in April 1896 Ainsworth had to send to Fort Smith for reinforcements. Russell immediately set out with 1,500 Maasai and Kikuyu for Machakos, where they killed 200 Kamba.[46]

Ainsworth was disturbed in 1892 to hear the Company was considering pulling out of Uganda and Machakos. What he did not know was that IBEAC was in grave financial difficulty. Uganda had proved incessantly troublesome and most disappointing from a commercial point of view. Frederick Lugard, left in charge there in December 1890, took over as a defence force some 600 Sudanese troops left behind by Emin Pasha. It was as well he did, for he had to make full use of them in perpetual skirmishes and battles, and unrest arising from unChristian squabbles between Roman Catholic and Protestant missionaries. IBEAC gained not a penny profit from the turbulent country and decided to pull out in 1891. But to keep its missionaries safe, the Church Missionary Society offered to support the Company with £30,000 if it would continue its occupation of Uganda until the end of 1892. After public opinion in England was stirred, IBEAC stayed there until April 1893. Lugard went to England in 1892 to urge the prolongation of British rule, and the British Government sent a mission of inquiry to the region under Gerald Portal. On 31 March 1893 Portal raised the Union Jack in Kampala in place of the Company flag. The Company was not blind to the possible implications of this – perhaps the British Government would also assume the expense of policing the area from Uganda to the coast.

The Company's fortunes continued to decline in East Africa. As early as 1891 Frederick Jackson wrote to Gedge about it: 'There can be no doubt old chap that the whole blooming show is rotten to the very core and I tell you honestly that if Berkeley [the Administrator] can not pull the thing round, there will be a general "bust" up within a year or eighteen months. I really don't see how it is possible to go on much longer.'[47] Ever since Frank Hall had first arrived at Mombasa he had known that IBEAC wanted to pull out of East Africa (by October 1893 the Mombasa staff had been reduced to six). It was common talk among the Company employees that threats to close the stations in the interior were a ruse to get the British Government to take over the show. Hall was therefore anxious to do a good job of making the road between Fort Smith and Athi River, reasoning that if he impressed Portal with his work, he would be taken on by the British Government. The trouble was, once it no longer possessed Uganda, the Company was unable to develop the East African interior. For the time being it retained its two posts at Machakos and Fort Smith, and one at Eldama Ravine on the western side of the Rift Valley. Finally the British Government decided to take over responsibility for the region when it became abundantly clear that the Company really meant it when it said it was going to pull out. In March 1895 the Company men received three months' notice and on 1 July the British Government took over East Africa from IBEAC for £250,000. Company personnel were simply adopted by the British Government, so for the time being the only thing that changed was the flag flying above the forts. The Company seal was still used on official documents in Malindi in the 1950s, for lack of government replacements.

2

A New British Protectorate

The British flag brought with it the hope that a railway might be built. It was self-evident that Uganda could not be supplied or held unless transport improved, so vast were distances to the interior. In 1895 the decision was finally made to build a railway from the coast to Uganda. Its progress was dishearteningly slow, but the advance parties transformed life in the interior for the few whites who lived there. Before they came it had been a very lonely existence. In June 1893 Hall told his father in one of his regular letters home that it was a month since he had seen a white face.[1] Although generally resilient, he was occasionally subject to depression. In March 1894 he wrote to say that he was 'a bit in the blues and wondering whether the worry and bother, to say nothing of the solitude, of this life was worth the pay I was getting'.[2] He tried to counter his loneliness with pets, at first his dogs Shetani (Devil) and Romp, and later a pet baboon and gazelle. In 1895 he boasted: 'My menagerie and museum are noted features of the station.'[3]

At one time Hall had a good Goan clerk with whom he spent the evenings, but his replacement was hopeless and the inter-racial evenings came to an end. In the administrators' letters and diaries there is of course no mention of taking African women as a solace, but it probably happened. Ainsworth was believed to have an African woman companion and in 1898 J. H. Patterson, engaged in constructing the railway, entered in his diary: 'Sleep in same hut as Whitehead [Richard] [the District Officer at Ndi] and his temporary Swahili wife.'[4]

Because they were on the caravan trail, the men in Fort Smith and Machakos saw briefly but fairly regularly white men passing through on their way to Uganda, and the occasional newspaper correspondent or sportsman on a shooting safari. Ernest Gedge, who had been on Jackson's initial journey inland, joined *The Times* of London and went to and fro more than once, while in 1892 Eugene Wolff, the German traveller and correspondent, passed by. But the most welcome of the arrivals were the railway survey party in 1892 – 'an awfully jolly lot', said Hall.[5] The geologist J. W. Gregory came in May 1893 to explore the Rift Valley and climb Mt Kenya. The result of his visit was the remarkable book, *The Great Rift Valley* (London, John Murray, 1896). A small, frail-looking but wiry man, a teetotaller, Gregory travelled by himself. He was not harmed by the Kikuyu because they considered him a lunatic, and they never hurt lunatics. Indeed, when they found him wandering about by himself they took him back to Fort Smith.[6] Lionel Declé, a French journalist and photographer domiciled in England, arrived in April 1894, having walked from Cape Town. Then when Edward Russell arrived to be Hall's assistant in 1894 Frank Hall became less lonely, for the two men got along famously. Hall found Russell 'always happy and jolly and takes kindly to the work'.[7] On home leave in 1898, Hall married Russell's sister Beatrice and brought her out to Fort Smith the same year.

In December 1893 an extraordinary sight met Hall at the gates of Fort Smith: standing before him was a white man, his wife, and six children ranging from six weeks to six years. It turned out to be Stuart Watt and his spouse Rachel, former CMS missionaries at Mamboia in Tanganyika, who had decided to set up their own, independent mission, in Kikuyuland. Hall refused to let the mother and her children go any further, because of the dangers, but Stuart Watt insisted on leaving to search for a mission site. Watt was an Irishman, a former traveller in the wholesale tea trade before he became a missionary, and, in Hall's opinion, 'a raving lunatic'. Recently he had helped his wife bury their baby, as she described:

I awoke at 2 a.m. and thought it strange that all was so still. Reaching out my hand over the little cot, I was terrified to find how cold was the body of my dear little son . . . My husband emptied one of our iron cases, and with a heavy aching heart I lined it with a linen sheet, and in it we laid the earthly remains of our precious child . . . The body of our little one was carried into the forest, and deposited underneath the shelter of a large euphorbia tree.[8]

Hall cleared his room for Rachel Watt and the children, relegating himself to the medicine room. Eric Smith, the fort's founder who was passing through, expressed an opinion of Watt's plans that was 'curt, emphatic and anything but scripturally expressed', while the CMS Secretary wrote to Watt: 'I pray to avert you from the catastrophe which your scheme appears to court.'[9]

But Stuart Watt returned safely to the fort from his foray in Kikuyuland. Meanwhile Hall had had an excellent Christmas with Rachel Watt and the children – Martha, Tooty, Eva, George, Freddie and Clara – who had not been a bit of trouble. He wished they would stay, as did the fort's Africans, for while they were there Hall 'couldn't even cuss properly and not a man got flogged'.[10] Rachel Watt mended all Hall's clothes. The Watts abandoned their plans for Kikuyuland, going instead to Machakos, where Ainsworth allowed them to settle at Ngelani, eight miles north of the fort. Their mission was not a great success – indeed, Ainsworth somewhat unjustly said he saw little evidence of any missionary activity by them. In order to be self-sufficient, they imported fruit trees from Sydney and established a fruit farm.[11] On many occasions Ainsworth had to send his askaris to convey Rachel Watt and her children to Machakos fort for safety.[12]

Christmas with Mrs Watt and the children was followed by other convivial social events, as more whites penetrated the interior. On 10 November 1895 there was a musical evening in Fort Smith, with eight whites there, two on drums, and one each on a French horn, melodion, pennywhistle and bottles.[13] That year six whites sat down to a Christmas dinner of oxtail soup, patties, roast beef, boiled and roast chicken, plum pudding, mince pies, stewed peaches, savory, sherry, beer, champagne, liqueur, whisky and soda, and coffee.[14] Apart from such feasting and revelry, the men in the interior took care to keep themselves informed about events at home in Britain, as well as international affairs. Under the Company regime there was a monthly mail from the coast, which brought up the *Zanzibar Gazette* and newspapers from home. Hall and Ainsworth exchanged newspapers when they had read them, and Hall's friend, the Post Master at Mombasa, collected all the used newspapers he could find and sent them up to Fort Smith. Hall's father also sent newspapers regularly from England which allowed his son to develop a great interest in the question of Irish Home Rule, though many thousands of miles away, in a different continent, and dealing with people utterly different though no less adamant in their views than the Irish.[15]

Once the British Government had taken over in 1895 what was now called the East Africa Protectorate (EAP), and once the railway was begun, settlers and traders were not far behind. The firms of Smith Mackenzie and Boustead Ridley, long established at Mombasa, now began to build stores upcountry. Smith Mackenzie had a store at Mumias by 1896, and their agent G. W. Lewis formed the Mirimbi Coffee Syndicate in Kikuyuland, under the management of Charles Kitchin. On 11 March 1896 Walter Trefusis, Smith Mackenzie's agent, arrived at Fort Smith and fixed on a piece of land off the road below Kinanjui's village, as a place to erect a store.[16] It was to be run by Mr and Mrs John Walshe, who were building it in July.[17] They invested in some goats – Mary Walshe was seen on the road from Machakos, unconcernedly driving a herd of goats alone to Fort Smith. Her husband was far behind, struggling with his donkey cart's detached wheel. As a teenager, Mary Walshe had left Ireland for Australia with her first husband. Within twelve years he and their two small children were dead. Mary then went to Rhodesia where she met and married John Walshe with whom she trekked up to East Africa. Small, fierce and red-headed, with a weather-beaten face, Mary Walshe was as tough as they come and not of the same social class as Frank Hall, to whom such things mattered – indeed, the only saving grace of Dr William Ansorge, he said, was that he was a gentleman. Mary was called 'Bibi Kiboko' (whip woman) by the Africans, because she was unsparing with her kiboko, or rhino-hide whip.[18]

In October of the next year, 1897, two Cape wagons drawn by oxen under the charge of C. S. Feltham, arrived in Fort Smith to provision the Smith Mackenzie shops in the interior.

Mrs Watt and Mrs Walshe were the first non-missionary women in the interior, but they were soon to be followed by the first administrator's bride. James Martin, now in charge of the fort at Eldama Ravine, married Augusta Elvira de Sousa, daughter of a Zanzibar Goan, in 1896 and brought her upcountry, arriving at Fort Smith on 20 September. Eight days later James Wallace and his wife Mary appeared in Fort Smith, and a few days after that two other married couples: Henry and Helen Boedeker and James and Mary McQueen.[19] Both Mrs Wallace and Mrs McQueen were pregnant, and the second and third European children to be born upcountry in the EAP made their appearance on 1 December 1896 (a son, Francis George Kikuyu, to Mary Wallace) and 16 May 1897 (a son John, to Mary McQueen), doubtless both assisted by Boedeker, who was a physician. The first white child to be born upcountry had been J. A. Stuart Watt, at Ngelani on 23 August 1895.[20]

What brought these Europeans to East Africa? Henry Albert Boedeker was a Eurasian, possibly half Parsi or half Burmese, who had studied medicine at Glasgow University.[21] There he met, fell in love with and married the daughter of Sir Henry Wardlaw of Tillicoultry.[22] As marriage to a half-caste was considered below the lady's station, fear of social ostracism made the pair decide to emigrate to East Africa, a place they had read about. Before he left, Boedeker prudently went to see Sir Clement Hill, in charge of East Africa at the Foreign Office, 'who was extremely gracious and was pleased at our coming out as the first settlers in the country as far as Kikuyu was concerned'.[23] A military man who met the Boedekers in Naivasha in 1900 reported that Mrs Boedeker 'had a Glasgow accent, I regret to have to record', and that Boedeker himself 'didn't look as if he could set the Thames on fire, being an insignificant little person, with a decided touch of the tarbrush, I should say'.[24]

Boedeker had persuaded Mary and James McQueen, a blacksmith from Dumfriesshire, and the brothers James and David Wallace and their wives, from Galloway, to accompany them to

Africa. The wife of the physician David Wallace had become ill
after the birth of a daughter in Mombasa, and she and her husband
returned to Europe. The other Wallace couple and the McQueens
had walked the 330 miles to Fort Smith from the coast, to be
followed shortly afterwards by the Boedekers.[25] It was, therefore,
a large gathering at Fort Smith which bade Frank Hall a happy
birthday on 11 October 1896 – in all, thirteen white men
and women.[26] The subsequent Christmas and New Year were
particularly happy and well-attended celebrations at Fort Smith –
there are thirty-two white faces in the New Year's Day photograph stuck into Russell's diary.[27] And his entry for that day is
uncharacteristically brief: 'Sore heads'.

How did these white newcomers expect to make a living?
Farming was a possibility and the first settlers bought land from
Africans. They were not the first whites to acquire land, for
missionaries had beaten them to it. Granting land for missions to
occupy and cultivate was regarded as permissible under Company
rule – for example, in 1894 Ainsworth had 'granted a site for a
mission station' for Watt, though in effect the land became a private
farm. According to Ainsworth's assistant Lane, the land the Watts
obtained had been unoccupied by Africans.[28] Though IBEAC was
happy to grant land for missions, it forbade the private purchase and
ownership of land while it was in charge of East African territory. Its
Administrator Sir Francis de Winton had issued a proclamation in
April 1891 proscribing all dealings in land between Europeans and
Africans, a measure designed to preserve the Company's monopoly.
When the British Government took over East Africa in 1895,
it issued no guidance about the purchase of land. Hall and
Ainsworth therefore had to be pragmatic when the first settlers
came. Eventually the British Government announced on 29 April
and 31 August 1897 that land purchases from Africans had to be
registered with a government magistrate. This had already been
done for all the land bought so far. The declaration provided no
advice about the rights and wrongs of whites acquiring land, or
how extensive their acreage could be.

Hall believed that Europeans could buy land as freehold from any

Kikuyu who claimed it. What he did not know was that there was no individual ownership of land among the Kikuyu. The companies Smith Mackenzie and Boustead Ridley were 'granted small areas of land which were purchased from the natives with Mr Hall's full approval and the consent of the people who owned the land', paying for it with cattle and trade goods.[29] 'Mr Hall,' said Boedeker,

> was most particular in the dealings with land purchased from natives. Each case was examined separately. The land to be sold was inspected by both parties in his presence, boundaries agreed upon and a sale price fixed by the natives. The deeds of purchase were drawn up and the transaction completed legally in Mr Hall's office at Fort Smith when he witnessed the signatures of both parties to the documents, which were then sent to Machakos for registration.[30]

When the Boedekers arrived they stayed at Fort Smith for three months while they negotiated for land. Boedeker applied for a piece of ground from Kinanjui and was offered an uncultivated area quite close to the fort. On learning that Boedeker was a doctor, the Kikuyu volunteered the land as a gift, but Hall demurred and recommended Boedeker make a deed of purchase in the same way as Smith Mackenzie and Boustead Ridley had done. Five cows, three bales of unbleached cotton cloth (Amerikani), two sixty-pound loads of beads and four loads of brass wire were handed over to Kinanjui and Kamani ya Kinyaga who claimed the ownership of part of the land. The boundaries were fixed by trees. As for the land obtained by the Coffee Syndicate at Mirimbi, on 6 February 1896 Thomas Gilkison, left in charge of Fort Smith while Hall was away with his leopard injuries, went to Mirimbi himself to measure up the land.[31] The same procedure must have been adopted with the Wallaces and McQueens. Gradually, therefore, a few whites were privately insinuating themselves into East African territory.

Britain's momentous decision to build a railway led to the opening up of East Africa to the rest of the world. The coming of the railway meant that land for the track had to be acquired from Africans. The 600 miles of line from the coast to Lake Victoria took six years to build and cost far more than the original estimates. In charge of the construction was George Whitehouse, the chief engineer, who reached Mombasa to assume his post on 11 December 1895. With him came several white engineers, many of them previously employed in India. As local labour in the numbers required was unavailable, thousands of manual workers were brought from India, the first of them arriving in Mombasa in January 1896. They were to alter profoundly East African society and commerce. Since the only harbours at Mombasa were on the island, first of all a bridge 1,732 feet long had to be built to take the line to the mainland, and this of course delayed the project. Though wood for the bridge was plentiful inland, paradoxically it would have required a railway to bring it to the coast, so all of it had to be imported from Norway; it did not arrive until April 1896.

A temporary viaduct was erected, which served until the permanent bridge was opened in 1901. The actual plate laying began in May 1896 and the gangs of workmen immediately faced serious problems. Pushing the line across the Taru desert was appallingly difficult due to the lack of water, though the road already constructed did of course help with the work. Finally the Tsavo river was reached, only for a worse fate than thirst to befall the workers: death by man-eating lions. The diary of J. H. Patterson, builder of the bridge over the Tsavo, poignantly recounts the losses. One night he noted that the only remains to be found of a man taken from the hospital by a lion were a few well-picked bones and a finger with a silver ring, which he duly sent to the man's wife in India. Almost every night he entered in the diary: 'Lion took a coolie last night.' During this dreadful period he heard the news of his first child's death. 'Poor, poor Francis,' he wrote to his wife. 'How I feel for you in your trial.'[32]

Eventually, in 1899, the line reached the swampy plain on which Nairobi would be built. It had long been the intention of the engineers to locate a depot at this gateway to the highlands, before the perilous descent into the Rift Valley – 'Kikuyu being the central point on the line of the projected railway, and the sanitary and climatic conditions being such as to point to its adoption as a place of residence especially suitable to Europeans, it has been considered advisable to locate the manager's office at this place.'[33] For almost the first time, the line began to cross land intensively cultivated by Africans. They were all compensated, and land for one mile on each side of the track was bought by the railway. Then came the difficult descent into the Rift Valley, where the ground fell steeply for 700 feet, to a ledge with a minor drop of 200 feet, beyond which was another fall of 500 feet into the Kedong valley. It took a long time to build this section, but meanwhile materials were lowered to the floor on a rope incline so the construction of the track could proceed across the valley.

The line as far as Naivasha was opened for traffic on 15 August 1899, and Hall gave a grand party at Fort Smith to celebrate. A marquee was pitched and draped with flags, and a horseshoe table was laid. Thirty whites, including five ladies, sat down to a lunch of salmon and lobster salads, beef, beefsteak pie, partridges, hams, tongues and fowls. Then, for those still peckish, salads, blanc-manges, 'shapes', jellies, tarts and custards were brought to the table. This Lucullan feast was followed by a shooting match – residents against the railway. Hall now closed his visitors' book 'as we can't have globe-trotters and railway passengers mixed with the old pioneers'.[34] A new era had begun.

There were two trains a week each way for the public. Passengers were not allowed to travel on the rope incline into the Rift Valley, and between Kedong and Escarpment stations women were carried in hammocks. At last, on 20 December 1901, the rails reached Lake Victoria at Ugowe bay, along a new route which cut 100 miles off that of the original survey, though there were as yet many temporary deviations and bridges. In March 1902 there was one more year's work to be done on the railway before it was finally finished.

As early as May 1895 Andrew Dick, while running private caravans to the interior to acquire ivory, had built a store at Nairobi river, but presumably this folded when he was killed by the Maasai in the Kedong valley the following year.[35] The ubiquitous James Martin then founded a camp at Nairobi river in 1896, to recruit

Africans for railway construction on Whitehouse's orders. On 19 September that year Edward Russell went 'to Nairobi to see Martin and his new bride'.[36] This is the first mention of Nairobi as a place. George Ellis, helping Sclater make his road, set up camp there at about the same time.[37] In 1897 R. O. Preston established the railway advance camp at Nairobi, consisting of tents and a few corrugated-iron shacks. He described the area as 'a bleak swampy stretch of soppy landscape, devoid of human habitation of any sort, the resort of thousands of wild animals'.[38] In 1899 the McQueens went to live there,[39] and the dwelling they built for themselves became the first private house in Nairobi. Ainsworth established a temporary camp in Nairobi under the charge of Dr S. L. Hinde in April 1899, just before the railway line reached the place. Two months later the first consignment of corrugated iron arrived in the vicinity and now buildings were roofed with that durable material rather than with grass.

There was a huge influx of Indian workers as the railway reached Nairobi on 30 May 1899. It was soon discovered that the site was not ideal, for the subsoil was soft and sticky when wet. The railway camp began to harbour a great number of rats, jiggers, fleas and other vermin. The more senior officials' houses were, therefore, built on a hill beside the site, which became known as Nairobi Hill, and later Secretariat Hill or Hospital Hill or merely the Hill. Somewhat feeble efforts were made to drain the plain. In 1900 Nairobi had 8,000 inhabitants, most of them Indians. All in all, of the 31,983 Indians who worked on the railway, 6,723 elected to remain in East Africa after the final repatriation of 1902. Many of them set up shops in the Nairobi bazaar, and for the moment the town was very much an Indian one.

It was difficult to make salubrious a place which was growing so fast. On 4 March 1902 the insanitary conditions caused plague to break out in the Indian bazaar: there were sixty-three cases and nineteen deaths. A German physician, Dr Lott, an expert in bubonic plague from neighbouring German East Africa, was called upon to help with the emergency. He surmised that the plague had been introduced into the bazaar from India, by gunny bags of rice or a consignment of sweets, or perhaps foul cotton waste from Karachi. An order was immediately given to burn down the bazaar; later it was rebuilt on another, more sanitary site. In 1902 there were serious efforts made to drain the swamp and turn it into market gardens. A bridge and causeway were built across it and a water supply laid on for Nairobi town from the Kikuyu forest. But for many years there was still no proper sanitation – a night-soil cart removed the buckets of waste in the dark and dumped their malodorous contents in the river.

A young, twenty-two-year-old chemist, Herbert K. Binks, who had come from Yorkshire for adventure, described what he saw:

> To the south the landscape was blemished by two huge corru-gated-iron buildings; one was the railway shed, the other the railway workshops. Leading from the station in a northerly direction was a wide track known as Station Street . . . About four hundred yards from the start of the street there were a number of corrugated-iron houses on its left. They were the residential quarters of the railway employees. To the right, running parallel with the main track were nine corrugated-iron buildings, flatteringly called stores or shops. The first one was double-storey, and some humorist called it a hotel. This was Victoria Street.[40]

The hotel was run by Mayence Bent (née Woodbury), who was the common-law wife of W. S. Bent, a railway worker and president of the Nairobi 'Railway Strike Committee' of 1900. It occupied the upper floor of a store run by Tommy Wood, who bought the building from the Armenian M. MacJohn in November 1901. Tommy Wood was a purveyor of everything, from hardware to clothes made by Mrs Bent, and his shop doubled as a meeting place and tea room. By 1902 there were some thirty European settlers in and around Nairobi to patronise the store. Colonel Richard Meinertzhagen described it as a wood and tin shanty sometimes known as Wood's Hotel and sometimes as the Victoria Hotel.[41] The following year a bungalow next door to Tommy Wood's was built by Dan Noble, the Post Master, as the first 'proper' hotel, run by May Bent and called the Stanley Hotel. Then in 1903 a butchery opened (a cobbler had operated from Wood's store from 1902). The roads fronting the shops were earth tracks, dusty in dry weather and muddy in wet.

A few miles from this unprepossessing place the earliest settlers experimented with farming. P. E. Watcham, who arrived in 1899, imported a Berkshire boar to cross with Seychelles sows, and other farmers grew potatoes for export to Zanzibar, where there was a demand for them. In 1902 A. E. Atkinson, who had come in 1897, imported a shorthorn bull to cross with native cows. In the same year all the land acquired by the railway for a mile either side of the line was transferred to the Protectorate Government. At the same time the boundary with Uganda was shifted and the region from the Rift Valley to Lake Victoria, which had previously been in Uganda, became part of the East Africa Protectorate.

On the coast, Mombasa grew as it became the major port for the new country. By 1902 its small white community consisted mainly of officials and businessmen. The trolley transport system had been extended, using track from the abandoned IBEAC railway, and now all white residents had their own trolleys and teams of African pushers. Trolley lines led to all the residential bungalows. The main line across the island to the old harbour via Fort Jesus, from the bluff above the new Kilindini harbour (since the advent of the railway this deeper harbour had been used for larger ships) was double-tracked, but elsewhere if trolleys met, the one carrying the more junior official was simply lifted from the track to let the other pass.[42] Along the track lay a few scattered railway officials' bungalows, but mostly thick vegetation. The round huts of the police barracks were midway across the island, and the town overlooked the old harbour. Macdonald Terrace was an impressive new street. Here were the High Court, an imposing building with a clock tower, and the Grand Hotel (a two-storeyed edifice owned by a Greek named Thrasubulos Dallas) with, next door, the Cecil Hotel. With the Protectorate came the first banks: the National Bank of India and the Chartered Bank.

In the 1890s firms came to Mombasa from Ceylon, Aden,

Germany and Britain, and by 1903 there were enough commercial houses to form the Mombasa Chamber of Commerce. With the increase in population a water supply was necessary, for the original wells were no longer adequate. A distilling machine was obtained and from 1896 to January 1901 sea water was distilled. After that a piped supply was installed from Changamwe on the mainland, though in the old town the traditional water-seller long plied his trade. Beside the massive Fort Jesus lay Mombasa railway station until another was built a hundred yards away in 1900 on the south side of Garden (later Treasury) Square. Opposite Fort Jesus was Vasco da Gama Street, home of the Indian-owned Africa Hotel, the route to the old harbour. Fort Jesus was flanked by the Mombasa Club, and, on the other side, the European hospital, beyond which were located several bungalows for white residents. Beside the hospital, a new house had been built in 1898 for the senior British official, on the site of the later Government House.

A coast businessman Reginald (Rex) Boustead had prospered from the caravan trade to Uganda and commercial activities in Mombasa.[43] The upstairs room of the Boustead Ridley Mombasa office, in Vasco da Gama Street near Fort Jesus, began to be used as a European club. Membership expanded to such an extent that in 1897 Boustead acquired a plot of land opposite his office, on which he built the Mombasa Club, still occupying the same site today. Consisting of a single storey containing a bar, billiard room and card room, it opened in January 1898, with membership open to Europeans and Americans only. It became the hub of the white community. In 1897 there were sixty members, most of them civil servants. Women were permitted to use the club before 6 p.m. On the coast south of Mombasa, there were no European settlers, apart from Charles Anderson on an estate at Ramisi, busy experimenting with vanilla and tobacco. He also acquired the Magarini plantation at Mambrui confiscated from a rebel Swahili.

To police its new territory, the British Government took over IBEAC's motley personnel. Askaris, in other words the most trusted porters provided with guns, had guarded the original IBEAC caravans. Then Sudanese soldiers had been taken over from Emin

Pasha, while other Sudanese were recruited in Cairo. Baluchi mercenaries in Mombasa's Fort Jesus had been inherited from the Sultan of Zanzibar. These various forces were used both in Mombasa and upcountry, as well as in the troublesome coastal area north of the Tana river, known as Jubaland, and especially at Kismayu, where the Somalis caused much trouble. IBEAC had also recruited some Indians from the neighbourhood of Delhi as police, which the Company put to garrison the rebellious town of Witu. In 1895 the British Government inherited 866 IBEAC troops: 415 at Mombasa and the coastal province, 176 in Ukamba (Machakos and Ndi), 180 in Tanaland and 95 in Jubaland. Of these, 255 were Sudanese. The number of white officers is not known, but was probably four.

In 1895–96 the British Government unified the troops under the name East Africa Rifles, and kept three companies of them in Jubaland. The regiment, with its headquarters in Mombasa, was commanded by the inefficient Captain George Hatch. Three hundred troops from a Punjabi regiment were seconded to the East Africa Rifles to deal with coastal troubles, but the Somalis remained truculent. By 1897, when the territory's troops numbered 1,120 men under the command of four white officers and three retired white officers, there occurred a mutiny of the African Sudanese troops in Uganda so serious that some East Africa Rifles troops were sent there, as well as other soldiers brought from India to assist in putting down the mutiny. Detachments of Indian troops also enabled an expedition to be sent to Jubaland in 1898.

Nevertheless, the Jubaland sub-commissioner, A. C. W. Jenner, was killed by Somalis in 1900. The Indian contingent returned to India in 1900, leaving an East Africa Rifles regiment of 1,000 men to keep order in the country. They got scant help from the police, for in 1898 the police force consisted of only two British officers and seventy-seven NCOs and men, all stationed at Mombasa. Elsewhere in the Protectorate, police work was done by African station askaris. By 1901, however, there were 650 police, led by four white officers, as well as the special railway police. They were stationed at Nairobi, Mombasa and Kisumu. It was hardly a force capable of keeping order in such a vast country.

Although the Company had pursued limited goals in the interior, mainly the maintenance of communications with Uganda, the British Government envisaged extending administration over the whole area from the Rift Valley to the coast. Upon the British assumption of responsibility for the region in 1895, Sir Arthur Hardinge, the British Agent and Consul-General in Zanzibar, now became in addition Commissioner for the East Africa Protectorate. He divided the country into four provinces, each under a sub-commissioner, with subordinate districts to be administered by district officers. The whole protectorate, from the coast to the Rift Valley, where Uganda began at the Kedong river, was to be run by twenty-two white officials. The law to be administered, both criminal and civil, was to be that of British India, and Pax Britannica would be imposed. But, initially at least, things did not run as smoothly as they had under the Company.

Inland the former Company's agents, now employed by the government, noticed a marked deterioration in their lives. Months went by without mails, and for the first time plum puddings were months late for Christmas. Attempts were made to improve communications. A telegraph line was built alongside the railway as it went inland – it reached Entebbe in Uganda in 1901 – but Africans repeatedly stole the wire to adorn their bodies, for it was the height of fashion to wind it round one's ankles, calves and arms. At the beginning of 1898 the German East Africa Line, from Hamburg, began to call at Mombasa once a month. Postage stamps were issued. Hardinge begged for a British line to call at Mombasa, to no avail, though the Austrian Triestino line began a monthly service from Trieste in 1900. To assist the ships, three buoys were placed to mark the reefs outside Mombasa and a port light visible at thirteen miles was erected on the shore. In the year 1901–02 thirty-two ships used Kilindini harbour, one of them the first Shell Transport Company's oil steamer. Communications, therefore, could not be described as attractive to potential settlers.

Hardinge spent most of his time on the mainland, touring his provinces, but there was much of muddle and indecision in his rule. 'Hardinge,' said Frank Hall, 'is a wonderfully clever diplomat but as an Administrator perfectly hopeless. He looks on everything as a huge joke, and as long as the revenue increases and everything slides along without any increase in expenditure, he is perfectly satisfied.'[44]

Frank Hall had had his wife with him at Fort Smith since September 1898, but he was becoming disenchanted with his job, having discovered how uncongenial was the establishment of the British administration he had formerly favoured. Particularly galling was the elevation of Ainsworth, with whom he had never been particularly close, even when they were the only white men administering the interior. Now Ainsworth became sub-commissioner of Ukamba, one of the four provinces created by Hardinge (the other three were on the coast). It meant a great increase in office work and Hall complained that he was spending most of his time 'slinging ink', with 'silly despatches' and the 'bilious effusions' of Ainsworth.[45]

> I wish I could see my way to get another billet and get clear of all this snobbish, brass button and uniform business, so-called an Administration, whereas not a single officer upcountry has ever been twenty miles from his station, and we know less about the natives than we knew seven years ago. The administration has been cut down to allow for a toy army which never does anything but drill and blow bugles, while the officers have a state-aided shooting trip . . . We are not allowed any money to expend, we have no facilities for moving around our Districts, and are little more than police officers guarding the track of the Uganda Railway.[46]

Even more irksome were the regular audits. Frederick Jackson, now in charge of Eldama Ravine, suggested an occasional judicious fire as a solution.

Then disaster befell the Africans. The EAP was stricken by famine and smallpox in 1899. Hall was burying six to eight people a day, and extracting lymph from those infected to give to those who had not yet had the disease. He was also trying to feed 370 people who had congregated round Fort Smith. In the midst of the crisis, in August 1899, Ainsworth was ordered to transfer his headquarters from Machakos to Nairobi, now the most populous centre since the advent of the railway. It had been decided that the headquarters of Ukamba province was to be Nairobi. According to Frank Hall, Ainsworth deliberately put all the administration officials on one side of the river whereas the township and railway people were on the other, one and a half miles away. But George Whitehouse, the chief railway engineer, told Ainsworth which bits of land the railway would not require and which he could therefore use, and that was the reason for the placement.

Hall was transferred to Machakos, out of Ainsworth's way, and Fort Smith, only eight miles from Nairobi, was regarded as no longer of use and abandoned. Hall was sad to see the demise of 'his' stronghold, the scene of so much of his effort, where he was often alone and in danger, literally holding the fort. He reckoned the real reason for his move was Ainsworth's jealousy, since he was much too friendly with the railway people. In contrast, Ainsworth and his wife 'are rather barred by all'.[47] Hall's social snobbery was uppermost in his dislike of Ainsworth – 'These fellows, brought up behind a counter, get too big for their boots and make life unbearable for others.'[48] Mrs Ainsworth's sister was the wife of Hall's cashier at Machakos, and as thus was not considered a fitting companion to Hall's wife Beatrice, though how the two women avoided each other in so small a place is a mystery. But Hall set to in his new post, and tried to feed the 1,100 starving famine victims at Machakos. A third of the Kamba people died, he estimated.

Heartily disliking the Kamba, a tribe in his view inferior to the Kikuyu, Hall went to see Hardinge, who was wise enough to put him back among the Kikuyu by asking him to establish a new station, at Mbirri, forty miles from Nairobi. By May 1900 he had selected a site for the new fort, and it was soon built, with a large, solid stone wall and ditch around buildings and offices. Perched on top of a hill, the fort was strong and secure. No sooner had they settled there than Hall and Beatrice suffered the severe shock of hearing of the death of her brother Edward Russell at his recent posting, Shimoni on the coast. The EAP was still hazardous as a domicile for Europeans, and Hall lamented that the administration had lost six men in six weeks. In each of his subsequent letters to his father he listed more European deaths. Soon it was his own turn. He contracted dysentery and died at Mbirri on 18 March 1901, with Beatrice and Dr William Radford, recently summoned from Nairobi, beside him. His last words to his wife were 'How bright!'[49] 'His memory', wrote Radford to Hall's father, 'will live long among the Kikuyu as a man to be feared, respected and loved.'[50] Other friends wrote, too, saying Hall was loved by everyone, being the most popular man in the region. J. H. Patterson, later famous for his book *The Maneaters of Tsavo*, said: 'He was a most lovable man, with a thorough knowledge of the Kikuyu nation. These people knew him as Bwana Hora, and although he often chastised them, they came to love him in the end as they have loved no white man before or since.'[51] A public subscription was got up for the placing of a memorial brass in Mombasa cathedral, and Mbirri was renamed Fort Hall, a name which persisted until Kenya became independent of British rule in 1963, when the town that had grown up at the spot was renamed Murang'a. As for Beatrice, who had adapted so well to the inconveniences and dangers of Africa, and had brightened the living quarters of the forts with pretty curtains and cushions, she went to stay with the Hindes before returning to her family in England.

One of Hall's first actions at Mbirri had been to arrest an Englishman in the area, John Boyes from Hull. Boyes had entered the region in June 1898 with donkey wagons in search of food to sell to railway caravans and to troops going up to suppress the Uganda mutiny. He had made contact with one Kikuyu faction under its leader Karuri and another under Wangombe of Gaki. Karuri and Boyes allied to fight those who would not co-operate with them, and it was not long before complaints were made to Hall at Mbirri and Boyes was arrested. Boyes was acquitted of a charge of dacoity (gang robbery). He later bought land near Athi River and lived out his life in Kenya.

Sir Charles Eliot succeeded Hardinge as Commissioner in 1900. In contrast with his predecessor, he had decidedly firm ideas about the future of East Africa. He said it was only a few years since the place had been a human hunting ground, where the native tribes warred with each other to get slaves to sell to Arabs, and therefore 'we are not destroying any old or interesting system, but simply introducing order into blank, uninteresting, brutal barbarism . . . East Africa is not an ordinary Colony. It is practically an estate belonging to His Majesty's Government, on which an enormous outlay has been made and which ought to repay that outlay.'[52] What he suggested as a means to do this was an influx of white settlers to develop the country and utilise the railway. The East Africa Protectorate was soon to be transformed.

In twelve years a white nation had made inroads into a part of Africa that would be for ever changed by the contact. It was not a one-way traffic in ideas and culture, for the whites, too, were heavily influenced by Africa and the Africans. Their civilisation was modified and altered, not as profoundly as that of the Africans, it is true, but in significant ways.

3

The Early Settlers

For the land was new and all strange to me,
Who was used to the beaten track,
And of course a man's bound to be green at first,
Till the country has burnt him black.[1]

Thousands of young men had left Britain just before the turn of the century to fight the Boers in South Africa, and many of them fell in love with the African continent, with its tawny colours and wide open spaces. Britain was at the peak of its imperial might, and welcomed adventurous and enterprising young people into its new colonies. Confidence was high, the ambition to civilise seemed laudable and communications were vastly improved, with steamship and telegraph minimising the world's distances. East Africa was soon talked about as a field wide open for new endeavours, because it had a railway to the interior. The railway was a powerful magnet which drew whites to the East African Protectorate after the conclusion of the Boer War at the Peace of Vereeniging in 1902. And how to make it pay was the largest problem faced by Sir Charles Eliot, who became Governor in 1900.[2]

The son of a Wiltshire clergyman, educated at Cheltenham and Balliol College, Oxford, Eliot 'possessed a brain so acute and a memory so retentive (it has not inaptly been compared with fly-paper) that no subject, however abstruse, held terrors for him; and what others accomplished only with heavy travail, he took unconcernedly in his stride'.[3] No longer was the EAP to be an adjunct of the Zanzibar administration, for in 1902 Eliot established a secretariat in Mombasa with the young, ambitious Alfred Claud Hollis at its head as his private secretary and secretary of administration.

Claud Hollis, a barrister's son, had been privately educated in Switzerland and Germany. At the age of twenty he went to German East Africa as an employee of a German company. Then in 1897, when twenty-three, he joined the EAP administration as an assistant collector (or district officer as it became known). With fluent German, he was an asset to a governor whose neighbouring territory belonged to the Germans, and Eliot made him his private secretary in 1900. Hollis was a very proper man, perhaps rather narrow-minded, and much more studious than his fellow administrators. He was looked on with favour by the Foreign – and, later, Colonial – Office, and regarded as efficient and conscientious. The settlers saw him differently – he was not their sort of person, being, in their view, stuffy and pro-native.

This is something that could not be said of Eliot. He held the contemporary and common opinion that Africans, particularly the Maasai, were savages needful of civilisation, and the way to do this was by the example of white immigrants, whose endeavours would also make the new railway pay. He set out to encourage immigration from South Africa, where many of the men who had fought in the Boer War had stayed on. One of these was Robert Foran, later a policeman in Nairobi:

In common with many others, I had been greatly unsettled by two and a half years' war service against the Boers. I pined for new adventures; felt the call of the wild strong within me; and Africa, the land of golden sunshine and joyous memories, had set her seal upon my heart. The vast, sunlit expanse of the yellow veld appealed enormously to my imagination. I was loath to bid it farewell.[4]

Eliot was encouraged in his efforts by a British Government as yet untroubled by the morality of the European civilising mission. He was happy to undertake a vigorous propaganda campaign for settlers – during the two and a half years from July 1902 twelve Parliamentary command papers were published to encourage settlers, and the British Emigrants' Information Office issued a pamphlet containing information on the EAP.[5] Under the Foreign

Secretary Lord Lansdowne's instructions, Eliot deputed Arthur Marsden, his Chief of Customs, to visit South Africa, that reservoir of Afrophile Europeans, and drum up some immigrants. No admirer of the common man, Eliot was not prepared to have any old white riffraff – people had to prove they had the means to set themselves up and cultivate the land or earn a living in some other way. He wanted members of the middle or upper classes, with assets of at least £300.

Eliot knew that farming – crops and cattle and sheep – would become the staple of the economy. South African financiers had established a syndicate and sent prospectors to examine the mineral potential of the EAP in 1903, but the results were a sad disappointment – East Africa had nothing. Shares in the East Africa Syndicate were held by men in the Chartered Group, the South African Gold Trust and Consolidated Goldfields, and prominent men in South Africa, such as the Duke of Abercorn, Earl Grey, Lord Debbigh, Lord Harris, Otto Beit and others. Although they were disillusioned by the EAP's lack of minerals, they bought the rights of the Australian Tom Deacon, who had found soda at Magadi, and further consoled themselves by concentrating on a huge land grant given them by the Foreign Office for agricultural purposes. Another vast area – 150 square miles – was granted to Lord Delamere in 1903.

Eliot was delighted by the highly favourable report of Robert N. Lyne, director of the Agricultural Department of Zanzibar, whom he had deputed to report on the agricultural prospects of the EAP's highlands. Lyne and Alexander Whyte, temporarily transferred from Uganda to inspect the EAP for its agricultural capabilities, produced paeans of praise for the country, and particularly the highlands where the soil was rich and the labour cheap. Convinced that the EAP should become 'a white man's country', Eliot followed the Foreign Office example and made a vast land grant to R. B. Chamberlain, a South African newspaper editor and the owner of freehold properties in Potchefstroom, Transvaal, a town he wanted to leave because it had been overrun by Asian traders in the past two years.

This large land grant caused Eliot to fall out with the Foreign Office. Having listened to complaints from the EAP officials Frederick Jackson and Stephen Bagge,[6] Eliot's subordinates, that their superior was granting to white newcomers land which rightly belonged to the Maasai in the Rift Valley, it decided that it could not endorse the large grant given to Chamberlain and ordered Eliot to withdraw it. Infuriated that the Foreign Office should thus undermine him, Eliot resigned. His successor Donald Stewart refused to reopen the matter, particularly after Chamberlain sent interminable letters of complaint containing 'abusive and undignified language' which he found 'insolent and offensive'. Chamberlain continued to make a noisy fuss until, with a change of government in London and the advent of Winston Churchill at the Colonial Office (which took over the EAP from the Foreign Office in 1905), he had the decision reversed in 1907.

Chamberlain and his colleagues A. S. Flemmer and Russell Bowker conducted a campaign in South Africa to bring more whites to Kenya. Fortunately from their point of view, South Africa was suffering an economic depression. From September 1903 to March 1904 they interviewed ten to twenty potential settlers daily. They even negotiated a reduction of fares of 20 per cent and a substantial increase in the baggage allowance on the German East Africa shipping line. By July 1904 they had sent fifty men to spy out the land in the EAP, many of whom remained there, to join the core of white railwaymen staying on after the completion of the Uganda Railway.[7] Among the new arrivals were V. M. Newland, the brothers Leslie and Henry Tarlton, Hugh Cowie, Hugh Heatley, Frank Watkins, and the partners A. F. Duder and M. H. Dix.

The enthusiasm was catching. Soon even more whites were embarking on ships sailing up the East African coast to view the prospects of the EAP, some of them Australian veterans of the Boer War. To those who decided to stay in the EAP, Eliot distributed land mainly in the Kikuyu and Mbagathi districts in 1902–04, compensating any Africans found living on it. He preferred a chequerboard policy of settlement, intermingling whites and Africans, to make it easier to obtain African labour and, in his view, to civilise the native peoples more swiftly. In contrast, John Ainsworth and some of the other officials preferred a policy of setting up reserves of land for Africans, because they envisaged a wholescale erosion of African land rights by the chequerboard policy. Ainsworth often 'bunched up' Africans, giving them land near other Africans in exchange for land in what were becoming white areas. His view was underscored by the Land Commission of August 1905 which established the principle of a reserves policy in relation to future European settlement.

At the end of 1903 there was a rush of settlers from South Africa to the EAP, all wanting to buy land. Unfortunately the tiny Lands and Survey Department hastily set up in April 1903 under the former Uganda Railway employee Reginald Barton Wright, assisted by one surveyor and an Indian clerk, could not cope with the influx. But Barton Wright was an enthusiast, keen to help all new-comers. Since hardly any of the areas thrown open to Europeans ('alienated' was the term used) had been mapped, the immigrants were told to inspect land suitable for farming, pick out a block, sketch it with landmarks such as rivers or trees and register their claim with the lands officer. The officer then wrote to the sub-commissioner of the province asking if he had any objection, such as that the land was heavily populated by Africans. If the sub-commissioner did not demur and it was found that the land had not been already registered, a simple sketch of the area was made by a draughtsman in the Survey Office and the applicant's name registered. It was a rough and ready, rickety system and it was hardly surprising that it caused overlapping.

After a claim was accepted, the applicant was allowed to camp on his land and begin the arduous process of clearing it of bush and trees while the legal title was being prepared. It took months until titles were issued, because Eliot could not increase the staff of the Survey Office. He was in the Catch-22 situation of being unable to appoint extra staff because they were not in his estimates, and being prevented from estimating for staff by never knowing how many whites would be arriving. Things improved in 1906 when more staff were indeed appointed and the Survey Department, with its own director, was separated from the Land Department.

Whereas in 1902 there were only seventeen whites involved in agriculture in the country, in 1903 seventy families or firms received grants of land in the EAP: serious white colonisation of the country had begun. Some of the grants were for homesteads (500 to 640 acres), some for 1,000 acres, which was supposed to be the legal maximum, and three for larger areas. The white population of the EAP increased by 290 that year. The following year 300 applications for grants of land were made, of which 230 were successful. After Eliot, with his anti-Maasai prejudice, had gone, in 1904 an agreement was made with the Maasai to secure them certain lands for reserves. This left open to white settlement the whole of the Rift Valley as far south as Naivasha, and the heights of the Mau and Aberdare hills on either side of the valley.

* * *

I love all waste
And solitary places; where we taste
The pleasure of believing what we see
Is boundless, as we wish our souls to be.[8]

People emigrated to East Africa for a score of different reasons, celebrating the individuality of human beings in the face of conformity in their home country. They seemed exhilarated rather than dismayed by the miles of virgin, untilled land. These new farmers were encouraged by the director of agriculture, Andrew Linton, who set up two government farms to experiment with crops and animals. The government farm near Nairobi introduced imported sheep, cattle, goats, pigs and chickens to see which would survive; it also cross-bred with local animals. It conducted experiments with varieties of imported fruits, vegetables and grain. The other government farm, at Naivasha, concentrated on domesticating and hybridising zebras. But by 20 June 1904 there were only fifteen zebras left out of the herd of 100, most of which had died from internal parasites. They had been savage to the point of ferocity and unapproachable in the stalls or fields. Very few of them had been broken to pull carts. Zebras were not even edible – British immigrants thought the meat had an unpleasant smell and was altogether too like horsemeat. The government farm then concentrated on the importation of blood stock and the grading up of native herds. It held an annual sale to settlers of grade stock.

The newcomers camped on their land in tents until they built grass huts (bandas) and rondavels of mud, wattle and grass thatch. These were whitewashed and floored with polished cowdung. Basic necessities such as lamps and candles could be bought in Nairobi, or in local Indian shops called dukas springing up every-where, but for those too poor to afford them hippo fat made an excellent substitute fuel. Rawhide from wild animals was used for rope, while nails were as gold and preserved, however bent. Pioneering was not for those who valued luxury or even comfort – rather it appealed to those proud to produce from virgin soil things to eat or sell; those who enjoyed the battle with nature, that enemy always trying to return the land to its untamed state; and those who relished the victory of personal will over a wild world. Some of them 'felt that they were doing something good and even great, and that in their efforts they were earning the praise and even, possibly, gratitude of their fellow-citizens at home'.[9] Even as late as 1913 the white population of the EAP consisted almost entirely of young men. Very few people were over thirty and only a small number of government officials were over forty. There were far more men than women.

The life was not easy and most new farmers lost rather than made money. Yet the years of toil brought whites closer together, as they shared the common bond of poverty. And working the soil binds men to it, so they were reluctant to quit, becoming, as the saying was, 'frozen in'. They found they could no longer live away from the wildness and the freedom and the vast empty spaces and, of course, the sunshine. On a more mundane note, they had to pay no direct taxes and were offered reduced freight on the railway from February 1904. They also, though illegally, travelled free on the railway, seldom bothering to buy tickets. The farmers began to bring in wives and to have children. The children, of course, knew no other country and imperceptibly became Kenyan.

The farmers' main fears were of African risings, lack of labour and good land being tied up in tribal reserves. The problem of acquiring African farm labour was perennial. One of the snags was that many settlers had an ill-concealed contempt for Africans fuelled by missionary and empire publications calling them 'savages', and this attitude prevented them from keeping labour for long. It was a vicious circle, for those who ill-treated Africans failed to find labour and became negrophobes. A district commissioner (DC) writing in the Kiambu political record book listed the settlers for whom Africans refused to work, and maintained that immigrants so under-mined officials that government servants should not be compelled to obtain African labour for them.

Many DCs felt that their first loyalty was to Africans. Yet settlers expected administrative officers to encourage Africans to labour on their farms. To them the ideal DC was one who would keep Africans quiet, make them come out to work when required, and not interfere in the disciplining of employees by white farmers. DCs approached chiefs to persuade young men to go out to work, and appointed chiefs who would do their bidding. The Kikuyu chief Kinanjui grew rich by imposing fines of goats on males who refused either to work for whites or to provide substitute labourers. He also flogged reluctant labourers. A hut tax was introduced by the government in 1901, mainly to persuade Africans to work for wages in order to pay it. It had limited success and by 1910, when the labour situation was critical, a poll tax was introduced to encourage into work those African males, mainly of the warrior class, who did not pay the hut tax.

The government made some attempt to protect labour from the excesses of employers – for example, the Masters and Servants Ordinance of 1901 specified various forms of contract and imposed obligations on employers concerning the treatment of their em-ployees. It was of limited use – in the Ukamba province in 1908–09 there were 235 labour complaints against employers: 185 Africans had had their pay refused, six had been beaten, and for twenty-one their pay was overdue. In contrast, some farmers treated the Africans well and retained the same labour for years. Those who kept labour in the slack season had far less trouble getting labour in times of scarcity than those who paid off the entire staff once planting was done.

Flogging was a common punishment on farms, as Noel Smith described to his mother: 'If you know of anyone anxious to go grey quickly, send them out here to handle niggers',[10] and 'My Africans wanted a 10 instead of 11-hour day, so I flogged the nearest, and a few more, then got them to flog the others.'[11] When the farmer H. M. Harries found an African beating a valuable pig, he flogged the man so badly that he was in hospital for three months. Harries was charged with giving him over 100 strokes and pleaded guilty to inflicting 'simple hurt' under extreme provocation. The jury accepted his plea and recommended mercy, but the judge demurred and Harries served three months in prison.

Captain Longrey Hawkins, who lost 400 rupees in a robbery, was charged on three counts of causing 'grievous hurt'. He had tortured three African suspects by putting their fingers in a vice and tightening it until they confessed. One of the men died. Hawkins was sentenced to two years' imprisonment and fined 7,000 shillings. A subscription was quietly opened in several districts to pay his fine, and he served his sentence.[12] Jasper Abraham, son of the Bishop of Norwich, flogged an African to death. On being charged with murder he claimed the African had wished himself to death – a well-known phenomenon. There was an uproar in Britain at Abraham's sentence of only two years' imprisonment despite a guilty verdict. The Colonial Office ordered that in future such a trial should take place in a district other than that where the crime had been committed. In 1927 the Supreme Court of Kenya ruled that whipping was degrading but it continued as a form of punishment on a few farms. One of the reasons for the floggings was extreme frustration arising from theft, particularly of expensive livestock. Stock farming could be heart-breaking in these early years, until grade animals were available in large numbers.

Farmers experimented with a variety of crops. Potatoes became the most important crop in the highlands in 1902, but they did not export well and farmers began to plant coffee instead.[13] By 1909, 400 ostriches were being farmed for their feathers, and John Shillington was so annoyed when his herd was stampeded by one of President Theodore Roosevelt's safari party shooting on his land that he complained to the DC.[14] After fashions changed during the First World War, ostrich farmers had to diversify. John Ainsworth introduced sisal, which flourished. American maize seed, vastly superior to the local type, was also imported, and many varieties of wheat were tried in an attempt to escape the rust to which it was prone. Wattle and fruit flourished, while experiments with tobacco and sugar cane failed. But the greatest success of all came with coffee, despite its pests of cutworm, coffee leaf disease, the antestia bug, thrips and caterpillars, and the unwelcome attentions of bucks and hares. It was first planted in a commercial way near Nairobi in 1899 and began to bear in 1903.

Among the early settlers were peers and members of the upper classes – they went to the EAP in greater numbers than to other colonies. The EAP attracted them as a place where vast acreages of land could be acquired cheap, where servants were plentiful and the shooting superb. Barons (Hugh) Delamere, (Bertram) Cranworth[15] and (Charles) Hindlip were regular residents, whereas Lord Kitchener was an absentee landlord, but his elder brother, H. E. C. Kitchener, who inherited the earldom and the Kenya land, was a permanent resident. Several descendants of peers lived in the EAP, such as the brothers Galbraith and Berkeley Cole (sons of the Earl of Enniskillen), Mervyn Ridley (related to Viscount Ridley and brother of Cranworth's wife), Denys Finch Hatton (son of the Earl of Winchilsea), Robert Carnegie (son of the Earl of Southesk) and 'Ronnie' Cardross (son of the Earl of Buchan), a dreamer with long hair who set up a farm on the road to Ngong with John Van de Weyer and spent the winters in the EAP.[16]

Delamere, truculent and fierce and individualistic, became the leader of the whites, despite the evil temper and violent tendencies of his younger days. He had first come to the country for sport and exploration in 1898 and had fallen in love with the Rift Valley.

He mellowed as he aged, cut short his long hair, exchanged his rags for smart dress, and, with his alert brain and brilliant repartee in the Legislative Council, became the representative of settler opinion, guiding the farmers who 'are never more happy than when ticking off on their fingers, in unsparing detail, the shortcomings of a mean-spirited, muddle-headed, wasteful and pusillanimous Government'.[17] Galbraith and Berkeley Cole, brothers of Delamere's wife Florence, soon joined their sister in East Africa. Galbraith Cole paid his sister a visit in 1903, decided to stay, and applied for land in Laikipia at Ndaragwa. He travelled there via the Rift Valley, taking his wagon to pieces to get it over the Aberdare mountains. Then the government took over the Laikipia area for the Maasai, giving Cole land in the Rift Valley in exchange, at Kekopey, on the eastern side of Lake Elementeita. Galbraith's brother Berkeley farmed at Naro Moru.[18]

Another wealthy immigrant was William Northrup McMillan, son of the founder of the American Car & Foundry Company. He went to the EAP via the Blue Nile in 1903, with his wife Lucie Webber, of Northampton, Massachusetts, a talented artist and musician. He bought land near Ol Donyo Sabuk, a mountain near Thika, and started a farm that he called Juja. Immensely rich, he ordered a farmhouse of asbestos and steel, designed by an English architect, to be made for him in Britain and transported to Nairobi in sections. Juja was begun in 1905, on a high bluff overlooking a river; by 1908 it had electric light, a telephone, an ice-making plant, bungalows for farm workers, a bachelors' mess (in which McMillan started the Juja Club in 1910), farm offices, a dairy room and post office and telegraph station. In the farmhouse itself, surrounded by verandahs shaded by vines and bamboo blinds, were luxurious teakwood chairs, a huge telescope to see game, a pianola and running water, and the walls were ornamented with the horns of wild animals of every sort. Although McMillan spent between £50,000 and £60,000 on the place, Lucie did not like it, and before the First World War he bought for her from Ewart Grogan the stone house Chiromo, in Nairobi.

When young, McMillan was tall and muscular, with a Texas

drawl which abruptly faded as his wife drew near. In middle age his weight increased to such an extent that no diet could control it. The Africans called him the man who had to spit sideways, or Mkora (rogue) because he had so many properties that he could not settle anywhere (the McMillans also kept a house in Berkeley Square, London, and rented Bicton, Lord Clinton's seat at East Budleigh, Devonshire). He rode in a buckboard driven by four white mules until cars came to the EAP, when he acquired a Cadillac with a specially wide and strengthened front seat, on which he spread with his frail-looking, slender, gentle, white-haired wife beside him. At over twenty stone, he developed pleurisy and heart trouble, and died at Nice in 1925 at the age of fifty-two. His body was returned to Kenya, to be buried on Ol Donyo Sabuk at a site he had chosen himself. Carrying his immensely heavy coffin up the mountain was a problem, but the grave was eventually attained, on an open space overlooking the vast plain below and the Ithanga hills beyond, beneath one old, gnarled tree. There was a wild beauty about the place.

Every society needs its benefactors, and the McMillans were the EAP's. They were exceedingly generous, financing the building of the YMCA in 1911, the Scott Sanatorium which was so useful in the First World War, the McMillan Library built later in Nairobi, and many other enterprises. They also ran Chiromo and Juja farm as soldiers' convalescent homes in the First World War. McMillan was knighted for his philanthropy – his Canadian birth allowed him to enjoy this British accolade. The grounds of Chiromo were used for many charitable activities: for example, on 5 October 1918 there was a garden fete, attended by Karen Blixen, in aid of the Star and Garter Fund. Mrs John Ainsworth ran the white elephant stall, Mrs Henry Boedeker acted as fortune-teller, and Mrs Leslie Tarlton supervised the refreshment tent. The occasion was followed by a night of 'fun and frolic', to the music of the KAR band.[19]

The white population of the EAP swelled from 391 in 1897 to 5,570 at the end of 1918 (2,493 men, 1,523 women and 1,554 children). Of the 5,570, 598 were officials, 1,195 farmers, 496 businessmen, 123 missionaries, 57 professionals and 22 unclassified.

Though numbers of whites were still small, they were soon to be increased by the post-war settlement of ex-servicemen in the EAP.

*   *   *

The coming of so many whites was not unopposed by Africans. The Nandi people were the most turbulent. To subdue them, Governor Eliot obtained 400 troops from India in 1900. In 1905 another expedition against the Nandi exploited age-old enmities and used Maasai levies rather than Indian troops. But the Nandi were skilful fighters. The government troops had to march in columns stretching hundreds of yards along narrow paths through the dense bush, and meanwhile the Nandi lay in wait, concealed in the tall grass a few feet from the route. Then they dashed across the path stabbing with their spears before they disappeared into head-high grass again. At night they attacked with flurries of poisoned arrows. Eventually the Nandi succumbed to British rule. The military force required to keep the settlers and the government safe was surprisingly small, so white military officers were few in number – there were only forty-five in 1904. In 1902 the East Africa Rifles became the 3rd battalion of the King's African Rifles, which raised its strength in 1904 by absorbing two companies from Uganda. By 1912 there were twenty-four British officers and one warrant officer. The rank and file were all non-white.

The police provided a second line of security. In early days there were the railway police (mainly Indians), Mombasa police and station askaris. In 1901–02 the force was reorganised into one body under the command of a commissioner and inspector-general, and in 1904 twenty European police officers and instructors were in charge of 1,600 non-white policemen (among them 200 at Mombasa, 200 on the railway, 150 at Nairobi and 250 at Kisumu and Lamu). They often worked in tandem with the KAR – they were, for example, present on the expedition against the Nandi in 1905, and, the year before, they helped the KAR to pacify the Embu. In 1907 the Kisumu police were sent to deal with the Kitosh and Kabras people.

A small body of township police under R. M. Ewart looked after the civilian population of Nairobi. In order to control a few undesirable whites, who had come up from South Africa in 1903, the Foreign Office sanctioned the creation of ten new police officer and subordinate grade posts, which could be recruited locally. The men appointed succeeded in expelling the unwanted whites. Since settlers refused to submit to the authority of African policemen, a tiny contingent of white constables was appointed in 1908 to deal with settler matters.

The law enforced was the law of England until 1895, when a change was made and the Indian Penal Code adopted. IBEAC had instituted a British court in Mombasa in 1890, presided over by an English barrister, A. C. W. Jenner (descendant of Edward Jenner of smallpox vaccination fame), who was later murdered in Jubaland in 1900. Upon the British Government taking over responsibility for the EAP in 1895, a Protectorate Court was appointed, with a judicial officer having jurisdiction over all British subjects and foreigners. Appeals could be made to the High Court at Zanzibar until 1902, when the EAP acquired its own High Court. Law courts were built at Mombasa and Nairobi, and in 1903 the number of legal officials had expanded to two judges, two magistrates, a Crown advocate, a registrar and a government solicitor.

Miscreant whites were sent to Mombasa, to be imprisoned in the vast ex-Portuguese bastion of Fort Jesus, a building which doubled as a lunatic asylum. There were two whites among 549 prisoners there in 1898. Africans were sometimes publicly hanged if they had murdered whites, in order to deter others. The practice came to a virtual halt in 1909, with the public hanging of an African for the murder of Thomas London, a sailor on a cable ship.[20] The first hanging of a white man occurred in 1912. One Grobbelaar, a Boer, was accused of murdering his wife. The trial was held in the local theatre in Nairobi because the magistrate's court was too small, such was the interest aroused. Usually white juries found persons of their own colour innocent of murder, but in this case they did not, perhaps because Grobbelaar was a Boer.

The distressing tendency of settlers to take the law into their own hands was made clear for all to see when Ewart Grogan publicly beat up an African before Nairobi town hall in 1907. The white town magistrate was booed and mobbed by a crowd of 200 armed white settlers, while a white policeman was knocked off his bike and hustled when he tried to stop the flogging. It was a nasty incident, which could have ended in bloodshed had not the African policemen present exercised superhuman restraint.[21]

The British South Africans were not the only immigrants from that part of the continent. Their former enemies, the Boers, also found their way from South Africa. To escape an economic depression in their own land, several went to German East Africa from 1903 onwards, but finding life almost as harsh there, thirty-three of these families trekked into Kenya in 1906, among them Piet Van Dyk, P. L. ('Flip') Malan, Abraham Joubert and Martinus Engelbrecht. Twenty-five of the families settled in the Nairobi or Athi River area, and eight went to the Uasin Gishu plateau. They were not quite the first Boers to arrive. One of the Van Breda brothers had come to the EAP in 1903; in 1904 the Arnoldi family, another Van Breda brother and John de Waal made the journey; in 1905 six families, including the Steyns, came; in 1906 twelve more families (excluding those from GEA) appeared; and in 1907 a further seven families joined them, all grasping the opportunity of a more prosperous future in a new country.[22] Tragedy struck the Van Breda family when W. J. ('Bon') Van Breda was murdered by two Elgeyo tribesmen on his farm in 1907. After no notice was taken of this crime by the authorities, six months later ten of the neighbouring farmers got together, met at Arnoldi's Drift with arms and ponies, and staged an expedition to intimidate the DC. The Governor hurriedly sent KAR reinforcements up from Nairobi, the murderers were dealt with and the incipient rebellion fizzled out.[23]

The largest influx was yet to come. Jan Janse Van Rensberg, a prominent Transvaal farmer from the Bethel district, was a *roikop*, someone who had collaborated with the British in the Boer War. Such people were often ostracised in their home districts. In 1906 Van Rensberg was told about the EAP by two British hunters; he went to have a look and visited Fort Hall, Molo and Eldama

Ravine. He also took the chance to gather information about the Uasin Gishu plateau from Frans Arnoldi. What he saw and heard impressed him mightily. After he returned to South Africa, he gathered together fifty-eight Boer families over the next two years and sailed back up the coast to Mombasa, arriving on 12 July 1908. The party consisted of 247 people, forty-seven wagons and ninety horses. In Nakuru they bought oxen to pull their wagons and trekked up the other side of the Rift Valley, to Londiani and onward to the Uasin Gishu plateau, where they selected farming land near Sergoit rock. In 1911 another large group, sixty families led by C. J. Cloete, a prominent farmer from the Bethlehem district of the Orange Free State, arrived on the Uasin Gishu plateau, which now housed 900 Boers, a quarter of the country's white population. By 1916 there were 1,177.

The attitude of the British settlers towards the Boers was mixed. Oblivious of the *roikop* element, Lord Cranworth voiced his disapproval of 'the formation in our midst of a solid mass of utterly disloyal colonists, speaking their own language and having their own church'.[24] He was correct in thinking the newcomers were disinclined to mix with the British, for the Boers set up separate schools for their children and worshipped in their own churches. Their isolation was enhanced by the plateau's remoteness from the rest of the country. In the rainy season it could take six weeks to travel from Londiani along the dreadful road to Eldoret, a new settlement in the midst of the Uasin Gishu farms. But the Boers were reluctantly accepted because they were crucially useful to the British farmers of the EAP during these years before tractors became available. Since they were the only ones who could train and handle teams of oxen, they undertook all the contract ploughing for other farmers. Many of them became hired hands on non-Boer farms, and they specialised in training oxen. Others ran transport – for years J. H. Engelbrecht carried goods and people by ox wagon between Nairobi and Thika to Nyeri, Naro Moru, Nanyuki, Meru and the Northern Frontier District. He and his enormous wife and nine children lived on Arnold Paice's farm thirty-two miles from Nyeri.

British settlers often castigated Boers for their poverty, while turning a blind eye to hardship among those of their own nationality. On her honeymoon in the EAP, Madie Cator met a distressed Englishman who hadn't a penny – one Kirk from Johannesburg. In an endeavour to address the problem, in 1906 an Immigrants Ordinance was issued to restrict immigration to those with sufficient means. All white immigrants had to provide adequate security by deposit or bond of £50.

By the end of the First World War less than half the adult white male population of the EAP were farmers – only 1,195 out of 2,493 people. A large number of the rest were engaged in business activities in the towns. Mombasa had the largest population of white businessmen, and they were of many nationalities: German, Austrian, Italian, Dutch, American and Greek.[25]

Nairobi, in contrast, had few foreign businessmen – in 1910 there was only Ignatius ('James') Marcus. The prominent British businessmen in Nairobi in 1910 were Thomas A. Wood, a tough little Yorkshireman and general merchant who arrived from South Africa in 1900;[26] A. H. Wardle the pharmacist; the general merchant J. H. S. Todd; the retail chemist A. E. Standring; the transport merchant A. H. Murrow; outfitters W. Maxwell & R. Brady; the grocers D. & J. Mackinnon; safari organiser W. C. Judd; timber merchant Ewart. S. Grogan; ironmongers J. H. Gailey & D. O. Roberts; land and estate agent S. C. Fichat; accountant F. J. Firmin; wine merchants E. Felix & A. F. Favre; stockbroker R. O. Preston; building contractor Stephen Ellis; jeweller Ewart Dobbie; W. D. Young of the Dempster Photographic Studio; wagon-builder C. Bonser; draper G. W. Cearn; butcher H. W. Rowe of the Colonial Meat Co.; and land and estate agent Hugh Cowie.

The best-known firm in Nairobi was the estate agents, auctioneers and safari outfitters run by V. M. Newland and Leslie Tarlton, who came up from South Africa at the close of 1903 after fighting in the Boer War as troopers in the Australian Light Horse. They started with ten acres in what became the suburb of Parklands to the north west of Nairobi, but soon began business in a corrugated-iron shed as Nairobi's first auctioneers and estate agents. Their enterprise was so successful that they were able to open a branch at no. 6, Piccadilly, London, the destination of all who required kitting out for safari or emigration to East Africa. Another large firm was the Boma Trading Co. run by Jack Riddell, Freddie Ward and Marquis Ralph Gandolfi Hornyold.[27] It specialised in running stock from Somalia and Abyssinia through the Northern Frontier District. But its smuggling of illicit ivory and other illegal activities led to its closure by Governor Percy Girouard. These firms, together with the Indian and Goan businesses, provided everything that the people of Nairobi required. Following the example of Mombasa, in 1919 they created a Chamber of Commerce to protect their interests.

The Governor and his officials were highly critical of Nairobi's firms. They were, they claimed, unbusinesslike, discourteous and too content to muddle along giving generous credit while holding stock of cheap and shoddy manufacture. In 1908 an inspector of the National Bank of India visited a branch of the bank established in Nairobi since 1900 and forced a wholesale call of credit and reduction of overdrafts. Several weaker traders went out of business, but others still continued their casual ways. The arrival of Percy Girouard as Governor in 1911 tightened things up, boosted confidence and encouraged many newcomers to come from Britain with capital in their hands. Land boomed in price, there was a marked development in trade and the safari business increased by 50 per cent.

From the early days one of the main attractions offered by the EAP was the hunting and shooting of big game. Despite the introduction of game laws in 1900, dividing the best game areas into two huge reserves in which no hunting was permitted except on licence from the Game Department, there was considerable poaching of ivory by white hunters. Among the most successful of these was Arthur Neumann[28] who once shot eleven elephants in a day. A shy and hypersensitive man, he avoided social intercourse, concentrating on shooting elephants in the Mt Kenya area until the government banished him in 1904. Another culprit was Cecil Hoey[29] who poached ivory around Mt Elgon, shooting without a licence. To elude the game allowance of only two elephants a year, he smoked the tusks until they looked old and claimed he had found them lying about in the wilderness. It was a lucrative business, for the profit from two tons of ivory (forty-two dead elephants) could set a man up for life. Dr A. E. Atkinson, Lord Delamere's companion on his original journey to the EAP via Abyssinia, Alfred Arkell-Hardwick, W. D. M. ('Karamojo') Bell and Henry Rayne were all involved in illicit elephant hunting – on one safari alone Bell acquired 14,000 pounds of ivory.

Big-game hunting appealed greatly to young men at the end of the nineteenth century, brought up as they had been on tales of excitement and the derring-do of hunters such as F. C. Selous, R. Gordon Cumming, Sir W. Cornwallis Harris, Rowland Ward, Sir Samuel Baker and William Cotton Oswell. The sport presented challenge in its most elemental form; daring and danger combined were a powerful drug. Life becomes more significant and intensely lived when one is in danger of losing it.

After the 1890s, word of the superb hunting available in East Africa spread far and wide and the safari business became most profitable. The first of the visitors sent by the travel firm Thomas Cook came in 1909 and included Sir Frederick Treves, rescuer of the Elephant Man. Considerable profits were derived from outfitting these European sportsmen, and from equipping and leading their safaris. In response to the demand, the profession of white hunter emerged, with its attractive gypsy lifestyle, as did that of game ranger. The EAP's white hunters of the time were R. J. Cuninghame, Alan Black, Henry and Leslie Tarlton, William Judd, Cecil Hoey and Marcus Daly. John Boyes made a living by the sale of ivory and rhino horn, and Arthur Blayney Percival, one of the first of the EAP's game rangers in 1901, had a profitable sideline in capturing and exporting cheetah cubs to India, where maharajahs used them for hunting.

White hunters could earn two to three guineas a day for leading safaris, the cost of which averaged £250 for a two-and-a-half-month trip. Three to four hundred safari parties visited East Africa annually during the first fourteen years of the twentieth century.

Their members were obsessed with the tape measure, to size the skins and horns of animals they had bagged. The trophies were cured by the firm of Rowland Ward and sent to the client's home country, and thus the hunter rendered immortal the animals he had shot. A code of behaviour grew up: for example, it was not considered sporting to kill a rhino, and shooting on the plains did not rank as highly as that in the bush because the etiquette of hunting required animals to have a sporting chance. The hunter was supposed never to leave a wounded animal, but to track and despatch it properly. Some men believed that if a hunter could not see an animal well enough to place the vital shot he should not fire at all. On the other hand, one prolific author of hunting sagas, Chauncey Hugh Stigand, maintained that the sportsman should never let the Africans think a white man was afraid of anything.

The American Paul J. Rainey was the first to introduce to the EAP the hunting of lions with imported hounds, formerly used for the hunting of cougar. Two hounds would follow the scent and put up the lion, and the rest would then be released to surround the animal and keep it in one spot until the hunter could approach to shoot it. Rainey killed over a hundred lions by this method. Big-game hunting was always very dangerous, and there were several deaths, particularly from attacks by lions. Basil Culverhouse de Gex, Walter Stuart, William Harrison, Arthur Godfrey, Halford Lucas of Ol Donyo Sabuk,[30] Fritz Schindler, George Grey, J. W. T. McClellan[31] – these were the names of those lions had killed and were recited as a dreadful warning of what could happen to others.

Fritz Schindler was a strange Swiss white hunter of nervous disposition who had despatched sixty lions in his time, despite being an erratic shot. A good raconteur, he was always reckless to the point of madness when hunting and if he had spectators would indulge in foolhardy actions, such as going up to a dead lion to cut out its heart and eat a piece of the meat. He said an old Maasai had told him this would give you strength. He was working on the Magadi railway in January 1914 when he decided to help the American photographer Cherry Kearton to make a film of a lion hunt. During the filming, an enraged lion, chivvied all morning

from place to place, mauled Schindler so severely that his abdomen
was split open. He died shortly after he was taken to hospital.
Another lion victim was George Grey, the brother of Edward
Grey, later British Foreign Secretary. George Grey was well known
for raising a corps, Grey's Scouts, in the Matabele rebellion of 1906.
Riding on the Athi plains with Sir Alfred Pease, a local farmer, he
was galloping within fifty yards of a slightly wounded lion when it
charged him. Pease pumped several shots into the beast at close
range, but this only maddened it. It leapt upon Grey and lacerated
him so badly that he died. Grey's is still one of the best-preserved
tombstones, too many of which bear the legend 'killed by a lion', in
the old Nairobi cemetery at the foot of the Hill.

The Athi plains teemed with lions. Several men who made their
homes there – Alfred Pease and Philip Percival (Blayney's brother)
and the cousins Clifford and Harold Hill – were happy to entertain
such notables as the Duke of Connaught, Theodore Roosevelt and
Stewart Edward White, in order to escort their guests to lion shoots
at Wami hill nearby. At the foot of the hill was a cluster of rocks
called the Pulpit, beside a winding game trail leading down from
the top. The sportsmen hid in the Pulpit while Kamba tribesmen
beat the lions down the hill towards them. Seldom did a visitor fail
to bag a lion. As for Clifford and Harold Hill, proprietors of an
ostrich farm on the plains, Clifford shot 160 lions and Harold 135.

The visit of the American President Theodore Roosevelt in 1909
brought much free publicity to the country. In Roosevelt's introduction to *African Game Trails*, his book about the safari, he evoked
the allure of the EAP with the words: ' "I speak of Africa and golden
joys"; the joy of wandering through lonely lands; the joy of hunting
the mighty and terrible lords of the wilderness, the cunning, the
wary and the grim.'[32] Roosevelt and his son Kermit employed Bill
Judd and R. J. Cuninghame as their white hunters, and they also
stayed with the wealthy American settler W. N. McMillan, on
whose estate at Ol Donyo Sabuk six lion dens were left alone for ten
months to be ready for the distinguished visitor. Such ploys were
necessary because Roosevelt, with his poor eyesight, was often quite
unable to see game clearly visible to anyone else.

The presidential party shot nine lions, five hyenas, eight elephants, seven hippos, six buffaloes, and thirteen rhinos, of which nine were white – well over the permitted limit. There was one human casualty – H. Williams of Lumbwa, attacked and fatally injured by a lion while accompanying the hunting party. There was some criticism of this animal slaughter in the press, but Roosevelt explained that he was providing specimens for museums, as was indeed the case. His African porters gave him the name of 'Bwana Tumbo', flatteringly translated in the American press as 'the portly master' but actually meaning 'Mr Big Belly'. His visit to the EAP attracted many more sportsmen and other tourists, as did the publication in 1907 of J. H. Patterson's *The Man Eaters of Tsavo*, about the lions who used the builders of the Uganda Railway as daily rations.[33]

The typical garb of the big-game hunter was khaki shorts or trousers, and a khaki shirt with a pocket on the left but none on the right lest it catch the toe of the rifle stock. The shirt had long sleeves rolled up, to be let down in thorny country. In the pockets would be a magnifying glass for making fire, an empty cartridge case carrying disinfectant crystals of potassium permanganate and a pair of small tweezers for extracting thorns. The early white hunters sometimes behaved very badly towards Africans. A. E. Atkinson pitched camp in the middle of an Embu shamba and helped himself to the crops to demonstrate how powerful he was. Unsurprisingly, his loads were stolen and two of his porters killed. So Atkinson retaliated by shooting twelve Africans and burning a village.[34] When young Claude de Crespigny was on safari he chased with a hog spear an African who had brought him a warm rather than cold beer and accidentally killed him. At his trial, to the cheers of the court, the white jury acquitted him of culpable neglect in using weapons, saying that they knew their duty to a white man.[35]

Safari leaders had to be good organisers rather than managers of men, for the actual direction of the porters was done by the headman or neapara, who relied on flogging as a sanction. Karamojo Bell believed that Africans hardly felt the beatings and certainly did not resent them, for 'nature is kind to her not too clever children'.[36] The hunter Gorell Barnes regarded the practice as perfectly permissible, for 'the black man does not think for himself; he expects his Bwana to do that for him'.[37] The white hunter always had a gunbearer, whose job it was to hand his master another rifle while he reloaded the original one. Men of the gunbearer class were never flogged – a sarcastic scolding was generally sufficient for them if they transgressed, declared Stewart Edward White, though a more serious fault could be punished on the spot by the white man's fist.[38] The white hunters' lives were so dependent on the efficiency of these gunbearers that they often developed a strong bond with them, as Robert Foran described:

> Hamisi bin Baraka . . . was invariably a tower of strength on all my safaris . . . The story of his long and faithful service, genuine loyalty and stoical courage under all circumstances, coolness and efficiency during critical moments with dangerous big game, complete understanding of my varying moods, splendid comradeship at all times, and tragic death in saving my life from an enraged bull elephant . . . I shall ever honour Hamisi bin Baraka and can never forget this great-hearted African.[39]

*   *   *

After Governor Eliot resigned in 1904 he was succeeded by the ex-soldier Sir Donald Stewart. Though Claud Hollis remained as the Governor's private secretary, he did not entirely approve of his new boss. He said of him, 'Though indolent, he was a disciplinarian, who thought no country could be properly administered until (to use his own phrase) the natives had been licked into shape.'[40] Intolerant of any nonsense from the settlers, Stewart was a better friend to the military than to his civil officials, often dining at their mess. Keen on sport, he was a convivial host, fond of company, a hard drinker, and he never went to bed until the early hours of the morning or rose much before midday.

Stewart's personal staff (the Secretariat transferred now from Mombasa to Nairobi) lived with him at Government House, a bungalow on the Hill taken over from George Whitehouse, the builder of the Uganda Railway. Hollis and another member of the Secretariat, N. A. Kenyon-Slaney, could not tolerate the late drinking hours of their superior, and moved out to their own place. Stewart did not last long – on 1 October 1905 he died of pneumonia following a leg wound caused by a fall from his horse while jumping a ditch. By that time the civil administration, composed of eight departments in 1901, had grown to fourteen departments. A new Government House, of mock-Tudor style, was built in 1905.

Stewart was succeeded by Sir James Hayes-Sadler, a peaceable, portly man with a face like that of a surprised sheep.[41] Though of pleasant personality and socially popular, he was disastrous as a governor because he could never make up his mind. He would reply to all suggestions and requests with a letter saying he would give 'sympathetic consideration' to the subject, a phrase which became a joke among settlers and officials. The Colonial Office thought him 'amiable and conciliatory to the verge of timidity'[42] and when he left office in 1909 downgraded him to the governorship of the Windward Islands.

He was succeeded by Sir Percy Girouard, a French Canadian born in Montreal and formerly the director of railways in Sudan, Egypt and South Africa. Girouard had married into Transvaal society but his wife thoroughly disliked the EAP and the partnership crumbled shortly after he completed his tour in 1912.[43] A short, dapper, handsome man with boyish energy and enthusiasm, he talked with a clipped accent and sported a monocle. He got on better with the settlers than with his own officials, of whom he was very critical in his home despatches. One was 'hopeless and supine', another 'self-satisfied and pig-headed', and a third 'mistrusted and unpopular'. None the less, Girouard commanded the respect of his own Secretariat, possibly because he was a great delegator despite his forthright views. No respecter of authority, he pushed through a railway to Thika against Colonial Office opposition. He had no compunction, either, about granting Lord Kitchener, a friend from Sudan days, land in the EAP on very favourable terms.

The Governors' subordinates were initially men taken over from

IBEAC, but gradually a professional class of colonial civil servants was recruited in Britain. The lot of such young men, posted to remote stations miles from any white men or women, was to suffer loneliness, despair and sexual frustration for those who did not have African mistresses. Officials had to seek permission before they could marry, and some districts were barred to white wives. It was very common to have a local mistress, and in 1903 one DC in the Nandi district had a whole harem. The missionaries, and some settlers, deplored the use by officials of African women as concubines. The settler W. Scoresby Routledge complained to the Governor that the Nyeri DC, Hubert Silberrad, kept concubines. The matter was raised in Parliament where one MP, Cathcart Wason, created a stir when he said that officials lacked the same facilities as MPs, who could just walk outside and take their pick of white women. This drew the attention of Downing Street to the affair and prompted the issuing of the Crewe circular in January 1909. In it Lord Crewe wrote:

> It has been brought to my notice that officers in the service of some of the Crown Colonies and Protectorates have in some instances entered into arrangements of concubinage with girls and women belonging to the native population. The moral objections to such conduct are so generally recognised that it is unnecessary to dwell on them . . . [I stress] the grave injury to good administration which must inevitably result . . . [Please] warn them of the disgrace and official ruin which will certainly follow from any dereliction of duty in this respect. (Enclosure A in Circular of 11 January 1909, Confidential, Downing St.)

The taking of African mistresses none the less continued. One official poured scorn on the circular with the verse, to be sung to the tune of 'The Church's One Foundation':

> Pity the Poor Official
> Whene'er he gets the stand
> He may not have a bibi[44]
> He has to use his hand.

And so he saves his money,
His character – his job,
And only has to answer for
His conduct to his God.
Oft times on an outstation
Your ardent nature pined
For the dusky little maiden
Who in your arms reclined.
Now you must put her from you,
Pronounce the stern decree
Your nights are cold and cheerless
But promoted you will be.[45]

The weariness of government boma life, the heat, the tropical illnesses, the over-indulgence in alcohol – all these were touched upon in a district officer's verse:

'Ship me somewhere east of Suez.'
The man who could write such rot
Should come and live, and the best years give,
Of his life in this God damned spot
I'm sick of the 'spicy breezes',
I loathe the 'coral strand'
And the surf that roars on the reef-girt shores
Of this Godforsaken land.
I'm weary of dusky maidens,
 I'm sick of all the things
 One has to eat; and the prickly heat
That the whisky and soda brings.
I loathe these doddering palm trees
With their everlasting quiver;
Oh for some grass, an English lass,
And a Sunday on the river.
Old Mac[46] the Government doctor
Gave me at best a year
Here's ten months gone, and I still live on,
If you call it living here.

> I know my number's hoisted,
> For I'm only skin and bone,
> But I shan't much grieve for the life I leave
> When I start for the great unknown.

These lines were written by K. D. J. Duff, a young district officer (DO) at Kipini, a remote fishing village on the coast north of Malindi, who committed suicide at Garsen shortly afterwards, on 3 July 1919.[47] He was suffering from syphilis, acquired either locally or during English escapades, as he detailed in other stanzas of his verse. Duff had been taking mercury and potassium iodide for the sores on his legs, which refused to heal and which the Tanaland medical officer thought were syphilitic when he explained to authorities in Nairobi why Duff had been absent from work for three weeks in February.[48]

On receiving a very depressed letter from her son, Duff's mother had set out from England and made the difficult journey to Lamu by steamer and further south to Kipini by coastal dhow. She arrived at or just after his committal to the ground beside the officials' bungalow and cursed the DC, Captain A. O. Luckman, whom she held responsible for the tragedy because he had sent Duff on foot safari when he was unwell (and then followed him up the Tana river in the government launch). The strain was too much for Mrs Duff – she had a seizure and was transported to Lamu, where she died.[49] That is the story which has come down to us orally, but her grave is not listed among those of Europeans in Lamu, and it is possible that she returned to Britain or went to Nairobi. She may well be the Mrs M. Duff who died of 'insanity and heart failure' in Nairobi Lunatic Asylum on 17 July 1923.[50] That she visited her son's grave in Kipini is certain, because a local elder remembered her there.[51]

Duff was laid beside another DO, C. G. Pitt, the graves being tactlessly positioned in view of the DC's house, beside that of C. T. Mitchell (who died on 8 June 1914), manager of the Belazoni Estate of rice and rubber five hours upstream.[52] Clifford George Pitt had gone mad (possibly as a result of sunstroke or malaria) and thrown himself into the Tana river. He was pulled out but lost consciousness and died near Kibusu on 5 February 1915. Two ghosts were said to haunt the DC's house, one of them of C. Pitt and the other of Mrs Duff. Kipini was therefore an unpopular station and from the early 1930s a ghost book was kept there. Today Africans will not go near the DC's house, now in ruins, because they say tormented spirits haunt it.[53]

Outstation work such as that at Kipini could generate a feeling of power. Alas, the concomitant sense of self-importance could result in pomposity, pretension, a tendency to quarrel with one's fellow officers ('when Tin God meets Tin God there is bound to be trouble'[54]) and resentment at directions from Nairobi impinging on one's own domain. Sometimes the young men's sense of power and prestige degenerated to paranoia and illegal actions, such as the burning of huts belonging to tax defaulters.

In 1897 there were twenty-two administrative officers in the entire EAP territory, although the effective strength was nineteen because there were two vacancies and four men were off sick. Many of them were former IBEAC men, and as late as 1907 five of the six provincial commissioners (PCs) in the EAP were Company men, the last of whom, C. R. W. Lane, did not retire till 1923. Between 1900 and 1914 there was a steady increase in the number of administrators (in 1904 there were 240 of them), and 140 district officers were recruited.[55] They had no preliminary training but were required to take a Swahili test after a while, and from 1907 a law examination. In 1909 the Colonial Office introduced a three-month course in London which included surveying, accounts and law. This was not, however, taken by those recruited in East Africa. The administrative officers were home recruited, locally recruited (chosen for experience rather than education) or transferred from other African territories.

The officials were under the control of the Secretariat responsible to the Governor. Secretariat officers considered themselves a cut above field officers – after all, they had to pass a spelling test. All the words in the following sentence had to be spelled correctly: 'It is agreeable to perceive the unparalleled embarrassment of the harassed pedlar whilst gauging the symmetry of a peeled potato, before a Committee of Judgment.' This fitted them to be masters of men. Such a requirement would have prohibited the illiterate but splendid James Martin, DO at Eldama Ravine, from serving in the Secretariat.

Though mainly middle-class, administrators came from very mixed backgrounds. Alfred Jenner, murdered by the Somalis, was the son of a baronet. In former life he had been a barrister. Frank Hall was the son of a soldier and the nephew of Lord Goschen. J. W. Tritton was the son of a master mariner. There were many parsons' sons, such as Stephen Bagge, J. R. W. Pigott, F. W. Isaac and J. W. T. McClellan. There was no pattern in the former lives of the early officials, although there was a strong military element. Three had ranched in America, one was a tea-planter in Ceylon who subsequently spent two years in Australia as an explorer, another was a lay artisan in the Church Missionary Society and yet another a doctor who had seen Congo service. Many came from South Africa – at least five had served in the Imperial Yeomanry there, and one in the Transvaal Civil Service. One was formerly in the Cape Mounted Rifles. There were also a former classics master, gold assayer, bank clerk and lumberjack.[56]

As more posts were filled from Britain, so the level of education of the officials rose, because the Colonial Office favoured university men. Between 1895 and 1914 a third of the officials had been to university and half to public school. Of the eight cadets who went to the EAP between November 1911 and March 1912, three had been to Oxford and three to Cambridge.[57] Outdoor types fitted the bill better than the studious – indeed, by 1914 there were three Oxford rowing blues and one Cambridge football blue. The new breed of administrator had a strong sense of duty to the African and a respect for seniority. He was, perhaps, a greyer man than his exuberant, adventurous IBEAC predecessor.

The officials faced great danger to their health in their postings. Of the twenty administrators present in 1897 seven died within ten years. Between 1901 and 1910 eleven officials died, and between 1911 and 1920 sixteen. Most of them died of blackwater fever, a complication of malaria when the urine turns wine-coloured as the blood cells break down.[58] There were some suicides and murders. Three men were killed by Africans, one by an Indian sub-assistant surgeon and one by a fellow white man, Dugmore. Drink, which took the edge off loneliness and boredom, was the curse of the isolated district officer and some died from its effects, whereas wild animals accounted for at least one death.

Those who survived had to fulfil a variety of roles. The DC was tax-gatherer, registrar of births, marriages and deaths (at this stage for whites only), doctor, presider at executions, judge, supplier of water, road- and bridge-builder, and sometimes digger of latrines to eradicate hookworm. One DC, disappointed that the Africans would not use the latrines, said that he now knew the meaning of a 'bottomless pit'. DCs organised sports competitions on special occasions and James Bond Ainsworth, brother of John Ainsworth and similarly fond of Africans, held dancing competitions among the Kamba, joining in round the evening fire in his pyjamas and gumboots.

The officials were divided into first and second classes, and there was a rigid table of precedence. The Nairobi Club admitted only first-class officials, so Parklands Club was opened for those of the second class, often non-professionals, people such as police officers. Second-class men could also use the Railway Institute, begun as a club for the forty-five whites who ran the Uganda Railway. There was great emphasis on correct dress and the wearing of uniforms (khaki field dress and 'white undress uniform for ceremonious occasions'), and in Nairobi and Mombasa it was obligatory to leave visiting cards. Most people deplored the card system but it did have the advantage that everyone got to know each other.

Sometimes firm friendships developed between settlers and officials, particularly when officials began to marry among the settler population, although an attitude of antagonism persisted among many. J. O. W. Hope was one of those rare officials who was universally liked and respected, by both his colleagues and the settlers. Another popular official was Shenton Thomas, who ran the Secretariat with one other official during the First World War. One of his assets was his skill at cricket, which made him very welcome at the Cricket Club.

The administrators were not well off, being paid a starting salary of only £250 a year. They did, however, have free housing (or a housing allowance) and six months' leave in Britain every two and a half years. They were not allowed to hold land or any other investments in the EAP. A circular reminding them of this inspired a letter from H. C. E. Barnes[59] of the Audit Department to W. J. Monson[60] in the Secretariat, asking whether there was any objection to his holding a six-by-four-foot plot in the cemetery, and confessing that 'on Saturday last I held for a negligible period a pecuniary interest in a horse, but I trust that in view of the fact that the said horse failed through a misunderstanding to reach the starting post, my action in this interest may be overlooked'. Monson, a round little man and versifier of some skill, replied, 'The eager anticipation of opulence, doomed, as it almost always is, to speedy disappointment, has been found to be very prejudicial to the efficient performance of public duty.'[61] Tongue in cheek, Barnes asked for a pay rise with the lines:

I've audited the year's accounts Appendix A to G
And found therein some grave mistakes where no mistakes
should be.
The cash account submitted is on paper cheap and thin,
The nasty stain across the front is evidently gin.
The Treasurer not only shows an ignorance of sums
But displays his nasty habits by the imprints of his thumbs.
The total of expenditure a serious flaw presents.
In casting you will notice there's an error of five cents,
Though the total of the debit with the credit side agrees,
You'll find the debit side is pounds, the credit side rupees . . .
Before I close the year's report I've one thing more to say:
Now don't you think it's nearly time I had a rise in pay?
An increment of fifty pounds is not a bit too large
Believe me, Sir, obediently, the Auditor in Charge.

In order not to have to raise salaries after the First World War, the Governor abolished the rule forbidding officials to own land, so that they could supplement their incomes.

Officials were frequently poorly housed, as one wife remembered:

The queerest house we ever had was at Baricho, a substation from Nyeri. The 'house' was a two-roomed grass verandah, with a thatched roof and walls made of river rushes plaited over the basket like frame of withies. The floor was mud and the walls were full of tarantulas. There was only a gap in the walls for a front door, as the former officer who had built it had a theory that a leopard never went through an opening if it had a narrow passage with a right-angled turn at the end . . . The odd thing was that the mud huts which formed the office, gaol and African quarters were well built. The gaol had a magnificent door studded with nails in the Zanzibar style. The station was very proud of this door. When prisoners got sick of their loss of liberty they always dug their way out of the mud walls and left the door intact.[62]

*   *   *

After farmers, government servants and businessmen, the fourth largest group of whites in Kenya was the missionaries. By 1910 there were eighteen different missionary bodies maintaining seventy mission stations under seventy-two white clergy and 169 lay workers, many of them white. They had about 5,000 African adherents, although it is true to say that many of these had attached themselves to missions to avoid having to labour for whites, because the missions negotiated deals with DOs whereby properly registered students were exempt from this obligation.

The government had deep reservations about missionaries. In the early years they could comfort themselves with the thought that few missionaries would survive their lonely sojourns in remote districts. For example, up to 1900 the Methodists sent twenty-five whites to mission stations, of whom seven died of fever and two were murdered, and of the rest only four withstood the climate for any length of time. Soon, though, cooler upland stations were opened and missionaries came in great numbers. So scandalised was the government about the behaviour of A. Ruffelle Barlow in Kikuyuland in 1905 that they deported him as potentially dangerous to the integrity of the European population. His crime was to drink beer with Africans, eat their food, dance with them and become fluent in the Kikuyu language. This sort of racial mixing led to his arrest, but he was allowed back into the EAP after a year provided he promised to avoid repeating his earlier behaviour.[63] He became a proficient linguist, publishing in 1914 *Tentative Studies in Kikuyu Grammar and Idiom.*

Of the missionaries the most successful were the Roman Catholics, who were almost entirely self-supporting and regarded by the government as a good example to Africans, because they provided industrial and technical training. In 1899 they opened the famous 'French mission', St Austin's, at Kabete outside Nairobi, and built the Ste Famille church there. Another Catholic mission was that of the Mill Hill Fathers, who had been in Uganda since the 1880s. They moved slightly south to open missions at Mumias and Kisumu in 1895. A third Catholic group, the Italian Consolata Fathers, set themselves up near the new government station of Nyeri in 1902. They had four or five sisters, dressed in a light grey habit trimmed with white, and the same number of priests and lay brothers, who wore no distinctive dress. On the 400 acres granted to them by the government they planned to grow vines and olives, neither of which proved a success, so they turned to education in technical matters.[64] By 1911 they had four schools, in Nyeri, Limuru and Fort Hall. Altogether the Catholics had seven stations among the Kikuyu by 1903.

A rival to the Catholics was the well-financed Church Missionary Society, whose relations with the government were 'armed neutrality at the best and daggers drawn at the worst'.[65] Established in the EAP since the 1840s, the CMS moved inland with the railway. Harry Leakey opened a mission at Kabete in 1902, from which the CMS spread until they had ten missions upcountry by 1908. The CMS missionaries were low church, often verging on

Puritanism, and were the loudest of the mission sects in their protests against certain African customs, practices regarded as best left alone by officials. It was the CMS who urged the government to take action against customs such as infant marriage, the dragging of the dying out of huts to leave them exposed in the forest, the similar exposure of twins or deformed children, pre-marital intercourse and, in 1918, female circumcision. The officials harboured deep reservations about this interference in local practices, undermining as it did the control of Africans by their traditional authorities. They feared detribalisation, and a weakening of colonial authority exercised through the medium of African chiefs. But the missionaries saw this as an abdication of responsibility and resented the government's unwillingness to act in favour of Christian morality. Occasionally the government would issue a general admonition against certain practices, but no effort was made to enforce compliance.

The settlers likewise looked askance at the missionaries, who were inclined not only to propagate the dangerous notion of equality in the sight of the deity but also to disapprove of settler lifestyles. Settlers gambled and drank and generally enjoyed themselves when they came to town after months of hard work farming in the wilderness. They were not a godly lot and some of them had African concubines. The EAP's first bishop, William George Peel of Mombasa, complained about how settlers kept themselves aloof from the mission community – for example, in his thirty-two years at Mombasa the missionary H. K. Binns had never entertained or been entertained by non-missionary whites.

The settlers deplored the Europeanisation of Africans who went to mission schools. They did not want pious Christian subordinates working for them; neither did they like uppity, educated Africans or those who wore European dress. A more liberal opinion was that Africans were better in their natural state of undress:

They do not seem to be troubled with many notions regarding decency, being evidently of the sensible opinion that the only object of clothing is to keep one warm; and as the parts of the bodies they think it most necessary to keep warm are not those which we blind followers of convention consider it most necessary to keep covered, the results are rather shocking to a new arrival in the country like myself, but I daresay it is only a matter of getting accustomed to it![66]

Apart from the CMS and the Catholics, many other, smaller, sects also opened missions. One of the most energetic of these was the Scots mission founded at Kibwezi by Mackinnon which moved in 1899 to Dagoretti. By 1909 it had five schools in Kikuyuland, and by 1919 thirteen. It abandoned its independence and linked up with the Church of Scotland mission, with its headquarters at Tumu Tumu from 1909.

The German Protestants (the Neukirchen mission) concentrated on the Tana area, opening a chain of missions along the river. The missionaries were interned in the First World War and their eighteen stations handed over to the Methodists. The United Methodist mission moved to Meru in 1913. Its counterpart, the American Methodist mission, caused protests among settlers, because the black and white sisters indulged in the tactile habit of kissing each other, and, even more deplorable, the white sisters were seen to be fondling black babies. Non-missionary whites were shocked by such behaviour, for surely it was wrong to encourage too familiar and sentimental intercourse between white and black?

There were two other American groups, the Africa Inland Mission and the Seventh Day Adventists. The former occupied Kijabe and then moved across the Rift Valley to Eldama Ravine, Lumbwa, Kapsabet, Kabarnet and other places. The Seventh Day Adventists arrived in Kisumu in 1902 and settled on Kaimosi as the site for their headquarters. Two of them wrote home for their wives and a third, Arthur B. Chilson, asked the home committee to choose him a wife and send her out. The only specifications were that she should not have red hair or wear glasses. His marriage must have been a success because he lived to a great age, not dying until 1979; his wife died six years later. Visitors to their mission were likely to be offered green corn and pumpkin pie.

In 1910 Richard Gethin, a trader in Kisii, was unimpressed by
the calibre of the Seventh Day Adventist missionary pastors
Herbert Sparks (a South African with a Cockney accent) and
Cascallon, who seemed more interested in trading for buffalo
hides. Cascallon saw an old Luo asleep under the shade of a tree,
put his hand on the African's head, kicked him awake and said,
'Son, you are saved.' Then he roped him in to carry a load on the
safari.[67] As for Sparks, he gave up being a missionary when the
trade in ostrich feathers and buffalo hides came to an end and
started the Lake View Hotel.

A very rare occasion when missionaries and settlers were united
in a common cause was over the Zionist plan to establish a Jewish
homeland in the EAP, in response to pogroms in eastern Europe.
In 1903 Joseph Chamberlain, the Colonial Secretary, paid the
EAP a visit and afterwards offered some of the land to the Zionist
Federation as a home for the Jews.[68] Governor Eliot had his
doubts, but suggested the Uasin Gishu plateau as a suitable area.

When word of Chamberlain's offer reached East Africa there
was immediate opposition from the settlers. Lord Delamere sent a
telegram to *The Times* and a meeting was convened in Nairobi
at which the Revd P. A. Bennett maintained that missionaries
violently opposed the scheme. Some speakers at the meeting
objected to the poverty of the Jews and their supposed lack of
agricultural knowledge. Delamere wrote a pamphlet,[69] Lord
Hindlip joined the protests[70] and the *African Standard* waged a
virulent anti-Semitic campaign. Bishop Peel joined the settlers in
opposing this large-scale Jewish settlement. As it happened, the
threatened influx of Jews never occurred because an exploratory
committee sent out by them found the proffered land to be
unsuitable. It is not true, as was claimed later, that obstacles were
put in the way of the committee by settlers.[71]

The whites in the EAP required the services of professionals
such as doctors, lawyers, surveyors and teachers, to keep their
society running smoothly. There was also a veterinary service,
begun by Robert John Stordy for the Uganda Transport Service in
1898; he became Chief Veterinary Officer of the EAP and Uganda

in 1901. He remained the sole vet in the country until 1904 when more vets went out to deal with an outbreak of rinderpest, whereupon he became Chief Veterinary Officer, a post he held till 1921, when he went to Peru before retiring to Kent. He was a popular man, a genial Scot of great cordiality.

The first PMO (Principal Medical Officer) to the EAP was Dr Walter H. B. Macdonald, appointed in 1895 with two sub-ordinates, Drs S. L. Hinde and H. E. Mann.[72] These men had to cope with the severe smallpox epidemic of 1898–09, which coincided with famine. Their task was assisted by the arrival in 1898 of William John Radford, Medical Officer of Health in Nairobi from 1904 to 1907. Gradually a few other doctors joined them: among them C. A. Wiggins and C. L. Chevalier (1901), E. J. Eynstone-Waters (1902); R. A. Moffat (transferred from Uganda, 1902); P. H. Ross, bacteriologist (1902); W. O. Pritchard and H. L. Henderson (1904); and V. A. L. Van Someren (1905). By 1904 there were forty European doctors, nurses and pharmacists. In 1906 James Will, formerly of the Uganda Railway, became PMO, and in the following year A. D. Milne.

Thereafter there were many increases in staff, as the doctors' initial responsibility for the health of officials and their families spread to the care of the African population as a whole. Private doctors for the settlers established themselves in the main settler areas, men such as Dr R. W. Burkitt, famous for his odd ideas and unorthodox treatments, Gerald V. W. Anderson, A. J. Jex-Blake (son of the headmaster of Rugby School), and Dr Violet Clarke and her husband. Government doctors were also allowed to treat settlers, and among those who did so were J. Langton Gilks, PMO in Nairobi, and H. L. Henderson in Nakuru.

A few of these early doctors were decidedly eccentric – perhaps that was why they had gone to the EAP in the first place. In 1913 the Acting PMO was Major James Augustine Haran, an enthusiastic walker. As he left the windows of his house uncurtained, at night passers-by could see him standing upright in front of a sloping board atop a tall packing case, reading a book intently by the light of two tallow candles. He had absolutely no social life.[73] As for Dr

Burkitt, a Dublin graduate and son of the vicar of Athenry, he was in religion a low-church evangelical. He rented a small hall in Nairobi where he conducted a service for Africans every Sunday. That was acceptable though peculiar in settler eyes, but he was also an earnest follower of the British Israelites and believed explicitly in the 'Prophecies of the Pyramids', being convinced that the end of the world was due in 1921. Though charitable, he would never let anyone who could afford it escape payment, for settlers were notorious for reneging on their doctors' bills. Burkitt had a very large practice, in which he was joined by Dr J. W. Gregory, and amassed a considerable fortune.

*   *   *

The Governor Sir Charles Eliot had said that the EAP was 'a white man's country', and one could be forgiven for thinking that it was well on the way to becoming one when the First World War broke out, so rapid had been the developments since the coming of the Uganda Railway. And yet the number of white settlers was still small, and agricultural problems still acute. Vast tracts of the country remained vacant of whites. Henry Rayne touched on the emptiness and remoteness when he remarked: 'Beyond Jie we passed naught of interest [in Karamojong] save a lonely grave, in which natives said a European had been laid to rest. Who he was they knew not. Perhaps someone in the great outside world often wondered what had happened to him; well, here he lay, with lots of elbow room to be dead in.'[74] The settler Mavis Birdsey echoed the sentiment when she said, 'We shall die here, be buried in lonely graves and years later people will plough over our graves and plant crops and there will not be a landmark where we have been.'[75] She was more right than she knew.

4

European Settlements before the First World War

Oh, my God above, the silence I love,
And I love the great, vast plain;
And I love the life, the toil and the strife,
I love the hardships and pain.
My trophies are all on every wall,
My skins are upon the floor,
They are all around and upon the ground,
And hanging behind the door.
Now beside me here, I can touch the spear
I took from a Masai chief,
And here is the skull of a buffalo bull,
Still covered with lumps of beef.
The timber I cut and I built this hut,
I worked with the sweat of my brow;
I broke up the ground, and I fenced it around;
The crops are ripening now.[1]

The society developed by the whites in the EAP before the First
World War did not ape the one they had abandoned in Britain.
With so few white immigrants, there was less class consciousness
than in Britain, because settler whites pulled together against the
local equivalent of the working class – the Africans. White
immigrants came mostly from the middle classes, though there was
a significant upper-class element. While less conventional than
their fellow countrymen who chose to stay in Britain, the newcomers had typical upper- and middle-class Edwardian attitudes,
and were believers in hard work and people 'knowing their place'.
Sport and education and hygiene were important to them. But the

land they found themselves in forced them to adapt their ideas and ideals to novel circumstances. They created a distinctive society in the EAP.

Nairobi became their administrative and cultural centre. At the beginning it was a railway town, with the railway offices and workshops near the station. Close by were the railway hospital and dispensary, and lines of corrugated-iron bungalows occupied by subordinate railway staff, including Europeans. Those boasting baths had no internal plumbing, and the baths emptied through a hole in the floorboards into the earth below. Lions and zebras and other wild animals roamed the area at night, and it was courting disaster to leave a pet dog on a verandah, for it might, be taken by a leopard. In the centre of First Avenue (the avenues were numbered one to eight) was the railway school for European children. At the end of Third Avenue, on the side of Nairobi next to the Hill, was the Railway Institute, where dances, concerts, plays and religious services were held, of all denominations except Roman Catholic, whose adherents worshipped at the French Mission, St Austin's, outside Nairobi at Kabete. Marriages and funerals were also held at the Railway Institute.

As the railway was completed, many of the bungalows in railway town were dismantled and the corrugated iron used elsewhere. In 1900 the importance of the new settlement was recognised when a municipal administration was appointed by the Governor, who nominated annually four suitable residents to act with him as chairman – a committee that became the municipal council in 1919. On Victoria Street, a continuation of Main Street stretching from the west end of the station as far as the Nairobi river, several stores were built, including Tommy Wood's and branches of Mombasa firms such as Boustead Ridley, George Stewart & Co., and Huebner (associated with Hansing & Co.).

Climatically, there is no doubt that Nairobi was a pleasant place to live. At 5,000 feet, the heat never became too oppressive, maintaining an average of 75 degrees F (22 degrees C). After the sun rose at 6.15, the early morning could be pleasantly misty and cool, and was a favourite time for riding, while from 4 p.m.

onwards, until the sun set at 6.45, the temperature was perfect for sporting activities. The town grew slowly and haphazardly. In no way did its houses resemble those the settlers had left behind in Britain, because the only building materials were corrugated iron, grass, wattle, wood and mud. There were as yet no stone quarries, though the Anglican minister Revd Philip Alfred ('Pa') Bennett, a CMS missionary from West Africa who became the first resident chaplain to the white community in Nairobi, managed to cut sufficient stone to build himself the first, and for quite a while the only, stone house in Nairobi. This did not go unnoticed among the white inhabitants, always inclined to criticise the missionaries for seeking their own comfort before anything else.

Ainsworth as PC tried to beautify Nairobi by planting flame trees (*Spathodea nilotica*) and fast-growing blue gums along the streets. Townspeople tried to help by making gardens, but the black cotton soil and the insolent zebras grazing on their flowers by night often defeated them. The unsurfaced roads were unpleasantly dusty in dry weather and a quagmire in the two wet seasons (April–May and November). By 1903 Ainsworth had connected Nairobi by road to the neighbouring settlements of Dagoretti, Kiambu and Fort Smith. By 1910 most people were using bicycles to get around Nairobi; there were so many of them that the next year compulsory registration of cycles was introduced, to minimise theft. Women did not use bicycles – they were carried in rickshaws, some owned privately and others touting outside hotels and in the streets. As a leisure activity young men rode their bikes out of town and along animal tracks, to shoot at game. Towards the Ngong hills the land remained thickly wooded and the game plentiful. Hostesses often served legs of buck and Thomson's gazelle chops to their dinner guests. Gradually bikes were replaced by cars. The first motor car was brought to Nairobi in 1902 by Major George Edward Smith, of Sclater's road-building crew. It was a strange-looking vehicle, with a door for the passengers at the back. The number of imported cars increased and in 1911–12 two garages opened in Nairobi to do the very necessary repairs.

Nairobi saw many small improvements by 1904. Most useful

was the construction midway up Main Street of a wood and corrugated-iron post office standing on iron stilts and run by Dan Noble. A few Indian traders had shops on Victoria Street, Main Street and Station Road (parallel to Victoria Street and later known as Government Road). By that year, Main Street also had a large, one-storeyed municipal office doubling as the high court when the judge was on circuit, and the office of Tonks & Allen, Nairobi's first legal firm, beside a small mosque. Opposite the mosque was a Hindu temple and behind it three rows of corrugated-iron shanties comprising the Indian bazaar. At the end of the third row was the double-storeyed police station facing public gardens laid out in 1904 by A. M. Jeevanjee, Nairobi's richest Indian merchant. The big Jeevanjee market was opposite the police station, with nearby a small row of corrugated-iron huts serving as government offices. The town's buildings, by 1910 more likely to be built of brick and stone, came to an end with the police barracks, jail, Land and Survey Office, African hospital and dispensary. Then came Nairobi River, the source of the settlement's water supply, and across it Ainsworth's bungalow and one or two other houses. The segregation of white and Indian living areas was established in these years, following the practice in India. Africans working as house servants began to live in huts beside their employers' dwellings, and the rest lived in African areas. The three races did not mix socially. The whites considered themselves at the top of the social hierarchy.

As more people came to join the white community, the forested area beyond Ainsworth's bungalow was built on and became known as Parklands. By 1906 the boundaries of Nairobi were ten miles in circumference and the membership of the municipal committee had risen to twelve people, now nominated annually by the PC rather than the Governor. There were 108 business premises and 244 dwelling houses in the town, eighty-seven new buildings having been erected during the year. Six and a half miles of Nairobi's roads had been metalled, there were 300 yards of stone drains and one and a half miles of earth drains, and a new, thirty-foot-span stone bridge replaced the rickety wooden bridge across the Nairobi river.[2] In 1905 a serious fire in Victoria/Main Street burnt down twelve of the wood and iron buildings, which had the happy result that a fire station and watchtower were built in 1907. The town was growing rapidly.

In 1909 a slaughterhouse was erected, followed in 1911 by a sizeable hall used for entertainments and auction rooms and the large store Whiteaway Laidlaw. In 1912 these were joined by a Jewish synagogue and Nairobi House, an imposing two-storey structure on the corner of Government Road and Sixth Avenue.[3] In the same year was built Donald Garvie's theatre,[4] where the Amateur Dramatic Society occasionally produced plays. It was a corrugated-iron building on Government Road with planks for seats, and became a bioscope when films were shown. If a doctor was needed in the town and he happened to be at the cinema, the film was stopped and a slide put on the screen to show him where to go.

There were other places of entertainment, this time of a carnal kind. Even before Nairobi swelled with soldiers in the First World War, there was a brothel used by whites. Situated down a small alley, it was known as the 'Japanese Legation', because its prostitutes were Japanese women who had come up from Zanzibar soon after the railhead reached Nairobi. There was also the 'government whorehouse', in a bad state of repair in 1909, when a stiff letter was sent to the authorities, saying 'I am reminding you yet again about the white ants in the Government whorehouse.'[5]

By 1903 the civic authorities had started to drain Nairobi swamp, and a water supply was being laid on from some permanent springs near Kikuyu station fifteen miles away, to replace the insufficient water from the first reservoir built on the Nairobi river near Chiromo, the house on present-day Riverside Drive. A new, deep reservoir was constructed, with sufficient capacity to provide over a million gallons a day, and a pipeline was laid to holding tanks. This served Nairobi well for a few years, until in 1911 the increase in population meant that the four-inch main had to be replaced by a nine-inch one, to increase the supply.

Lacking water-borne sewage disposal, the town was a malodorous place. Everyone had bucket latrines, which were emptied each night into the night-soil cart. The excreta was then deposited in trenches near the river. People were recommended to add dry earth to the buckets to lessen the smells. Household refuse was put into large receptacles, then collected and buried. But hygiene remained unsatisfactory and in 1912 a sanitary commission was appointed.

After night fell at 6.50 p.m. the streets were lit by Kitson lamps, which shed such inadequate light that in 1906 the East African Power & Lighting Co. was established, with capital of £30,000. The company completed the building of a dam at Ruiru, on the road to Thika, in 1907, and with three turbo generators and a total capacity of 500 bhp it supplied power for commercial uses from April 1909. Electric street lighting came to Nairobi in 1911, though the power frequently failed.

Although 300 miles from the coast, Nairobi was not cut off from the outside world. There was a public telephone call box at the post office which built for itself a fine and for the moment completely isolated new building some way down Sixth Avenue. This was a little far for the public to walk and the new Nairobi Chamber of Commerce asked for telephone boxes to be put in more convenient places, such as the railway station, Parklands, the police station and central Nairobi. The EAP had been admitted to the Postal Union in 1895, and the first provisional stamps issued in 1896–97. The first permanent issue of EAP stamps went on sale in 1898. The telegraph had followed the railway, reaching Nairobi in 1898 and Entebbe in 1901, though Africans persisted in stealing the copper wire between Nakuru and Kisumu. In 1912 two new telegraph lines were opened – Magadi Junction to Machakos and Kisumu to Eldoret. Two years later the Eldoret telegraph line was extended to Sergoit. Telegrams were the only fast way to transmit information, because it took three months to get a reply from Britain to any letter written from the EAP. At first the mails were carried by the German East Africa Line, whose Hamburg steamers began calling once a month at Mombasa from the beginning of 1898. There was also a British India (BI) steamer once a fortnight from India. In 1901 the Austrian Lloyd line from Trieste also began calling monthly at Mombasa.

The number of Nairobi's European inhabitants steadily increased. In 1906 there were 579 of them (together with 63 Eurasians, 510 Goans, 3,071 Indians and 9,291 Africans); in 1909 the number had risen to 799 and in 1910 there were 834 (of 1,337 in the province of Ukamba). The number rose to 968 in 1911 (476 males, 275 females and 212 children), to 1,200 in 1912–13 and to 2,036 in 1915–16, a figure inflated by the war.[6] This was still a pitifully small number, but paradoxically gave the town a spirit and cohesion that would otherwise have been absent. The whites banded together and began to exert political pressure to consolidate their position.

Not long after the advent of whites in Nairobi, a club culture developed on lines similar to those elsewhere in the British empire. The country's first club – the Mombasa Club – was founded in 1896–97. This reflected what was happening in Britain, where London clubs were at the height of their popularity. (Even today, *Who's Who* lists at the end of each short biography the clubs to which the entrant belongs.) Clubs in the EAP were an essential part of the social fabric, embracing and uniting as they did people of their own kind in an alien country. As Nairobi town developed, the first club to open there was the Railway Institute in 1900, for the white employees of the railway. The Railway Institute deteriorated with age, and in 1915 a new one was built, with a magnificent view over the Athi plains.[7]

With the coming of white officials in some numbers, the Nairobi Club was founded. It originated with a meeting held in Nairobi on 14 October 1899 to discuss the starting of a social club. The meeting decided to ask Boustead Ridley, proprietors of Mombasa Club, to construct the building, as they had the Mombasa Club. The firm erected a simple corrugated-iron building, soon found to be inadequate. The committee then decided to put up its own building, a rambling wood and corrugated-iron affair, later to become the Secretariat when the club moved to a stone building in 1915.[8] This new building was financed by issuing a prospectus and inviting members to put up loan certificates, each 100 rupees in value. Thus the necessary funds were raised and the club was built on Nairobi Hill. The Hill was reserved for senior railway and government officers' bungalows (often put on stone pillars because of white ants' insatiable hunger for wood), the Governor's residence and a few offices of government departments. Also on the Hill, behind the Governor's house, were the corrugated-iron cantonments of the King's African Rifles. A sports ground was laid out nearby for the use of the members of Nairobi Club, and this became the affiliated Gymkhana Club.

Nairobi Club was frequented mainly by first-class officials (those earning above £250 a year). Despite the early absence of deep class divisions in the EAP, in contrast to those existing in Britain, whites such as the more junior railway engineers, engine-drivers, and lower-rank policemen were not accepted in Nairobi Club. Lowlier officials of the second class had their own club built for them, at Parklands. It was in existence by 1912, held dances and entertainments, and like the Nairobi Club had tennis and cricket facilities. The settlers, too, wanted their own place, so the Travellers' Club opened in Government Road, opposite the Stanley Hotel. And when a wealthy visiting American on a hunting safari, J. Archie Morrison, put up the money, the Muthaiga Club was erected a few miles from Nairobi, on land sold by the Sandbach Bakers after they returned to England in 1911.[9] The main portion of the building, painted a distinctive pink, comprised public rooms around a peristyle, and a squash court and several single rooms. Later, double rooms and a ballroom were added, and the peristyle became an interior lounge with a glass roof. Muthaiga Club had a golf course, whose greens were 'browns' covered with sand, consisting of only two holes initially, the first from a drive in front of the verandah, and the second back to the start. The club was opened with a party held on New Year's Eve of 1913. The writer Elspeth Huxley's parents were present at the party, a very small affair enlivened by the over-loud playing of the KAR band; as there were too few women the dancing was of limited success. From such modest beginnings the Muthaiga Club was to burgeon into a famous settler haunt, the favourite meeting place of the later Happy Valley crowd. In the 1920s its walls were hung with the impressive pencil portraits of legendary Kenya characters by Ray Nestor. He had arrived in Kenya in 1912 to work in the Survey Department and when he died aged 100 in 1989 he left a remarkable pictorial record of the country in drawings and watercolours, published as *An African Sketchbook*.[10]

The Muthaiga Club was packed in race weeks, when Nairobi was at its most populous and bustling. The first race meeting had been held at Machakos in 1897 in honour of Queen Victoria's jubilee. No sooner had the first buildings come to Nairobi than a race course was laid out at Pumwani, on its north-eastern outskirts. The first races held there, on a wet 24 December 1900, were marked by tragedy – R. W. Buchanan, unwise to enter a race on account of his fifty-five years, fell from his horse and died the same night. The East African Turf Club was founded and by 1912 Nairobi had three race meetings a year, when settlers flocked to Nairobi from all over the country. It was the chance of a lifetime for an unmarried girl, because settlers from distant districts were unlikely to have seen white women since the last races and were 'ready to see beauty in the most meagre charms'.[11] Apart from racing, other popular sports were hunting, tennis, polo, pig-sticking and cricket. The first cricket match was played in Nairobi on 23 and 25 December 1899, the teams being A–L and M–Z.

Race weeks exacerbated Nairobi's big problem: too few hotel rooms. Visitors were now arriving in some numbers to see whether they would like to settle in the country, but they could find nowhere to stay while they enquired about business opportunities or the buying of land. On the other hand, no one wanted to invest in building hotels when they did not know how many visitors might need them, or how many future settlers there might be. The hotel run by May Bent sufficed for a while, together with the adjacent tea room rented by Tommy Wood. Major Henry Rayne, a New Zealander formerly working for Boustead Ridley in Mombasa, and his brothers J. A. and J. F. Rayne, took the building over in 1904 and renamed it the Masonic Hotel. Henry Rayne joined the KAR, but one of the brothers ran this two-storeyed wood and corrugated-iron establishment with his sister Mary, a kind woman who nursed many a sick bachelor back to health.

After Victoria Street's buildings burned down in 1905, the inde-
fatigable May Bent hired the wooden upper floor of B. Choitram's
stone shop in Government Road where she opened another
Stanley Hotel. As the building was unfinished, much use was made
of camp beds and tarpaulins, and because this coincided with a
great inrush of settlers from South Africa, any accommodation
would do. Even in 1910 beds were set out in dormitories of eight
beds each. Dan Noble, the post master, was May's manager, an
Irish girl Biddy acted as receptionist, and May's happiness was
complete when Fred Tate, Nairobi's stationmaster and the pianist
at the Railway Institute, married her in 1909. His was a musical
family, for he was the brother of the soprano Maggie Teyte, who
had elaborated the spelling of her name. In 1911, financed by the
farmer W. E. D. ('Wednesday') Knight, May transferred the
Stanley to the corner of Sixth Avenue and Hardinge Street, and it
became the New Stanley Hotel. There it remains today, although
the buildings have been replaced by a modern structure.

With accommodation so sparse, the new settlers camped on
ground provided by the Anglican chaplain, the Revd 'Pa' Bennett,
in front of the Manse, his house behind the jail on the far edge of
the hill. In 1904 fifty families lived there in tents for nine months.
Although the occasional officer of the law in the person of an
askari could be seen strolling past the tents in his uniform of bare
feet, khaki shorts, red fez and red belt, there were many robberies
in the camp. However, there was great comradeship among the
campers and all the food, brought to the tent flaps by African
women hawkers, was very cheap.[12] Tentfontein, as it was called,
was approached from the end of Victoria Street by a track following
the course of the Nairobi river.

On Christmas Day 1904 a third Nairobi hotel opened, the
Norfolk, opposite the town jail at the end of Government Road,
parallel to Victoria Street . Owned by Major C. G. R. Ringer and
his partner R. Aylmer Winearls, it was built of stone, with a tiled
roof. With its French chef Louis Blanc, it was in a different class
from the other Nairobi hotels and soon eclipsed them, its bar
becoming the town's favourite meeting place. The Norfolk's fame

spread far and wide, so much so that when there was a serious fire in the building not long ago, the news was published in international newspapers. In 1906 the Norfolk was taken over by the capable and likeable H. C. Blancke, a Swiss hotel expert brought out as manager, who left it in 1913 to start a leather factory. In those years it paid off its mortgage overdraft and made a clear profit of £20,000. Its peak year was 1908, when women began to go to the EAP in considerable numbers.[13] As more young civil servants arrived, they rented houses together or lived in boarding houses. The best known of these was Mrs Begby's, a wood and corrugated-iron building in Parklands, which became Nairobi's fourth hotel, the Salisbury.

The newcomers needed facilities for their rites of passage. At first the Railway Institute was used to celebrate marriages. The doctor C. A. Wiggins claimed that his marriage to Ethel Beatrice Elliott, daughter of C. F. Elliott, Commissioner of Forests, was the first to take place there, in 1903, with Bishop George Peel of Mombasa officiating, the Governor Sir Charles Eliot as witness and C. C. Bowring, the Treasurer, as best man.[14] The first Church of England service was held in Nairobi on 2 February 1902 in the Railway Institute, led by the Revd 'Pa' Bennett, the first resident chaplain to the white community in Nairobi. Since his stipend, paid by the Colonial and Continental Church Society, was a mere £100 a year, he supplemented his income by spending six days a week running a fuel contractor's business at the Rift Valley escarpment. In 1904 he was succeeded by the Revd W. Marcus Falloon, nominated by the Colonial and Continental, who remained until 1916.

A church building committee was formed on 1 August 1902. Two years later the Anglicans had their own church, St Stephen's, known as 'the tin tabernacle'. Built of corrugated iron on a cement base, at a cost of 12,500 rupees, it was consecrated by Bishop Peel on 26 December 1904 and served its purpose for thirteen years. The vet Robert Stordy was a church warden, and he and the chaplain had to contend with an active high-church group within the congregation which disapproved of evangelical missionaries. The members of the group wanted to choose their own chaplain rather than the one the CMS provided, to have sole control over the organ they bought, and to reserve some of the church furniture for themselves for reasons of hygiene. In face of their threat to secede, church services were held at 9.30 on Sundays so that whites did not have to sit on benches recently vacated by Africans, and the CMS was careful to appoint non-evangelical chaplains to Nairobi town. With the rise in the white population of Nairobi to 580, of whom 120 lived in Parklands, in 1906 it was decided to build another church, St Mark's, in Parklands, and it was consecrated on 9 September 1910. The following year St Paul's church at Kiambu was built of local stone.

There was racial segregation in death as in life. Dead Europeans were buried in a cemetery at the foot of the Hill. As the population expanded this was enlarged to twenty acres, but the ground was so rocky and unsuitable, and graves so difficult to dig, that in 1916 a new cemetery was opened on Forest Road, at the junction of the Fort Hall–Kiambu roads. The graves of pioneers can still be seen in both cemeteries, though some of the inscriptions have worn from the gravestones, many of them leaning like shoulders bowed in grief.

Death was an ever-present threat for Europeans in the EAP. At the turn of the century people doubted whether whites could live permanently in Nairobi, or indeed anywhere in the EAP, without their health breaking down. This was one of the reasons why government servants were given such generous leave allowances. 'It is still doubtful', said the visitor Gorell Barnes, ' . . . whether conditions are favourable to the permanent residence of Europeans, or whether there may not be a slow deterioration in the future generations.'[15] A major problem for whites was thought to be the sun, whose 'actinic rays' would damage European bodies. These rays even penetrated through clouds, so no one was ever safe. Thus sola topees, looking like policemen's helmets and made from the Indian sola plant, were worn on the head (pith ones were useless because they went soft when it rained). Women and children wore double terais (two wide-brimmed felt hats placed one inside the other lest the sun penetrate a single layer).

Other horrors were the 'Nairobi eye', a small red flying ant which caused intense irritation to the eyes, and the ubiquitous jigger or burrowing flea – *Tunga penetrans*. Once the characteristic itching was felt beside a toenail, the sufferer would be wise to ask an African to dig out a sac of eggs the size of a small pea from beside or under the nail. Using needle-like thorns, the Africans were skilled at removing the sac whole – if it broke, the victim was in trouble and could lose a toe. Then, of course, there was malaria:

> There's a theory that we hear about,
> Of course we know it's true,
> That all the ills we suffer from
> Are really only due
> To those horrid little insects
> That are buzzing night and day,
> And the place will be a paradise
> When they are cleared away.[16]

Malaria was common in Nairobi, particularly after the rains when stagnant water lay about. The swamp was also a perpetual breeding ground for mosquitoes and not until it was cleared was the incidence of malaria reduced. The illness was especially prevalent at Kisumu, in the area around Mumias and on the Uasin Gishu plateau. It is not true that mosquitoes did not live above a certain height, as was thought for many years. To combat malaria people would often take five grains of quinine a day as a prophylactic, a practice frowned upon by doctors because the medication prevented them from detecting the parasite in blood slides. Some people took one grain a day and five on Saturdays and Sundays. When fever struck, the dose could be increased to twenty or thirty grains. Many people, miles from doctors, treated themselves, but one doctor, C. A. Wiggins, reckoned that the incidence of malaria was far higher in those who took quinine that in those who did not.[17]

When malaria developed into blackwater fever, there was little hope for the patient. The treatment was to give pints of water and doses of bicarbonate, and the sufferer had to remain very still in bed and not be moved. As the disease progressed and the blood vessels broke down, the patient's skin took on the vivid yellow colour of jaundice. After the third day there would then be a lapse into unconsciousness, followed by death. There were many tragic cases, such as that of Leslie Williams, aged twelve, whose mother, a nurse, returned home after the death of a blackwater patient for whom she had been caring, to find her own son had developed the fever. He, too, died.

Another common ailment was bubonic plague which if untreated had a mortality rate of 80 per cent and if treated of 60 per cent. Pneumonia was a regular killer, as was typhoid fever. Whites generally avoided acquiring smallpox, which was more a disease of the Indian community. There were few antiseptics, apart from carbolic acid crystals in glycerine and permanganate of potash, to treat wounds inflicted by thorns or wild animals. Some people swore by the healing properties of paraffin for wounds. Cocaine, ether and chloroform were available for surgical operations, though chloroform was dangerous. Treatment for lockjaw was turpentine applied to the tongue by means of a feather pushed through a gap in the teeth. It was prudent to have such a gap. In remote places, far from a dentist, people stopped their teeth with gutta percha. Lion fat, rubbed on before bedtime, was reckoned an excellent balm for strained or rheumatic limbs. Six whites of eggs shaken in a bottle of barley water and one tablespoon of brandy were thought to be a certain cure for dysentery.[18]

A European hospital opened in Mombasa in 1891, but Nairobi had to wait until 1912 for a similar institution and even then it only had two standpipes outside the building rather than running water within, as well as the usual bucket latrines. An analysis of illnesses and deaths shows how difficult it was for the doctors to practise medicine successfully in such a climate without any, as yet uninvented, antibiotics. To take as an example the Ukamba province, which contained Nairobi: in 1906–07 there were among the whites 19 cases of measles, 7 of enteric fever (that is, typhoid fever), 13 of plague and 2 of chickenpox. In the following year, 1907–08, there were 12 deaths, or 20.7 per 1,000 (compared with 23 births, or 39.72 per 1,000). In 1908–09 there were 5 births and 4 deaths, in 1910 (when statistics began to be given from

January to December) 15 births and 4 deaths, and in 1911 22 deaths in Nairobi, a shocking 11 of them in children under the age of sixteen months. The birth-rate had risen to 30.3 per 1,000, and varied little in 1915 when it was 31 per 1,000 (that is, 83 births) as compared with a death-rate of 16 per 1,000. But infant mortality among the whites was still dire, at a rate of 96.27 per 1,000. The main ailments throughout the period were pneumonia, enteric fever (typhoid), malaria and tuberculosis. Four whites died of plague in Nairobi in 1917, and in 1918–19 there were nineteen white deaths from Spanish influenza.[19]

To deal with diseases of the mind, a mental hospital, Mathari, was opened outside Nairobi in 1910, with space for two whites among its inmates. Most people who went there were alcoholics, but extreme loneliness could also destabilise men's minds:

> When a man's alone in the Bush for long,
> His mind and body alike go wrong;
> Day after day, week after week,
> With never a comrade with whom to speak,
> With never a sight of a white man's face,
> Cut off from the world in that awful place . . .
> He had weird fancies and restless nights,
> With sudden startings and needless frights;
> He had fits of rage, like a naughty child,
> When he raved and screamed like a man gone wild.
> The fever took him and laid him low,
> Froze him and burned him from head to toe;
> With every limb on the rack with pain,
> And his mind astray from his tortured brain.[20]

The hospitals were firmly racially segregated. This was difficult for Dr Rozendo Ayres Ribeiro, a Goan medical doctor resident in the EAP since 1899, who sometimes treated whites in his surgery and pharmacy in Victoria Street. His anti-malaria tablets, made to his own formula, were moreover much sought after by the settlers, though he was never accepted socially by them. Ribeiro was unique in that he rode a zebra to visit his patients.[21]

From the point of view of disease, Africa was more dangerous than India. Even so, most whites kept their children with them and did not send them back to Britain to be educated, unlike their counterparts in India. This practice was a reflection of the number of farmers (many of them Boers) among the early settlers, and of the poor salaries paid to government officials, who could not afford the expense of a British education. Some of the older children, particularly boys and offspring of the titled settlers, were sent to Britain for their education, but this became less common as the years rolled by and money dribbled away and fortunes failed to be made. Sending children overseas was heart-breaking for mothers: often they could not afford to accompany their offspring and were obliged to put them into the care of someone travelling on the same ship.

Instead, good education had to be provided locally. In 1898 the Roman Catholic fathers started a school in Mombasa for the many European children arriving with the new railway employees. Upon reaching Nairobi in 1900 the Uganda Railway set up its own school there for the children of its white workers. Soon this educational establishment decided to accept settler children as well, and the teachers, A. J. Turner, a thin, dour man, and his wife A. M. Turner, had a total of thirty-eight pupils by 1904. The school roll shows that many of these came from schools in India (because their fathers had previously worked on railways in India), a few from schools in South Africa and one from the Loreto Convent, Nairobi, a small school begun by Roman Catholic nuns and sometimes called St Joseph's Convent.[22] By the second term of 1904 ten pupils had left Mr Turner's school out of a roll of seventy, but by August 1906 his roll had risen to ninety-nine.

In January 1903 Tommy Wood's store announced that a Miss Ellis had opened a day school in one of the upper rooms, but this establishment cannot have lasted long because nothing more is heard of it. In the same year another school was founded, at Kijabe on the edge of the Rift Valley: the Rift Valley Academy, run by the Africa Inland Mission primarily for the children of missionaries. Young Hermann Klaprott went there in 1910 as a boarder, and with him were the Hoddinotts (children of Kiambu farmers), the Arnoldis from the Uasin Gishu plateau, the Aggetts from Rumuruti, Beatrice Hall from Limuru, Irene and Agnes Birdsey from the Uasin Gishu and one or two American lads, the sons of missionaries.[23]

With the completion of the railway, Mr Turner's school became the general European school in Nairobi, known as Nairobi School. It became a boarding establishment accepting children from all over the country and was taken over from the railway by the government in 1908. From 14 March to 27 April 1908 the place was closed due to an outbreak of typhoid fever. Turner was on leave abroad at the time, but his deputy, Matthew Kell, officiated in his stead.[24] Of the children who left school in 1908 on completion of their studies, eight gained employment – among them, one each on the railway, in the Land Office, Electric Light Co., Post Office and the school itself as a pupil teacher. The education offered by Nairobi School was therefore adequate if not outstanding, though it is true that one girl was studying for the College of Praeceptors examination.[25] In 1915 Cambridge Local Examinations were substituted for those of the College of Praeceptors.

In 1910 the school was moved into the old European police barracks on Nairobi Hill. New buildings of wood and corrugated iron were erected, as boarding blocks for 130 boarders, two miles away by the old Buller's Camp near Nairobi Club. There were now 107 on the roll, including at least one child born in Nairobi – Jean McQueen, born on 9 November 1899. The children's ages ranged from six to twenty-three, the older ones being Boers who had started school much later than their fellows. Somewhat ignominiously, they had to sit beside children much younger than themselves as they proceeded up the seven standards. Possibly because of their families' reduced financial circumstances, a few children came to Nairobi School from two new schools established in the past few years: Mrs Pailthorpe's at Parklands and Miss E. B. Seccombe's in Nairobi.

By 1918 Nairobi's Chamber of Commerce was complaining about the unsatisfactory state of education in the town. Nairobi School, it said, had inadequate sports facilities, its existing buildings were undesirable, and there was insufficient space for boarders. Many people were now having to send their children to South Africa to be educated. After a deputation was sent to the Governor, he appointed a Commission to examine the requirements of the education system in the country.[26]

Elspeth Huxley (née Grant), later a noted writer, left Miss Seccombe's school at the end of 1923 and enrolled in Nairobi School, in order to learn Latin for entry to Cambridge University. There was only one other girl in the top class. Elspeth found the teaching spasmodic, with some teachers always on leave and the headmaster courting the matron and often away. She failed to get into Cambridge. In 1923 the fees for Nairobi School, which now had seven teachers, were ten or fifteen florins a term. Since this was about £60 in present-day terms, many parents were unable to find the money and there was a government poor vote of £400, to help those too indigent to pay.[27]

With increased numbers of white settlers spreading throughout the country, schools soon had to be provided in places other than Nairobi. A primary school for white children was established at Nakuru in 1911, two miles from the town on the slopes of Menengai crater, as remembered in the school song:

> High above the dusty highway
> Where the creaking wagons go,
> With a canopy of deepest blue above,
> In a circle of the mountains,
> With a placid lake below,
> Stands the school we shall remember with our love.

At the same time, the provision of education on the Uasin Gishu plateau was under consideration. In 1909 Professor Fraser from India had been sent to see what the plateau needed. He suggested that a Central School be built in Eldoret, but the government demurred. Education on the plateau was contentious, because many Boers wanted their children taught in Afrikaans, whereas the government thought this would be divisive. And so the farmers of the Uasin Gishu had to provide their own education for their children –

between 1911 and 1912 six farm schools were opened on the plateau.
Three did not last long and were closed by 1915 though the farm
school system lasted till 1939. The Revd M. P. Loubser, a Boer pastor
who united the three Dutch Reformed churches around Eldoret and
established a single place of worship, would not compromise on the
language of instruction and started his own school, Broederstroom,
in 1911, with all lessons in Afrikaans. He also began a second school
at Sergoit. Two teachers were hired from South Africa – P. Pienaar,
who taught fifty students, and D. I. de Villiers – but they both
returned to South Africa in 1916.

The government could not delay indefinitely the education of
white children on the plateau and in February 1915 the Central
School was finally opened at Eldoret. By June of the following
year it had fifty students. A new block was erected next to an old
corrugated-iron building at the end of the road beyond the
Roman Catholic church, and Mr and Mrs Humphries were
appointed as the headmaster and his assistant. F. W. Humphries,
of medium height, sturdy and well set, with a fine-shaped head
and dark hair greying at the temples, had a dark moustache and
twinkling brown eyes. He was a wonderful teacher and keen
gardener. Mrs G. Humphries, with grey eyes and brown hair
plaited and wound round at the nape of her neck, was able to keep
perfect discipline. Their daughter Marjorie (Margaret Georgiana),
a piano-player with a pleasant singing voice, had recently left
school and helped with the teaching. Miss Bleakman was the
games mistress. There was boarding for twelve girls, but boys had
to lodge with people in the town – for example, Hermann
Klaprott's brothers boarded with the Steyn Pohls. The Eldoret
District Commissioner S. W. J. Schofield regularly invited the
boarders to tea. In 1919 a new boarding block, containing two
long dormitories, a dining room, staff quarters and recess rooms,
was built at the top of the hill to cater for sixty boys and girls.[28]

Private and public education systems emerged side by side in the
EAP. As in India and South Africa, there was firm racial segregation.
Segregation even occurred, though voluntarily, among whites, with
Boer and Briton attending different schools on the Uasin Gishu

plateau. Pupils frequently developed intense loyalty to their schools, and even when scattered all over the world after Kenya was returned to the Africans, they kept in touch with each other through flourishing old school associations. This seems to compensate them to some degree for having had to leave the country they were born and raised in.

Until 1907, when Nairobi became the official capital of the EAP, Mombasa was the country's major town; then it was eclipsed by Nairobi, less malarial and more central to the farming areas. It was Sir William Mackinnon's vision that had brought IBEAC and the whites to Mombasa in the first place and in 1900 a statue of him was unveiled, in what became known as Treasury Square, by the Governor Sir Arthur Hardinge. The sculptor could not have known Mombasa and its ever-present sultry heat, for the poor man is dressed far too warmly in a heavy coat and high collar, and is committing an unpardonable sin by holding rather than wearing his hat and thus putting himself at the mercy of the lethal actinic rays of the sun. Birds built their nests year after year in his conveniently shaped hand and still do so a century later.

As the main town of the EAP, Mombasa soon acquired an Anglican church for conducting rites of passage. In 1897 the diocese of Mombasa came into existence, with William George Peel being consecrated as bishop on 29 June 1899.[29] Just after the turn of the century Mombasa cathedral was built, with a dome to match the mosque and other Muslim buildings of the town. The chair of Bishop James Hannington, murdered in Uganda in 1885, was placed within. Many brides were married there, having met their fiancés on leave in Britain and travelled out by ship to join their loved ones. It was common for the betrothed pair to have their wedding in Mombasa cathedral before going upcountry.

The wedding of Hilda and Leslie Macnaghten, of the Public Works Department, was typical. In 1906 the bride arrived in Mombasa by ship in the morning, and was taken to a bungalow by two ladies she did not know. She was helped to dress in a wedding gown and veil she had brought with her, and was given a bunch of oleander picked from the garden as a bouquet. From the bungalow she went straight to the cathedral in a trolley pushed by two Africans and decorated with white flowers – oleander, jasmine and frangipani. William McGregor Ross, of the PWD, whom she had never met, gave her away before a small congregation lacking any of her relatives.[30] On the same day she and her husband embarked on the overnight train to Nakuru. On arrival there she was seated on a white Muscat donkey and rode eighty miles to Turkana country, to find her new home was a banda with no doors or windows. She played the gramophone in the evenings for a touch of home, but found herself surrounded by Suk and Turkana, tribespeople mystified by Harry Lauder's laughing song. Just over nine months later she lost her new-born twins in Nairobi.[31] Such was pioneering life.

The Roman Catholic cathedral of Mombasa was not built until 1918. Made of coral blocks quarried locally, it had two towers, the first of which unfortunately collapsed and had to be rebuilt. The ambitious Brother Gustave, in charge of the construction, designed its roof as a copy of Westminster Cathedral, and as an added adornment inserted richly coloured stained-glass windows.

Like Nairobi, Mombasa suffered from a lack of good hotel accommodation. The Grand Hotel, on Macdonald Terrace, looked good, with its fine wide verandah upstairs, but its mosquito nets were torn, some rooms had curtains instead of doors, and rats came into the bedrooms. It was run by Gerald Wright Anderson and Rudolf F. Mayer, who treated complaints contemptuously, with advice to go to the Greek hotel owned by M. Filios, in Ndia Kuu, an infinitely worse establishment. Thankfully the Grand Hotel was pulled down in 1904 and the Standard Bank of South Africa erected in its place. Almost next door to the Grand was the Cecil Hotel, built in 1904, with an Armenian proprietor, M. MacJohn. Then there was the Africa Hotel in Vasco da Gama Street, Indian owned and managed and notorious for fleas and bedbugs.

The advent of Mombasa Club (see Chapter 2) was soon followed by the opening of the Sports Club, with its fine cricket ground, next door to the European cemetery. An activity less enervating than playing cricket in Mombasa's heat was sailing round the island, in the cool sea breezes. Captain Henry Pidcock, the Port Officer and deputy governor of the jail, was an excellent companion on such expeditions, familiar as he was with the peculiarities of wind and current. On return to land, refreshment was taken at Mombasa Club, where drinking started at 11.30 a.m. with a stiff whisky, brandy or gin. Many people drank too much because of boredom, loneliness and the fact that spirits were only three rupees a bottle. Other entertainments were dinners at Government House, children's parties, picnics on the mainland and swimming parties.

Mombasa Club's billiard room flooded in the rains, a catastrophe which prompted the PWD to lay a concrete drain in 1905, across Vasco da Gama Street and past the club into the sea. This expedient also relieved the flooding by the police station at the lower end of Ndia Kuu. By 1904 Mombasa had a two-storeyed Government House and in the following year the PWD completed a new Treasury and Audit Office. Mombasa buildings were not con-structed of corrugated iron, like those in Nairobi, but rather of coral rag covered with cement and whitewashed. They were therefore much more substantial-looking, and Mombasa began to take on the aspect of a proper town rather than an ugly conglomeration of shanties, as was Nairobi at that time.

What Mombasa needed most was a deep-water pier at Kilindini so that modern ships could berth beside the shore. This would be more convenient for passengers who had been transported ashore in small boats, and it would also benefit merchants, then paying huge lighterage charges for the portage of goods to ships. In February 1911 the Nairobi Chamber of Commerce requested the construction of a deep-water pier, and a loan was raised. Three years later another loan, of £610,000, was secured for harbour works, though the outbreak of the First World War caused the plans to be abandoned. An aid to navigation was, however, completed in 1903, when a smart black-and-white striped lighthouse, with a beam that flashed every four seconds, was erected at Ras Serani. It proved to be a popular meeting point for the white children of the island, who gathered there every afternoon to play.

The white population of Mombasa remained small because no

land in the vicinity was suitable for farming. Indeed, in the whole coast province there were a mere 227 whites in 1907. Before 1914 most whites were civil servants or businessmen, with a few planters trying, mostly abortively, to establish plantations of cotton, sugar cane, rubber, sisal and coconuts along the coast. In 1912 there were seven planters at Shimoni, employed by the East African Estates Co. on their rubber and coconut plantations. At Rabai there were six planters, outnumbered by the eight missionaries, at the Ceara Rubber Estates, but by 1914 the firm removed them because the price of rubber had fallen. After rubber proved a failure, attempts were made to replace it with coconuts. Powys Cobb had a large sisal plantation at Kilifi, an isolated success story among the few sisal plantations at the coast. But the coast planters were a less persistent group than upcountry settlers, and by 1914 most had gone, defeated by the mosquito and the humid climate. In 1913–14, Mombasa town had 422 whites (303 males, 68 females and 51 under twenty-one). Of these 97 of the males were officials, 131 non-officials, and 75 foreigners. Because of the First World War numbers fell to 318 whites in 1915–16. Numbers picked up a little after the war and Mombasa's population in 1918–19 was 336, 14 having died from Spanish influenza. By 1920 numbers had still not returned to over 400.[32] Nairobi had well and truly taken over as the EAP's major town.

Kisumu on Lake Victoria owed its foundation to being the site chosen as the terminus for the Uganda Railway, which reached the Lake in 1901, and the point where goods and people bound for Uganda were shipped to Entebbe. Kisumu was laid out by the Provincial Commissioner Charles W. Hobley[33] on the north side of Ngowe bay on Lake Victoria, on a low, flat, grassy plain only just above flood level. The place was a death trap, swarming with mosquitoes, so Hobley's successor Stephen Bagge moved the town to a healthier site on the other side of the bay in 1903–04. The new town consisted of corrugated-iron huts, a railway workshop, the DC's office, a dak (government) bungalow, a few Indian dukas, African huts and a pier. On the low volcanic ridge behind was the DC's bungalow, soon to be joined by other government and private bungalows as the town grew. Rocks from the new site were used to make walls along the road. Unfortunately these became infested with rats and snakes, so had to be removed, the rubble being put on the foreshore to create Connaught Parade.

The need to transport people and goods across the lake to Uganda meant that boats of some size had to be employed. And yet this was a place with no experience of building boats beyond small African vessels. The problem was solved by ordering boats made in Britain, then dismantled and sent in package form to Kisumu. There the engineer Richard Grant put them together in the Uganda Railway workshop. The *William MacKinnon*, laboriously carried in pieces by porters from the coast and launched in June 1900, was superseded by the *Winifred*, which took to the water in 1903, and the *Sybil* in 1904. Both were steamers of 600 tons, built by Grant from sixty-pound packages. Then, in 1907, the *Clement Hill*, of 1,100 tons and 200 feet, was launched by the Duchess of Connaught. The following year the *Nyanza*, of 1,146 tons, was launched by Lady Hayes-Sadler, the Governor's wife. The manning of these wood-burning steamers was organised on naval lines, with captains and first officers recruited from the British and Indian navies.

Even after Kisumu's move to a better site, mosquitoes and malaria and plague and sleeping sickness dominated the area. The egregious John Ainsworth, removed from Nairobi to Naivasha (1906) and Kisumu (1907) by Governor Hayes-Sadler, thought there was a 'fear complex' there, engendered by an obsession with the climate. An assistant District Officer committed suicide in the residency, and a few weeks later an assistant surgeon shot himself. Shortly afterwards a Treasury officer also killed himself. Commerell Cowper-Coles, senior prospector for the East Africa Syndicate, died of blackwater fever and the government geologist, Edward Eaton Walker, of an infected mosquito bite. 'Generally speaking,' said Ainsworth, not normally known for lugubrious wit, 'Kisumu was not, at this time, a place for a melancholy man.'[34]

Ainsworth cleared and drained the swampy land and made war on rats and on officials wearing shorts to work. He would not allow naked Africans to come into town. He finished Connaught Parade in 1906 and laid golf links, improved the road between Kisumu and Mumias, and cleared and drained Mumias, another death trap. The Yala river was spanned by a suspension bridge and the Lumbwa–Sotik–Kericho road made suitable for wheeled traffic. With these improvements more white women went to live at Kisumu and the town assumed a more cheerful aspect. In 1906 the Broughton-Knight memorial church was brought out in pieces from Britain and erected in honour of E. Kegley Broughton-Knight, a blackwater fever victim who died at Karungu, south of Kisumu, in 1904. Hilda Macnaghten, now removed from the Suk and Turkana, and their failure to appreciate Harry Lauder, played the harmonium on Sundays for any of the sixteen white inhabitants of Kisumu who chose to attend the church.

The DO's wife, Marion Dobbs, has left an account of the town in 1906.[35] She was initially wary of the place because fifteen different men had occupied her husband's post in the previous two years, but she buckled down and made the best of it. All drinking water was boiled and filtered and had the flat taste removed by aeration with a soda water syphon, the bulbs for which were readily available in Indian dukas. The local milk was likewise strained and boiled, but Ideal unsweetened evaporated milk in tins was a welcome substitute. Butter also came in tins, emerging with a vivid orange colour and strong cheesy flavour. Yet, if it was beaten up several times in fresh filtered water and salt added, it became a passable imitation of the real thing. As for eggs, they came from the local hens and were tiny. It was essential to place them in water before purchase, when at least half would float and show they were rotten.

Office hours were nine to twelve and two to four. After tea tennis was played, and there were always people for supper, for the tiny white community stuck together. In the evening hippos would come out of the lake to graze and ruin gardens. They were harmless ashore, but dangerous if bothered in the water. The DO Botry Pigott was drowned on Lake Victoria at Karungu, when a hippo passed beneath his raft and up-ended it. He was eaten by a crocodile.

Business was in the hands of the Indians and of P. H. Clarke, the first white merchant in Kisumu. A cattle trader originally in charge of safaris from the coast, he was helped to put his business on a sound footing by Otto Markus of Mombasa, by the small white population of Kisumu clubbing together to raise funds for him, and by Stephen Bagge giving him contracts to rebuild Kisumu on the other side of the bay. He did well and joined Boustead to launch the firm Boustead & Clarke.

Kisumu's neighbour Kericho, 6,500 feet above sea level and cold, had a vital part to play in the EAP's economic future. In 1904–05 tea bushes grown by the DC Hugh Partington in the prison garden flourished mightily. They attracted attention after the First World War, and tea gradually became one of Kenya's main exports.

On the Uasin Gishu plateau the town called Eldoret grew up. It had two types of white inhabitants: Boer and Briton. Among the British were the Hoeys, Swinton Homes[36] and Pardoes,[37] while the Boers consisted of wealthy families such as the Cloetes, Van Rensburgs, Van Rynevelds and others, and poor farm labourers.[38] Following the Van Rensburg trek, the government divided the land into farming blocks, one of which, no. 64, was leased to Willie Van Aardt who found it unsuitable for farming because of its poor soil. Instead, in 1909–10 a few dukas and a post office were built there – telegrams went by heliograph to Kapsabet, the nearest point where there was a telegraph line. The farmers called the place Sixty-four, but the post office gave its address as Eldore River, a river which merged with the Sosiani (or Saucy Annie as the locals dubbed it) in the vicinity. Eldoret was known by both these names until early in 1911. Then the Governor Sir Percy Girouard paid an official visit and at a luncheon in his honour the speaker asked whether in remembrance of the visit the town could be called Girouard. The Governor replied that this would be an impossible name as no settler would be able to spell it and no African pronounce it. In view of the wonderful prospects of the young district, he added, it was a happy omen that its present name should be so like Eldorado. He suggested the inhabitants should add a 't' to the Eldore of

Eldore River, as many place names in the district ended with this letter, and call the place 'Eldoret'. And so they did.[39]

The post office, a stone building of two rooms run initially by the Kemps and then by Mrs E. O. Milne, was joined in 1910 by a DC's house, of stone with a thatched roof, and a clerk's house. At the same time two British businessmen, Herbert Wreford Smith and John McNab Mundell, left their mining interests in the Orange Free State and built a hotel and bar of wattle and daub. Social life centred on this bar, known colloquially as the 'Rat Pit'. On 28 March 1913 several plots in Eldoret were sold by the government, which had surveyed the place in some detail during the previous year. Smith and Mundell (general merchants), Harris and Redmond (blacksmiths), the Standard Bank of South Africa and the Sosiani Syndicate bought plots of land there, and around the same time A. A. Ortlepp, whose property was adjacent to Plot 64, also sold pieces of his land. A bridge was built across the river and by August 1913 three shops had opened in 'Ortleppville'. Late that year the Pioneer Hotel, managed by the fearsome Mrs Ortlepp, opened its doors.

By 1916 there were four European shops (John Rifkin and Meyer Rosenblum opened a second blacksmith's), and five Indian and Goan stores on Plot 64, while Ortleppville still had three shops. One day the haberdasher's shop, of wood and iron on stilts, went up in flames. As for the Standard Bank, of wattle and daub, it was run by John Clifton Shaw, a Scotsman generous with his credit, who believed that 'You canna far–r–m on a shoestr–r–ring' and lent considerable sums of money to struggling farmers. There were twenty-seven adults and fifty-five white children resident in the nascent town, whose main street was wide enough to turn a wagon and sixteen oxen.[40] The European population of the plateau as a whole rose steadily after 1911, to 900 (1912), 1,220 (1913), and 1,177 in 1916, when many were away at the war.[41]

At the beginning the whole area was alive with game, except for buffalo and elephant, and yet in a few years the plateau was bare of wild animals. The government encouraged the killing of zebra because they carried ticks, but most of the damage was done by the

Mt Kenya

An African family at Njoro, 1905

Fort Smith, 1890s

The grave of George Grey,
old Nairobi cemetery

Tommy Wood's hotel and shop, 1901

Descending the Rift Valley, 1899

The opening of the railway, 1899

Nairobi station, 1899

Nairobi, 1905

A Boer settler family, 1909

Standing: de Silva, Charles Kitchen, Francis Dugmore;
seated: Charles Lane, Elvira Martin, Frank Hall; *on ground*: James Martin

Standing: Frank Hall, Frederick Jackson, Lennox Berkeley, Eric Smith,
Frederick Snowden; *seated*: Mrs Snowden, Helen Boedeker, Charles Lane

Bazaar Road,
Nairobi, 1909

Boxbody cars

The East African Mounted Rifles and a train sabotaged near Voi
by the Germans, 1915

The Masara Hunt
at Government House,
Nairobi, 1913

H. Conway Belfield,
Governor, and his family,
1913

The Theatre Royal,
Nairobi, 1913

shooting of animals for food and to eliminate nuisance. Having laboriously planted oats, wheat and maize, the Uasin Gishu farmers did not want their crops devastated by wild game. The European and Boer communities did not always mix well, for the British regarded some of the Boers as lazy and indigent, while the Boers disapproved of the farming methods of the British. But the very isolation of the plateau (in the rains it took six weeks to travel from Londiani to Eldoret by wagon or Whitelock's stage coach) meant that there had to be some co-operation between the two white communities and in 1910 the Uasin Gishu Farmers' Association was formed with mixed membership.

Mavis Birdsey's family lived eighteen miles beyond Eldoret before the First World War, next door to the Van Rensburgs and to Herbert Wreford Smith, formerly the Birdseys' neighbour in South Africa. Nearby was Guy Lovemore, auctioneer and employer of the transport rider Tommy Hall, a wild man in charge of a fleet of transport wagons between Londiani and Eldoret who died young. Agnes Birdsey, the older sister, taught Mavis and the neighbours' children in a farm school. These people had very little hope of medical attention – there was only one doctor, an Indian sub-assistant surgeon, until the arrival in 1911 of Dr William Heard, who rode long distances upon a mule to see his patients. One neighbour, Robert ('Daddy') Muirhead, who lived alone and far from the others, had a good library and would lend out his books, except perhaps to Mrs Ortlepp with whom he had a running feud because she said his dogs chased her water donkeys.[42] There were rare shopping trips to Eldoret, but on the whole the farms were self-sufficient. Families made soap and candles of hippo fat, and baked their own bread in anthills. Farmers visited Eldoret for social activities, such as dances or fancy-dress parties attended by the five handsome, stately Stephenson girls, when the American Louis Johnson would play his violin and Mrs Shaw, wife of the bank manager and a professional singer, would sing duets with Marjorie Humphries, the daughter of the head of the Central School.[43]

Soon after the rise of Eldoret, whites occupied the land to its north, with the impressive massif of Mt Elgon to the west and the

Cherangani hills to the east. Beyond the Nzoia river, the place was known as Trans-Nzoia, an undulating terrain covered by trees and scrub and watered by little streams flowing into the Nzoia river. No Africans seemed to live there in any numbers. In October 1913 the government held a sale of recently surveyed farms on the Trans-Nzoia. One of the surveyors, D. G. Crofts, had died – his grave was visible below the Endebess bluff – but this deterred no one and twenty-six families bought farms (there were about fifty-six people in all). Among them were Henry Mitford-Barberton,[44] A. C. Hoey, Charles and Edmund de la Harpe, J. Bertram Steyn who had fought for the British in the Boer War, George Robert Chesnaye (a nephew of Earl Roberts), D. Avery Johnston and his brother Cecil, Charles Stradling, Gordon Hewitt, Claude Wright, Mary Bowker, Gert and Hans de Jager, Abel Erasmus, John Kemp, Alexander K. Macdonald and G. K. Glanville. In 1915 they were joined by Odin Sunde and his wife Olufine, Norwegians who had gone to South Africa in 1902, and their five children. Sunde built a sawmill on Mt Elgon, making the waterwheel for the mill himself.

It was a far from easy life. African runners were sent to get the mail from the post office and store established at Soy, forty miles away. The white death-rate was high. Henry Mitford-Barberton died of malaria at Soy in 1920 and his wife Mary of blackwater fever in 1928. G. K. Glanville lost his two young sons to blackwater fever. A. K. ('Wanderobo') Macdonald, who had lived in Paraguay, Australia and Abyssinia – indeed, he called one of his daughters Nesta after the Abyssinian Ras of that name – and had written *Picturesque Paraguay*, was also to suffer from blackwater fever and die in 1918. Nesta, famed for riding across the veld on a sledge made of a thorn tree in the shape of a wishbone, which was drawn by four oxen and slithered across the grass as smoothly as on ice, died of the same illness soon afterwards. Both father and daughter were buried near the round hill of Saboti. A few years later Macdonald's son Noel also died, of malaria. The cairns of stones over the three graves disappeared over the years. Macdonald's wife Matilda, a good woman who followed her restless husband around the world, had more than her fair share of sorrows.

John and Bessie Kemp arrived from South Africa in 1908 with their baby Colin. They obtained a farm ten miles from Eldoret, subsequently ran the post office and store at Sergoit, and bought a farm on Mt Elgon in 1917, where they grew coffee and lived a hospitable existence holding tennis parties on a court they had built. Their son Colin was accidentally impaled on an African spear set as a game trap to catch bushbuck; he severed his femoral artery and bled to death two miles from home. The great wailing of the farm employees brought neighbours to the scene and Colin was carried home on a sheet of corrugated iron to be buried on the farm. John Kemp died a few years later.[45] These were the sort of people Kipling recalled with his lines:

> There's a Legion that never was 'listed,
> That carries no colours or crest,
> But, split in a thousand detachments,
> Is breaking the road for the rest . . .
> The ends of the Earth were our portion,
> The ocean at large was our share.
> There was never a skirmish to windward
> But the Leaderless Legion was there . . .
> Then a health (we must drink it in whispers)
> To our wholly unauthorised horde –
> To the line of our dusty foreloopers,
> The Gentlemen Rovers abroad.[46]

They were adventurers, people who refused to be resigned to the mundane inadequacies of life, men and women born without a sense of doubt who took joy in lands where there were no roads and developed intense feelings for the spirit of places.

White settlements also grew up around Mt Kenya. The government established a post at Nyeri in 1902 – an enclosure surrounded by a ditch and mound of red earth encircled with barbed wire. There was a causeway guarded by a sentry, and inside a white-walled, tin-roofed house and several bandas and sheds. By 1909 missionaries had come to the area and held services for Europeans once a month in the new courthouse. Five years later, the white population had risen to fourteen, including three women, and the amenities included flower gardens, tennis courts and golf links. By 1920 the place had a bank, hotel, two garages and a few shops. People still remembered the splendid ngoma (African dance) held to celebrate George V's coronation in 1911, when twenty-one sticks of dynamite were ignited as a substitute for a twenty-one-gun salute. All over the country the imperial event was commemorated in diverse and innovatory ways.

Beyond hilly Nyeri was Nanyuki on the plains, a small administrative centre in 1913. The South African W. S. Bastard and his sons Seager and Willie farmed cattle and sheep nearby on their land running down to the Uaso Nyiro river, while Berkeley Cole and E. M. Vaughan ('Pat') Kenealy farmed on the mountain side of the road. On the other side of the mountain an administrative post was established at Embu in 1906, in response to African raiding of caravans from the north. The young Stephen Seymour Butler was left alone there for months with his KAR company, an experience he described as the most enjoyable of his life. He shot to feed his men, walking twenty miles every day through this vast natural zoo where lions were two a penny. One day three naked Embu girls, wanting to see a white man, went into his banda, 'their mouths and eyes as wide open as they could go. They stood thus, silent, for about a minute and then, all together, burst into screams of laughter and rushed from the hut.'[47]

Administration spread ever northwards and two years later a station was opened at Meru, in 1908. The DC was the energetic E. B. Horne, known as 'Shorthorn' because he was the smaller of the two Horne brothers, both of them government officials. He busied himself building irrigation ditches, roads and paths, houses, fences, and an eighteen-hole golf course with bunkers and water hazards. Explaining that it was easier to get caddies than golfballs, Horne stationed supernumerary caddies round the edge of the course whenever he could persuade a passing traveller to play.

Horne lived in a two-storeyed house, the peak of Mt Kenya visible behind and the Aberdare range in front, with a mud-floored hall 'in which a huge hatstand rose gauntly from a great pool of water'. In the dining room was an enormous mantelpiece supporting a Union Castle ship's funnel down which water poured when it rained. From the tall, Gothic roof, came the sound of millions of insects munching away at the timbers. 'One night, on opening our bedroom door,' said Madeleine de la Vie Platts, whose husband relieved Shorthorn when he went on leave, 'I found with flesh-creeping horror that my hand had rested for a moment on the black coils of a snake wound round and dangling from the handle.'[48]

Beyond Meru were Rumuruti and Isiolo, two stations established to ease the passage of stock southwards from Somalia and Abyssinia. Before 1911 there were two stores in Rumuruti, one run by an Indian and one by a Somali. The DC, A. J. M. Collyer, lived there with his sisters Margaret and Olive, the latter a wonderful plantswoman whose beautiful garden was admired by too few travellers, such was the isolation of the place. After the Maasai were moved southwards in 1912, Rumuruti declined in importance, though it remained the residence 'of a lonely, sunburned white man with the high accents of Belgravia', the inspector of horses, cattle and camels.[49] Isiolo, on the fringe of the Northern Frontier District, a closed area where whites required permits to travel because the terrain was too barren and the possibility of rescue nil, was a quarantine station for the control of cattle diseases, in the charge of the stock inspector J. E. McDonough. McDonough was quite a character. After a spell as a medical student he went through the South-West African campaign and finished the First World War in East Africa as a medical officer, though not medically qualified, with the rank of captain, RAMC.

The Rift Valley settlements of Nakuru and Naivasha arose as stopping places on the 1890s caravan route to Uganda. Naivasha soon boasted a hotel, owned and run by Charles Cottar, an Irishman.[50] Lord Delamere lived nearby, and if he happened to be in the hotel at 11 p.m. he would produce boxing gloves and offer twenty rounds to anyone. The free-for-alls that ensued were enjoyed by the exclusively young, male clientele.[51] A few years later the hotel was destroyed by fire and the Bell Hotel took

its place. Delamere also indulged in wild high jinks in the hotel
bar at Nakuru, a hot, dusty cow town, and had his neck fractured
during a rough-and-tumble there. That bar was likewise the
scene of a famous fight between the Stanning brothers and a
family of Boers, the Van Klypers, and every now and then Harry
Watt would arrive from Fort Ternan with his drinking cronies
and take over the hotel for a week. He was involved in at least
two cases of alleged murder of Africans on his farm, but was
acquitted both times.

There were many other little settlements developing within the
EAP, as white farmers took up land, Indian entrepreneurs set up
dukas, or the government established small administrative posts.

> So give them a passing thought sometimes,
> Those men of the earlier day;
> The men who have founded the track we tread,
> The men who have 'paved the way';
> Who have died at last on a fevered bed,
> Or in a red-hot fight been killed,
> Just a thought for the workers of yesterday,
> The men on whose bones we build.[52]

5

The First World War

Where were our lads when the call was made
And what did Nairobi do?
See how our citizens on parade
Are waiting to answer you!
Then steadily, Railway and Parklands,
Steadily Town and Hill,
Marching along, twenty score strong,
To be even with Kaiser Bill.
Not in the Stanley or Norfolk Bars
Not on the tennis courts,
Not on the links or in motor cars,
But marching about in shorts.[1]

The banal last line of this song, sung at a rally at the Theatre Royal in Nairobi in September 1915 to the tune of 'The Old Brigade', belies the seriousness of the First World War for the EAP. It may seem odd that the war should have had the profound effect that it did on that nascent country, so remote from Europe, but German East Africa was just next door to the EAP – less than fifty miles away at certain parts of the border – and the white citizens of both countries were determined to fight for the land they were beginning to tame with domestic animals and crops, and to regard as their own.

As news of the outbreak of war reached the EAP, so farmers flocked to Nairobi to join up. Freddie Ward, an ex-Guards officer, was in charge of the recruiting at Nairobi House. There were no uniforms available but recruits handed in their shirts for local ladies to sew the letters EAMR (East African Mounted Rifles) on the shoulder. Single, breech-loading rifles were laid out on a table in Nairobi House until Davies Evans, a veteran of the Boer War, insisted on having modern magazine rifles, some of which were hastily procured. The rest of the men were armed with lances that Eric Gooch, an ex-Lancer, had made at his own expense. Fortunately they disintegrated as the wood dried out. In all, 1,200 men were enrolled, and the rest returned to their farms. Horses were commandeered from farmers – Brian Havelock Potts was allocated Elspeth Huxley's pony Neusi, which later saved him from a pack of wild dogs.[2] The Governor's attractive daughter, Monica Belfield, so often watched the drilling in Nairobi that the soldiers of the newly formed EAMR came to be known as 'Monica's Own'.

Martial law was declared and enemy aliens rounded up. The merchant Otto Markus, confined to his house in Mombasa, was surprised that his former friends disowned him, except for his legal adviser G. G. Atkinson who brought him food. The other Mombasa Germans and Austrians were assembled in the building of the Westdeutsche Handels & Plantengesellschaft, where Wardles chemist later traded. They were placed under guard on the first floor before being put on a train to Nairobi and incarcerated in the common prison, to which they had to walk from the station carrying their luggage on their backs. They were treated like criminals and lived under deplorable conditions, until those considered too old or unfit for military service were sent to a girls' school (probably the Convent). As Austrian consul, Markus was allowed to go home on an Italian ship, but other aliens were transferred to imprisonment in India.[3]

The Nairobi and Mombasa Chambers of Commerce ensured that alien firms were no longer allowed to trade. This caused problems for Sammy Jacobs of the Dustpan, owned by Lumm Bros. He had to leave the council chamber while the matter was debated.[4] After the war there was an awkward discussion about whether Rudolf F. Mayer, of Anderson & Mayer, was an enemy alien, especially as he had served with British forces during the war, as an intelligence officer. This did not, however, save him and he was struck from the register of the Chamber of Commerce.[5]

The Germans took the British border post of Taveta on 15

August 1914. Troops of the EAMR were posted to fly-infested Kajiado on the border, where lions played havoc with the soldiers' ponies at night. There was insufficient drinking water for the men, so on 18 September 1914 an attack was made on Longido hill, a place well supplied with waterholes, but the Germans beat back the British, killing eight of them and wounding four others. The dead included young Alton Forrester, one of four brothers who came to East Africa in 1912 and took up farming at Rumuruti.[6] He had joined up a week before.[7] In November there was another engagement at Longido which caused the deaths of Lionel Tarlton, F. C. de Cerjat (a Swiss), H. H. Sandbach and seven others.[8] The wounded were returned to Nairobi on the Magadi soda train with a red cross painted on the side. Shortly afterwards the Germans retreated from Longido.

Other troops guarded the railway line. They employed Kamba trackers to follow German raiding parties trying to blow up the line, and fortified the railway bridges with twelve men each (six for the less vulnerable ones). Orders were given for all locomotives to be centralised at Nairobi, and engineer B. L. Bremner had to find space to stable them. He was obliged to run one train each way on the line every day, and to keep three trains standing ready in steam twenty-four hours a day. He worked day and night in the railway workshops to build an armoured train, while having his machines commandeered for the making of munitions. There was a great deal of improvisation. P. C. Ford, the railway workshop manager, was very cunning and able to do everything he was asked.[9] His men even managed to make the shot and shells for two old Armstrong guns.

At the outset of the war there was a rush for foodstuffs. Prices went up and flour sold at 80 shillings for a 140-lb bag. A committee was immediately appointed to regulate prices and the government seized all the petrol in the country. Mombasa, in a vulnerable position on the coast, raised a Defence Force. All adult whites joined it and dug trenches near the lighthouse. A decision was made to attack from the sea Tanga on the GEA coast. Troops were brought from India and 4,000 men disembarked near the German port. Unfortunately the hapless British commander made a strategic error by allowing the Germans in Tanga twenty-four hours to surrender, an ultimatum which gave them time to hurry troops to the defence of their port.

Fighting took place in the rubber plantations beside Tanga on 3–5 November 1914, and the British suffered very heavy losses, with 780 killed and wounded. In this battle the Germans were not the only enemy – the soldiers also faced swarms of marauding bees. Contrary to belief, the Germans did not put the bees in the way of British troops – the insects were disturbed by the firing and attacked men on both sides, also stampeding one of the German companies (East African bees are much more hostile than those in Europe). The British were forced to withdraw. While they licked their wounds they realised they were not strong enough to invade GEA and would have to concentrate on guarding the border until rein-forcements arrived from South Africa under General J. C. Smuts.

Meanwhile, in England, a new battalion was formed to fight in East Africa by Colonel Patrick Driscoll, famous in the Boer War as the commander of Driscoll's Scouts. Now, at the age of sixty, he raised the 25th battalion of the Royal Fusiliers, otherwise known as the Legion of Frontiersmen, from adventurers from all over the world. It left London in April 1915, a heterogeneous collection of men, among them several big-game hunters including the famous F. C. Selous, James MacQueen, George Outram and Martin Ryan, the well-known naturalists Cherry Kearton and Angus Buchanan, musicians from the old Empire band, a circus clown, Texas cow-boys and an ex-colonel of the Honduras army always accompanied by a little private who was his bodyguard in Honduras. MacQueen had only one arm, having lost the other after an encounter with an elephant in 1908, but this did not hinder his recruitment. He was killed at Dodoma in November 1917, and Francis Brett Young used him as a model for M'Crae in his novel *Marching on Tanga*. Other recruits were Privates Macrae who had been with Shackleton's polar expedition, and Synnott, the ex-heavyweight champion of Australia. Altogether 1,200 Frontiersmen fought in the battles of Bukoba, Maktau, Kasigau and Lupigora ridge.

By the battle of Lindi there were only 120 survivors, of whom a mere thirty-eight returned from the fight.[10]

Selous, now sixty-three years old, served for two years before he was struck in the head by a sniper in the Beho Beho hills in December 1916 and killed instantly. Charles Bulpett sent a telegram to his friend W. N. McMillan, also a member of the Legion of Frontiersmen but confined to duties in Nairobi because of his size: 'I cannot tell you how sorry and shocked I feel about Selous. To think too that a man of his value has been put of [sic] the world by a dirty nigger.'[11] 'W.S.' penned a memorial verse:

> Midst that fair hunting ground where oft he faced
> Leopard and lion and the zebra chased,
> Heedless of stealthy prowl or furious roar,
> Our great Selous is sleeping evermore.

A memorial to Selous was unveiled in the British Museum of Natural History in 1920, and in his memory a magnificent bronze model of a buffalo, designed by J. L. Clark who had hunted in East Africa, was placed in a prominent position in the main lounge of Nairobi Club. The model was later adopted as the crest and badge of the Kenya Regiment.

Another force raised privately was the Arab Rifles, led by Major Arthur Wavell, cousin of the later field marshal. He had converted to Islam, undertaken a pilgrimage to Mecca and settled down at Malindi, north of Mombasa, on a sisal plantation. When war broke out he raised a company of local Arabs and established a post at Mwele, thirty miles south of Mombasa and near the German border. He wore Arab dress and shared the life of his men. Both Germans and British sent out patrols along the coast, either side of the Ramisi river. They used the same camp sites and left messages for the enemy giving details of the other side's officer casualties. The Germans then determined to march up the coast to take Mombasa, but were held twenty-five miles from the town by Wavell and his men. Wavell was later killed in an ambush, and after his death the Arab Rifles melted away.[12]

The women of the EAP were kept busy nursing the sick and

doing other war work. Nairobi's women formed the Women's Field Force Fund, which collected money and bought material to make pyjamas. Each woman in Kericho, for example, made two to four pairs a month. There was also the Women's War Work League, otherwise known as the Weary Women's Wrangling League, which sent eggs, vegetables and magazines to the troops – 100,000 eggs were sent from Kericho alone. Hospital trains were met and women helped the professional nurses, among them Violet Donkin, who was to have married Fritz Schindler had he not been killed by a lion. She ran the Scott Sanatorium at Kijabe, and saved the life of many a soldier suffering from dysentery, by disobeying the doctor's orders and refusing to administer constant purging. Financed by W. N. McMillan, the Scott Sanatorium had been opened as a convalescent home in June 1913, but was commandeered by the government in the war. It closed after the war.

Other women ran men's farms while they were away at war. Cara Buxton, owner of the farm Kipsaas near Kericho on the Lumbwa road, worked particularly hard. She supervised several properties, travelling from farm to farm accompanied by a single African, two mules with bulky saddlebags holding the wages in rupees for all the farms' staff, and a sack containing her belongings. She must have lived in great discomfort. One day she found herself making a coffin and burying the post master who also ran the hotel – 'somehow that kind of thing one never has anything to do with in England'.[13] She kept Arthur Barclay's farm and shops running and even opened two new stores for him, trading in flour, honey and blankets for Maasai skins which she railed to Mombasa for leather exports to Europe.

The war was also fought on the Lake Victoria front. A tug was painted grey and armed with an old muzzle-loading nine-pounder. And a four-inch gun was rescued from the *Pegasus*, sunk at Zanzibar by the *Koenigsberg*, and put on the *Winifred*, which sank the German armoured tug *Mwanza* on the lake. Reginald Kenneth Rice, telecommunications expert, rushed from the telegraph station at Mombasa up to Lake Victoria to establish a telegraph receiver on the *Clement Hill*, to intercept German messages. For example, on 14 December 1914 Major von Stümer's despatch to Captain Braunschweig was intercepted: 'Despatch of troops here impossible. Wire situation in that place to Commando, from whom I am demanding reinforcements. Hold the line on the River Mara and Mwanza.'[14] The interceptions were invaluable – at one point the British learned that the Germans had left logs of firewood hollowed out and filled with dynamite stacked on the lake shore, ready for British troops to find them and use them and be blown to smithereens.

Local volunteers were rushed from Kajiado to Kisumu when it was heard that the Germans were on the march in the vicinity. They boarded the *Winifred* and sailed to Karungu to cut them off and prevent them attacking Kisii and Kisumu. But the port was already occupied by Germans who drove them away and marched on Kisii on 11 September 1914. Having been given news of their approach by native scouts, the local whites hurriedly left their dinner tables and evacuated the settlement. Prudently, they released thirty prisoners from the jail to carry the specie stored in the strong room.

After they had departed, the local Africans looted the Europeans' houses and the Germans occupied the station. Then Lieutenant W. J. T. Shorthose, with forty KAR men and six settlers, bravely marched from Kericho to retake Kisii, observed from the hills by Africans who had a morning's entertainment watching white men shoot at each other. As far as they were concerned, one white man was as bad as another and they did not much mind who was in possession of Kisii. Captain E. G. M. Thorneycroft was killed and Charles Grey, brother of Sir Edward Grey, British Foreign Secretary, was wounded and had to have his arm amputated. He was killed by a buffalo in Tanganyika in 1928. As Sir Edward had already lost another brother to a lion, he must have had a jaundiced opinion of East Africa.

Thinking the British force was larger than it was, the Germans decided to retreat, and the British reoccupied Kisii. The settlers and officials returned to find everything looted, except Mrs Spencer's piano. Its notes had sounded when Chief Orrere of Bassi sat on it, whereupon the looters thought it was a devil and left it alone. Jasper Evans's house was intact, having been used as a hospital for German wounded, six of whom were still there. Before he left he had put all his bottles of liquor on the dining table with a note saying he was sure the Germans were thirsty after their long march, so please take the liquor and leave the house as it was. The casualty list was forty-five African soldiers and fifteen whites killed on the German side, and twenty African soldiers and one white killed on the British side. The German whites were buried in a common grave, with Father J. A. Wall of the nearby Nyabururu Roman Catholic mission taking the service.[15] Thorneycroft was buried near the tennis court.[16]

By mid-1915 the British were doing so badly that more recruits were needed. However, an appeal led to only five offers to join up. In September Ewart Grogan, fired with patriotic zeal, arranged a public meeting at the Theatre Royal, Nairobi. He made a speech of fiery eloquence urging national service for the EAP – this was really aimed at the Boers on the Uasin Gishu plateau who were, it was felt, not pulling their weight. But it was only a small minority of Afrikaners who refused to serve in the British forces. Conscription was introduced in December 1915, and in mid-1917 seven Afrikaners were brought to trial for not reporting for duty, and were given six-, nine-, and ten-month prison sentences.

At the end of 1915 the Germans invaded the EAP in the Tsavo area and took the mountain Kasigau. They attacked Ndi station on the railway on Christmas Day. It was only the arrival of troops from South Africa under Jan Smuts in early 1916 that put the enemy on the defensive. GEA was finally invaded in spring 1916. There ensued a war of manoeuvre, with an excessively heavy sick-rate. As the soldier Noel Smith wrote to his mother, 'Of course nature and the mosquito are far greater enemies to our advance than the Germans.'[17] In 1917 there were 1,423 military admissions to hospital for malaria per 1,000 soldiers. Altogether there were 40,527 admissions of soldiers for malaria that year, with 2,291 deaths, mostly of Africans from the highland regions who had not suffered the illness before.[18] Smuts reoccupied Taveta in March 1916 and soon captured Moshi, Arusha and Kahe. It was all bush fighting, with no spit and polish, and the troops were often hungry, despite the herculean efforts of the African Carrier Corps, who carried all the supplies and died in large numbers doing so.

The troops were fed with game shot on the Athi plains by men from the Army Supply Depot camping there for the purpose. No less than 40,000 head went to furnish the soldiers with meat – far more game was killed inside the reserve in those war years than had been shot outside it in the ten years before. Hartebeeste (known locally as kongoni) and wildebeeste were the most popular meats, and zebra was rejected as unpalatable. As for giraffe, the animals were seventeen feet tall and though not specially shot for meat, they had to be destroyed because their necks kept breaking the telegraph wires. They were almost exterminated in some areas. Rhinos were not shot for food but proved to be such a nuisance to the troops that they, too, were almost eliminated in some parts. The survivors became very savage and game rangers wondered whether the rhino population would ever recover.

Smuts pushed southwards in pursuit of Von Lettow Vorbeck, the German commander, whose tactics were to retreat and lead the British troops a merry dance. In southern Tanganyika supply lines were so stretched that the British troops suffered great hardship from rats, scabies and malaria. The rats were particularly insolent, eating clothes and pulling blankets from sleeping men. There were no chaplains in the field to encourage the soldiers or bury the dead. Doctors were few. One of them, Owen Berkeley, of the Indian Medical Service, wore a huge yellow turban and hated discipline. When asked for the marching-in state of his troops, he replied, 'I never march anywhere in state. It is as much as I can do to get along.' As so often in war, the biggest and strongest men suffered the most from illness.

In November 1917 the Germans eventually crossed the Rovuma river into Portuguese East Africa. There they stayed for nine months, regrouping and re-equipping themselves with the assistance of the not unsympathetic Portuguese. When the British got to the Rovuma river they were confronted by a large group of German civilians who displayed hatred towards them, including a small boy who spat on officer Cornelius Durham's boot. He patted the boy on the head and said, 'Good shot!' The British escorted the German civilians to the coast.[19]

Von Lettow turned northwards in September 1918 and re-entered German territory. When war in Europe ended on 11 November 1918 he was still in the field in Northern Rhodesia, occupying the town of Fife with 2,000 men. Many of the EAP's pioneers had lost their lives. Among the names on the war memorial at Muthaiga unveiled by Governor Edward Northey on 23 July 1920 were T. H. Drake, H. M. Lambert, J. N. F. Pixley, H. H. Sandbach, R. R. Tate Smith, A. H. Thompson, R. F. C. Tompson and R. B. Woosnam – pioneers every one of them. The names of all the British whites lost in the East African war are inscribed on the war memorial in Hyde Park, London. The thousands of Africans who lost their lives, some of whom donned their white officers' headgear so that they would be shot at instead, lack a memorial on which all their individual names are inscribed.

6

Post-war Adjustment

The war had forged a feeling of bellicosity and solidarity among those who had previously been scattered and separate settlers. Shared misfortune had been a great stimulus to friendship. Victory in the conflict had reinforced the whites' self-confidence and belief in the invincibility of the British empire. At the end of the war the EAP's men returned to their farms and civilian jobs and settled down to resume their former lives with an energy renewed by the feeling that they had fought hard for the land they had chosen. This confirmed them in their belief that if they farmed it well, it was justly theirs. Their numbers were soon to be swelled by new immigrants. The number of whites in the EAP rose from 5,438 in 1914 to 9,651 in 1921. Broken down into occupations, the three largest were agriculture (28 per cent in 1911, 36 per cent in 1921 and 39 per cent in 1926), government (26, 21 and 22 per cent), missionary (16 and 6 per cent), industry (9, 10 and 10 per cent), commerce (4, 18 and 19 per cent) and professions (3, 3 and 4 per cent).[1] The farming lobby was therefore the strongest, but numbers in commerce and industry were increasing.

*   *   *

At the end of the First World War the British Government had to find jobs for thousands of demobilised military personnel. The colonies were obvious places of settlement for them, in particular Kenya, as the EAP was renamed in 1920. With a white population much smaller than that of Southern Rhodesia, it seemed to have plenty of space. Now the Kenya Government followed White-hall's instructions and alienated more land for Europeans – some of it formerly in African reserves – while dividing into smaller farms other, already alienated, land. In all, 2,540,000 more acres were made available for white settlement. For the ex-servicemen there were to be 500 A-farms, of approximately 160 acres each and containing a high proportion of arable land, and 850 B-farms of from 500 to 3,000 acres each.

The farms were distributed by raffle. Men and women who had served in the army, navy or air force for at least six months were allowed to submit a series of numbers, in the order of their choice, as there would be many applications for the better farms. If an applicant's name was drawn early, the chances of getting better land were good, because there were too few applicants for the hundreds of free A-farms available. Kenya residents (including government servants) could also apply if they had served in the armed forces, as could citizens of other colonies. The rule against officials owning land had been relaxed in 1918, after pressure from the Civil Servants' Association. Governor Sir Edward Northey bought a coffee farm. Both the former Governor Sir Percy Girouard and Acting Governor Sir Charles Bowring applied for land on their retirement.

In some cases people formed syndicates and obtained as much as 10,000 acres. Four-fifths of the A-farms went to local applicants, two-thirds of them from Nairobi and one-sixth of them government officials. Only a quarter of the B-farms went to local applicants. The total number of non-local applicants allocated farms was 731, of whom 685 emigrated to Kenya.

Many of the new immigrants travelled out on the *Garth Castle*, arriving in Mombasa on 25 December 1919. One of the party, C. T. Todd, said that none of them 'realised what a complicated business farming is, and we had not visualised the difficulties that would present themselves in territory that was nothing more than an empty wilderness and where we were totally ignorant of local conditions. We were to learn the hard way.'[2] In most cases the farms were too large to be worked economically by new settlers with limited capital and no agricultural experience. The government encouraged the planting of flax, providing the new farmers with seed. But in June 1921 the price of flax dropped from £500 to £50 a ton. Many of the soldier-settlers then abandoned their farms and returned to England. But some stayed on, taking any job they could get – for example, Todd went foot trading in the Northern Frontier District, exchanging goods for ivory and rhino horn with the Suk and Turkana.

Yet by October 1923 three-quarters of the 1,031 farms allotted had been occupied and a quarter had fulfilled the development requirements in full. A quarter of the farms had been sold by the allottees and a fifth had reverted to the government. By late 1926, 900 farms had been settled on 1,600,000 of the original 2,450,000 acres. But up to 90 per cent of the original farms had been transferred from the original allottees. Only 286, less than half, of the non-local allottees remained in Kenya in 1925. The intentions of the original scheme had not been fulfilled. If the British Government had hoped to populate Kenya with whites and develop the country cheaply, it had failed. However, the scheme had other, lasting effects.

The extra land taken over by the government for the scheme led to ill-feeling among the Africans, as the settler frontier was pushed ever further into what they considered was their land, whether they occupied it or not. T. R. L. Nestor, of the Survey Department in Nairobi, described how his theodolite was stolen and his survey beacon pulled out as he was cutting through African bean shambas while surveying for soldier-settler land in the Ithanga area.[3] Furthermore, the South African influence in settler affairs was diminished, because many of the new farms were in the Uasin Gishu area.

Three men who were to become influential political leaders came out under the scheme: Lord Francis Scott, Ferdinand Cavendish-Bentinck and A. G. Keyser. And the social impact of the new settlers tended to reinforce the upper- and upper-middle-class nature of Kenyan white society. If one examines the class structure of the soldier-settlers, it emerges that sixty-five of the non-locals appeared in *Burke's Peerage*, and forty-eight in *Burke's Landed Gentry*. There were several professionals: 25 doctors, 4 nurses and a dentist, 14 lawyers, 20 civil or mining engineers, 9 vets, 5 accountants, 2 clergymen, an architect and an entomologist.[4]

A second, similar scheme was implemented, for officers disabled in the war: BEADOC (British East Africa Disabled Officers Colony). The land allotted to this project by the government was 25,000 acres near Kericho, and training grants were provided for applicants. Each of seventy disabled officers put £600 into the venture. They intended to establish a co-operative flax-growing settlement with individual ownership of land and the provision of common facilities. C. M. Dobbs, the DC at Kericho, a tall thin Irishman with glasses stuck together with sealing wax and a stained and battered soft hat, worked hard with his wife Marion to help the newcomers. When the first batch arrived on 3 January 1920, among them a doctor and several engineers, Dobbs arranged for porters to carry their belongings and pitch tents on the land allocated. He tried to recruit cooks for the newcomers but could find nobody suitable. No official with any knowledge of that part of Kenya had been consulted, or a lot of money would have been saved and the men would have been told about difficult local conditions.[5]

The men cleared their land, and built a dam, factory and temporary houses for themselves. Then they were joined by their wives, the first of them the spouses of Hugo Daly and Norman Birkett. This livened things up, for some of the wives were fond of dancing and would drive five miles or so in evening dress to dance to a gramophone on mud floors. Despite, or because of, being in a co-operative, not everyone got along well with each other. The wilderness, unfortunately, can act as a catalyst, exaggerating the faults of some though bringing forth the finer points in others. After the fall in the price of flax, some BEADOC members left the colony, others went to the towns, while yet others swelled the number of white landless people working as farm managers or on construction contracts, such as the new Nakuru–Eldoret railway. The sale of their land gave them their money back after a few years, but by the time it was discovered that tea did excellently in Kericho, the money was gone and BEADOC had disbanded.

*   *   *

Soon the newcomers were to be plunged into political crisis. In early 1920 the settler whites faced a huge predicament, when the first general election was held in Kenya. The Europeans had been given eleven single-member constituencies for elections to the Legislative Council, and the Indians, who vastly outnumbered them, followed the example of their compatriots in India and demanded their own political representation. They also supported the Africans, themselves beginning to make political demands. A despatch to the Governor of Kenya from Lord Milner in Downing Street caused great alarm to Kenya's whites. It read, 'I could not countenance any restrictions which would place the natives of India at a disadvantage as compared with other immigrants.'[6]

This was shocking to settlers as yet unsure of their political position in the new country of Kenya. The whites realised they would be outnumbered and overwhelmed if Indians were allowed to vote and to own land in the highlands, and their reaction to Milner's pronouncement was to plan sedition. The whites had learned to love and respect Kenya, to worship its *genius loci*. They did not have the same feeling for their own cold, wet country, or they would never have left it. The feeling among them was so strong, and so skilfully fostered, that rebellion against the government seemed the only possible response. They did not want the right to belong in Kenya to have to be fought for and earned by each succeeding white generation. Through the Convention of Associations,[7] to which all districts sent delegates, the whites demanded complete segregation of Indians, restrictions on Indian immigration, no alienation of land in the highlands to Indians and the restriction of Indian representation in the Legislative Council to two nominated members. Mindful of the dangerous situation in India, and its close links with East Africa, the British Government refused to comply.

The Convention of Associations then formed a Vigilance Committee of five settlers chosen in secret, with sub-committees in all white settlement areas. Being mostly farmers, the white settlers were already armed. Meetings of settlers in the various districts were held, and a declaration signed: 'That we the undersigned hereby solemnly declare that during the present crisis we will place ourselves under and obey the orders of the officer commanding this District, chosen by ourselves, who shall in turn be under the orders of the Central Committee.'[8] At Nyeri, where Richard Allsopp was in command, the whole of the white population was placed under military discipline. Marmaduke Wetherell, the Medical Officer at Eldoret who had been six years in India, raised the temperature by saying that the unrestricted immigration of 50,000 Indians to Kenya would spell the practical extermination of the native because they would contaminate water with *bacillus coli* and cause typhoid fever and dysentery. This statement caused the missionaries to join the settlers in a rare act of collaboration. A petition with 3,060 signatures was sent to King George V and Delamere went on an abortive mission to South Africa to try to get the support of Jan Smuts, who had led the East African troops in the First World War and was now Prime Minister. The Kenya whites boycotted all Indian businesses.

General Philip Wheatley, a fiery former Indian army officer with a soldier-settler farm at Nanyuki, went on a whirlwind tour with Powys Cobb around the different districts – 'I have been asked to tour the country and set it alight.'[9] At the meeting he addressed in Eldoret, the settlers passed the resolution put by Colonel G. A. Swinton Home, 'that this meeting hereby solemnly pledges itself to oppose by every means in its power including armed resistance any political concessions to the Indian community'.[10] Tommy O'Shea, owner of the Ford garage in Eldoret, took out a full-page advertisement in the *Uasin Gishu Weekly Advertiser* with nothing on it but the words 'Johnny Get Your Gun'. It seems extraordinary that the whites engaged in sedition, but when the alternative is possible disaster, a man will gamble.

Lists were drawn up of the number of arms people possessed and everyone was allocated a role to play when rebellion broke out. Wheatley told his father:

> The Colonial Office have made the most abject surrender to the Indians and everybody is wild. So much so that there will be great difficulty in holding some of the fellows back, but we are

doing our utmost . . . The pledge of secrecy is off . . . Now we fight in the open. As the country is solid on the point, absolutely so, despite the assurance of some politicians that our resistance is all bluff, we shall win.[11]

Wheatley was told by a government official that they had got him as a marked man, and the intelligence department scrutinised his mail – 'I couldn't even order a dozen of whisky without the latter being considerably delayed, or even suppressed altogether, by some B.F. who in his muddled mind conceived that an order to enable me to alleviate my thirst conveyed some cryptic information which might possibly be subversive of law and order.'[12] The highlands were divided into twenty-seven mustering districts under seven group leaders who reported to Wheatley, the Commander-in-Chief. In fact, Wheatley was dangerously indiscreet, as was his colleague J. E. Coney at Kitale who said hostilities would begin in a fortnight, giving a 'wild and harmful distortion of the facts'.[13] Meanwhile influential contacts in London briefed newspaper editors and members of the House of Lords, while the settler force was put in a state of readiness.

The Governor, Sir Robert Coryndon, abandoned his original feeling of amused tolerance, but decided against the arrest of the white leaders of the rebellion because no jury would convict them. Deportation was impossible because of the numbers involved, and a declaration of martial law would have been injudicious.[14] The officer commanding troops said he could not rely on his men to obey their officers in case of disturbance, since many of their former officers in the First World War, to whom they felt great loyalty, were now settlers engaged in the rebellion. Neither could reservists be trusted, because most of them were employed on farms and thoroughly supported the rising. Of the administrative officials, only 20 per cent had views opposed to the settlers, while 80 per cent said in the event of a rebellion they would find pressing duties in a portion of their district far removed from the disturbances.

The Governor made arrangements for all ammunition dumps to

be transported to Mombasa and put in the sea to prevent them being seized by the settlers. He told his private secretary, Eric Dutton, to find out exactly what was being plotted. Dutton discovered that the settlers planned to take over the railway, whose head, Sir Christian Felling,[15] was probably on their side, and that they had among them railway engineers, drivers and guards. In Mombasa they intended to seize the cable station, wireless (radio) station, stock of petrol, repair shops and all military equipment. The settlers had among themselves railway engineers, drivers and guards. Dutton also learned that the Governor would be captured and some light occupation or amusement found for him in the Aberdare mountains.[16]

Because the situation was so serious, the British Government summoned Coryndon and settler leaders to London. Lord Delamere, C. Kenneth Archer (leader of the Convention of Associations, previously a lawyer in Nairobi and now a coffee farmer at Ruiru) and Tommy Wood, a prominent Nairobi businessman, were chosen as the settlers' delegates. Meanwhile Mombasa, which had held itself aloof from the rebellion, was brought into line with the highlands when Sitaram Achariar, editor of the Mombasa Indian paper *The Democrat*, charged the whole race of Englishwomen with being of low character, adding that most of them 'had to procure an abortion before being finally led to the altar'.[17] The white population of Mombasa became so intensely excited about this slur on their ladies' honour that Judge Joseph Sheridan committed Achariar to prison for his own safety. When the Governor and delegation reached London some weeks later, a compromise was worked out, and the rebellion died away. Essentially the settlers had got what they wanted, winning on all points of substance. From the evidence it does seem that they would have carried out the threat of military action had matters not been resolved satisfactorily.

*   *   *

Economic conditions in Kenya were harsh in the years immediately after the First World War. Some of the whites succumbed to penury or became vagrant. The *East African Standard* of 28 August

1920 called for the police to do something about the increasing number of European tramps on the streets of Nairobi. In response, the League of Mercy expanded its operations and in 1919 Lady Northey, the new Governor's wife, founded the Lady Northey Home in Nairobi to provide a day-care centre for the children of European women working in Nairobi and a place where the children of poor whites could be maintained free from 'the contamination of contact with Africans'. The Uasin Gishu Plateau Relief Fund was established in April 1920 to help whites who wanted to be sent home to Europe. The Salvation Army came to Kenya in the 1920s and made the poor whites of Nairobi its particular concern. It founded two hostels there for indigent men and women and also ran an employment bureau in conjunction with the town clerk.

A few of the whites had reached rock bottom because of alcoholism. The Mathari mental asylum on the outskirts of Nairobi was home to many of them – indeed, most of its white inmates were alcoholics. The admission rates of whites were: 1921 fourteen, 1922 thirteen, 1923 seven, 1924 fifteen, 1925 twelve, and 1926 sixteen. In the first three years after the introduction of the soldier-settler scheme eleven indigent or undesirable Europeans were deported, and in 1926 fourteen.[18] In March 1922 a meeting held in Nairobi to discuss European unemployment requested that 100 men be taken on by the Uasin Gishu railway and any shirkers deported. A flag day was held that month for the white unemployed.

The problem was exacerbated by the post-war rise in the world price of silver, which encouraged the Indian rupee currency of Kenya to appreciate against sterling. The government decided to cut the link with the rupee and move to sterling, and fixed the rupee at two shillings in 1920. Many settlers had taken out bank loans when the rupee was worth a shilling and fourpence, so their overdrafts doubled overnight. The following year the price of flax crashed, and there were also falls in the prices of coffee, sisal and wool. The land market collapsed and rural indebtedness was huge.

And yet, united in their common poverty, white farmers were reluctant to leave. There was something about Kenya that answered an emotional need in them. Perhaps it was the crunch of dry grass under the feet, the smell of red dust, the sound of rain tap-dancing on corrugated-iron roofs, the cadences of coucal birds, the pink snow of Mt Kenya at dawn – all these chained people to the country.

In self-defence, the producers began to organise themselves into co-operatives. The Kenya Farmers' Association sprang up in 1927 as an amalgamation of maize marketing organisations, and in 1929 the Kenya Co-operative Creamery was formed. Freight became more regulated. When the question of licences for motor vehicles carrying cargo was being discussed in the Legislative Council, the Chief Native Commissioner said, 'Under that clause do you mean to say that if I go off to Machakos with a case of whisky in the back of the car, I have to take out a licence as a carrier?' 'Oh no,' said Delamere, 'we don't intend this to apply to the daily ration.' Things began to improve and Kenya entered a period of relative prosperity from 1924. The area under white crops doubled in the six years up to 1929, while the number of farmers swelled from 1,122 in 1919 to 2,097 in 1930.

Maize, wheat, coffee and sisal were Kenya's main crops.[19] There were hopes that gold would be found in quantities sufficient to work profitably. In 1927 gold was being mined by the Kisumu Syndicate Mine at Migore camp near Kisii, and the Kenya Gold Mining Syndicate was working nearby. Then came two disasters: an invasion of locusts and world depression in 1929. Farm managers were forced to take work for as little as ten pounds a month. Others found work as locust officers, their job to poison the hopper locusts before they took to the air. There were two types of locusts: the big brown which came from Southern Rhodesia via Tanganyika, and the desert red from Abyssinia, Somaliland and Sudan. Swarms stretched for thirty miles and darkened the midday sun. If washing was left on the line the locusts would eat it, and they stripped the crops bare. Traffic came to a halt when roads were made too slippery by crushed locusts. Town roads were cleared by brushing the locusts into the drains and poisoning them with arsenical spray. After the locust swarms,

Kenya was hit by world depression in October 1929, and the total trade of the country fell from £18,066,190 that year to £10,597,969 in 1930.[20] Civil servants had to suffer a reduction of 10 per cent in their salaries, and many farmers went bankrupt. Kenya was in trouble.

* * *

A new means of communication – by air – saw its inception in the Kenya of the 1920s. The invention of the aeroplane was a boon to Kenya and soon air travel, which shrank the world, would transform the colony's links with Britain. Aircraft had played no significant part in East Africa in the First World War, but after the war the first aircraft to reach East Africa, on a flight to South Africa, was a Vickers Vimy Commercial. It landed at Kisumu but subsequently crashed at Tabora in Tanganyika. Small aeroplanes then began to reach Kenya, the first of them owned by John Carberry,[21] and several people learned to fly, among them Beryl Markham,[22] Maia Carberry, Denys Finch Hatton and Tom Campbell Black. Florence Wilson[23] opened a small airport outside Nairobi to accommodate these planes and to house the company she started in 1929, Wilson Airways, which provided charter flights within East Africa.

Such charter flights were used by many of the wealthy big-game hunters, including the Prince of Wales. But what people most wanted was an airmail service to England, and passenger flights as well, if possible. Imperial Airways sent Sir Alan Cobham to reconnoitre a route to South Africa via Kisumu in November 1925. He managed to land safely at Kisumu and successfully completed the journey to the Cape. A seaplane service carrying mail from Kisumu to Khartoum was attempted in January 1927, but the aircraft crashed. And yet by 1929 Kisumu had become the southern terminus of the Nile route from Cairo and Khartoum, and there were plans for a regular passenger service, which began in 1932.

As yet, however, the Europeans still went 'home' by ship – a three-week journey through the Suez Canal to Italy or France, and then by train to Britain in order to avoid the gastric calamities of the stormy Bay of Biscay. Some people took the longer, southern route round the Cape of Good Hope. Newspapers printed the dates ships docked at Mombasa, and there was always a frisson as the passengers embarked and saw who their shipmates were. There was invariably someone they knew on board; their enjoyment of the voyage could be determined by the random choice of their fellow passengers who could either make or mar the journey.

Communications within Kenya were becoming slightly easier, though roads were still bad. But agriculture had been given a boost by the expansion of the railway in the 1920s. A branch line to Thika, opened in 1913, was extended to Nyeri in 1926 and Nanyuki in 1930. A line to Uganda which avoided Lake Victoria was also planned. There had been pressure to build such a track since 1913, when Ewart Grogan, owner of a timber firm at Timboroa, wanted the railway to come to his sawmills. A survey of the Nakuru–Eldoret–Mumias–Uganda route was therefore undertaken the following year. The war intervened and matters came to a halt, but pressure began again in the early 1920s. Lord Delamere, Grogan and the Rift Valley farmers wanted the line to begin at Nakuru, but a cheaper option, branching off the line to Kisumu at Mau, was favoured by William McGregor Ross, head of the Public Works Department. The large landowners prevailed. The line was begun at Nakuru, and it reached Kampala in Uganda in 1930. It came to Eldoret in 1925, thus ending the isolation of the Uasin Gishu farmers.

A branch line into Tanganyika from Voi, built for troops in the First World War, operated for goods, and the line built just before the war to Magadi continued to transport soda, joining the main Mombasa–Nairobi line at Konza. Apart from opening up the north west of Kenya, the railway came at an opportune time for farmers failing on their land. Many took supervisory jobs on railway construction and so were able to remain in Kenya until economic conditions improved. But a few of the settlers had mixed feelings about the expansion of the railway:

Oh, I realise that we civilise,
And the work that we do is fine,
When we lay the trails for the gleaming rails
Of a pioneering line.
But soon they'll push, till there's no more bush,
And never a bushman's shrine,
And when that day's come where will be the home
For a soul that is made like mine?[24]

The railway had been modernised since the early days of non-corridor carriages and disembarkation for meals. Some of the trains now had corridors and restaurant cars. Passengers no longer had to bring their own bedding, but rather could hire it on the train. The biologist Julian Huxley was intrigued to find that the trains had bottle openers built into the wall of the lavatory compartments.

*   *   *

The Kenyan whites were fortunate in the three Governors they had in the 1920s. General Sir Edward Northey was Governor of Kenya from 1919 to 1922 and presided over the country's change of name from the East Africa Protectorate to Kenya in 1920. Kenya, the name of the country's highest mountain, had been applied to one of the original provinces, when it was pronounced Kenya with a short e. However, the powers in Whitehall decided that the pronunciation should have a long e, and Keenya became the pronunciation until independence in 1963 when it reverted to Kenya with a short e.

A delightful man with no liking for protocol and ceremony, Northey kept a zoo of wild animals in the Government House grounds and let his wife raise chickens in the attics. In contrast to the Government House of the past, his period of office saw a round of brilliant parties, frequently enlivened by the appearance at dinner of cheetahs under the table. He failed to make provision for his zoo when he left and his successor complained about the considerable expense of feeding the animals. Eventually London Zoo took most of them, though Northey, by now a private resident in Kenya ('I can promise that I shall never embarrass you by any political discussion or statement of opinion'), asked whether his successor wished to keep the lions and two leopards.[25] After the Northeys left, the Medical Officer of Health had to inspect Government House because Lady Northey had never cleaned out the attics, now deep with chicken droppings.

Northey was succeeded by Sir Robert Coryndon, famous in the past as a hunter, a talented artist and woodworker, a first-class poker player who could tear a pack of cards in half and drink anyone under the table though was generally reasonably abstemious, one of Cecil Rhodes's private secretaries who had become Governor of Uganda and Southern Rhodesia.[26] Coryndon was a good handler of men and won the trust of his officials and the regard of Lord Delamere. Delamere was still regarded as the settlers' leader, not least because he was like one of those round-bottomed Russian dolls that can never be knocked over, no matter how often they are pushed.

Coryndon liked Africans and urged the complementary development of both African and white production, dreaming of new buildings, new railways, new harbour works. He preferred things that could be built in the present, that he could go and inspect, a sore trial to his private secretary, Eric Dutton, the possessor of artificial legs who none the less climbed Mt Kenya. Years earlier Rudyard Kipling, travelling with Coryndon on the *Kenilworth Castle*, had written on a piece of ship's notepaper the poem 'The Proconsuls' and had dedicated it to him:

> They that dig foundations deep,
> Fit for realms to rise upon,
> Little honour do they reap
> Of their generation,
> Any more than mountains gain
> Stature till we reach the plain.

During the visit of the Duke and Duchess of York in 1924 Coryndon was not looking well. Noticing his grey sheen, Dutton asked what was wrong, to be told, 'I believe I am going to have twins.'[27] In fact, he was having trouble with his pancreas. J. Langton Gilks, director of medical services, visited Coryndon in bed one morning but was not unduly alarmed. Dr P. A. Clearkin visited shortly afterwards, was horrified at what he saw and urged immediate admission to hospital. But this was delayed until the evening, even though Coryndon was unconscious, because the Chief Justice could not be found to swear in the Acting Governor. Dr H. H. V. Welch, resident surgeon at the European hospital, a drug addict who had been MO at Wajir before the war, operated and found acute haemorrhagic pancreatitis from which Coryndon could not be saved. He died within a few hours and Welch submitted his resignation on health grounds, which was accepted. In fact no surgeon could have saved Coryndon, though Welch later tried to blame his death on the anaesthetic Clearkin had administered, claiming that the Governor's heart could not stand the operation at such a height as Nairobi's.[28] The Duke of York attended the funeral of the man who had so recently been his host and the country was left feeling bewildered and discouraged.

Coryndon was succeeded as Governor by Sir Edward Grigg, once military secretary to the Prince of Wales, and former parliamentary private secretary to Lloyd George after being a General Staff officer in the Guards, a man who rejoiced in ceremony. There were changings of the guard twice a week and tailcoats had to be worn at garden parties. On state occasions the Governor held a levée after dinner and all members of the civil service with 'first-class appointments' were obliged to attend in full evening dress with white kid gloves and decorations. Also invited were important members of the unofficial community who were lined up by ADCs and bowed to the Governor standing on a dais with members of the Legislative and Executive Councils grouped behind him. The settlers, who remembered Lady Northey dancing with abandon on one of the tables at the Muthaiga Club, and called her daughter 'Careless Flo', thought it all rather risible.

Government House, which looked like a small seaside hotel or a Swiss chalet,[29] was exchanged for a Palladian mansion designed by Sir Herbert Baker at a cost of £60,000. On account of the cost, and because the settlers suspected Grigg's eagerness to achieve was to promote his own future not theirs, the Governor was not popular with the settlers, although Lord Delamere tried to get along with him. The trouble was, said Delamere, that Grigg changed his mind so often that it was difficult to bear, and his incessant cables home to Britain ruined any course he espoused – 'he certainly is the worst diplomat possible'.[30] However, Delamere's step-children and Grigg's younger boy John remained playmates despite the new *froideur*.

Tall and good-looking, with charming, gracious manners, Grigg was possessed of imagination and enterprise. He and his wife did much for Kenya. Apart from Government House, Grigg approved the construction of the law courts, railway headquarters and offices. This example encouraged private enterprise to build the National Bank of India, the Standard Bank and the municipal market, converting Nairobi from an insignificant town of mainly wood and corrugated-iron structures into a fine, modern place. He was also more pro-settler than the settlers suspected. 'I am quite clear', he said in 1927, 'that an abandonment of the official majority [in the Legislative Council] in Kenya is now desirable, in order that a sense of responsibility may be built up and the way prepared for responsible government', though he still wanted to retain considerable powers of veto 'if the mettlesome Kenya horse is not to pull the whole wagon off the course in moments of excitement'.[31]

It was Grigg who persuaded the Prince of Wales and Duke of Gloucester to visit Kenya. This placed the country on the map and encouraged further capital to be invested. But Grigg's fundamental aim was to unite the three countries of Kenya, Uganda and Tanganyika, much to the horror of Tanganyika's Governor, Sir Donald Cameron, who thought a white bastion might thus be created and the advance of the Africans consequently delayed. The British Government sent out the Hilton Young Commission on Closer Union to examine the matter. In the opinion of one of its members, Sir George Schuster, Grigg and Leo Amery, another member, had plotted together to fix the report, and Hilton Young was privy to the plan. Schuster was mistakenly regarded as tame, but he concluded that closer union was a personal ambition of Grigg, a man determined to make a big career for himself by becoming Governor-General of the three united territories. Schuster had been at New College, Oxford, with Grigg, a Winchester scholar there, and had conceived a dislike for the man. As a result Hilton Young had to write a minority report, which was not what was wanted, and the idea of closer union was shelved.[32] Grigg's misfortune was to be in Kenya during a world depression. He was consequently regarded as extravagant, a man of grandiose schemes. In another period, he might have been viewed as far-seeing.

*   *   *

Throughout the terms of office of these three governors, Kenya's white population steadily increased – from 5,438 in 1914 to 12,529 in 1926.[33] The country was not so dangerous to health as it had been before the war, or these people would not have come. After the war medical facilities for settlers and Africans alike improved, and more doctors arrived. However, there was still much 'do–it-yourself'. Martin Mahoney, of the 5th KAR, described assisting a doctor, who had hurt his hand, at an operation on the arm of an African. Mahoney administered the chloroform and removed the bone which was sticking through the skin. 'In the evening he [the patient] came and asked for his bit of bone, but as the dogs had already chewed it up, we could not give it to him.'[34]

By 1924 there were thirty-three British MOs in the Medical Department (among them seven in Nairobi, three in Mombasa and one each in Kakamega, Kisii, Fort Hall, Chuka, Nakuru, Narok, North Jubaland and Moyale). There were also four part-time European district surgeons and several Indian sub-assistant surgeons. Their jobs were various – 'Life was enlivened by the odd exhumation and the occasional post-mortem performed under a thorn tree in cases of sudden death, usually murder.'[35] In Nairobi there was the PMO, Dr J. Langton Gilks, and his deputy, Dr C. J. ('Dan') Wilson, together with Dr A. D. J. B. Williams, and Dr W. H. Kauntze at the head of the Medical Research Laboratory. Because there were insufficient assistant surgeons in the settled areas, doctors were granted free farms on the under-standing that they would practise medicine in specific districts. From 1924 all recruits to the Colonial Medical Service had to do a course at the London School of Hygiene and Tropical Medicine.

The commonest illnesses were still malaria, blackwater fever, typhoid fever, and bacillary and amoebic dysentery, the last of them often accompanied by amoebic abscess of the liver. Tropical ulcers were a regular nuisance. Mumias was still one of the most dangerous spots, with serious morbidity and mortality among the government staff there. There were six graves in its European cemetery, five of them of blackwater fever cases. And then another DO, Mackenzie Hamilton Fraser, also died there of the same cause. The DC, Edward Vincent Hemnant, who had summoned Dr P. A. Clearkin from Kisumu in a vain attempt to save his colleague, ordered the local village carpenter to make a rough coffin out of some of the shelves in his office. They found an old KAR bugler to sound the Last Post, Hemnant read the burial service, rain dripped down relentlessly and mosquitoes feasted on the mourners. In exactly one month, Hemnant himself would occupy a grave next to his assistant, in a coffin made from the rest of his office shelves.[36] The Mumias station was then closed down and moved to Kakamega.

Dr R. W. Burkitt was still practising, though by now he had an assistant, Dr J. W. Gregory. The Nairobi European Hospital surgeon was Cliff Viney Braimbridge, a keen cricketer who kept fit by skipping before breakfast. He gave long service to the Nairobi Club, where a room was named after him in the Gymkhana section, following his death in 1964. Dr Gerald Anderson, with his distinctive pince-nez, and his young assistant, T. Farnworth Anderson (no relation), had their consulting rooms in the *East African Standard* building in Sixth Avenue, since Gerald Anderson was the son of the newspaper's proprietor. As there was no maternity hospital and white women in labour were not admitted to the European Hospital, they had to give birth at home, assisted by peripatetic midwives. Towards the end of the 1920s two new nursing homes were opened, the Eskotene and the

Maia Carberry, the latter founded in memory of Maia Carberry, Dr Gerald Anderson's sister, who died in an accident to a light aeroplane. Both these homes accepted maternity cases, so domiciliary midwifery tended to die out.

In 1927 the European Hospital in Nairobi had twenty beds and its counterpart in Mombasa eleven beds. There was also a twelve-bed European hospital at Nakuru, now a town of 400 whites, with wards opening on to a long, stone verandah. Eldoret, too, had a European hospital, controlled by the Eldoret Municipal Board and the Uasin Gishu District Council, with a staff of a matron, three nursing sisters and a housekeeper, and a cottage hospital opened at Kitale in 1923. Nurses for these hospitals were reunited in England by the Overseas Nursing Association.

The practice was to keep a nurse for two tours (i.e. five years) and then not re-engage her, perhaps because, as the recruiting brochure stated: 'Owing to the peculiarities of the East African climate experience shows that women are peculiarly liable to nervous troubles after several years' service at high altitudes in tropical countries.'[37] This was nonsense and deeply resented by nurses who wanted to stay in Kenya. Many did so by marrying local men – the high rate of marriage by recruits put a strain on the service, so constant were the changes of staff. The headmaster of Nakuru School found himself a bride among the sisters at Nakuru War Memorial Hospital, who all lived together in a bungalow beside the hospital. Nurses were always welcome at social events – indeed clubs usually gave them honorary membership. The recession at the end of the 1920s saw nurses' pay cut by 5 per cent from £200 a year, and the period before leave stretched to three years from two and a half.

*   *   *

Nairobi's expanding population meant that there was a regular core of churchgoers, while non-regulars used the church to make meaningful the rites of passage for birth, marriage and death. The Revd Falloon was succeeded in 1916 by Alexander Thornton Down, whose stay was brief. In 1920 William Joseph Wright became the fourth Anglican chaplain of Nairobi; he stayed for eighteen years before leaving East Africa in 1938. A bachelor known as 'Padre' Wright, he surprised everyone by getting married shortly before he retired. Though earning the miserable pittance paid to the chaplain, he made a shrewd investment by buying shares in Paka Neusi, a Kakamega goldmine. The CMS continued its dominance of Anglicanism in Nairobi when its missionary the Revd George Burns became canon, and later archdeacon, of the diocese. A tall, heavily built man with a rosy face, white walrus moustache and bald head with a tonsure of white hair, he was an evangelical, a breed not too welcome among Nairobi's whites.[38]

Having chosen Temple Moore as architect, the Nairobi congregation built a new church, All Saints, from grey stone quarried at Government House. It stood halfway up the hill, looking down on central Nairobi. The lower portion of a tower was added in 1922 to house a peal of bells given in memory of Henry Maclaren Lambert (killed on active service on 13 May 1915) and his brother Archie Fox Lambert (killed on active service two days later), who farmed ostriches on the Athi plains. Four years later All Saints became a cathedral. In 1930 two bays to complete the nave were added, thus allowing the north tower, which for eight years had stood in solitary splendour, with its southern face open, to be joined to the building.

The Roman Catholics, too, swelled in numbers with the coming of new settlers. Mombasa already had a Catholic cathedral and Albert Walter,[39] the country's statistician and a keen Catholic, formed a Kenya European Catholic Association in 1926, its object being 'to bring Europeans together to organise Catholic action in all its forms and eventually to embrace all classes and races of Roman Catholics in Kenya'.[40] The first meeting was held at St Austin's mission just outside Nairobi on 7 November 1926, and thereafter social gatherings were organised every month, generally on a Sunday afternoon at the Convent or at St Austin's where tennis was often arranged and followed by a talk and benediction. The Association was a great success, with Sir Joseph Sheridan, soon to be the country's Chief Justice, as the first president. Its only difficulty came from the opposition of some of the Catholic fathers, especially Father Cornelius McNamara of the Holy Ghost fathers, who objected to the society being solely European.

However, Walter also organised the setting up of a branch of the Society of St Vincent and St Paul, so that Roman Catholic action could assume a more multi-racial significance. There was much need for this among the Seychellois, Goan and African populations, though there were some desperately needy cases among Europeans as well, and branches were established in Mombasa and Kisumu. Hampers were distributed at Christmas and arrangements made to provide midday meals for coloured children attending convent school in Nairobi.

Relatives of those wanting to get married sometimes built their own church for the wedding, as a settler described:

> In December 1913 [my sister] was married to Bennet Mousley in Eldoret. Our little bamboo church was specially built for the occasion. Our kind neighbours in-spanned [yoked] their oxen and trekked to the 'whipstick bush' about 30 or 40 miles to cut and carry the bamboos and load them on to their wagons. They also had to bring cedar posts for the uprights, and then the church was thatched with grass which was cut by them.[41]

Missions, too, enjoyed a post-war boom. Africans began to enrol in greater numbers in mission schools, recognising the advantages in terms of wealth and the range of jobs open to the educated. While some members of the administration supported the missionary attempts to educate Africans, others were perturbed about the detribalism and consequent loss of government control that this engendered. Matters came to a head over the post-war labour question. Settler demands for increased supplies of labour culminated in 1919 in a circular issued by Governor Northey ordering administrative officers to 'exercise every possible lawful influence' to get Africans on to the labour market. The bishops of Uganda and Mombasa, and Dr J. W. Arthur of the Church of Scotland Mission, issued a memorandum sharply criticising the policy. Pressure from Britain ultimately got the Northey circular withdrawn, but no local cancellation was issued and it remained in force *de facto*.

Africans' opposition to labour demands, and the general misery they suffered from displacement, became formalised under Harry Thuku of the Young Kikuyu Association. When Thuku was locked up in Nairobi in 1922, Africans filled the streets from the Norfolk Hotel to Jeevanjee Gardens and a large crowd of them blocked the area around the police headquarters in Government Road, while across the street the photographers Martin and Osa Johnson were dodging about trying to find a good vantage point for their cameras. Some Europeans mingled with the rioters and motorists tried to barge their way through. The white officer guarding the police station either tripped or was manhandled to the ground, and suddenly there was a burst of gunfire. The crowd panicked and scattered. Those running down the street collapsed as they were shot in the back by armed askaris headed by the white officer. Altogether twenty or thirty Africans were killed and seventy or more injured.[42] It was a foretaste of African dissent, but unwisely put down by the white settlers to inflammation of the Africans by Indian agitators.

Dr J. W. Arthur had been in the country since 1907 but had had limited success in solving African grievances. The problem, according to his friend McGregor Ross of the Public Works Department and a great advocate of African development, was that 'to do effective work, he [Arthur] would find himself faced by an organised group of European bandits in the Legislature who are clamorous, insatiable and vindictive'.[43] Arthur did not have the strength to take issue with these people, unlike Archdeacon W. E. Owen of western Kenya, an outspoken opponent of white settlement as well as a thorn in the flesh of his own colleagues. Owen was loathed by C. M. Dobbs, PC of Nyanza, who reckoned he put words into the mouths of Africans.[44] Handley Hooper, at Kahuhia, had similarly strong views as Owen, but was far more circumspect when advocating African interests. As for Harry Leakey, the CMS missionary in Kiambu, he listened to African grievances and vigorously opposed the soldier–settler scheme because it removed more land from Africans.

The missionaries were divided in their attitude to the Kikuyu practice of female circumcision. The matter came to a head in 1929, with the distribution in the Dagoretti–Limuru area by emissaries of Dr Arthur of papers for signature by mission boys. The boys had to promise to oppose clitoridectomy or be excluded from mission schools. Offended by this attack on tribal custom, the recently formed Kikuyu Central Association petitioned the Colonial Secretary in London, but the government did not want to get involved. Its attitude was one of benign neglect. The CMS took a less extreme attitude than did Dr Arthur of the Church of Scotland, though Leakey tried to persuade the Kenya Government not to issue a passport for a visit to England by the secretary of the Kikuyu Central Association. To make their point, Africans broke into a room in the Africa Inland Mission at Kijabe and forcibly circumcised Hulda Stumpf, a white missionary, who died from her injuries. Those Africans expelled from the missions also began to form their own independent churches and schools, which became foci of opposition to white rule.

*   *   *

Abroad, Kenya was famous for its big-game hunting and fearless white hunters. People travelled there from all over the world to enjoy the romance and danger of shooting wild animals and going on safaris led by white hunters, and they were significant contributors to the country's revenues. Many of them were VIPs or members of the British, Belgian, Swedish and other royal families. The Duke of York (later to be George VI) went on safari in 1924 and the Prince of Wales went big-game hunting on two occasions, in 1928 and 1930, the second time with his brother the Duke of Gloucester. Several people also came in search of specimens for zoos and museums. For example, Carl Akeley went to Kenya in 1926 to seek specimens for the great African hall of the New York Museum. He was accompanied by William R. Leigh, the painter of the American West, and his talented colleague Arthur Jansson, who were to sketch and paint for the hall backdrops. For eleven years afterwards Robert Rockwell mounted and modelled the specimens sent to the USA by Akeley for the African hall, including four elephants.[45]

The firm Safariland, founded in Nairobi in 1903 by Victor Newland and Leslie Tarlton, still supplied everything needed for shooting safaris, from their shop in Nairobi and its branch in Piccadilly, London. Henry Tarlton thought differently from his brother Leslie – he opposed hunting and kept an open-air zoo for the preservation of game on his land at Ruaraka. He hated trespassers, ran white men off his farm and was murdered in 1933 while fishing at Ruaraka.

Kenya's first game warden, R. B. Woosnam, had been killed in the First World War and Archie Ritchie, a man of magnificent physique who had once served in the French Foreign Legion, took over as Chief Game Warden in 1924. His task was to preserve animals for shooting by big-game hunters and to control poaching by Africans. It was Archie Ritchie, having retired to Malindi, who saved the life of the Governor Sir Evelyn Baring in 1959, when Baring swam out to sea to rescue an Indian girl in difficulties. Among the white hunters were Pat Ayre and the dashing Pete Rattray, who captured the heart of the daughter of Lord Furness on one safari.[46] She married him. A man of squarish build and firm expression, Rattray had a farm seven miles up the Isiolo river where he tried to break Grevy zebra to harness. He managed to get some to pull ploughs. It was common for women to fall in love with their white hunter on safari. Bror Blixen, Karen Blixen's husband and a veritable Don Juan, took full advantage of this, and many men most wisely declined to entrust their wives or daughters to his safaris. The white hunter Philip Percival, A. Blayney Percival's brother, had robust views about his clients, proclaiming that he did not 'care a damn about these people who can split a pea at three hundred yards. What I want to know about a man is how good he is on a charging buffalo at six feet.'[47]

Robert Ruark gave a good description of the life of the big-game hunter:

The heavy work for a hunter is not so much the location of game and the supervision of the final kill as the camp routine. He supervises a tiny portable city – administers loading and unloading in exactly the right order, ordains the pitching of camp, selecting camp, looks after the water supply, supervises the skinners and trackers and gunbearers and porters and cooks and body servants. He must be an expert mechanic – he must be able to rebuild a motorcar from the spare parts he carries and improvise those parts he has not . . . The hunter finally combines the duties of a sea captain, a bodyguard, a chauffeur, a tracker, a skinner, a head-waiter, a tourist guide, a photographer, a mechanic, a stevedore, an interpreter, a game expert, a gin rummy partner, drinking companion, social equal, technical superior, boss, employee, and handy man. The difficulty of his position is magnified in that he lives in the pockets of his clients for long weeks, and unless he is a master of tact, nobody is speaking to anyone else when the safari pays off in Nairobi.[48]

Denys Finch Hatton was renowned as a superb organiser of safaris, and it was he who was chosen, with Bror Blixen, to lead the Prince of Wales on safari in 1930. He kept the Prince safe, in contrast with the episode a few years earlier when the Duke of York's life was put in danger in 1924. A dead zebra had been put out as a lure for lion, and at dawn the next day the Duke of York and his white hunter, Andy Anderson, who was lame, went out to see whether the bait was taken. A lioness on the carcass turned and charged. Anderson shot her, but not fatally, and she slunk into the bush. Anderson went off to get two dogs to track the wounded animal, but unfortunately while searching for her they put up two buffalo which charged. The Duke shot at the leading buffalo at twenty-five yards, badly wounding it, and then shot and killed the second buffalo.

For the Duke the episode must have been thrilling, for it is a truism that one has never lived until one has almost died. Locally he was extolled for his coolness, courage and fine marksmanship, but the British newspapers got hold of the story and were scandalised at the danger the King's son had faced. A horrified Governor Coryndon set off for the royal camp and told Andy Anderson never again to leave his guest in such circumstances. There followed a reproof from the King, who had not been well disposed to the Duke of York's visit to Kenya from the start. Coryndon telegraphed his regrets.[49]

There arose at this time a new breed of big-game hunter: the photographer. Prominent in this category were Cherry Kearton, and Martin and Osa Johnson, all Americans. As early as 1929 Kearton was writing: 'I let myself hope that the day will come when all men will realise that animal life is not theirs to take . . . You will not preserve wild life by licences nor by shutting off certain areas; you will save it only by altering the popular point of view, so that indiscriminate slaughter shall no longer be tolerated.'[50] Martin Johnson even took an eight-roomed bungalow in Nairobi where he set up his own darkroom, installing fifty-gallon developing tanks. He let A. Radclyffe Dugmore, the son of the unfortunate Dugmore who so bothered Frank Hall in the 1890s, develop hundreds of his own photographs in the laboratory, and extended the same facility to Carl Akeley.[51]

Rudolf Mayer of the *East African Standard* supported the photographers by refusing to print pictures of dead animals. In 1924 Theodore Waldeck and Albert Smith undertook an expedition north from Nairobi towards Abyssinia to photograph game and gather specimens for museums. G. H. R. Hurst, a photographer who started the production of Tusker beer, still going strong today, was killed by a charging elephant when attempting to photograph it. Such people were appreciated by the pioneer A. Blaney Percival, who 'had a brusqueness of manner that at first was a little disconcerting, but . . . it grew out of a downright exasperation with the so-called big-game hunters who came, in increasing numbers, to fatten their egos with trophies, no matter how obtained, and whose lust to kill would in time become a menace to African wild life.'[52]

As the 1920s drew to a close, Kenya's whites were firmly entrenched as settlers. Their beliefs about the British empire and the part they were playing in it were common to almost every British man and woman of the time. Elspeth Huxley expressed the feeling well with the words: 'It is hard to credit what a good opinion we had of ourselves in those days. There was the Empire, and there we were at the heart and centre of the world. No one questioned our position. Everyone else was a barbarian, more or less.'[53]

7

White Society in the 1920s

Soldier-settlers and members of BEADOC by no means accounted for all the whites who went to Kenya in the 1920s and whose numbers swelled from 9,651 in 1921 to 12,529 in 1926, and 16,812 in 1931. Who were these people? Their political leaders provide clues to the answer to this question. In general, there were two political groupings: the large landowners co-operating with the land speculators, and the small farmers allied to the businessmen. In the first group were Lord Delamere, Ewart Grogan, the brothers Galbraith and Berkeley Cole, W. N. McMillan, Powys Cobb, Robert Chamberlain and A. C. Hoey as large landowners, and V. M. Newland, J. C. Coverdale, W. C. Hunter, H. F. Ward, J. H. Gailey, T. J. O'Shea and A. C. Tannahill as the group of lawyers and land agents who represented the land speculators. By mid-1920 this first group's power was waning – Cole and McMillan died in 1925, while Cobb, Hoey and Chamberlain abandoned politics.

The second group – the smaller farmers and businessmen – was successful in Kenya's first election for the Legislative Council in 1920, winning eight of the eleven seats. However, the following year the large landowners returned to politics, though it was not long before the small men – lesser farmers and owners of stores and hotels, contract ploughmen, timber millers, transport riders and brickmakers – came into their own. The lesser farmers were now esconced in large numbers in the north Uasin Gishu, Trans-Nzoia, the north-east Rift Valley and western Kenya, and they wanted an independent role in white politics, since their interests were different from those of the large landowners. They started their own newspapers and developed distinct political identities. Their lot was far from easy – they sank all their funds into land, lost most of their capital, and borrowed money at high interest rates. They were given a temporary boost in 1925 when the concept of colonial development through loan financing was introduced – by January 1926 Kenya had contracted for loans of £5 million from London – and this prevented them from going under.

The loans had an important side-effect, for they made it advisable for settlers to co-operate to some extent with both the home and Kenya governments, and there was therefore a dwindling of the power of large landowners and speculators who had traded on policies of self-government and encouraged European dissidence over the Indian question in the early 1920s. At the same time, African discontent at white rule, increasingly evident in the 1920s through the development of African political organisations (often thought to be due to the subversive influence of the missionaries and the Indians) served to consolidate the small settlers' benevolent feelings towards Britain, because it was obvious that Kenya's whites could not put down a large African rising, but would be dependent on the importation of imperial troops. This was a sobering reality. The small men were further boosted by a white population increase of 35 per cent between 1926 and 1931, which was confined largely to the towns. Indeed, Nairobi's white population increased by 145 per cent from 1921 to 1931, while the whole white population increased by only 75 per cent.[1]

This made it inevitable that there would be changes in white political leadership. The new leaders were people like J. G. Kirkwood, owner of the Kitale hotel; T. J. O'Shea, Sinn Feiner and autodidact economist who ran the Ford garage in Eldoret; E. M. Vaughan ('Pat') Kenealy, an outspoken stockfarmer of Nanyuki who hailed from South Africa; and the hyper-energetic Olga Watkins who stood for 'the women on the back verandahs of their houses'.

The political structure did not entirely mirror the social structure of the whites. Essentially the whites of Kenya became a society of landed gentry in the 1920s, with Africans representing the working class, and Indians comprising the lower middle class of clerks and traders. Among the whites, too, a class structure developed.

Whereas in the early days such a structure was difficult to sustain because of the small number of whites, who inevitably had to pull together, now numbers had so expanded that classes developed. At the bottom of the heap were poor whites, many of them Afrikaners. The whites in skilled manual trades came next – there were 740 of them in the 1931 census. Then came engineers and railwaymen, many of them locally born. Although in 1930 only 50 per cent of the whites had been in the country for less than five years, the numbers of whites born locally rose from 1,140 (12 per cent of the population) in 1921 to 2,063 (16 per cent) in 1926 and 2,910 (17 per cent) in 1931. Many locally educated white lads were working with Africans in the garages and railway workshops of Nairobi. Some of them were from Afrikaner families, but by 1931 the Afrikaners, who had formed such a large proportion of Kenya's whites earlier in the century, had shrunk to only 7 per cent of the European population.

Then came the huge mass of lesser farmers. The primary occupation of white males in Kenya was agriculture. Altogether 1,893 of them farmed in 1921 and 2,199 in 1926, a 16 per cent increase over five years.[2] Of these 503 people were involved in coffee farming, 343 in maize and 231 in stock – the remaining farmers did not specify their type of farming. In fact, many farmers did a bit of everything, growing crops as well as keeping cows, pigs and sheep.

These were people generally of middle- or upper-middle-class origins, with birthplaces in Britain and Ireland (54, 51 and 50 per cent in 1921, 1926 and 1930) and the British empire (27, 26 and 24 per cent).[3] Most of them had been to public school. Many had military pensions. They came after hearing of Kenya from friends and relatives, and also by entering into farm pupillage, a system established in 1923 by the Convention of Associations. Another source of information was the Kenya Land Advisory Committee, formed in 1922 with funds from Sir Northrup McMillan to attract 'the right kind' of settler. The East African Trade and Information Office, established in London, also provided instruction and advice. Its 1927 report stated that 155 settlers (many with wives and families) had gone to Kenya that year. One-third were wealthy people (everyone had to give a statement of capital) and the rest were young men who planned to become farm managers after a period as a pupil on a farm learning the job, or people who went to have a look round, to see if they liked the place.[4]

These settlers belonged to the twenty-seven farmers' associations round the country, bodies which discussed such matters as compulsory dipping and branding of stock, the provision of third-class carriages for whites on the railways because fares were so high, and the unproductive expenditure of the government on District Officers. The Lumbwa Farmers' Association viewed 'with alarm the practice of certain individuals giving meat and cigarettes to native labour'.[5] All this may seem petty, but the harder the bargain they had to strike with nature, the more rules they needed in order to survive.

Their social life was not always class-ridden. People happily intermingled – for example, F. R. Rainsford of the Nakuru police had no qualms about calling on Lord Francis Scott accompanied by his wife Tissie and her friend Tossie, both of them Gaiety Girls. There was a heavy use of alcohol (in 1926 56,937 gallons of whisky were imported) and the white population spent £150,000 on the demon drink every year. Everyone was very hospitable. When people turned up without invitation they were welcomed to meals and drinks and asked to stay the night. Everyone went to anyone's aid when called upon in an emergency, whether at night or over impossible roads.

The better-off farmers could afford to build large houses for themselves. Captain S. H. Carnelly raised a double-storeyed Elizabethan-style house on the shores of Lake Naivasha where crested cranes pecked out the putty from the window panes and admired themselves in the glass.[6] Loresho, Lord Delamere's house, was a beautifully appointed residence at Kiambu, and Lord Francis Scott's house, Deloraine, a tastefully furnished two-storey building at Rongai. John Carberry owned Seremai, a lovely house near Nyeri, six cars and an aeroplane.

There was no electricity on the farms or in the remoter areas, and everyone used paraffin lamps. Cooking was done on cast-iron, wood-burning Dover stoves, irons were heated with charcoal, meat was kept in mesh-fronted safes, and there were no refrigerators. Water was heated in forty-four-gallon drums over an open fire in the evenings. Clothes washed in water coloured red from silt went pink so Reckitt's blue was employed to restore a semblance of their original white. For the poorer white farmers, life was hard. The Klaprotts, who ran a milk business at Eldoret, fabricated from skins their own bridles and shoes, the latter worn by the children only when they went into town. They made their own clothes, and spun silk to sell to Nairobi traders. Since nails were expensive and difficult to get, cedarwood houses were joined together with wooden pegs. Hair was cut with old safety razor blades.

One farmer's clock was a stick in the ground which threw a shadow, except at midday. In Kakamega 'we have no real time here but set our watches to 6 o'clock when the rim of the sun shows over the hills'.[7] Furniture was locally made – for example, Kavirondo seats were constructed of withies roughly bent into the shape of a chair, with a triangle of goatskin hairy side up to sit on. The withies stuck into the sitters' backs and the goat bristles into their legs, while any nails caught on their clothing. There were stools carved by the Kisii from one block of wood, with beads stuck on the top. Cars were 'box-bodies', constructed from the chassis of American cars, with locally built bodies. They were curious contraptions shaped like large boxes in which farm machinery or sheep could be carried, their roofs supported at the corners by lengths of angle-iron, with canvas curtains to roll down when it rained. The ratio of automobiles to Europeans was one in four, much higher than in England, although of course cars were far more necessary in Kenya, with its enormous area and lack of public transport, apart from the very limited railway.

Houses were made out of whatever material was available – wood, corrugated iron, grass, reeds, stone or sometimes only mud:

My house is made of mud with holes of various sizes and shapes to represent doors and windows. The floor is nothing more than mother earth . . . Everything is continually covered in sand, mud or white ants and consequently any degree of comfort is impossible . . . It is remarkable how much the office owes to petrol boxes and tins . . . The insects at night are most trying and appear in large numbers in the form of moths and beetles of all descriptions, that it is almost impossible . . . to read or write, and quite futile to consider any supper but bread and cheese. Scorpions, tarantulas and snakes are also numerous.[8]

Another farmer described how the walls of his grass house grew more and more dilapidated,

the dogs making doors through them at their pleasure. We had quantities of rough stone quarried out, and by dint of hewing and hacking with much grazing of hands and grunting and sweating, we built a very passable rough stone wall, cemented with mud, all round the house up to window level. Above that we built mud and wattle up to the roof, plastered with cow dung, and whitewashed. Next we put in a cement floor, all with our own fair hands, and there we were all snug again and very proud of our handiwork.[9]

One farm pupil on Berkeley Cole's land at Naro Moru lived in a mobile cabin. At the end of the day he sat outside in his greatcoat, a book and his pipe for company as he toasted his feet by the fire. The Maasai shepherds would glide out of the darkness and squat down to listen to his gramophone or chat. They told him tales of hunting and raiding, fables and folklore, while he described England and how the white man lived. He provided his own food by hunting buck and birds – sandgrouse and partridges – for the pot. All drinking water was boiled and filtered, and milk in remoter areas came from tins – condensed and over-sweet from Nestlé, or the thick and creamy Ideal evaporated milk so delicious on tinned peaches.

In Kenya the settlers cultivated a way of life, made more agreeable by the employment of several servants, that was disappearing in England. The cheapness of servants opened to them many aristocratic pursuits such as polo, racing and hunting. There were four domestic servants for each household of two whites in

Kenya (that is, 200 for every 100 whites, compared with 44.3 domestic servants for every 100 in Mayfair, London). There is no doubt that being able to afford servants was so attractive that it lured Europeans to stay in Kenya. Settlers communicated with their African employees in a simplified version of Swahili, often called 'kitchen Swahili'. Officials who were forced to learn the true Swahili of the coastal region criticised settlers for not using that language. But upcountry Africans simply did not understand coast Swahili, so it was useless to speak it to them. The incoming whites also acquired status as a ruling class over the Africans. Life in Kenya was very comfortable until the newcomers were hit by the hard economic fact that farming in Kenya was usually unprofitable.

The top social stratum in Kenya was occupied by the British and foreign aristocracy and the moneyed upper middle class. In the 1920s the pioneer aristocracy were joined by the large professional businessmen Lord Howard de Walden in Trans-Nzoia, Sir John Ramsden at Naivasha and Lord Egerton of Tatton at Njoro.

There were a few from the upper and moneyed classes, such as Lord Erroll, who used Kenya as a sexual playground, but this was only a small minority. Indeed, there were only fifty-seven divorced persons resident in Kenya in 1926. Far more representative of the top social stratum in Kenya, those with social rank, land and supposed money, were Lord Delamere, Lord Cranworth, Mervyn Ridley, Lord Francis Scott (son of the Duke of Buccleuch), Nellie Grant (from the Duke of Westminster's family), Sir Northrup and Lady McMillan, Denys Finch Hatton, Galbraith and Berkeley Cole, F. W. Cavendish-Bentinck (later the Duke of Portland), Powys Cobb (from a rich Welsh mining family) and members of the Buxton family such as Rose Cartwright. There were scores of members of families of baronets and knights and other scions of the aristocracy. Kenya had more people from this social elite than Southern Rhodesia, with its population of 30,000 to Kenya's 9,651 in 1921. And yet these people, about 300 in all, were still heavily outnumbered by the middle-class whites.

People from the best regiments or most prestigious public schools (an annual Eton dinner was held) also belonged to the social elite. Among them were Frank de V. Joyce, F. O. B. Wilson, A. C. Lewin, A. H. L. D. Coke, L. R. Gascoigne, Arthur Fawcus, G. C. Sladen, R. O. R. Kenyon-Slaney (son-in-law of Lord Aberdare), A. R. A. Cartwright, W. A. Conduitt and his wife Lady Viola, W. H. Wilson, Charles Taylor and many others. It was not essential to have money to belong to the elite – Nellie Grant, for example, always had very limited funds.

The so-called rich farmers were often anything but, and Delamere was in dire financial trouble in the late 1920s. From 1926 to 1930 the sales from his farms averaged annually about £30,000 gross, but everything was swallowed up and more by the interest on his mortgages and overdraft. Nor could he clear his debts by selling land because no one was buying. As for Powys Cobb, a man driven by a fierce inner impulse always to be doing something new, he had already had to sell his beautiful farm Keringet, and in 1930 was forced also to sell the second farm he had created from nothing. In the past Cobb had made large profits from farming but he always ploughed it back, as did almost all the farmers. Then two or three bad years left him with nothing and he had to start all over again. 'The pioneer mind', lamented Delamere, 'only sees forward. If it did not it would never do what it does. But it seldom consolidates for the same reason.'[10]

*   *   *

The government servants formed another social entity, though one much riven by insistence on strict adherence to hierarchy. The caste system in government service was very marked, with officials graded first, second or third class. In Kisumu, for example, those of lower rank in the technical departments and police were not accepted as members of Kisumu Club. They could have gone to the Railway Club, but the railway people were very clannish and reluctant to mix with other whites. But because the sick-rate among the lower ranks of the civil service was so high, the medical officer in Kisumu broke down the caste system by advocating that the 'untouchables' should be allowed to join the Kisumu Club. At first they were accepted for sporting activities only, but eventually they were admitted as full members. The doctor claimed that the sick-rate went down enormously after this.

In the early days in Kisumu the farmers deeply resented the officials, with their freedom to travel and six-month furloughs to Britain every thirty months, but gradually more officials retired and became farmers themselves, and some farmers' sons joined the civil service, so these old barriers were progressively broken down.[11] There was still a residual feeling among officials, however, that settlers failed to support them. In 1929 the Colonial Secretary's wife, Daphne Moore, said the settlers browbeat officials. In retaliation, the DO Gerald Reece went out to dinner one night in Kisumu wearing a tailcoat and Dundreary whiskers made from the DC's wife's hair, and had himself announced as Lord Maldemer – a dig at Lord Delamere.[12]

The strange, eccentric public servants inherited from IBEAC were now a dying breed, though one or two of the new intake vied with them in oddity. One such official, a superb bird shot, was S. W. J. Schofield, DC in Eldoret. Very fond of liquor, he once 'lost' his false teeth down the latrine at the Pioneer Hotel while vomiting. His subordinate, asked to retrieve them, commandeered prisoners from the local jail to do the job for him. Eventually the teeth were found in the DC's pocket. Schofield used to send a convict in prison clothes to drive a wagon to Londiani to bring his liquor supplies to Eldoret; he once fell flat on his face when he bent forward to kiss the hand of Lady Northey, the Governor's wife. After his African cook deserted him, he instructed the police to find him another, which they did by shamefully trumping up a charge against a good cook working for the bank manager's wife. The man was remanded to prison and became the DC's cook.[13] Schofield was, however, an exception. The calibre of colonial officials was improved when a new rigorous selection process was instituted in the 1920s and colonial officers were obliged to take a course before they left Britain.

Professionals belonged to another social group, as did those involved in commerce and industry, most of them living in the towns. These were people whose interests had been ignored by the early politicians, and they became more united and vociferous as the 1920s proceeded and their numbers expanded. Then there were the foreigners, who generally fitted into their economic class. Seven per cent of Kenya's whites were foreigners in 1921 and 1926, and 9 per cent in 1931.[14] Some of them were Italian, French, Danish and Swedish aristocrats, who found their friends among the British aristocrats.

Life in the towns was very different from farming life. All Kenya's towns swelled in size during the 1920s, Nairobi and Mombasa in particular, though one newcomer in 1929 still found Nairobi 'an uninspiring collection of tin roofs scattered about the plain'.[15] By 1921 its white residents numbered 2,339, an increase in fifteen years of 1,697, or 264 per cent. By 1926 it was necessary to appoint a Local Government Commission under Mr Justice Richard Feetham to look into the governance and town planning of the rapidly expanding two main towns of Nairobi and Mombasa. Sanitation was, as it had always been, a huge problem in the capital – 'the conditions which prevail, when judged from the point of view of public health, can be described only as unsatisfactory and, indeed, highly dangerous'.[16] All the town roads were still bordered with wide, deep drains and there was as yet no water-borne sanitation. Carts drawn by Ankole bullocks with huge horns took away the contents of bucket latrines by night.

In 1926 there was a large fire in Nairobi. Among other buildings the Salisbury Hotel,[17] Moore's bookshop and a gunsmith's belonging to Charles Heyer were burned down. Not long afterwards, a block of buildings between Hardinge Street and Government Road went up in flames. The firefighting equipment of Kenya's capital was utterly incompetent to deal with the blazes, consisting as it did solely of a length of hose wound round a contraption like an outsize cotton reel. When this was connected to a hydrant, the water pressure was just enough for a thin stream to trickle out of the nozzle. The water supply was clearly inadequate for current needs and the roads were in a poor state of repair, not having been designed for motor vehicles or their speed. Although Muthaiga suburb had become a township in 1922, the estates of Upper

Parklands, Westlands, Upper Hill, Kilimani and Thompson's, owned by individuals or companies and divided into small residential plots, had unsatisfactory roads, water supplies, refuse removal services and house drainage. Much drainage and filling work was also needed to stop mosquitoes breeding.

The Public Works Department, which should have seen to such matters, was hardly dynamic or efficient. It was run from 1905 to 1922 by William McGregor Ross, who had joined the Uganda Railway in 1900 as a junior assistant engineer.[18] An ambitious and outspoken man of intemperate character, he was arrogant to a degree. He was heartily disliked by settlers for his attacks on them, and by his colleagues on the Legislative Council, peopled in his opinion by 'a troupe of farmers and hardware-merchants' and 'the dregs of the settler community'.[19] McGregor Ross's language was frequently tactless and extreme and Governor Northey was determined to be rid of him. In 1921 there was such an uproar about the PWD's ineffectiveness that a commission of inquiry was held. Its report was damning, as the *East African Standard* described:

> The abiding impression of a perusal of the document is that of an administrative officer purposefully and with calm deliberation accumulating in his own hands one after another of the public activities of the country, with a gaze embracing many future years, but withal with an impregnable vanity, serenely unperturbed by blatant evidences of failure in those duties for which he was first commissioned. [Ross displayed] unruffled indifference to criticism.[20]

McGregor Ross was obliged to resign. Feetham's report on local government finally appeared in 1929 and its recommendations were put into effect the same year. H. T. Martin, the Municipal Engineer of Nairobi so despised as a town planner by his subordinate Henry Elliott Fitzgibbon, left Kenya and things began to improve.[21]

The development of Mombasa, run from July 1920 by a District Committee, was similarly problematic. Though in 1921 two deep-water berths were begun, four years later the port was still being worked in the main by two lighterage companies which handled all cargo, the East African Lighterage Co. and the African Wharfage Co. Cargo was brought from ship to shore by lighter, to the government wharves at Kilindini, the wharf at Mbaraki, a private pier at Shimanzi at the north end of Kilindini harbour belonging to the Magadi Soda Co., and the old harbour. It was not until 1926 that two deep-water berths were opened at Kilindini,[22] and in 1929 they were joined by two others. This improved the shipping situation, greatly increasing capacity. It also, for a while, transformed the white population of the town, because the construction company imported some of the toughest of South Africa's poor whites as workers. On pay days they got drunk and raced around the town, firing off revolvers.

In 1921, 378 white males, 170 females and ninety-five children lived on Mombasa island. Of the men, 108 were government officials, six lawyers, five planters, and the rest involved in commerce or shipping.[23] That year the sanitation of the town was improved, by the construction of a concrete excrement tank with a chamber leading to a chute into the sea at Ras Serani. The Mackinnon market was completely reroofed and provided with concrete stalls, and town roads repaired. With the coming of the motor car the trolley lines were removed, and a motor ferry service crossed to the mainland at Likoni. The following year a large slaughterhouse was erected. But Mombasa also had 20,000 non-whites living in insanitary conditions in the old town. Illness among whites was a constant problem, with ever-present malaria and intestinal problems such as typhoid fever. Though there were only 742 white men, women and children in Mombasa in 1922, there were 607 inpatients that year in the European Hospital.[24]

The town badly needed a town planning scheme, now that the fourteen miles of roads had taken their present pattern across the island, and in 1925, with the white population swelled to 1,077 on account of the harbour works,[25] a loan of £129,000 was voted for betterment, and £50,000 for the improvement of the old town. Electric lighting was extended in the town, though it was shut off in the streets at 11 p.m., far too early in the opinion of the local paper, the *Mombasa Times*.[26] A kindergarten for white children was built in 1926, and twenty older children travelled to Nairobi to boarding school.

By 1929 the area between Kilindini Road and Mbaraki was being covered rapidly with bungalows for Europeans. A causeway at Makupa was opened to the mainland, which meant that a site for the airport was selected on that part of the mainland rather than at Likoni.[27] There was another important development in 1928, when a private company was formed to build Nyali bridge across to the northern mainland. This had the effect of relieving congestion on the island by encouraging settlement on the mainland. That year some good hotels were erected and several fine shops opened. The town grew more slowly than Nairobi – there were 1,250 whites in Mombasa in 1930, thirty of whose children attended the elementary school.[28] Royal Navy ships regularly called at the port and were eagerly welcomed by local Europeans, who organised festivities, games and entertainments for the visitors. When passenger liners docked at Mombasa, white women flocked aboard to make use of the ships' hairdressers.

While the older towns grew in size a new one emerged – Nanyuki, beyond Nyeri and Naro Moru, on the way to Isiolo. In 1920 Major and Mrs L. R. Gascoigne erected the first shack there and opened a post office and store (previously mail had come by runner from the Naro Moru post office on Berkeley Cole's land). The Standard Bank of South Africa began to visit once a week from Nyeri.[29] By 1922 Nanyuki had acquired a hotel, another store, an Indian carpenter and wheelwright's shop, a large and expensive policeman's house and, believe it or not, a race course and polo ground. The two sports facilities were built on seventy acres of ground 'commandeered' by Major-General Philip Wheatley, the soldier-settler in command of the rebellion of 1922–23 against Indian immigration.[30]

The whites of Mombasa and Nairobi developed their own social habits as their numbers increased. A practice common to both places, and one which continued to cause the utmost dismay, was that of leaving calling cards. The custom was particularly followed by government officials, as described by the daughter of one of them:

> There was also the terrific business of 'calling'; you always 'called' in the afternoon. I would drive Esme round in the car to visit, perhaps half a dozen houses in a single afternoon. We had a special card case with embossed cards (it was considered vulgar to use printed cards) giving your name and address, large cards for women, smaller cards for men. Calls had to be paid on new arrivals and senior officials, leaving cards again after you had visited for dinner. Every home had either a special slit topped card box into which you put your cards, or a silver salver on a small table on the veranda. The salvers were more fun, as a hasty but discreet glance would tell you who else had called that day.[31]

Daphne Moore, the wife of H. M. Moore, Sir Edward Denham's successor as Kenya's Colonial (Chief) Secretary in 1929, deplored the business of 'calling' – 'We paid 16, which brings the number I have returned to 74. There are about 60 now outstanding. Several people were in, damn them. Others we saw afar off and gave them time to burrow into the flower-beds or hide behind the sink. One says "Hodi!" [is anyone in?] under one's breath and then throws the cards into the spitoon [*sic*] and runs.'[32] On one occasion she drove out to Muthaiga to pay calls 'and paid exactly one. We found a Mr Carnelly in and were shown his garden, his two swans, his tame goose, his dog, his cat and his porcupine. We would also have been shown his mongoose but it had fortunately disappeared.'[33]

White Kenyan society was becoming altogether more self-sufficient. People resident in Nairobi could now rely entirely on local produce: butter, eggs, poultry, beef, mutton, pork, bacon, ham, cheese, fish, sugar, coffee, tea, flour, and fruit and vegetables. There was a cannery for pork products and vegetables at Uplands, and jams were made near Machakos. Locally made shoes were available, though some footwear was still imported. Imported clothing was very expensive, and most women made their own clothes or had Indian dressmakers do it for them. Office hours were from eight till four, and then followed tea and sport. People

met for sundowners during the brisk dusk from 6.30 p.m., an
alcoholic occasion except among missionaries, who would offer a
choice of water or water with Eno's fruit salt. The sundowner was
an opportunity for much overlapping of social strata in clubs and
hotel bars.

As in India, the society created by the whites in Kenya was one
in which sport and clubs played a prominent part. People wanted
to socialise with others of their own kind, and clubs and hotel bars
were natural meeting places for those who travelled into settlements over appalling roads to get supplies or conduct business.
Several pleasant hours could be spent in the club as the local garage
repaired one's battered vehicle of conveyance. Clubs often arose
from organised sporting activities – for example, the Makuyu Club
sprung from the polo games enjoyed by the early farmers of the
district. Polo was an extremely popular sport among Kenya's
whites after the First World War – Governor Northey even
sacrificed an eye to the game.

Njoro Club, founded in February 1921, was one of the earliest
provincial clubs. In 1924 the Nanyuki Sports Club built a grand-
stand and dance hall, and instituted annual gymkhanas – an
amalgam of racing, polo and paper chases in which people from all
over the colony participated. The Nyeri Polo Club was founded in
1920 by soldier-settlers who had formerly played in India. There
were golf clubs throughout the country. Eldoret had a Gymkhana
as early as 1919, to be followed by Nakuru and Laikipia. Eldoret
Club was founded as a golf club in 1922, and its example was soon
followed by Kitale Club, completed in 1925. Thomson's Falls
joined them with a race course in the latter year. The Elgon Club
was established in 1928. There were, in addition, a number of
hunts in Kenya. The Masara hounds, the first of these, came to an
end when their owner committed suicide, it was said for the love
of a lady. Nanyuki began the Loldaiga hounds in 1924 and the
Lumbwa hounds were founded in 1926.

Apart from polo and golf, the clubs offered cricket, tennis,
rugby, hockey and football. The twenties saw the opening of the
Nyanza Cricket Club, Fort Ternan Cricket Team, Nairobi's

Kenya Kongonis Cricket Club (which became the controlling body of Kenya cricket in 1932), Turbo-Kipkarren Tennis Club (which split into the Kipkarren Club and the Turbo Country Club) and the Subukia Valley Tennis Club and Sports Club. Kenya's fine weather made outdoor sporting activities much more practicable than in Britain, thus allowing the numerous clubs to survive. Sport was a priority among many settlers. 'Truly,' said Julian Huxley, after seeing Nyeri's full-size cricket field, golf course, tennis club and polo ground while on his visit to Kenya in 1930, 'the British are a remarkable race. No imperialists save perhaps the Romans have ever exported their domestic habits and their recreations so whole-heartedly all over the empire.'[34]

Everyone indulged in sport, but intellectual activities had a less prominent place in Kenyan white society, though Nairobi had a natural history museum, later to become the Coryndon Museum, and a public library was planned. There was a variety of newpapers over the years, the one with most staying power being the *East African Standard*, run from offices in Sixth Avenue.[35] The British East Africa Broadcasting Corporation began putting out radio programmes in 1928, from 7 to 10 p.m. every night. A typical evening's entertainment, that for 12 October 1928, was:

> 7 to 7.30 gramophone records
> 7.30 to 8.30 military band of the KAR
> 8.30 to 8.45 British official wireless press, local news
> and information bulletin
> 8.45 to 9 Royal East African Automobile Association road
> and rainfall report
> 9.30 to 10 dance music.

Despite the high level of education among the settlers, Kenya was not a cultured society. 'Of a large and important section of white people . . . officials as well as settlers,' said Julian Huxley after a visit to Kenya in 1930, 'it is not unfair to say that the *Tatler*, *Punch*, a few magazines, detective stories and second-rate romantic novels, represent their intellectual and cultural level.'[36]

Kenya's limited population could not at this time have supported an orchestra or professional theatre. There were no picture galleries. The one theatre – the Theatre Royal in Nairobi – doubled as a cinema. It hosted amateur theatricals of dubious merit. There was also a travelling cinema which went from hotel to hotel putting on silent films. Whenever it visited Kisumu, Elizabeth ('Peter') Le Breton was called upon to play the piano, with her eyes glued to the screen.[37] Her attitude was typical of the settlers of the 1920s:

> If at first you don't succeed, try, try again . . . is the only way to tackle a difficult job or get anything done. It applied very much – entirely really – to our social life and all the little pleasures that bring enjoyment to many and give scope for hidden talents. If you want amateur theatricals you form a society and with luck build your own theatre. Music? Then you scout around and find willing performers. A flower show? The same procedure. A little talent and a lot of enthusiasm will get you where you want to be – Nowadays it has a new name – Do It Yourself. For fifty years or more in Kenya we were the first DIYs.[38]

Another example of this attitude was the formation by Brian Havelock Potts of a band of eight regular players to perform at the Elgon and Kitale clubhouses. The piano-player was a seventy-year-old ex-Cambridge organist. Julian Huxley would not have been impressed – he thought that anyone to whom music and the visual arts were important made a real sacrifice in coming to the tropics.

Local schools could not be relied on to raise cultural standards, though attempts were made to improve them in the 1920s. But the pressure on the few white schools from the sharp increase in numbers of pupils was unrelenting and strained them at the seams. The sex ratio shifted from 570 to 790 females for every thousand males over the twenty years from 1911, so there were even more children to be provided for. Very few children were now sent to Britain or South Africa for schooling, because the 'actinic rays of the sun' which settlers had thought might produce inferior offspring, had proved to have no such effect. The education commission established in 1918 by Acting-Governor C. C. Bowring had advocated that the co-educational schools at Nairobi, Nakuru and Eldoret should be complemented by a boys' secondary school at Nairobi. This would be designed to offer an education as good as that in British public schools.

Such high ideals faced the hurdles of finance and lack of super-lative teaching, and Nairobi had to wait thirteen years for the boys' school. In 1925 the performance of children in Nairobi European School, still the one government school admitting white children of all ages, with its shield-and-lion crest designed by W. A. Berkeley of Nyeri and its motto 'Servire est Regnare', was so far below that of their Indian counterparts that the results were suppressed.[39] At the time R. W. Wotton, who had been in charge of the junior section from 1921 to 1924, was the acting head.[40] The Governor visited the school to see what was going on and reported that the present wretched classrooms should be scrapped and extra boarding accommodation provided.[41] Two years later it was found that 12 per cent of white children were not attending school, and on the Uasin Gishu plateau the number was 20 per cent. To exacerbate matters, the railway administration, which accepted a fair proportion of the leavers from Nairobi European School, produced a report claiming that 40 per cent of their white intake had the makings of a 'poor white' class. This news caused great alarm among whites anxious to maintain a social position they might lose if all members of their society did not conform.

Something would have to be done. The immediate solution was to make boarding fees as low as possible, so that white children from remote districts and poor farms could attend school. There was also a free list for those who were unable to pay anything. The Governor's visit had done the trick. Twenty-five acres were allocated for the use of the school, a rugby field was laid out, and a new school building was opened in 1928, with twelve fine class-rooms, offices, stores, flush latrines, wash places, cloakrooms, showers and a large central hall on the upper storey, with the words around the wall in black letters: 'O God help me to win. But if in thy inscrutable wisdom thou willest me not to win, O God, make me a good loser.' There were three dormitories for

girls and five for boys. Nairobi European School now had 350
pupils, of whom 102 were boarders and thirty-two were on the
free list. Before leaving, pupils sat the Cambridge Overseas School
Certificate. Primary schools were also planned for Parklands,
Westlands and Kilimani.

The secondary school for boys proposed in 1918 was to be built
at Kabete, on the outskirts of Nairobi, on a piece of land alienated
in 1922 for such a purpose (the Prince of Wales School, which
opened in early 1931 with Captain Bertram W. L. Nicholson as
headmaster). Secondary-level girls would have to bide their
time. For the moment they occupied the upper floor of Nairobi
European School's new buildings, under the headship of Miss
Grace Kerby, who had begun to teach at Nairobi European School
on 1 February 1924.

A government boarding school was also opened at Kitale, and
there was a government day school at Mombasa for primary pupils.
Nanyuki School came into being in 1927, with mainly Afrikaner
pupils. And yet there was still no compulsory education for whites.
To help pay for all this, an education poll tax was levied on all
whites from late 1926. There were vociferous protests, but a flat-
rate poll tax on whites was instituted in order to prevent the rise of
a poor white class. As it was, the government was paying 29 per
cent of the cost of white education.

At the same time there was considerable expansion in the
number of private schools, which seemed to provide the sort of
education many parents required for their children. There were
seven by 1929. The largest was the Loreto Convent School for
girls, near Nairobi. Another private girls' school was Limuru
School, founded in 1923 by A. B. McDonnell. Kenton College at
Kijabe high up on the edge of the Rift Valley escarpment overlooking Mt Longonot, founded in 1924, and Pembroke House at
Gilgil begun in 1927 when it broke away from Kenton College,
prepared boys for the British Common Entrance examination,
as did the Hill Preparatory School in Nairobi. One of the head-
masters of Kenton, Captain F. R. Cramb, had won an MC in the
First World War so Kenton boys had blazers striped in purple and

white, the colours of the award. Every Saturday morning the matron, the possessor of a wooden leg, dosed the pupils with Epsom salts.[42]

The Central School in Eldoret, a government school, had better results than Nairobi European School. Established in 1915, by 1916 it had fifty students, and by 1919 three-quarters of its students were from Boer families. Broederstroom, with its curriculum taught in Afrikaans, continued until 1939. During the 1930s the farm schools collapsed. But for the time being they provided alternative education for whites in this remote part of Kenya, made more accessible by the opening in 1925 of the railway to Eldoret.

Other distant places, like Rumuruti, had problems educating their children. In 1925 the Rumuruti youngsters were taught in a private home, but in July 1928 a school opened in the old Laikipia Gymkhana for twenty-one children of Afrikaner settlers in the district. It closed in 1930 when the Afrikaners migrated. The remaining children continued at a private school under a Miss Van Dyk. At Nyeri Eric Sherbrooke-Walker, the proprietor of the Outspan Hotel, tried but failed to start a school. Education in Kenya was, therefore, beginning to develop along the lines of the private/public school system such as existed in Britain. The Kenya Government was anxious to retain the social structure that had developed and to prevent the rise of a poor, uneducated white class. The creation of schools gave the whites confidence in their future in Kenya, instilling in them a sense of permanence, however misguided.

Kenya's white women developed into a tough breed as they struggled with the punishments of nature, and domestic problems, and servants with very different customs from theirs, and the tribal impenetrability of the people they lived among. They learned to outstare, even mock, failure. Towards the end of the First World War a women's organisation was formed in Kenya with the purpose of getting votes for women in the forthcoming elections: the East Africa Women's League (EAWL). It became a powerful force in the country and still exists today. One of its first successes, in 1919, was to get voting extended to white women over twenty-five, which made Kenya's white franchise more liberal than Britain's, where women had to wait until 1929 to get the vote, though propertied women had been enfranchised since 1918. In many ways Kenya's women were more advanced than their counterparts in Britain. The 1926 census reveals that 27 per cent of white females in Kenya were in employment, of whom 28 per cent were in the professions (mainly teaching and nursing), 25 per cent in commerce and 24 per cent in domestic service (the maids brought over from Britain by the aristocrats). Officials' adult daughters, especially in Nairobi, tended to work as typists in government offices until they married.

A new type of woman was seen in Kenya after the war, a person who stood in conspicuous contrast to the hard-working farmers' wives. C. T. Todd, recently arrived as a farm pupil, was astounded to see a topless white woman when he went visiting one day. He explained his surprise to himself by reasoning that in a community as small as Kenya's such people were so very obvious, whereas if they had remained in Britain, they would have been no more unusual than the other Bright Young Things. Some people reckoned that the rot started in 1924 with the publication of Florence K. Riddell's novel *Kenya Mist*.[43] The book sold 375,000 copies, and was reprinted eleven times before 1930. The author had come to Nairobi in 1919 with her business-man husband, and she ran a small private school. Her novel was a story of passion among affluent white renegades escaping the conventions of British society and the successful attempt by a woman settler to have a child outside marriage. It was serialised in the *Daily Express* under the title 'Love among the Lions'.

Two of the people who gave Kenya a bad name were Lady Idina Gordon and Frank Greswolde Williams's wife Ann. Lord Francis Scott, who arrived in Kenya in 1920, thought Greswolde Williams a funny little man, objectionable when drunk, with the rough manners of a stable boy. His daughters were 'rum 'uns' who could not read or write. 'To sum him up, he is a very kind-hearted little bounder.'[44] He was suspected of flying drugs into the country and his wife became a drug addict. Delamere often found her at

Muthaiga Club meandering about 'in a semi-conscious condition half the time'.[45] As for her husband, he was nearly thrown out of Muthaiga Club in March 1930, when Delamere gave him a good dressing down and made him write an abject apology, promising never to misbehave again.[46] His misdeed was to have offered drugs to the Prince of Wales during a visit to the club. Williams once admitted in a breach of promise suit that he was drunk most nights and proposed to most of the women he met.

Lady Idina Gordon also took drugs. Francis Scott thought she 'had done a lot of harm out here and behaves more like a barmaid than a lady. It is a great pity as others are apt to follow her example.'[47] It was she who started the fashion in shorts and bobbed hair. Then the murder of a white woman, Mrs Sims, in Trans-Nzoia in 1925 and the subsequent trial of one of her guests, C. R. Churcher, revealed the way of life, involving parties, big-game hunting and affairs, followed by a small minority of white Kenyans. The damage was done. A few people had given Kenya a bad name, but when the new Colonial (Chief) Secretary's wife arrived in 1929 she found Muthaiga a great disappointment after the lurid pictures she had formed for herself – 'instead of men in red shirts lurking with 6-shooters in every corner waiting to shoot their third or fourth wives lurking with co-respondents in every corner – there was no one else at lunch except one meek man worrying a solitary lettuce'.[48]

Although it was common for officials, and some male settlers, to have African concubines, white women never took African lovers. There was a law against this – Ordinance no. 7 of 1913, which read 'Any white woman who voluntarily permits any native to have unlawful carnal connection with her shall be punished with imprisonment – for a term which might extend to five years.' In 1924 the East Africa Women's League acquired some information about one Elsie Farley, nurse to the children of Cecil H. Crampton of Ngong Road. As a result, they wrote to the Governor claiming she was a menace to the white community. Nothing was done because the Commissioner of Police discovered that she was a half-caste Dutch and Cape Coloured woman living with a Somali in

Nairobi bazaar, and married to him. As she was not white, the Attorney-General said that no offence had been committed.[49]

Matters were different for members of the male sex, who commonly had black mistresses. This was particularly true of KAR officers and sergeants.[50] White women did not condone the practice and their opinion of men living with African women was low:

> Some of the men lived quite openly, or otherwise, with African women, and this was something white women found hard to take, diminishing as they felt it did, the white man in African eyes, and making white women more vulnerable to assaults by black men . . . No white woman would marry a man who, even if it was only a rumour, had lived with a black woman. He, it was considered, was letting the side down, and their opinion of him would be low.[51]

The ladies of the EAWL also urged film censorship; in this they were joined by *Mombasa Times* editorials railing against the 'shilling shocker' posters on the streets, which might affect adversely the Africans' opinions of whites.[52] In 1929 Tommy O'Shea made a speech in the Legislative Council urging film censorship – 'The idea is that Africans should not be shown films which put Europeans in an unfavourable light and it was suggested to ban films dealing with scenes of industrial unrest, bedroom scenes or scenes of "high life".'[53]

Sexual assaults on white women by Africans were extremely rare. There was one in 1922, in Eldoret, two in 1923 and three in 1924, two of which involved children and resulted in a petition calling for the death penalty for rape, signed by 1,500 whites. In 1925 there were three rapes and in 1925 five, one of an eighty-year-old woman in Kijabe.[54] Now some action was taken, and an act was passed by the Legislative Council on 1 July 1926 imposing the death penalty for rape. It was used only once, when an African raped the ten-year-old daughter of a missionary in 1928.

A stereotypical white Kenya woman at this time was the somewhat autocratic DC's wife. Of course not every official's wife was of the same type, but in some, it is true, power did go to their heads. They had an average of four servants and an important position in the community, entertaining as they did almost every night. Jack Strachey composed this verse about the formidable Jane, J. H. Clive's wife:

> We're not the sort of slackers who just lie about on sofas,
> We're out and out attackers and we hate the lazy loafers,
> We're England's working daughters and we're proud
>   of what we do,
> We're just about three-quarters of the white man's
>   burden too.[55]

Perhaps it was in reaction to Jane that Brian Bond, Clive's fellow DO, founded the Kisumu Purity League, which had ten maxims, two of which were: Work is the Curse of the Drinking Classes, and Sobriety is a Menace to Civilisation.

The women in Nairobi, in contrast to the settler wives who worked extremely hard to keep their heads financially above water, tended to entertain on an absurd scale and some were irritatingly kittenish, in the opinion of Daphne Moore, the Colonial Secretary's wife. 'Everyone seemed so busy trying to be naughty and to give the impression of being no end of a devil that the effect was rather artificial.'[56] Torr's Hotel, worthy of London, was the place they met in the mornings – by 1929 there were five hotels in Nairobi, the Norfolk, New Stanley, Torr's, the Salisbury and the Avenue.[57] But the wives also did 'good works' on committees of the flourishing Girl Guides, YWCA, League of Mercy and EAWL. Several indulged in amateur dramatics, putting on plays at the splendid new Theatre Royal opened in Nairobi in 1929.

The women were settling down, and if they put down roots, so would their menfolk. Through all the changes and stratification of Kenyan society in the 1920s, the women were running charities, offices, farms, societies and clubs, while at the same time they were bringing up their own children as little Kenyans, the new generation that was to secure the whites' position in the country.

8

The Difficult Years

Was this not Africa, enticing, alluring, gentle, soft; but look deep; beware! the green cloak of verdure may be hiding smouldering fire.[1]

The 1930s was a troublesome decade for Kenya. It witnessed the dying of hope and mounting of debt as world recession struck and drought and locusts tormented the land. Rain failed to come three years in succession, farmers could not meet the stare of the sun and locusts ravaged the crops. Every blade of grass, every crop and leaf, and even washing on the line fell victim to the insect hordes. They came from the north in red, relentless swarms and nothing, absolutely nothing, no banging of tins or swiping of blankets, no lighting of fires or trampling with cattle, would deter them from settling on farms:

> They flew straight into your face, clinging to your clothes [and] getting down your neck and into your shoes . . . We lit huge fires on patches of bare ground, fed on thick oily vegetation to produce clouds of choking black smoke. We beat innumerable tin cans, we burnt them when they settled for the night. We beat them with large leafy branches . . . and we trampled them with herds of cattle. Birds of prey by the hundred joined in, gorging themselves until they were unable to fly; eagles, kites, vultures and great flocks of storks. Nothing, however, appeared to make the slightest impression on the whirring, crunching, creeping hordes which could be heard munching away even when half squashed . . . Even trains were brought to a standstill by them, unable to get a grip on rails . . . All our beautiful ranges

of waving green grass, were beaten into a flat desert, broken by the skeletons of spiky stripped bushes, brown and forlorn under a now clear blue sky. Even a raging fire could not have done more damage. A great black depression like a leaden weight settled over the entire country.[2]

At the same time, world prices fell by more than half in the slump that punished the world. Kenya farmers found themselves in sorry straits. They could no longer afford to use their cars, house servants had to go and workers on the farms were sent away. Reduced to its essentials, life was hard, as farmers stayed alive by eating bull calves, home-grown vegetables and flour made from mealies or what little wheat was reaped. Some settlers had to live on posho porridge and skimmed milk.[3] It was a dreadful time (the last two months of 1931 and first four of 1932 were worst) and many whites gave up. Others closed their farms temporarily and made for the new Kakamega goldfields. Crop acreage ceased to grow – between 1929 and 1938 the area of land under coffee increased by only 4,000 acres, that supporting maize fell by more than half, and the wheat and barley acreage both dropped. Sisal, tea and pyrethrum alone showed any progression. Experimenting yet again, the settlers fixed their sights on pigs and pastoral dairy products. By 1939, however, most white landowners in Kenya were drowned in debt.

A coffee farmer remembered the time:

A drought that lasted for three years, and nearly broke everyone's heart. A drought that had not been known since the years of the great famine before the days of European settlement. A countryside burnt and blackened, rainy season after rainy season ending futilely with a few sparse showers that brought the first tender roots of grass up, only to wither again in the glare of the fierce African sun.

Coffee trees in their millions, covered with a fine crop of green berry, then wilting, drying, and finally being stripped to save their lives. Plantations with a hundred tons of coffee on the trees in some cases picked not a single ton of it. The drought broke in April 1935, but by that time it had ruined another crop. In 1935 the price of coffee dropped below thirty pounds a ton.

Some of us have lost everything, others with private means still left to them have given up in disgust and gone home. But most of us are still here, still smiling and carrying on, still hoping that one day the tide will turn. We don't talk about coffee as much as we used to, and you no longer see those solemn conclaves in the corner of the club bar where some knotty point of pruning or cultivation used so often to be discussed.[4]

It was too much for some unfortunates. Between 1 September 1933 and 31 December 1934 the Salvation Army in Nairobi dealt with twenty-one cases of distressed white families or individuals. Their report noted:

> an old man having spent a number of years in the Colony felt the time had arrived for him to return to Rhodesia; he arrived penniless having tramped many weary miles – arrangements were soon made for his repatriation . . .

> an elderly lady with three boys were accepted into our Hostel whilst the boys' five sisters proceeded to the Lady Northey Home, the mother of the children having been sent to prison – upon the mother's release the case was taken up by us and now through the kindness of the Unemployment Committee arrangements have been made to send the whole family back to England . . .

> a man wandered into Nairobi looking very dirty and tired – he had no work or money and had slept out on the roadside for a few nights . . . Arrangements were immediately made for his repatriation.[5]

Indeed, repatriation was almost invariably the solution, as Kenya rejected those who might become 'poor whites'. Some people were too proud to be helped. In June 1935 a woman suffering from cancer shot dead her four children before shooting herself. At Christmas the Caledonian Society of Nairobi proposed to look after the interests of Scottish children likely to be overlooked by a Santa Claus operating on a heavily reduced budget.[6]

Catastrophe encourages fellowship and poverty breeds improvisation. Old felt terai hats were cut up for bedroom slippers or replacement piano hammer felts. Tumblers were made from old bottles by putting string soaked in paraffin around the line to be cut, setting fire to the string, then dipping the bottle mouth-down into a bucket of cold water, causing the neck to crack off along the line of the string. The rough edge of the tumbler lip was sanded down. Old boots were made into leather washers. No longer were the hides of wild animals sent for curing to Rowland Ward in Nairobi – now people did the job themselves with one part of saltpetre to four parts of burnt alum mixed into a paste with a little water and rubbed on the pelt.[7] It was a hard life, as a rhymester reflected:

> In starting to slake my wanderer's thirst,
> I made for the bush and plain;
> And much have I seen since I came here first
> Of pleasure and work and pain,
> Making of railways, ploughing of land,
> I've hunted, prospected and shot,
> At trading and planting I've given a hand,
> And ranching and heaven knows what!
> And I've made my friend and I've made my foe,
> And stuck to them each and all;
> And I'll stick to them still until either go,
> Or till I in my turn must fall.
> And when all is done and ye read this rhyme,
> Whatever the world may say,
> They'll have to own that I lived my time
> In a thoroughly manly way.[8]

It was mainly the farmers who suffered, for administrators were cocooned by their salaries from sharing in the poverty. 'After three bad years,' said one of them, 'we get good rains and good crops and then like a curse world prices fall. The root of my sympathy with these farmers lies in this fact, that month after month I go on drawing my admittedly inadequate pittance, but I do draw it . . . At any rate we officials have some security, but to sit down on one's farm and watch the rains pass over, or one's crops being eaten by locusts or some other scourge, or to reap one's crops and then find the prices dropping week by week, would drive me plumb crazy.'[9] It was calculated that the debts of white entrepreneurs in Kenya exceeded £8 million in 1931, causing banks to take drastic measures and limit overdrafts. The farmers' lot was eased by the establishment of a Land Bank that year, offering loans at very low interest rates, over a repayment period of thirty years. Most farmers took advantage of this and thus hung on to their land. In the first year of operation, applications for loans totalled £584,000, the first six months seeing 78 per cent of the applications being for the conversion of onerous private mortgages.

Though ostensibly this was a far from ideal time to foster immigration and encourage newcomers to Kenya, it was paradoxically argued that more white settlers were just what the country needed to ease it from the doldrums. An organisation designed to stimulate interest in Kenya was the Joint East Africa Board, formed in London in 1923 with Sir Sydney Henn at its head. And a new body, the Kenya Association, was set up in 1932 by the Convention of Associations to give publicity to the colony and undertake work involving 'the introduction of men and women of the right type into Kenya by judicious and soundly constructed migration and land settlement on up-to-date lines'.[10] Really its function was to revive the market for land, whose collapse had done so much to retard the country's progress. The new organisation portrayed the advantages of Kenya for a new type of residential settlement, designed to bring a quick return. Whites retiring from India and elsewhere were encouraged to buy small plots, usually around the towns. Advertisements stressed the beauty of Kenya, the country's great attraction. As a former Governor Sir Percy Girouard said, 'I notice one remarkable thing, that when I visit a settler, instead of showing me his crops or discussing the production value of his land, he invariably first shows me the view.'[11]

Unfortunately for the Kenya Association, the settlers' widely expressed dissatisfaction with the government painted the future prospects of the country in the darkest colours and thus discouraged further white immigration into Kenya. In contrast, in Southern Rhodesia officials and settlers were united in saying that their country was incomparable in every respect.[12] Moreover, white society in Kenya was more sharply defined than it had been earlier in the century, when all-comers were welcome, and now settlers were reluctant to admit certain potential buyers.

Prejudices abounded among those selling land. One of them wrote to the Association secretary complaining, 'I note that your last list of applicants for land is composed entirely of Dutchmen [Boers]. Do we want to convert Kenya into a Dutch colony? Any whites may be better than no whites, but I think we should try to get Englishmen as much as possible.'[13] Though the secretary agreed, he pointed out that it was important to increase the white population 'in consideration of the undoubted menace which threatens from other quarters', and that the right kind of Afrikaner made a good colonist.[14] The hypothetical menace was that posed by Indians, whose number, at 36,461, was double that of the whites. In reality, hardly any of Britain's inhabitants were attracted to Kenya at this time – from January to November 1937 there was only one enquiry from England and four from Rhodesia, one from the Malay States, three from South Africa, and one each from Ceylon, India, Texas and Brazil.[15] White immigration expanded only very slowly in the 1930s, the European population of Kenya rising from 16,812 in 1931 to 18,269 in 1936. Figures for the end of the decade are distorted by the outbreak of war.

Some of those who came were Jewish. The rise of Hitler in 1933 and the persecution of the Jews in Germany stimulated the Jewish community in Nairobi, and Edward Ruben in particular, to form on 17 December that year the Kenya Jewish Board of Deputies. The East African Jewish Guild and the Kenya Zionist Association heartily supported this development. The first seven Jewish refugees then arrived in Kenya. Anna Ortlepp of Eldoret, wanting to sell two farms in 1936, asked the Kenya Association to encourage the Council for German Jewry to become interested in Kenya.[16] In London there was a movement to establish a scheme to settle a number of Jewish families in Kenya, and the Plough Settlement Association came into being. Over thirty-five people were selected in Germany and sent to Kenya. When they arrived, the refugee Jews were looked after by a local committee and found posts as farm managers.

The Governor, Sir Robert Brooke-Popham, was cautious about the development because he thought that the country's racial problems were already sufficiently complicated and there was a large Arab population on the coast which might object: 'What I want to avoid at all costs is the formation of a regular Jewish enclave.' As long as they were scattered and absorbed into the community they would be an asset, 'but what with the Indians and the Goans and the Arabs and the Somalis, quite apart from the Dutch [Afrikaners], I feel that another community problem must be avoided'.[17]

It was not easy for the incoming Jews:

It took time and a lot of patience for that severe German-European upbringing to get used to and understand the – to him – primitive and sometimes even childish, African culture and customs. The anecdotes were numerous as each farmer came to Nakuru to share the experiences he had with his farm labourers . . . For instance, when something went wrong and the manager asked his head man for an explanation, this usually consisted of a blank look, an upward rolling of the eyes, the shaking of the head and the inevitable answer 'shauri ya mungu' (only He knows). What could be more exasperating?[18]

The Kenya Association was also involved in advising enquirers about employment possibilities in Kenya. Because only land-buyers were wanted, in 1936 those seeking information about jobs were told that prospects were not good, and people were discouraged from going to Kenya unless they had a position awaiting them or sufficient capital to make a start.

The Governor who had the misfortune to deal with the settlers at this difficult time was Grigg's successor Sir Joseph Byrne. A former Chief Secretary said of him, 'His greatest crime appears to be, so they say, damn stupidity.'[19] Byrne struck the settlers as vacillating and lacking in confidence and drive, the embodiment of an uncaring government in Britain. He indulged a plaintive manner, and he signally failed to respond to settler unrest, his attitude to the agricultural crisis being one of laissez-faire. He was out of his depth and showed it. 'I am bound to confess', said Eric Dutton in 1935, 'that never in my experience have I met a man so utterly incapable of governing, so utterly out of touch with the governed as Sir Joseph Bird [Byrne]. It is deplorable.'[20] The hotheads Ewart Grogan (a businessman), Ferdinand Cavendish-Bentinck (of Equator Sawmills and the emergent new leader of the whites[21]) and Claude Anderson (managing director of the *East African Standard* and son of its proprietor) ran rings round him. Their more moderate colleagues, such as the amiable but weak C. Kenneth Archer and Lord Francis Scott, who should have succeeded as leader of the whites on the death of Delamere in 1931, found the extremists difficult to control. A balancing body should have been the Convention of Associations, but it lost much of its power when it was reduced by poverty to holding a single session per year, and its place was taken by the elected members of the Legislative Council.

The chief items of disagreement between the Governor and members of the Legislative Council were the Governor's perceived reluctance to help farmers in the slump and his support for the introduction of income tax, proposed by the Moyne Commission of 1932. This infuriated the settlers, firmly of the opinion as they were that the cost of government was outrageous and the colony's financial affairs should be subject to their own control. Their personal poverty was the underlying force prompting them to demand that government be accountable, extravagance be curbed and incompetence rooted out. They were strenuously opposed to income tax and in 1933 Byrne was defeated over the issue – in the opinion of the former Governor, Grigg, this could hardly have caused greater loss of face for the government.[22]

The following year Byrne tried once more to introduce his income tax, speaking in the opening session of the Legislative Council like a complete autocrat utterly out of sympathy with the much harassed community he proposed to tax. Cavendish-Bentinck replied with an intemperate outburst. An offer to establish a committee undoubtedly saved a critical situation. Said C. Kenneth Archer,

> We are restive under a regime of laissez-faire. Nothing has been done for agriculture since the early days of the depression when Grigg was in command, and taxation is really beyond our ability to pay – these [sic] have culminated in public exasperation. This policy of drift in the face of recurrent losses year after year has rendered the farmer nearly desperate, and there may easily be a flare-up in the near future.'[23]

Then Sir Alan Pim was sent out from England to report on Kenya's financial position and he, too, advocated the introduction of income tax. As so often, life was a series of trade-offs and mixed choices, so a compromise was reached and light income tax began.

Another inquiry, the Morris Carter Land Commission, dealt with the demarcation of Kenya's crown lands, white highlands and native reserves. The settlers awaited its report, published in 1934, with high anxiety, because their future in Kenya depended upon its conclusions. They were reassured by its recommendations, which were on the whole satisfactory to the settlers, mainly because it accepted the principle of keeping the highlands white, though its allocation of the Lerogi plateau to the Samburu was regarded as a breach of faith. It took years for the recommendations to be implemented – another sore point with the settlers – and it was not until 1939 that a Highlands Board was set up, controlled by settlers, with power over land transactions in the highland region. No African, Indian or coloured person could buy or lease land in the privileged area.

The administrators carried on much as before during this decade, though their walking safaris through the districts were being replaced by car journeys, making them more remote from the communities they served. Impassable or absent roads kept some safaris going, as a DO's wife remembered:

> In those days we were out usually for about three weeks, walking fifteen to twenty miles a day. The day began before sunrise with a tray of tea and boiled eggs by the light of hurricane lamps and then a quick rush to get the camp struck, the last loads finished, the tent and beds in head-loads and then as the sun rose the porters moving off into the little twisting native paths, each man balancing his head-load comfortably on a pad of banana leaves. Soon someone would start a song with endless verses and the rhythmic tap of sticks on the loads. We did not always stay with the safari, but would be met by the local chiefs to go and inspect a dam, or a nursery of forest trees or a dispensary or a school. The best bit of the day was dinner by a huge fire, no dinner jacket, only pyjamas and mosquito boots and the moon rising and the Southern Cross.[24]

The DOs continued to deal with the mail and requests and complaints from the public of all races who came to the office. They collected taxes, prepared and checked accounts, signed payment vouchers and cheques, and supervised all activities in the government boma as well as building, road maintenance and bridge-construction. They trained tribal police, inspected the Kenya Police and oversaw the prison detainees in their jobs. They toured their districts regularly to scrutinise apparent deaths and check on *maskini* (beggars) exempt from tax; a surprising number of people turned out to be alive or far from poverty-stricken. Secret black books were kept of bad white employers.

Some administrators had time for their own hobbies: Robin Wainwright was a talented cabinet-maker, while G. B. Rimington was so skilled at training wild animals that he persuaded an ostrich to draw him in a light carriage. The administrators could hardly have functioned without their highly competent Goan clerks. There was only one white clerk: Robert ('Hoppy') Marshall in Nairobi, an eccentric Cockney with a war wound that made him limp severely. He doubled as the hangman, apparently having been given the job when providing the lowest tender of £5 for a white, £1 for an African and a promise to do the Indians free – a highly suspect story revealing Europeans' dislike of Indians. Administrators always had time for sport after tea. At Machakos the golf course was beside an area used by the local hospital for burying corpses. The soil was so shallow that hyenas were able to dig up the bodies and golf balls were always fetching up against skulls in the rough. When that happened the player was allowed a free lift.[25] The best-known sportsman was Percy Wyn-Harris, DC at Nyeri, who participated in the two expeditions up Mt Everest in 1933 and 1936, as well as climbing the Batian peak of Mt Kenya, only the second man to do so.

Administrators created the goat bag, to oil the wheels of empire. Because indenting for funds for various purposes was a tricky business, each boma had its own goat bag from which money could be disbursed for urgent necessities. The hoard arose from fines and taxes paid in goats to the government. Such animals were fed to the members of the King's African Rifles, but before they were killed some had kids. These were sold, as were the skins of their parents, to provide a useful income for the goat bag. To this little example of private enterprise the government turned a blind eye, and many a bush school was built from a goat bag. Otherwise, administrators were expected to display a high standard of conduct. There was a scandal when the DC Clarence Buxton was cited as co-respondent in a divorce case by the government analyst Maurice Fox. 'Intimacy' was supposed to have occurred in a car in the Nairobi Game Park, an accusation denied by Buxton on the grounds that there were too many ticks there. Buxton lost the case and was transferred to Palestine, though he later returned to farm in Kenya.

In 1937 the settlers were relieved to find Byrne replaced by Sir Robert Brooke-Popham, recently Inspector-General of the RAF and a much tougher character than his predecessor. When offering him the appointment the Colonial Secretary W. Ormsby-Gore said of Kenya:

Its internal make-up is somewhat notorious. The very vocal
British settlers, mostly of the ex-officer and public-school class, a
large Indian middle class of traders, artisans and some lawyers,
and three million African natives of the most heterogeneous
types in any colony in Africa. The administration of this complex is never easy, and quite frankly, the present Governor
Byrne and his wife have given little satisfaction socially or in
other capacities. The colony wants somebody who is a good
mixer, has plenty of self-reliance and a sense of humour quite as
much as an energetic administrator . . . [Nairobi is] the rather
active Power-house of all East Africa – the capital of a country
people fall in love with and acquire an emotional rather than a
strictly rational attitude toward – a paradise of big game with
superb scenery, but bristling with 'problems' and controversies,
many of them arising from the fact that at 6,000 feet above sea
level on the Equator everyone wants to run before they can
walk in an atmosphere which doesn't permit of quite such
strenuous exercise . . . There is an Imperial job to be done there,
and it requires someone with wide and varied experience and
outlook. I know it well enough to know it is a 'man's job' . . .
There are two superb – possibly too superb – Government
Houses built by Ned Grigg when he was Governor at Nairobi
and Mombasa respectively.[26]

Brooke-Popham found that Kenya's white colonists did not
speak with only one voice, except when it came to their dislike of
Indians. There were factions among them – some criticised the
elected members of the Legislative Council, while there was
special tension between those who lived in Nairobi and those who
did not, as well as between the personnel of different industries. He
discovered that the roads were appalling and government buildings
in a state of disrepair, but he put politics aside for a moment to
celebrate the coronation of George VI in June 1937. People of
every race joined in the fun and put on a spectacular display, with
march-pasts, sports, bonfires, fireworks and in Nairobi a torchlight
procession. Streets were decorated and from every car flowed

streamers printed with union jacks. A thousand people attended a Coronation Ball at Government House.

Brooke-Popham's short stint as Governor (he left when war was declared in 1939 in order to rejoin the RAF) was dominated by the rise of Hitler and rumours that the British Government was inclined to do a deal with the German dictator by restoring Tanganyika to Germany in exchange for a limitation of armaments. Hitler had been induced to reclaim Tanganyika by German colonists there and pressure groups at home. 'The Germans are behaving in a very strange manner in Tanganyika,' said a Kenya colonist, 'and a number of us who have a lot of secret information believe that they are working up till they are ready for a coup d'état.'[27] In 1937 there were 3,000 Germans in Tanganyika and more were pouring in by every boat. Ferdinand Cavendish-Bentinck founded the Tanganyika League to prevent the return of Germans to Tanganyika and of Tanganyika to Germany, and to arouse the interest of the world in this menace to Kenya. As it happened, however, Britain turned down the proposed return to Hitler of the former German colony.

For a while, though, the threat was real because Kenya was already insecure on its northern border after Mussolini occupied Abyssinia in October 1935. Deserters from Italian troops and 5,000 refugees trekked southwards into Kenya, and were settled in a camp at Isiolo. If the country of Tanganyika to Kenya's south had been ceded to Germany, Kenya would have been squeezed between two hostile nations.

Byrne and Brooke-Popham presided over a country split in half in the 1930s. On one side were professionals, administrators and merchants in the large towns of Nairobi and Mombasa, and on the other were the needy farmers. To the outward eye, Nairobi was not a place of straitened circumstances.

Nairobi's aspect had altered under Grigg and now there were palatial new railway buildings, law courts, a town hall and two magnificent banks with pillared porticos. A gleaming, white, arched structure, the municipal market, housed fruit and vegetables more royally than the High Court its judges and magistrates. The new McMillan Memorial Library, with a classic dark-grey façade fronted with stone lions, sat solemnly beside the white, wedding-cake minarets of the neighbouring mosque. The City Park, formerly an unkempt patch of forest, had been laid out along the Muthaiga–Limuru road, with three sets of swings – for whites and Indians and Africans, though white children seldom went there. Nairobi had expanded, with the new white suburbs of Kilimani, Groganville, Kabete, Westlands and Ngong, all of them served by tarmac roads. The earliest suburb, Parklands, was closely built upon, though Muthaiga had more space between its houses. Nearby, the coffee country of Kiambu had itself become almost a suburb of Nairobi. There homesteads encircled by lovely gardens topped the summits of the ridges, windbroken and shaded by blue gum and *Grevillea robusta*.

As a town consisting mainly of largely professional and com-mercial whites, Nairobi was more prosperous than the countryside. The streets no longer bustled with khaki-clad white toughs in sola topees or double terai hats, and Africans in blankets. Now Africans wore all sorts of European clothing, and white women perched berets on their heads, or the lightest of felt hats. Summery frocks mingled with well-cut tweeds or corduroy slacks in green or blue or brown (grey flannels were absolutely out) and bright blouses and scarves. The ladies took elevenses in Torr's, though really it was better to be seen in the New Stanley Hotel. In town were four hotels – the New Stanley (the best), and Torr's, the Norfolk and the Avenue, while outside were the Salisbury, with a swimming pool, the Queenswood, Westwood Park and Grosvenor House. Recently rebuilt, the New Stanley was a magnet for elevenses, with its comfortable wicker-chaired lounge. The 'Happy Valley' crowd could be found there, as one startled newcomer noticed: 'The figure . . . was dressed like an advertisement for Sandeman's port, black sombrero, black cloak scarlet-lined, cigarette holder about a foot long . . . A vision appeared in the doorway, dressed in white slacks, shirt and terai, carrying a sheaf of arums, and on a white lead, a magnificent white Borzoi hound. Then with a cry of "Darling" advanced slowly to join Sandeman's port.'[28] Torr's had superior dance bands, such as Lou Green's (the musicians mainly Indian), on Saturday evenings. Those not wearing evening dress were allowed only into the bar on the balcony. Or for other evening entertainment there were now three cinemas in Nairobi – the Capitol in Government Road, the Playhouse by the market and the Empire (which doubled as a theatre) in Hardinge Street – whose films changed twice a week. And there were nightclubs too – Hoppy's in Government Road (Hoppy Marshall had expanded his interests), the Westwood Park and the White Horse Inn – though they did not admit single people, being fairly decorous establishments.

'Social life in Nairobi is mainly a sophisticated affair,' noted one observer; 'a procession of dinners, luncheon and sundowner parties, dances (private and subscription), cinemas, amateur theatricals and morning, afternoon and evening bridge. There are, of course, a great number of people who, either from choice or necessity, lead quiet uneventful lives, and whose one form of amusement consists of an occasional cinema.'[29] Drinking was heavy and hospitality boundless in those who led a more social life. Though hotels ceased to serve drinks after 11 p.m., clubs could continue to do so. There was an attempt to put a stop to this and a committee was appointed to look into the licensing laws in 1934.

Muthaiga had developed into a suburb of the better-off. There were more two-storeyed houses than bungalows there, buildings of grey stone, with long, low windows and roofed with local tiles. On the verandahs were tubs of maidenhair, arums, agapanthus, and begonias of the tall climbing variety with clusters of small, waxy, scented, pink and scarlet flowers. Beyond were lawns bordered by wide beds of scarlet or blue salvias and bushes of daisies, with a thick cypress hedge and pergola smothered in the creeper golden shower. Those living in Muthaiga rather saw themselves as a community apart.[30] There were Old Wykehamist dinners at the Muthaiga Club, and trips to Limuru, to the Brackenhurst Hotel for tea and golf.

As yet Nairobi boasted little of high culture, leading Llewelyn Powys, working on a farm in the Rift Valley and the brother of the writer John Cowper Powys, to observe:

It's curious being with these people who do not think, who do not 'have ideas'. I don't believe in the whole of Africa there is a single man or woman who could understand a line of poetry or who for one second gets a glimpse of the world as we see it . . . These men – these lads as they call each other – are free and fair and unsophisticated like a lot of jolly school boys. I think it is these wives who get on one's nerves, these wives with their preoccupations domestic and otherwise, with their dusty shoes, fat legs or thin legs.'[31]

Llewelyn Powys had come to Kenya to cure his tuberculosis but to his chagrin found the settlers had 'heads made of concrete', apart from Galbraith Cole, Lord Delamere's brother-in-law, who 'at least has a hawk's brain'.[32] Powys was exaggerating, for he was isolated on a farm and things were not as bad as he thought. Teachers and other professionals, and the better-educated farmers, had a lively intellectual life, though their numbers were still too small to support professional drama or music-making.

But by 1932 'meetings of a scientific character' were taking place at Nairobi's Museum, while Evan E. Biss held a poetry discussion group in his own house. There were regular lectures and readings from modern poetry in the McMillan Memorial Library, and the amateur Nakuru Symphony Orchestra gave creditable performances.[33] A sense of their own history in the country was developing among settlers and a new group, the Kenya Pioneers' Society, with the object of 'recording the history of the early occupation of the country', began to have annual dinners.[34]

Though the British class structure was more muted in Kenya than in the home country, the colony's society was highly racially stratified. Members of mixed marriages and their offspring – the 1931 census recorded 205 'half-castes'[35] – were ostracised and therefore kept very much to themselves. An exception to this rule was Ali Khan, formerly the owner of a transport firm in Nairobi, the proud possessor of carriages, a fleet of rickshaws, livery stables, and horses and mules for hire. He had married a white South

African woman in South Africa before he came to Kenya with her in 1904, from Rhodesia. Ali Khan was a fair-skinned Pathan, something of a gambler, whose business folded as the number of motor vehicles increased. He lost everything but was so well liked that Indians and whites clubbed together to put him back on his feet again. He expressed his thanks to the Europeans in the *East African Standard* of 1 December 1934. Another mixed marriage was that of G. Montgomery from Machakos, a DO dismissed for beating an African, who became a soil conservation officer and a Muslim and married a Swahili woman.

Whites very rarely sought the friendship of Africans, though there were some exceptions to this rule – George Nightingale was one of those who had more friends among Africans than whites, two of his companions being Ndola, headman on the Kinani sisal estate, and Nganga, an employee on a maize farm at Elementeita, but he was unusual and his conduct was frowned upon by members of his own race. When working on George Langridge's farm he was discouraged from becoming too familiar with African servants on the grounds that they had to be kept in their place in society – 'I was not told how long this convenient state of affairs was to last.'[36] Social stigma and ostracism were hard to bear, and immigrant whites with liberal ideas soon began to conform to the norms of Kenya's European society.

There were, however, regular liaisons between white men and African women. Llewelyn Powys consorted with African women, though they often disgusted him – 'great Gilgil trots [whores] poxed for the most part and without modesty . . . I see in the background three Kikuyu girls who have come from far. I shall perhaps select one when I come back from dinner tonight.'[37] Children sometimes resulted from the white–black unions. In the Northern Frontier District the policeman Derek Franklin came across several progeny of former administrative officers in the Moyale district. Half Boran, with handsome features, they received maintenance payments from their fathers via the local post office.[38]

Close bonds could and often did develop between whites and their employees because common humanity is difficult to suppress.

A. C. Harries of Limuru inserted in the *East African Standard* a touching obituary of Kamau wa Mbuthu, a faithful worker for twenty-six years until slain by a lion.[39] There was, too, an army of dedicated missionaries and Salvation Army personnel who devoted their lives to African welfare. The experience of Salvationists, living among Africans, having no cars and little contact with settlers, stood in stark contrast to that of members of the Happy Valley crowd or even of ordinary settlers. They made their own entertainments, edited the Kenya *War Cry*, kept aloof from missionary squabbles, and helped members of all races, taking in orphans, running schools and hostels and visiting women in prison.

The settlers had a grudging admiration for these good-hearted people, not least because the Salvation Army picked up the pieces when whites fell upon hard times or did not measure up to the standards expected of their race. A rest home for whites was run at Likoni by Salvationists, and they had hostels for indigent whites in Nairobi. Most Europeans were wary indeed of the potential appearance of 'poor whites', a group much despised in South Africa. On 15 May 1933 there was founded in Nairobi the Kenya Society for the Study of Race Improvement, with forty members. Its chairman was the energetic and forceful Rudolf Mayer, the largest shareholder in the *East African Standard* and chairman of the Nairobi Chamber of Commerce. Since he himself had been discriminated against, as a German, during and after the First World War and twice had his application to join the Nairobi Club turned down, it is odd that he lacked sympathy for other victims of discrimination. At the first meeting of the new society Dr H. L. Gordon of Nairobi gave a paper on 'Eugenics'.

To prevent the growth of a poor white section, there was continual emphasis on the provision of good education for white children. In 1934 the East African Women's League discovered that there were 357 white children of school age receiving no education, and most of them were Afrikaners. Afrikanerdom was resilient and determined to retain its cultural integrity in the face of British domination, and the government's plan to lift some of its children from 'poor white' status was unsuccessful. The more extreme whites advocated sterilisation and repatriation to South Africa of the Afrikaners they considered undesirable. Gradually, however, the Afrikaners became more reconciled to their children being educated in government schools, with English as the language of instruction, rather than at farm schools where pupils were taught in Afrikaans. The government made a concession in 1930 when it accepted that Afrikaans could be taught in schools as a foreign language if there was sufficient demand for it. In 1935 there were 113 Afrikaner children in farm schools compared with 122 at the government Central School in Eldoret (with a new principal, R. Hunter). When the Afrikaner Broederstroom School closed in 1939, most of its pupils transferred to the Central School. The school at Rumuruti, which had reopened, closed in 1937, and all 122 children of the district of primary-school age were forced to go to Nakuru School.

A grand new secondary school for white boys, the Prince of Wales School, opened in 1931, at Kabete outside Nairobi, with seventy-seven pupils and a junior school of thirty. It was housed in beautiful buildings, designed by the architect Herbert Baker, with yellow walls and green doors and a red roof. But the high cost of boarding at the Prince of Wales School meant that many Afrikaners were denied secondary education – in 1936 only three Afrikaners enrolled there. By 1939 there were 131 pupils and two new blocks were due to open to accommodate boys previously housed in marquees. Nairobi also saw the opening of two new primary schools – Parklands and Kilimani. Girls of secondary level were educated on the Hill in Nairobi, in the Kenya High School, as it was called from 1 January 1938, under the headship of Grace Kerby. There was therefore no need for children to be despatched to Britain for secondary education, though some settlers continued to send their offspring, particularly the boys, to public school at home. This was largely a matter of wealth and class. Prospects for school leavers in Kenya were limited. Some went back to help on farms, while others joined commercial enterprises.

*   *   *

With its cosmopolitan and trading tradition, the coast of Kenya remained culturally different from the rest of the colony. As the point of entry to the country, Mombasa always had to cater for scores of visitors, and in the 1930s it also became increasingly popular as a holiday destination. Modest hotels, consisting of simple bandas for sleeping and a larger building used as a communal dining-room, were built on beaches on the mainland north and south of Mombasa island. One of the first was at Bamburi beach seven miles north of Mombasa. Settlers began to make a habit of taking an annual fortnight's holiday on the beach, now that they were less fearful of the sun and its lethal rays.

In the town of Mombasa itself were five hotels: the Manor, Palace (with spacious verandahs), Rex, Tangana and Albion. There were also three outside the town: the Tudor House (with a large, thatch-roofed dance floor), the Azania on the south mainland opposite Kilindini harbour (established by Elspeth Huxley's father Jos Grant and reached by a ferry from the island) and Port Reitz, with its 'eat all you want' teas for one and a half shillings. There was also a boarding house, the Moorings run by Mrs Philips, and a pub known as Mrs Bill's. The eccentric Manor Hotel, more of a club than a hotel, had been started in 1914 by two sisters, Mrs Davis and Mrs Webber, and it grew in labyrinthine fashion. It became the meeting place for residents and visitors alike.[40] At the Manor Hotel dwelt a huge tortoise, two feet tall and four feet long, so equable in temperament that children took rides on its back as it wandered about the lounge and gardens, sometimes even making forays down to Likoni ferry. The creature came to an untimely end after the Second World War when a taxi accidentally ran it over.

For the entertainment of its visitors Mombasa had two cinemas, the Regal and Majestic, and to keep them spruce two laundries (Mrs Lund's European Laundry and Dias Laundry, both in Salim — now Digo — Road), and two European hairdressers. There were various developments to the port's benefit. The construction of Nyali bridge had greatly eased access to the northern mainland and allowed its owners, Nyali Estates, to sell plots on the mainland, as the CMS had done when they sold much of their land at

Freretown formerly used to house freed slaves. In 1931 a deep-water jetty was opened for Shell, Vacuum and Texaco, permitting the oil companies to disgorge petroleum products straight into bulk lines from the jetty to their tinning factories, for petrol was still sold in two-gallon debes. In the same year a fifth deep-water berth was opened for ships at Kilindini harbour. A further improvement occurred in 1934, when the Mombasa–Lamu road through Golbanti on the Tana river was realigned from Witu to travel through the forest via Nyongoro and cross the Tana at Garsen. But this was, alas, of little benefit to road traffic in the wet season, because there was still no way of avoiding a nasty pocket of viscous black cotton soil on a journey to Lamu. Mombasa was isolated as far as road traffic was concerned, for the 300-mile road to Nairobi was in a parlous state, and there was only a narrow, sandy track southwards to Tanganyika. Those wanting to travel up and down the coast went by sea, and the upcountry-bound took the daily train.

Because of the economic downturn, upcountry towns stayed much the same as they were in the 1920s. The Bell Inn remained the only hotel in Naivasha, though on the shores of Lake Naivasha stood Sparks Hotel. Apart from that, there was only a tannery in the little town. At the dusty, messy cow town of neighbouring Nakuru there were plans for a blanket factory in which Lord Egerton, in the process of building himself a large house near Njoro, was reported to be investing £80,000.[41] Overshadowed by the nearby Stag's Head, the Nakuru Hotel limped along with only a memory of the wild times of the past when Lord Delamere and his friends had rough-and-tumble in the bar.

Near Naivasha lay the Wanjohi valley, dubbed 'Happy Valley' by newspapers avid for gossip of a titillating kind. Some disreputable members of the British and foreign aristocracy lived there, people like the Earl of Erroll; Lady Idina, daughter of the Earl de la Warr and six times married; Comte Frédéric de Janzé and his wife Alice; Michael Lafone, married to the daughter of the Earl of Strafford; and Raymond de Trafford, a remittance man from a grand Lancashire family. They were very few on the ground (it is untrue that Kenya hosted scores of remittance men, as news-papers then and now claim) and were a stark contrast to the penurious farmers round about them. They developed a style of life and entertainment which shocked Governor Grigg and on which Governor Byrne kept his own counsel. On farms drinks were served at sunset, and afterwards people took their baths and donned dressing gowns and pyjamas for the evening meal. The quality and colour of your dressing gown indicated your social position – Peter de Polnay regarded Boy Long as his social equal because they both had Charvet robes.[42]

On Saturdays the country towns were thronged with settlers gathering at clubs and hotels for sports matches, racing and polo. Nanyuki was an especially sporty place, and to accommodate the visitors it had the Silverbeck and Sportman's Arms hotels, both built on the Equator. The latter was run by Mrs Hill-Williams (Mrs Hilly-Billy) and her daughter Kathleen (Twopence) and for 250 shillings you could rent a cottage for a month. Twopence became a member of the Oxford Group, a movement strong in Kenya at this time, and refused to sell alcohol at the hotel. Financial exigency forced her to relax her principles, but she still insisted on the Quiet Hours with staff each afternoon – an irritant to guests who had to cope with newcomers unable to command attention.

Rumuruti, to the west of Nanyuki, was a place of such poor land that every cow required eleven acres for its grazing. Rumuruti town consisted of three stores in a row, one of them belonging to a European. Farmers were honour-bound to shop at the white store, but most settlers then slunk round to the Indian dukas to take advantage of their lower prices. Near the Rumuruti club stood a house occupied by a major from India with buffalo and antelope heads upon the walls, its bookshelves crammed with books on India, and the floors and chairs draped with pelts of leopard and lion. This was a typical bachelor house – dwellings with a feminine presence had chintz on the chairs instead, or even Somali shawls. Several Afrikaner families moved to Rumuruti and in 1932 their dominee, Revd M. P. Loubser, laid the foundation stone of a magnificent new Dutch Reformed church. On Wednesdays and Saturdays, the two days on which a train reached Thomson's Falls with mail, Robert Kuhne drove a lorry from Thomson's Falls to Rumuruti with the letters and supplies. On mail days farmers went to Rumuruti town to fetch their mail and shop. Month-old magazines and weeklies were awaiting them – for those of British origin the *Tatler, Bystander, Field* and *Country Life*, sent by relatives in England, were their staple reading fare. Books from Nairobi Lending Library came in parcels and filled many lamplit evening hours.

The isolated farms of the Rift Valley and Laikipia enjoyed annual visits from a Chinese entrepreneur toting silks and other fine materials. He tempted farmers' wives dressed in corduroy slacks and aertex shirts to buy his wares and thus indulge their longing for a more luxurious life:

> The nearest I came to womanly things was when the old Chinaman paid his annual visit, arriving in his battered old van. The back of this was full of roll upon roll of the most beautiful Chinese silk, which he threw in shimmering waterfalls all over my armchairs . . . The old man was no fool, he knew that women in the bush were starved of beautiful things, and I always bought a few yards simply for the pleasure of being able to take it out of my cupboard occasionally, to stroke and enjoy its colour.[43]

In the lake region of Nyanza, Lumbwa and Kericho there was more development than in the rest of the country. By 1928 Kericho had proved promising for tea and in the 1930s four hundred tons of tea a month were railed by large companies such as the African Highlands Company and Brooke Bond from Lumbwa, a nascent town where Shell had built an oil distribution centre. The Kibos Cotton Ginnery had opened recently, while at Kisumu the Nyanza Oil Mills made simsim (sesame) and ground-nut oil and bottled mineral waters. Kisumu also had a soapworks, and there were firms which undertook general engineering and repair work, especially in connection with mining. For visitors there were the Kisumu and Marina hotels, both with precious electric light. There was, moreover, a regular bus service to Kakamega and Kitale on Tuesdays and Fridays.

Kakamega helped to save Kenya from economic ruin in the 1930s, for it was in that mosquito-ridden, hot and humid place that gold was found. Previously Kakamega had been an unhealthy station where five months' government service counted as six, but now it blossomed. There had been gold mining before in Kenya, particularly in the Lolgorien area near Kisii in the 1920s, but it had not come to much. Miners had suffered much privation there, with trypanosomiasis (sleeping sickness) rife and no hospital to treat the sick, and conditions harsh beyond belief. Among the prospectors at Lolgorien were Louis A. Johnson, American, tall and bony, a farmer at Turbo near Eldoret who lived in hope of better things, and his wife Fanny, tough and skinny, with untidy, wispy hair. Before he went to Kenya Johnson was a storekeeper in the Klondyke, where he learned to use prospecting pans. Now he formed a syndicate with a few partners who contributed finance, in blocks of £25, for one safari at a time to look for gold. His 1931 syndicate with J. A. Collins and G. G. Smallwood moved to Kakamega to explore the Yala river, where they discovered alluvial gold and the Kimingini reef. Back in Eldoret, Johnson raised further finance from Eldoret citizens forming themselves into the Eldoret Mining Syndicate with T. J. O'Shea as chairman. The new company obtained a concession, pegged a large number of claims and made useful sums of money.

News of the finds leaked out and a gold rush began. Farmers hit by the slump flocked to Kakamega, as did two banks and the dentist from Eldoret. Chris Teesdale, an expert on the mosquito, was stationed there. Prospectors erected posts to stake their claims, made dams in streams and set up washing boxes to collect the heavy gold as it sank to the bottom of the water. Shafts of fifty or sixty feet were also dug, and miners lowered by winch in buckets. Prospectors and their families lived in Kavirondo matting huts, made of reeds tied together with string. By 1932 there were 200 miners, a number which trebled by 1934. Then came an injection of capital from large companies such as Tanganyika Concessions

Ltd, Bewick Moering & Co. and the American millionaire de Ganahl[44] who came with other prospectors from the Yukon. This created a large number of jobs for desperate, failing farmers and money started to flow again. As for Johnson, he made sufficient money from his gold mining to return to the United States, purchase a geiger counter and make a uranium find. After three years only the larger companies were left in Kakamega, the two biggest mines being Rosterman's and Risks. In 1937 68,670 ounces of unrefined gold were won from Kenyan goldfields. The total value of the gold in 1934 was £69,000 (4 per cent of Kenya's domestic exports), but in 1941 it was £696,000 (15 per cent). One of the beneficial side-effects of the mining was that it unearthed palaeolithic artefacts which added to the world's knowledge of early man.

As the mines were in an African reserve, compensation for surface rights was paid to local people. Unhappy about the incursion of whites into their reserve, some Africans sent a petition to the British Parliament: 'We are in great distress of mind owing to the overflowing number of more than 1,000 Europeans into North Kavirondo in search of gold; and we are afraid that many more will come . . . In Africa bad Europeans does commits illicit acts of taking some of our girls and spoiling their good character thereby become bad women.'[45] On the other hand, many Africans did very well out of Kakamega, where they had a ready market for their produce.

The little town grew fast. Past Kakamega's two new banks and white-run shops, a dirt road ran across the river via 'Seven Dials', to 'Piccadilly Circus', the site of scores of huts already surrounded by gardens. Wherever the British went in the world they planted gardens. The road proceeded on to 'Golders Green', 'Palmers Green' and 'Hampstead Heath', the latter flat enough for the new airport built by de Ganahl. Families were welcome and at Christmas 1932 there was a party for ninety white children.[46] Among the new townspeople sundowner parties became a habit – they started at six and lasted till nine, and afterwards people went home for dinner, eaten in pyjamas, sweater, dressing gown and mosquito boots, and then to bed. Bachelors might go to the Corkscrew Bar or

Eldorado Hotel or Golden Hope dance salon to jig to the music of talented locals – Chris Bell on the drums, Reggie Taylor on the harmonium and Stan Daly on the saxophone and trumpet. But this must have been one of the best-behaved mining towns in the world, with most of the prospectors ex-officers and upright settlers. The Golden Hope, for example, played host to church services on Sundays, with Paddy Collier officiating. After church the Sunday routine in the government boma included tennis from nine to eleven, ping pong and beer from eleven to noon and gin and darts from noon to one.[47]

Bridge was a popular evening pastime, after a day in the sun. A newcomer from Britain, familiar with English snobbishness about 'tradespeople', was surprised to find behind a counter in a shop a woman he had played bridge with the night before – 'Wives of the European shop-keeping classes work, usually in other people's shops. In England they would probably be living in Hove on twopence ha'penny a year, struggling to keep up appearances. Here they don't worry. It's all democratic . . . You lift your hat to the woman behind the counter.'[48] Occasionally an expensive travelling cinema set itself up in a large store known as the Farmers' Mart and showed films such as *King Kong*. By 1938 the worst of the slump was over and the farmers returned to their farms. The boom town of Kakamega resumed its former sleepy existence, though the more successful mines continued to yield gold.

*   *   *

The barren north of Kenya, always called the NFD, was not a settler area. Only government servants were allowed to live there, in a region 300 miles from east to west and 400 from north to south. The area housed 26,000 people of the Turkana, Samburu, Somali and Boran peoples, owners of cattle, goats and camels and dependent on salt licks and waterholes, the subject of perpetual dispute between one group and another. It was bordered on the east by Italian Somaliland and on the north by Abyssinia. The population centres were at Lodwar, Wajir, Buna, Moyale, Mandera, Garbatula and Garissa, but most of the people were nomads wandering from place to place. It was so dangerous and waterless that white settlers had to obtain special permission to enter the area.

The southernmost government boma in the NFD lay at Isiolo where the superintendent of police, J. B. Grenfell-Hicks, was a buffoon and source of joy to the little white community. To him the nearby Archer's Post was Poacher's Arse. Though it seems strange, officials in the NFD often found that loneliness was welcome. Young men straight from university at home (as became the norm in the Colonial Service) loved the wildness and the dearth of people and the proudness of the races in the north. White visitors intruded on the peace. Yet cultural norms, ingrained in childhood, still prevailed. Officials and police took British attitudes to sport along with them into this barren land. On the exclusively sand and stone 'Royal Rudolf Golf Course' at Lodwar, palm nuts became golf balls, and in a desert miles from water, at Wajir, with its castellated, Beau Geste fort, was the Royal Wajir Yacht Club and a squash court doubling as the prison. A single-storey mud and cement building with a palm-frond roof, the Royal Wajir Yacht Club had a verandah in the shape of the prow of a ship.

After the Italian invasion of Abyssinia in 1935 the Kenya Government prudently stationed troops at Wajir, though the small town remained under civilian control. At sunset when a bugle sounded all stood still to watch the lowering of the union flag. Vincent Glenday, stationed in the NFD from 1914, was in charge from 1929 to 1939, in his headquarters at Moyale. He had a radio, but depended on small planes for communication, stores or special missions. In these early days of flight, navigation was precariously by sight, and compromised if clouds appeared. Glenday was assisted by the eccentric Scot, Hugh Grant, later to suffer death at the hands of the Maasai, but here in his element among the warriors of the north.[49]

The NFD also played host to H. B. Sharpe, an administrative officer who moved from station to station creating beautiful gardens for himself with prison labour. He was kept out of the way in the north by a nervous government fearful that his homosexuality might lead to indiscretion. When 'Sharpie' was stationed at Garissa he had two lavatories known as 'Haraka' and 'Baraka', after the proverb 'Haraka, haraka, haina baraka' (haste has no blessings). Haraka was near the house, whereas Baraka was further away and open, with a lovely view of the Tana river and a table full of magazines. Sharpie had his own private game park and bird sanctuary where he would stay for days learning the songs of the birds, till he could imitate them astonishingly well.[50]

*　　*　　*

Though farming in Kenya faltered in the 1930s, the country still derived revenue from wealthy hunters and tourists entranced by the beauty and wildness of Africa.

Oh, I love to lie at midnight in the clear and open veld,
And to watch the stars above me in the sky;
That's the time I do my thinking, and at times I've often felt
That's the sort of time and place I'd like to die.
It is good to be out somewhere all alone in Nature's arms,
When one lays one's blanket down and goes to rest;
And I've often thought of all her gifts, of all of Nature's charms,
That the glory of her silence is the best.[51]

Several firms, such as Gethin & Hulett's Tours and Shaw & Hunter, organised safaris, led by white hunters. Ten miles from Nyeri Eric Sherbrooke-Walker and his wife Lady Bettie, founders of the Outspan Hotel, built a wooden house in the branches of a fig tree in a forest glade and called it Treetops. Visitors could spend the night there, watching wild animals coming to drink at the waterhole below. There was a growing recognition that its big game might hold the key to Kenya's future and in order to preserve it, the accountant Mervyn Cowie started campaigning in 1933 for the establishment of national parks. Playing devil's advocate, he wrote a letter to the *East African Standard* under a *nom de plume*, to push the tide of opinion against hunting.[52] The Game Department waged a campaign against poaching – four keepers and a few scouts managed to get convictions of an average of 550 ivory and rhino-horn poachers every year. Most were caught in the hinterland of the coast by C. G. MacArthur, a man who almost single-handedly destroyed the age-old hunting culture of the Wasanya people in the region. The Game Department also started to control animal numbers, and the appropriately named J. A. Hunter was employed to cull lions on the Athi plains.

A famous visitor who did much to popularise Kenya as a tourist destination was Ernest Hemingway. He first arrived in 1933, and employed as his guide the noted hunter Philip Percival. Karen Blixen's former husband Bror Blixen became a friend and was taken fishing in the Bahamas by the writer. Hemingway regarded his shooting very seriously – his weapons were a custom-made Springfield, a 30.06 Mauser, a 6.5 Mannlicher, a twelve-gauge pump shotgun and a Colt Woodman pistol. His two stories 'The Short Happy Life of Francis Macomber', which deals with the defeat of fear when hunting wild animals (first published in *Cosmopolitan* magazine in 1936 and filmed in Kenya as *The Macomber Affair*, 1947); and 'The Snows of Kilimanjaro' (also published in 1936 and filmed in Kenya with the same title in 1952); and his non-fiction *The Green Hills of Africa* (1935), were all most evocative of the time and place and instrumental in enticing other visitors to Kenya.

Tourism was further encouraged by the advent of air travel in the 1930s. The aeroplane had a profound impact on colonial society, now that it took a mere eight days to reach Kenya from Britain. In 1930 an agreement was signed between the British Government and Imperial Airways to operate a passenger service to South Africa via Lake Victoria, which began in 1932. It was a tedious journey, travellers being taken from London (Hendon) to Paris by Handley Page 42, Paris to Brindisi by train, Brindisi to Alexandria via Crete in a Short Kent flying boat, Alexandria to Cairo by train, Cairo to Kisumu via Juba by Calcutta flying boat, and Kisumu to Nairobi in a three-engined Hercules.

In 1935 matters were simplified when Empire flying boats began to fly all the way from Southampton to Kisumu, though with numerous stops. Cumbersome and forced to fly low, the aircraft were slow and bumpy and for many passengers the flight was a misery of travel sickness. Together with the journey's expense (a return ticket cost the huge sum of £196), this meant that there was no decline in the number of ocean liners sailing to Britain and most people still went by sea. Within Kenya, Wilson Airways developed internal routes – in January 1935 it began a service linking Kisumu, Kakamega, Eldoret, Njoro and Nairobi, and many other routes were also flown. By 1939 the Wilson Airways fleet numbered sixteen aircraft before it had to cease operations in September 1940 after the outbreak of war. Society was transformed as mail, medicines, doctors, vets, spare parts, newspapers and books were carried throughout the country on these planes.

By the 1930s there were several hospitals for Africans with white doctors in charge. Some were missionary, but others belonged to the government. The doctors were reliant on Indian sub-assistant surgeons, frequently very skilled and superior to qualified new recruits from Britain in their knowledge of tropical ailments. As for government European hospitals, these existed in Nairobi (30 beds), Mombasa (11 beds), Eldoret (12 beds), and Kisumu (6 beds), while there was also the War Memorial Hospital at Nakuru created by private funds and various other tiny cottage hospitals. The private European nursing homes in Nairobi, the Eskotene and the Maia Carberry, were joined by a third, the Kenya. The Mathari Hospital in Nairobi still took white mental cases. The white doctors working in hospitals for Africans were part of the white community, in which they found their friends, but this was not the case with missionaries.

Missionaries were still despised for their inter-denominational squabbling, regarded by the settlers as narrow-minded, bigoted and unChristian, and for their education of Africans 'beyond their status', which frightened Europeans anxious to maintain their own superiority. The Roman Catholic Consolata fathers and the strongly Protestant Church of Scotland missions in Central Province were particularly antagonistic towards each other. There was a rule that a mission could not have a school within three miles of a rival mission's school, and one DO complained of the amount of time he had to spend pacing out the distance – 'I used to walk miles on my flat feet, seeing the school site and then walking up hill and down dale to the nearest school and seeing if it was three miles away or not.'[53] Only thus could he keep the missions sweet.

Though a few missionaries shared upper-middle-class and public-school backgrounds with settlers and officials, many were nonconformists or fundamentalists of a lower-class or American background who were shunned by other whites. The CMS, however, was more respected and continued to supply priests for the churches built in every town. These small churches, often of wattle and daub, with planks for seats, were built by private subscription and served by chaplains with huge chaplaincies, whose salaries were also met by subscription. With the rise in the price of petrol, parish visiting over the vast distances involved had to be severely curtailed in the depression years of the 1930s, though services were still held in churches, where goats were wont to wander in and chew the straw-filled hassocks. If the chaplain was unavailable couples could be married by the PC or a High Court judge. On one occasion a couple was told to be very punctual as a murder trial was to be held immediately after the wedding. Churches often doubled as law courts.[54]

Even the CMS, though, had its failures. One of their missionaries in the Taita hills was sentenced to death in 1939 for shooting his mother-in-law. Vladimir Verbi, a Hungarian and ex-ship's captain, now a CMS missionary, took to himself a new wife, an Australian younger than two of his sons by his first wife. She was invited to a dance in Voi, and to stay the night with friends. Verbi refused to let her go and locked her in her bedroom. Her mother found her daughter imprisoned, helped her get ready for the dance and sent her off in the car. Verbi returned to the house to find his wife gone, argued with her mother and fired two shots. He maintained to the police that he had been in the garden, his mother-in-law had called out, he turned and both barrels of his gun went off accidentally, shooting her dead.[55] Verbi escaped the hangman when he was acquitted on appeal, but the whole episode did little to endear missionaries to the settlers, though a nurse at Wesu African Hospital in the Taita hills remarked, 'I don't consider it murder as it happened in the Taita hills.'[56]

In Nairobi the Anglican cathedral expanded, and a south tower was added. In 1939 Wright was succeeded by the Revd Norman A. Lesser, a little man, much smaller than his wife and daughter. He came from Fitzwilliam Hall, Cambridge, though he was far from erudite or eloquent, but he got such fun out of difficult situations that his church was packed, with whites of course, for services were still racially segregated.

As the 1930s drew to a close and war was declared the whites of Kenya found themselves in great danger. With Mussolini in Abyssinia to the north, and Kenya too far from the mother country to expect any rapid deployment of reinforcements, it was fighting for its life again within the space of twenty years. And yet this was a defining time, when whites worked to consolidate and maintain what they had built, a time when the ordinary became extraordinary and unusual people thrived. There is no motive so strong as to defend that which one has acquired with great difficulty, and the 1930s had tested Kenya's Europeans to the utmost. Most of them had weathered the difficult years and were never going to surrender their hard-won land to foreign invaders.

9

The Second World War

Paradoxically, the Second World War saw the flowering of white enterprise in Kenya while sowing the seeds of its destruction. Britain's declaration of war against Germany on 3 September 1939 came as no surprise to Kenya, just as it was anticipated in London. For weeks local newspapers had stressed the accelerating danger, making settlers and officials mentally prepared for the conflict. The Kenya Women's Emergency Organisation (KWEO), set up at the time of the Munich crisis a year before under the aegis of Lady Brooke-Popham, the Governor's wife, and designed to allocate tasks to other organisations should war occur, now went into full operation. The KWEO registered 4,000 women for war work.

The East African Women's League set up a day nursery in Nairobi, financed by government and the municipality, to prevent children being left in the unsupervised care of African servants while their mothers were engaged in war work. The women thus freed from childcare were allocated the jobs of men called up on active service. They also provided the additional staff needed by the military authorities. This was despite a curmudgeonly article in the *East African Standard* claiming that there were too many persons of the female sex wanting to do war work: women with young children would be far better employed in looking after them at home than in sending them to hastily organised crèches whose owners might be guilty of profiteering.[1]

The KWEO took a comprehensive census of all the women of the colony, dividing them into five sections: clerical, nursing, canteens, transport and clothing. By 1942 the KWEO had registered 6,500 European women between the ages of sixteen and sixty, of whom 2,300 were engaged in war work outside their own homes.

About 500 of them were enrolled in the Auxiliary Territorial Service (ATS) and served with East African forces. In 1941 650 women were posted as clerks, typists and stenographers in military offices.[2]

As soon as war was declared censorship was imposed on all postal and telegraphic communications, petrol was rationed, maximum prices of food were set and published – to the disgruntlement of members of Nairobi's Chamber of Commerce – and Imperial Airways discontinued the carriage of passengers for the time being. There were dire warnings about trading with the enemy and lorries were requisitioned by the government.

Kenya had a sizeable German population of 700. DCs all over the country were told to round up the Germans in their districts and send them to Nairobi. It fell to the lot of G. B. Rimington, an eccentric DC and expert in training animals, to collect the Germans living near Voi. James Cooper described the scene:

The day that War was declared I was ordered to proceed to Voi, down the line, with Secret Despatches for the District Commissioner . . . The DC was . . . Rimington, known to his friends as 'Bloody Rim' owing to his language and favourite adjective . . . After breakfast he said 'Ever seen a baboon type its bloody name?' . . . Rimington called an orderly who entered leading a baboon on a chain. The baboon climbed on to the stool and with some persuasion typed a few letters but was clearly not concentrating. Finally Rimington said 'I told the Police Inspector to round up all the bloody Huns in the district.' There were a number of sisal estates in the area, German owned and staffed . . . We went outside followed by the baboon. There in front of the office was a child's bicycle. Behind this attached to the back axle by a length of cord was a soapbox on wheels in which sat a smooth fox terrier. Behind this, also attached by a length of cord was a smaller box on which sat a tabby cat. The baboon climbed on to the tricycle and we proceeded down the drive, the DC and I, dressed in a khaki bush shirt and those over-wide shorts then fashionable through which my thin legs protruded to end in blue puttees and boots with on my head one of those umbrella-like Wolseley helmets. It must have been a strange sight this procession of DC and Cooper followed by a baboon and his train with the orderly bringing up the rear as we went to inspect the first fruits of war . . . He left me visiting the Germans 'as he had better bloody things to do'. The Germans were held in the station restaurant or dak bungalow where they were enjoying beer in plenty. It was a convivial party that I interrupted and they welcomed me in. I wasn't sure that I ought to be drinking beer with Rimington's 'Bloody Huns' but they were most pressing – and promised they would put in a good word for me when the Third Reich took over in Kenya which would be only a matter of a week or two.[3]

The Germans were taken to the Vermont Memorial Hall and St Andrew's church hall in Nairobi. On the first night some of them had to sleep on the hard floor because there were too few camp beds. The Germans themselves insisted that the Jews and Nazis among them dined at separate tables. No German property was confiscated and German farms were taken over by British group managers who continued to husband them well. It cannot have been easy for British settlers to see German friends and neighbours imprisoned because of their nationality.

The women and children were not interned, instead being allowed to stay in their homes and visit their menfolk. However, those who lived on farms were forbidden to stay there without their spouses, possibly for their own protection. Only those German women who had expressed hostility to Britain or might endanger security were placed in a camp at Mau Summit run by the First Aid Nursing Yeomanry (FANYs) under Lady Sidney Farrar.

The men in the two Nairobi halls were soon moved to the Nairobi suburb of Parklands, to the Gloucester Hotel, requisitioned for the purpose by the government. A few days later some of them were freed – particularly long-term residents of Kenya sponsored by two British subjects. The Czechs were also released, as were

German Jews and those who had fled persecution in Germany. Eventually all those who remained in custody were moved to the reformatory at Kabete, specially adapted to house them for the duration of the war.

Meanwhile all able-bodied British white men between the ages of eighteen and thirty-five were called up. They joined the Kenya Regiment, a successor to the Kenya Defence Force. Membership of the latter had been compulsory for all white men between the ages of eighteen and thirty since its formation in 1928 as a territorial force whose main purpose was to help with the evacuation of white women and children in the event of an African uprising or rioting. Given khaki uniforms, .303 rifles and five rounds of ammunition (to be kept at home), the KDF had trained in the Eldoret district at weekends for 100 hours a year. It withered away after the founding on 1 June 1937 of the Kenya Regiment, because the Colonial Office suspected it might be used to support a new Vigilance Committee set up in 1935 under the chairmanship of Lord Francis Scott to safeguard settlers' interests and counter the unpopular Governor Sir Joseph Byrne. However, once war broke out, it revived as a 'Dad's Army'.

The Kenya Regiment, a far more efficient force, held annual camps in the Ngong hills. The new regiment was intended to provide a reservoir of trained junior leaders to cope with the increase in numbers of the African soldiers of the King's African Rifles in the event of war. When war was declared the Kenya Regiment expanded so rapidly that a new training camp had to be established at Kampala in Uganda – to the horror of mothers foreseeing their sons laid low by malaria[4] – and an Officers' Training School was built at Nakuru. The recruits at Nakuru were joined by the King's African Rifles' reserve of officers from Nyasaland and Tanganyika. By 1942, of the total available Kenyan white man-power of 8,998, 3,039 were serving in the forces. Of the remainder, 3,041 were in essential occupations, 1,092 had been discharged from the forces or were unfit and the rest were exempted because of age or other reasons. Kenya's white population was estimated as 22,808 in 1939, hardly sufficient to defend the country.[5]

The first months of the war were a time of uncertainty for Kenya's whites. Their main military threat came from Italian-held Abyssinia in the north and Italian Somaliland in the east and north east. Altogether the Italians had 250,000 troops stationed there, in comparison with East Africa's 8,500. The East African forces became part of Middle East Command and devoted themselves to watching Kenya's borders. They used four main routes to the north: Thika to Garissa on the Tana river, Isiolo to Habaswein and Wajir, Nanyuki to Archer's Post and Marsabit, and Kitale to Lodwar and the north-west end of Lake Rudolf. Troops of the King's African Rifles defended the northern positions at Moyale, Marsabit and Wajir in case the Italians invaded. Then Italy entered the war on Hitler's side on 10 June 1940 and the position became far more serious. Italians living in Kenya were immediately interned, though Furio, the charming Italian mechanic at Kitale Motors employed to construct on the roof of the hotel the first and only air-raid siren in Trans-Nzoia, and the only person who knew how to operate it, was allowed free under special guard.[6] On 1 July the Italians began to advance. It took them two weeks to occupy Moyale and force the evacuation of the British from the town, and then they halted, daunted by the prospect of having to cross the waterless desert southwards. They also occupied British Somaliland.

The railway workshops in Nairobi, the sole heavy engineering plant in the country, became the ordnance workshops of the East Africa Command. In the last six months of 1940 they designed and built bodies for twenty-two ambulances (250 were eventually built), manufactured seventy-two three-inch mortars, 25,000 screw pickets for barbed-wire, 600 four-gallon water tanks and supports for anti-tank guns, and created the armour for twenty-nine trucks of the East African Reconnaissance Squadron vehicles. They also made 30,500 anti-tank mines and hundreds of other tools, bombs, petrol tanks and guns.[7] They reconditioned all the railway engines which had been scrapped and were awaiting demolition, and kept them and the railways running throughout the war. It was an astonishing achievement.

The British Government knew that Kenya would have to be given help to defend itself. Six shiploads of reinforcements arrived in Kenya from Nigeria and the Gold Coast in West Africa, and South Africa also promised to send troops. The West Africans numbered 10,000 men, nearly 730 of them white and the rest Africans. The 10,000 South African soldiers, all of them white, began to arrive from mid-1940 in battalions with names such as Natal Carbineers, Transvaal Scottish and Cape Town Irish. They were billeted in tents in Nairobi's City Park where Anne Francis ran a canteen to feed them. The South Africans also provided a squadron of Spitfires, which soon put an end to the nightly Italian air raids on KAR soldiers stationed along Kenya's northern border. By the close of 1940 Kenya's forces numbered 75,000, of whom 25,000 were South African. Sir Alan Cunningham, the Commander of the East African forces, began his attack on the Italians in January 1941 with the battle of El Wak, a frontier station beyond Wajir. His forces advanced rapidly into Italian Somaliland and were able to capture the coastal town of Kismayu and a vast quantity of army stores. By the end of February Italian Somaliland was taken and the army turned inland into Abyssinia and occupied Jigjiga. British Somaliland was recaptured from the Italians by a force from Aden. After the success at Jigjiga the Marda Pass was captured and Harar occupied.

The South African troops took the lead, entering Diredawa and pushing the Italians westwards along the roads to Miesso and Asba Littorio. Then Addis Ababa fell to the KAR on 6 April and the retreating Italians were pursued along the road to Eritrea. Dessie was captured and the Italians' leader, the Duke of Aosta, taken prisoner at Amba Alagi in late May. He was removed to Kenya to be held in Lady McMillan's house at Ol Donyo Sabuk, where he died after contracting malaria. His illness was aggravated by an old tuberculosis of the lung. It was an embarrassing loss. After the fall of Addis Ababa a large body of Italian troops separated from those fleeing northwards and withdrew to the lakes region to the south and south west of the city. A series of battles led to their defeat. The Italian remnants crossed the Omo river to join General Gazzera's

forces near Jimma. Nigerians and the KAR chased Gazzera westwards until he was forced to surrender to the Belgians, and the
British victory over Abyssinia was complete. Kenya's whites could
breathe a temporary sigh of relief.

One of the most heroic individual actions of the war in Abyssinia
was that of Sergeant Nigel Leakey, son of Louis Leakey's cousin
Gray Leakey. He won the Victoria Cross for attacking on foot and
routing the Italian tank force at the battle of Colito. The story is
best told in the words of an eye-witness:

> The first thing I remember was Leakey shouting to his men,
> 'Come on! I can hear some lorries trying to get away. Let's stop
> them.' He was just going forward with three or four men. I
> thought they sounded most unlike lorries – more like tractors,
> and I said, 'Hell, look out! I think it's a tank.' Just about that
> time we heard several start up. They were in front of us in the
> thick bush. Then the noise stopped and for a bit we couldn't
> hear a thing. And Leakey was just going forward in front of my
> men when we heard a noise behind us. This time it was
> obviously a tank, and we could hear the noise coming nearer to
> us. Suddenly we saw it, about fifty yards away from us, not
> going very fast – keeping to the thick bush. Eventually it
> stopped behind the bush and Leakey did a sort of stalk as if he
> were stalking a buck or something, only it was a pretty quick
> one . . . He crawled right through the middle of the bush, up
> underneath the tank, and then leaped on to the front of it. I can
> remember seeing, as he leaped up, the chap pulled down the
> vizor in front. The tank went mad. It came out into the open,
> then on to the road, and went off like blazes, firing all that it had
> got. It had a cannon and two machine-guns on it, with an all-
> round traverse in the turret. Leakey was straddling the
> machine-gun, one leg on either side, and there he was, quite
> happy on top of the tank, struggling with the lid of the turret.
> After the tank had gone, I suppose, a hundred yards, I saw the lid
> of the turret come up. I then saw Leakey poke his revolver inside
> and fire four or five shots rapid [*sic*]. The tank immediately

stopped. Then Leakey jumped off and opened the side door of the tank, and pulled out two dead bodies. One was the Colonel commanding this lot of tanks. Inside the driver's seat was a miserable specimen, who hadn't been shot, so Leakey jumped in beside him, poked a revolver in his face, and made him drive the tank on to the side of the road. He then hauled the driver out, put an askari to guard him, and then he said, 'By God, we'll get the others – with this tank we've got 'em absolutely cold. We'll get the cannon to work.' And he struggled with the cannon for, I should think, three or four minutes, but couldn't find out how to get it to work. It was no good asking the driver. He was so frightened that he was hardly a human being. So Leakey said 'Oh well, I'll get 'em on foot,' and off he went with two askaris. I never saw him again.[8]

Leakey set out to catch the remaining Italian tanks, and these were last seen retreating, with Leakey climbing on to the back of one of them. He never returned and his body was never found, but the enemy tanks took no further part in the battle of Colito.

All this military activity meant that there were constant troop movements northwards through Kenya. The towns of Thika, Nyeri, Nanyuki and Isiolo lay on the road northwards. A military railway line was planned between Thika and Garissa, but only a few miles of track were laid, such were the difficulties of the terrain. Rather it was decided to improve the roads. Certainly a beneficial side-effect of the war was the tarring of some roads, such as a stretch north of Nanyuki, by troops tired of having their vehicles alternately bogged down or shaken to pieces by corrugations. The South African troops brought with them road construction companies made up of civilian road engineers and in a few months the roads to Wajir and Marsabit were the best in the country. The troops also bored for water all over the Northern Frontier District.

Army lorries returning empty from Abyssinia were used to transport china clay from deposits to the north east of Thika to a new pottery factory in Nairobi. The clay was also put to good military use as blanco for whitening. The NFD began to take on the aspect of an abandoned military camp. Army lorries pounded down the last 100 miles of dry earth road to Garissa, with its twelve-inch-deep corrugations three feet from crest to crest. Lorries had to maintain a steady sixty miles an hour over the corrugations, as they passed the remains of huge camps everywhere, with thousands of empty forty-gallon oil drums, and broken lorries, cars and refrigerators. One raw recruit, new to Africa, described the conditions:

> The fabulous N.F.D.! . . . it was one of the hottest places on earth . . . the traders had all left [Wajir], and the shops and little houses were all occupied by our troops. Around the perimeter was barbed wire, and among the wire were land mines. Wild watermelons grew under the wire, because there animals could not get at them. An askari was blown up as he plucked watermelons one day but it did not prevent the others from plucking more. It was ferociously hot, and for the whole of the three months that we were there we were thirsty. We never stopped being thirsty. There was not enough water in the wells for over a thousand troops and we were parsimoniously rationed. And the water was *brak*, as the South Africans say: bitter and salt. One could hardly drink it. We all suffered from an unpleasant condition of the bladder because of it.[9]

Maribou storks perched on top of the Wajir wells, gazing adoringly at their reflections. The only way to make the well-water palatable was to add lime juice to it.

After the fall of Abyssinia the South African troops went to fight in northern Africa against the Germans, but Kenya's military personnel did not diminish in number. The Vichy French had to be ousted from Madagascar, an island lying in a strategic position in the Indian Ocean. Diego Suarez, its harbour, was taken in May 1941 with the assistance of an East African brigade, and in September the rest of the island was taken.

After the entry of Japan into the war in 1942, troops were sent across the Indian Ocean to assist in fighting the Japanese in Burma.

One shipload met with tragedy. The 11th East African Divisional Artillery, 1,000 strong and accompanied by WRNS, members of the Women's Territorial Service and fifty-four nurses, were to be acclimatised in Ceylon before service in Burma. They embarked at Mombasa in the 7,513-ton *Khedive Ismail*, a BI merchant vessel. On 12 February 1944 a Japanese submarine torpedoed the ship off the Maldive islands and it sank in under two minutes. Of the 1,511 on board only 214 were rescued, making this the third-largest merchant sea tragedy of the Second World War.[10]

Another wartime tragedy was the loss of a South African Air Force flying boat and its thirty-five passengers on Lake Victoria. The person responsible forgot to remove from the wing flaps the wedges inserted to stop wind damaging the plane during the night. When the pilot tried to take off the plane dived into the water. A luckless DC, K. L. Hunter, had to take the funeral service as no padre was available.[11]

Kenya's second largest town, Mombasa, was regarded as under threat of attack from sea and air alike. The KWEO drew up plans to evacuate its women and children to safer zones in the highlands – altogether 833 upcountry homes were offered and arrangements made for the reception of evacuees. As it turned out, these plans were put into effect only to a limited extent at the outbreak of war, and the people evacuated soon returned to their homes.[12]

Mombasa took on the aspect of a fortress, with no one allowed to enter or leave without a permit. Blackout regulations were imposed. The Kenya Defence Force recruited those too old for active service, and men happiest at the nineteenth hole were now to be seen jogging round the seafront golf course, doing their training. The island became overcrowded with troops in transit camps, and to ease the situation the Fleet Air Arm established itself a little way inland, at Mackinnon Road. Most local whites also took military personnel to live in their own homes: 'We had a couple – she a Wren – who were very newly married and very much in love. When in the house they played two or three records endlessly on their gramophone of which "My devotion is endlessly deep as the ocean" nearly drove my mother mad.'[13]

The forces personnel were fed in canteens operated by local women – a popular job because it precluded evacuation. In 1942, when Japan entered the war, the town became more vulnerable, so coast guards and patrols were stationed up and down the coast, and receiving stations for victims of air raids (which never materialised) were built. People built air-raid shelters in their own gardens.

In May 1942 Mombasa became the naval base for the Eastern Fleet after the fall of Hong Kong and Singapore, and its harbour was crammed with battleships, cruisers and destroyers. At one time 200 war, auxiliary and merchant vessels were using the port and seven admirals were based there. The newly created 'K Boat Service' plied a busy trade transporting men and goods from ship to shore. Three more deep-water berths were opened in 1944 and the auxiliary anchorage at Port Reitz was also put to full use. A naval dockyard was built at Kilindini, while a large number of camps and naval buildings were erected on the island. Boom ships guarded booms stretched across the harbour mouth, and steel submarine fences were positioned to deter the stealthy approach of any hostile vessels.

Because the naval personnel increased Mombasa's population by 25,000, there were temporary food shortages. All boarding and guest houses were requisitioned with scant ceremony and temporary quarters were erected at great speed. The Fleet Club opened for ratings, the Officers' Club for officers, a Garrison Theatre was set up, and Government House became the officers' mess. Concerts were organised by local ladies at the Convent, to raise money for comforts. The military were not always on their best behaviour. After an obviously over-indulgent Christmas, on Boxing Day 1943 John Llewellin Phillips murdered Reginald C. Bradley at Liwatoni barracks on the island. Found guilty but insane, Phillips was sent home to Broadmoor where he killed another patient and then committed suicide.

Nairobi, too, grew in size during the war. The town was presided over by Gwladys ('Glady'), Lady Delamere, Lord Delamere's widow, now re-elected as its mayor. She flung herself into war work with great energy, while also enjoying evenings in the Muthaiga Club. This proved too much for her health – a first stroke left her partially paralysed and a second led to her death on 22 February 1943. So untiring and selfless had been her war work that her cortège was followed by scores of private cars to her place of burial.

Its population swelled with troops, Nairobi opened new night-clubs, such as the Equator off Hardinge Street, the Kudu and the 400, and beauty salons had a spate of prosperity. The newspapers' domestic columns were filled with announcements of wartime engagements and marriages. White soldiers patronised the British Legion canteen in Hardinge Street, run by Glady Delamere and Maud Fair, assisted by the tall, erect Lady Muriel Jex-Blake, a noted plantswoman. The canteen also provided cubicles where soldiers on a night's leave could sleep. Across the road officers dined in the Officers' Club. A huge NAAFI canteen opened in Government Road. Restaurants such as Chez Gaby on Government Road prospered, and the Mascot made Hoppy Marshall a rich man. He took piles of money home in a pillow case, to add to that he made from a match factory and the construction of camouflage nets. The war gave Nairobi a buzz it lacked at other times, and there was a surprising lack of tension between local whites and expatriate white troops.

With the influx of expatriate troops, the question of sexual relationships became important. The troops had regular lectures on the use of the 'Dreadnought', not the fearsome weapon of war suggested by its name, but a contraceptive whose use was advocated strongly – penalties were severe for those who concealed sexually transmitted diseases. Canary ward was a special ward for officers with VD in Mogadishu Hospital, during the British occupation of Italian Somaliland. It was common for officers to have Somali mistresses, a practice quite acceptable if handled with discretion.[14]

Early in the war, in fear of attack from the Italians to the north, Nairobi imposed a blackout on its residents, some of whom pru-dently constructed air-raid shelters, and ARP (air-raid precautions) wardens were appointed. Sirens were placed strategically, the largest being on top of Torr's Hotel. Despite the absence of any air raids the alarm would periodically go off, sending people to the air-raid shelter in the basement of the Standard Bank, and on one occasion into the hole being dug for the erection of a statue of Lord Delamere outside the New Stanley Hotel. The Long Bar in the New Stanley Hotel was the favourite haunt of local whites, whereas soldiers preferred Torr's, where 'Auntie' Turner, an old lady in a long dress, greeted them as they entered. After troops misbehaved and threw things down on to the dancers, they were banned from going into its gallery overlooking the dance floor, where Micky Migdoll's band 'The Serenaders' played (except on Sunday and Monday nights). Next door to Torr's was the Theatre Royal where Mervyn Cowie's wife helped to put on entertainments. Other recreation was offered by the three cinemas – with E. A. Vasey, later a prominent politician, as the manager/doorman of one of them, the Empire.[15]

Nairobi was in a quandary about what to do with its children at the beginning of the war. When Mussolini entered the war in June 1940, all schools were temporarily shut while sandbags were issued, barricades built and trenches dug. Then the boarders of the Kenya High School (the girls' secondary school in Nairobi) were sent to Eldoret, to be housed in the Eldoret Hotel, and the boarders of Nairobi Primary School and the Prince of Wales School also went upcountry. Day pupils of the two secondary schools were taught upstairs in the Nairobi Primary School, whose own day pupils were confined to the ground floor. There were air-raid drills for all pupils. WAAFs moved into the boarding blocks. After the defeat of the Italians in Somaliland and Abyssinia, the boarders of all three schools were brought back to Nairobi in 1942. In the evenings the girl boarders busied themselves with knitting long white 'operation stockings' for wounded soldiers undergoing surgery. Limuru Girls' School continued through the war years, though with a depleted staff. Daphne Moore, the Governor's wife, was unhappy with its teaching and removed her daughter to the Kenya High School. She said her daughter was bored at Limuru: 'There is no one of her own kind there, and the nicer girls (I mean as regards breeding) seem to be the least intelligent.'[16]

On the outbreak of war Governor Brooke-Popham, an ex-RAF man, thought his talents would be better employed in the Royal Air Force at home and resigned his post. Walter Harragin, Attorney-General and lately Acting Colonial Secretary, took over as Acting Governor. It was a popular appointment, for his tall, dark and humorous wife Marjorie was well liked and his beautiful daughters graced Torr's Hotel, still the hub of Nairobi social life. Both Mr and Mrs Harragin were present at a tragedy which overtook Nairobi on 12 September 1939: the burning of the Secretariat next to their home on Nairobi Hill. The Secretariat was housed in an old wood and iron building, the original Nairobi Club and later a hostel for women employees of the Post Office before being taken over for its present purpose. The building contained all the historical and current files of the country's government, and their conflagration was a tragedy and an immense historical loss. The alarm was raised by the nightwatchman at 1.15 a.m. when he knocked on the Harragins' window to alert them to the blaze. The fire brigade arrived in quarter of an hour, but the water pressure from the two-and-a-half-inch pipes was insufficient to quell the blaze. Fire appliances required four-inch pipes to get sufficient pressure to fight even a normal fire, and this one was abnormal because it was fanned by a strong early-morning wind.

The whole episode was deeply suspicious, occurring as it did just after the outbreak of war. Were there files in the Secretariat which someone wanted destroyed? An inquiry was held and blame was laid on an electric kettle found blackened and burnt out in the wreckage. It had been plugged into a lampholder, against regulations, and placed on a wooden stationery cupboard on top of a piece of cloth. It had no automatic cut-out mechanism. The supposition was that it had been inadvertently left on or switched on in error, but the truth may never be known. The Secretariat set itself up in the Law Courts and appealed to other departments to send it duplicate correspondence. A wag took up his pen:

The purifying flame of War.
How true these words have proved once more!
It's really quite amazing:
That ancient pile of iron and wood,
Which belched forth circulars that could
At times almost be understood,
Has ended up in blazing.
And those who there for years have slept,
Wrote 'passed to you' and 'file' and wept
And talked and waited, while they kept
An eye on decorations,
Are now turned out into the cold . . . [17]

One of the puzzling aspects of the Secretariat fire was that it began in the office of the Earl of Erroll, then deputy director of manpower. In January 1942 he was murdered, an event which reinforced the home country's jaundiced view of Kenya's whites – that they were a bunch of hedonistic wastrels. It was a myth which had become most durable. The affair received greater coverage in the *East African Standard* than the progress of the war. Erroll, seducer of other men's wives and caresser of secretaries' bottoms, would hang out in the foyer of Theo Schouten's hair-dressing salon, chatting up the clients, who preferred that establishment to Osa's, Nairobi's other hairdresser, with its smell of rotten eggs. Erroll's body was found early in the morning of 24 January slumped in the front of a car on the Ngong Road outside Nairobi, not far from the house of Sir Henry ('Jock') and Diana Delves Broughton. Joss Erroll and Diana had been having an open affair, despite the fact that the Delves Broughtons had been married only two months. Erroll was shot in the head, probably while driving the car, and his body had been pulled away from the driving seat so that the vehicle could be driven to where it was found by two early-morning milkmen. Jock Delves Broughton was arrested for murder, but the trial jury acquitted him – as everyone said at the time, no jury would condemn a man who might have killed the man who might have seduced its own members' wives. A broken man, Delves Broughton then went home to England and committed suicide with an overdose of morphine.[18]

There have been many theories about who murdered Joss Erroll, a mystery almost as widely discussed today as it was at the time. Many think Diana shot her lover in a rage; others consider Delves Broughton ordered his African chauffeur, who disappeared, to do the killing. It may be that the police were right to arrest Delves Broughton, if the memory of a police officer on the scene is to be believed:

> When I arrived at Broughton's home I was told that he had left for a safari in Laikipia. I called for the night watch, who was initially very hesitant and obviously afraid of losing his job, but after a general chat about his family tribe and his job, all in Kiswahili, I gained his confidence and after explaining his rights to him, he told me what he said was a strange experience during the night and early morning. He said Sir Delves had arrived back at his home that night with a certain lady whose name he did not know [in fact June Carberry, with whom he had dined at the Muthaiga Club] and after parking his car they went into the house and a light came on in a room on the second floor. Shortly afterwards the light was extinguished. Later another car arrived from which a *bwana makuba* [sic, in fact Joss Erroll] (very important man) and Sir Delves Broughton's wife arrived and another light went on . . . Shortly after the second couple arrived Sir Delves came out of the house and entered the *bwana makuba*'s car by the left rear door and lay down behind the front seat so that his silhouette disappeared. Some time later the *bwana makuba* came out, entered his car and drove off at very high speed, something Erroll was well known for, often having been stopped at police speed traps.[19]

Unfortunately the nightwatchman later retracted this statement and was not called as a witness at the trial. The truth may never be known, though a recent account claims that Broughton's murder weapon was concealed by June Carberry in Malindi for years before being thrown into the sea.[20] In 1942 the matter was a talking point for months in Nairobi, as an escape from the weary topic of the progress of the war. Servicemen on leave packed the trial, attended by Diana in a new outfit every day. Diana later married the Kenya landowner Gilbert Colvile, and then left him to marry Lord (Hugh) Delamere's son Tom, who had inherited his father's title.

However, the Happy Valley group were not typical of the Kenyan settlers, who worked hard in the war. As well as acting as co-ordinating centre for the Women's Branch of the British Legion, the East Africa Women's League, the Red Cross and St John Ambulance, the KWEO ran the War Workers' Hostel for FANYs in Nairobi, started a military library which collected 336 books in the last week of September 1939 alone, and inaugurated an Entertainments Section to put on drama, music and concert parties for troops. New singers and performers were always welcome. In the six years of its work the military library despatched 400,000 books from its headquarters in the McMillan Memorial Library.[21] Women working for the Red Cross made war dressings and turned their attention to providing comforts for the troops. All women were exhorted to knit socks and pullovers, to make shirts and other clothing, and all this was done without any subsidy. The *East African Standard* provided premises for the Comforts Depot.

Throughout the five and a half years of its existence the KWEO spent over £70,000 (at least £2 million at 2004 values) on comforts for the troops, the entire amount being raised from voluntary subscriptions. Among the items supplied were 101,000 glory bags, containing 22.5 million cigarettes, 15 tons of African snuff, 45 tons of sweets, 258 tons of sugar, 12 tons of Christmas puddings and cakes, 20 tons of coffee, 5 tons of tea, 12 and a half tons of marmalade, 150,000 writing pads, 90,000 woollen garments, as well as many thousands of toothbrushes, cakes of soap, razor blades and books. Most fortunately, recently established factories in Nakuru could supply locally made boots and blankets. Hospitality for the troops was not forgotten, and the KWEO set up a section to organise this. Leave for 34,000 white troops was arranged on private farms in the war – some soldiers returned to the same place over and over again. Thus everyone tried to do his or her bit for the war effort.

During September 1939 farmers awaited advice from the government about a wartime policy for agriculture. Britain then decided that it most needed butter, cereals, oilseed, flax, sugar, tea and sisal. A Settlement and Production Board recommended the establishment of a combined Training Farm and Secondary Farm School. Lord Egerton of Tatton made a generous gift of 500 acres of land for this at Njoro, and Egerton Farm School was born. It is now a university. Of immense practical value, special, short-term loans were made available to farmers for the cost of planting and cultivating crops, the purchase of fertilisers and the expansion of animal husbandry.[22] These were much needed, for locusts were again about, spreading from the north into Central Province as far as Nairobi. A dried vegetable factory was established at Kerugoya and it soon dealt with 20 tons of fresh vegetables daily.

Farmers left their farms in the hands of their wives or of group managers: older men and women appointed to care for a group of farms as well as their own. There were only 1,020 male white farmers left, while 800 women were now employed as owner-farmers, assistants or agents acting on behalf of menfolk serving in the forces.[23] About 40 per cent of the farms were left, and it is to the eternal credit of the wives that production doubled during the war. Cut off from neighbours by distance and petrol rationing, with husbands serving in the forces and sons joining up as soon as they left school, these women defied loneliness and anxiety and got on with the job. One of them described the lot of the farmer's wife at the end of the war:

My daily garb is a tattered pair of trousers and an array of oil-spattered shirts and sweaters, while my hands have to be seen to be believed. When I do dress up in my finery to go out, the earth roads are usually streams of dust or miles of slush and we get stuck in the car. After pushing our way through the mire, being sprayed with chocolate-coloured mud, my only wish is to be back in my comfortable farm clothes . . . I shall never forget the faces of some friends who arrived for a drink one Sunday night . . . to find me sitting in an engrossed fashion stitching up the tractor driver's leg with black thread and a darning needle . . . I have had to forgo all thought of a gleaming, spotless, farmhouse kitchen, mainly because it has been and always will be regarded as the Africans' club-house . . . Very important in our lives is the theatre which local farmers and their wives built themselves and on which we now depend for most of our entertainment.[24]

Nevertheless, the white farmers prospered during the war. When it began, their average indebtedness was £2,000 and the area they occupied was shrinking. During the war the whites recovered quickly. To obtain a constant supply of foodstuffs and other material for the forces flooding in from South Africa, in October 1940 the Kenya Government issued compulsory powers over production and labour. A year later the Kenya economy was placed on a war footing. Prices for European-grown maize were guaranteed, and grants were made for clearing land and planting maize, flax, wheat and rye. Settler farmers ran local production sub-committees and those who did not comply with their directives risked fines or imprisonment. The Department of Agriculture asked Nellie Grant, Elspeth Huxley's mother, to run a training centre on her farm in the Rift Valley Province, to teach Africans spinning and weaving. She obtained Italian prisoners of war to help her, acquiring a carpenter, a clerk, a man to run the irrigation, two brickmakers and two builders. They constructed a kiln and made bricks and roof and floor tiles for the new buildings, while Nellie went off to train African women in Nakuru prison.[25]

Between 1941 and 1943 there was a doubling in value of military purchases of maize, meat, vegetables and dairy products – from £750,000 to £1.5 million.[26] Maize had been sold for five shillings a bag in the 1930s; now it was fetching thirteen. Italian prisoners of war formed ploughing teams which moved around Kenya to break new land. Italians also operated combine harvesters supplied by the Americans. The government conscripted African labour to work on farms, an enormous help to farmers, and the Royal Navy was despatched to fetch bird droppings from the Seychelles as fertiliser. For the first time white farmers began to make substantial profits and became economically secure. The Afrikaner farmers shared in the prosperity and there is no further mention of a 'poor white' problem in Kenya. These were good times.

Food also had to be provided for the huge numbers of Italian prisoners of war (54,684 in 1944, which vastly outnumbered Kenya's white population)[27] and Polish refugees, as well as the troops in training for Burma once the Abyssinian campaign was over. In 1942 Kenya's white population experienced a rapid increase when 10,000 Poles were accepted from India and Palestine, whither they had fled from Hitler's troops, and 60,000 Italians from Somalia and Abyssinia were taken prisoner and sent to POW camps at Nanyuki, Nyeri, Naivasha, Gilgil, Londiani and other places. The two largest Italian camps were at Nanyuki and at Nyeri station, ten miles from Nyeri.

Trusted Italian prisoners were set free to work on farms. Those sent to help the Klaprotts at Kipkabus took over the milk round and made beautiful inlaid furniture.[28] The Italians quarried stone, erected farm buildings, did plumbing and electrical installation and impressed everyone with their skill as master craftsmen. They also tarmacked the road between Nairobi and Naivasha, over and down the Rift Valley escarpment. Near its foot they built a tiny chapel of thanksgiving, tucked into the side of the cliff and overlooking the site of the Kedong massacre nearly fifty years before. Indeed the Italians had a vast range of talents. A fine Italian orchestra gave concerts in Nairobi, and there were superb arts and crafts exhibitions. They also assisted with the archaeological investigations of Louis and Mary Leakey at Olorgesailie, on the floor of the Rift Valley.[29] The Italians were well liked by the settlers, despite difficulties of communication because so few spoke English.

Of the Poles who had escaped eastwards before Hitler's onslaught, 18,000, most of them women and very few of whom spoke English, found themselves allocated to camps in Africa in 1942. They arrived in Mombasa where Gwen Kempton, of the K Boat Service, had collected and dressed dolls and toys of all sorts for distribution to the children. Nairobi was their administrative headquarters (the officials all lived in the Gloucester Hotel in Parklands), and they were dispersed from a camp at Makindu to other camps in Kenya, Uganda (Masindi), Tanganyika and Rhodesia. Each Kenyan camp had a British commander, a kindergarten and a school. Orphaned children were looked after at a camp at Rongai, where a Polish school was opened. Lessons in Polish, given by professional teachers from among the refugees, and syllabuses and Polish books were sent out from the Polish government-in-exile in London. The Poles had their personal weekly newspaper, edited in Nairobi, and radio programmes of their own, broadcast from the Cable & Wireless studios at Kabete. The commentators got their news from listening to French radio broadcasts from the Belgian Congo and from tapes sent from London. At the end of the war several Poles stayed on in Kenya rather than return to a Communist state – 'Everyone expected to go back. It was such a shock to realise we couldn't go back.'[30] Many of them joined the firm of Dalgety.

In the war Nyeri and Nanyuki became important, prosperous, bustling towns, because they were en route to Abyssinia and later became centres for prisoners of war. The Silverbeck and Sportsman's Arms hotels at Nanyuki flourished under the patronage of white troops, the latter attended by officers and the Silverbeck by rankers. At the Silverbeck the South Africans' favourite song concerned a girl called Solly Marais down in the mealie fields.[31] Lord Baden-Powell, founder of the Boy Scouts, chose Nyeri as his home. He and his wife Olave, leader of the Girl Guides, lived in a chalet-bungalow in the grounds of the Outspan Hotel, with its magnificent grounds looking towards Mt Kenya thirty miles away. Upon Baden-Powell's death in January 1941, a grand funeral was arranged in the tiny, beautiful Nyeri cemetery. Detachments from all three services and top brass attended the long cortège marching slowly down the avenue of huge gum trees from the Outspan, while the band played Handel's funeral march. Thereafter local Cubs and Brownies were appointed to weed the grave at weekends, a pastime far from arduous and usually spent looking for four-leaved clover rather than performing the required task. On the headstone were Baden-Powell's name and the words 'Chief Scout of the World', together with the Scout and Guide badges and the tracking sign which to Scouts and Guides means 'I have gone home'.

Nyeri was not an easy administrative posting, having as it did such eccentric residents as John Boyes, self-styled king of the Kikuyu (no Kikuyu ever accepted his claim that members of their tribe had made him king) who was at perpetual war with his aggressive neighbour Paul Clarke, through whose land Boyes unfortunately had to pass to get to his farm; and John Carberry, the deeply unpleasant farmer imprisoned in Fort Jesus for flouting wartime currency regulations, and his wife June, one of the jet set liable to be found lying naked on her bed with her lover by her side.[32] It is unsurprising that when A. C. M. ('Mug') Mullins, the PC, retired from his Nyeri posting a number of missing files, presumably those concerning intractable problems, were found hidden in his office lavatory.[33]

When war broke out white politics in Kenya were momentarily suspended and settler political opposition to the Governor and Colonial Office died away. In January 1940 the new Governor and his wife arrived: Sir Henry Moore and his wife Daphne. Moore was no stranger to Kenya, having been its Colonial Secretary from 1929 to 1934. His predecessor Brooke-Popham wrote him a letter of advice, stressing that the real object of white settlement was not merely the material development of the country, but the creation of a nucleus where British ideals and traditions could be preserved and whence they would spread. Kenya should look north to England for guidance and not south to the Afrikaans-speaking community, while the British element must be paramount in the Highlands and not swamped by other European nations or the Jews.[34] The witty and rather wicked Daphne Moore (her private comments on others were always funny but rather cruel – she said the wife of Sidney Fazan, PC at Kisumu, always reminded her of a wicker wastepaper basket which had not been emptied)[35] threw herself with verve into overseeing all women's organisations, though she was sorely tried by infighting and the actions of Mrs

A. Turner. She also tried to curb in Government House the 'blatant extravagances' introduced by the Brooke-Pophams.[36]

The Legislative Council temporarily ceased to meet and white political leaders co-operated to exert influence on the wartime government through the Executive Council, on which settlers gained increased representation. Numerous committees and boards were established to control the economic life of the country, and correspondence flew to and fro on bright pink paper captured in reams from the Italians.[37] But this consensus did not last long and dissentient whites soon made their voices heard. One of them was Olga Watkins, who assumed Lord Erroll's place in the reconvened Legislative Council after his murder. She and F. J. Couldrey, editor of the *Kenya Weekly News*, and S. V. Cooke, the member for the coast, saw that Africans could not be excluded from politics for ever and urged their membership of the Legislative Council. Some of the more enlightened settlers now made efforts to understand Africans. Elspeth Huxley's mother Nellie Grant suggested that the Njoro Settlers' Association ask an educated African to speak there:

> I pointed out that really we had better know a bit more about the African than we did and the best way was to meet a real one. The time of the meeting led to much talk – it couldn't be in the Club House as usual because it wouldn't do for the educated African to see European ladies in the Bar (really 'cos J. Beeston etc thought they might get landed in the position of having to offer a bloody nigger a drink). I longed to ask why an educated African couldn't see this as a long succession of uneducated African bar boys had survived the spectacle.[38]

In October 1944 the first African became a nominated member of the Council – E. W. Mathu, a Kikuyu and former student of Balliol College, Oxford. Africans and Indians now united in opposition to European political hegemony and economic dominance, though it would take another eight years for rebellion to break out openly.

It took time for the Governor to see what was happening. Towards the end of the war a new Governor, Sir Philip Mitchell, reminded the home government that:

It is of the greatest importance on all grounds of Imperial policy and for the future well-being and prosperity of the native people that there should be a vigorous and well established British settlement in these highlands, for without it there is no hope of successfully overcoming the immense problems which confront us in this part of the world and of creating here a permanent structure of enlightenment and civilisation. The British people in East Africa are the key-stone of the arch and without them it will soon be no more than 'vast and trunkless legs of stone' . . . in the desert.[39]

This doom-laden prophecy simply illustrated the extent to which both administrators and settlers had been unable, and indeed unwilling, to bridge the gulf between themselves and the African inhabitants of Kenya. It was a situation which would have fateful consequences in the next two decades. But meanwhile, on 8 May 1945, the war ended.

10

The Final Years

Under the spell of this merciless sun the country, yes, the whole Universe, seems damned and throttled by the inevitable sequence of destiny; and all man's fondly cherished beliefs are as impalpable and unreal as the mirages by Lake Olbolosat. Africa, like one of her own black-maned lions, laps up the life blood of all the delicate illusions that have for so long danced before the eyes of men.[1]

As the Second World War drew to a close soldiers black and white returned to their homeland of Kenya, bringing with them new ideas and modern attitudes and experience of a wider world. The pre-war demarcation of races, the dominance of the whites, the denial of proper education to large numbers of blacks, the supremacy of the Asians in commerce, all these and other matters were beginning to be challenged by Africans who had seen other ways of life and heard different, more liberal, opinions as they fought abroad. And the first university-educated Africans were trickling back to Kenya and refusing to countenance the racial prejudice and job discrimination they suffered on arrival. Even a few whites began to question the status quo. Things were ready for change as pressure built beneath the volcano's none-too-solid crust. For the time being, though, most of Kenya's whites knew nothing of this.

Sir Philip Mitchell had become Governor of Kenya in 1944. With more progressive, multi-racial views than most of the settlers, particularly those who belonged to what he called the 'Muthaiga Club mafia', men like Lord Francis Scott and Mervyn Ridley, he invited Africans to lunch and garden parties at Government House.

The settler elite were not included and now seldom graced the building. They rather looked down upon the South African Lady Mitchell, with her lack of social skills and shyness and dislike of entertaining. Elspeth Huxley said,

> She was an oddity: short and tubby, almost as broad as long and, while not at all unfriendly, without that veneer of manner that can ease encounters between strangers. I can see her now, sitting on a chair too high for her, her feet dangling some distance from the floor, clutching a whisky and soda in her hand and looking like an amiable frog.[2]

Moreover, the settlers thought the Governor himself did not come from the right background for the job. On his part, Mitchell found it hard to hide that he considered most European elected members of the Legislative Council of low intellectual calibre, and that he wanted Indians, Africans and Arabs to join them, and on the front benches too – though he was in no doubt that colonial government would have to remain until there were far more educated Africans in the country.

Yet Mitchell had to work with the settlers. To harness them he vowed to make leading white politicians ministers of the government. At a stroke, therefore, the idea of settler politicians as an inevitable opposition to the administration came to an end. Men such as Ernest Vasey, Michael Blundell and Derek Erskine began to see the sense of Mitchell's views, accepted ministries and moved towards a type of multi-racialism. There was, however, a serious drawback in the novel strategy: African politicians, observing the breach in official defences, foresaw that a constitution like those of Rhodesia or South Africa might develop in Kenya. To counter this, they declined to co-operate in attempts to draw them into a very limited partnership. Senior government officials, believing the wave of unrest to be caused by a few power-hungry agitators rather than by genuine grievances, refused to admit there could be any shortcomings in government policy. This blindness was to lead to dangerous black rebellion.

Meanwhile, though, more whites continued to come to Kenya,

for the post-war years were ones of great prosperity. Prices of exports rose and capital flowed into the country, while there was sharp appreciation in the value of land and property alike. In 1948 a census was held, the first since 1931, and the figures that emerged from it showed that the country had 29,660 whites, 5,251,120 Africans and 97,697 Indians and Goans. This made whites 0.55 per cent of the population, compared with the 19.5 per cent (513,008) of the largest tribe, the Kikuyu. In 1953 it was estimated that there were 42,200 whites and in 1956 57,700.[3] Despite their steady increase, the Kenyan whites were not as numerous in 1948 as those in either Northern Rhodesia (50,000) or Southern Rhodesia (160,000). In this period there were on average 2,500 whites coming to live in Kenya every year. By 1950 the influx of newcomers caused a severe housing shortage in Nairobi and elsewhere. Hotels were also full, and sometimes had to limit residents to five-day stays.[4]

It was certainly not the Kakamega goldmines which brought new whites to Kenya, for during the war most of them closed down. The number of operating mills fell from fifty-three in 1939 to sixteen at the end of 1948, and production fell from £607,753 to £189,397.[5] Those which closed were mainly the small ones, and now only eighty-four whites were employed in the mines. Some of the new immigrants came as farmers, for once again a world war led to the introduction of a soldier-settlement scheme for Kenya. At war's end a Land Settlement Scheme was published detailing a comprehensive programme for further European settlement by the fuller and better use of land in Kenya.[6] It is somewhat surprising that this was implemented by a Labour government, but Arthur Creech-Jones, the Colonial Secretary, said in the House of Commons that 'European settlement must be viewed as an integral part of Kenya's development as a whole'.[7]

With a tragic lack of foresight a Settlement Board was appointed in Nairobi and a selection committee in London. The plan was twofold: an assisted ownership scheme, for applicants with £3,000 or over, and a tenant farming scheme, for those with £1,000 or more. Once again, it was not the yeoman farmer who was sought – rather, people who could control and work with

Africans were wanted. On the day that F. A. Levy went for his interview all his fellow interviewees were ex-officers.[8] Those who passed the selection committee were trained at Egerton Farm School at Njoro before taking up their farms. The original idea was to establish 500 families in Kenya, but the money allocated covered only 370.[9]

By June 1948, of the 800,000 acres of farmland settled by the new immigrants, all except 42,000 had been in European occupation before, and the rest was undeveloped Crown land. Since Africans were very suspicious and sensitive on the subject, the Kenya Government had been careful to encourage white farmers to sell parcels of their under-used land on which to settle the newcomers. Most of these pockets were around Kitale. By 1949 the Settlement Board was broke and regarded as defunct, and it was left to the new white political party formed during the war, the Electors' Union, to take up the subject of increased settlement, for it still intended to secure the position of the whites in Kenya by increasing their numbers on the land.

What failed to be understood, both in London and Nairobi, was that Kenya's Africans, more specifically the Kikuyu, would not tolerate this. It was left to the *Daily Herald* to suggest that 'Kenya is, in fact, a paradise for Rip van Winkles'.[10] But even as late as 1952 white Kenyan politicians were keen to encourage further white settlement and counter the left-wing British MP Fenner Brockway's campaign against imperialism. They included Michael Blundell, later so pro-African. Blundell was too thin-skinned to tolerate criticism or unpopularity, so he was always changing his mind, a disadvantage in a politician. The Settlement Board enjoyed a revival after 1951 and continued in existence throughout the 1950s, its aim still 'to secure the introduction to Kenya of the new farmers, the new farm managers and assistants, and the fresh private capital that a young country needs'.[11]

An immediate effect of the scheme was to raise the price of land and by 1948 it cost three times as much as it had ten years before. This was a great deterrent to potential settlers. What is more, young British men and women, apart from the few who refused to live under the Labour government elected after the war, no longer wanted to leave a Britain recently provided with free education and health services, for the vagaries of farming in a distant land. Residential white settlers, though, particularly from a newly independent India, continued to arrive, as did Europeans on government service, and professionals and those entering the commercial sector. These were urban immigrants who swelled the towns of Kenya. There was a steadily rising excess of white. immigration over emigration in the years 1946, 1947 and 1948, from 1,928 to 2,810 and 3,528.[12] Capital flowed into the country until the outbreak of the anti-white Mau Mau movement in 1952, when it was reduced by 90 per cent as fear mounted for Kenya's stability.

Up to 1950 economic development in Kenya was concentrated on the white settler. Africans were seen largely as subsistence producers to whom anti-erosion measures had to be applied. The whites, on the other hand, had to be helped with their farms, to provide cash crops and create traffic for the railway and revenue for the country – certainly not revenue for Britain, which derived no financial benefit at all. At times of difficulty, such as the great outbreak of pests and diseases in the depression years of the late 1920s and the 1930s, there had been great emphasis on improved services to white farmers in the shape of veterinary and crop research, while agricultural services to African farmers were pushed less firmly, by too few agricultural officers, and were often resisted by the Africans themselves, most of them wedded to traditional methods of husbandry and land tenure. Steady African population growth and fragmentation of land holdings also hindered their progress. By the end of the 1930s there was only one white agricultural officer for each African agricultural district, so there was little chance of doing anything other than advising. In contrast, the spending of £700,000 a year for research led to advances in the husbandry of coffee, pyrethrum, wheat and cattle on white farms. The Second World War, with its emphasis on increased food production, was a time of economic buoyancy for both white and black farmers.

Eric Smith

Left to right: Arthur Collyer, Olive Collyer and Eric Smith (*courtesy of Veronica Bellers*)

John Henry Patterson

John Boyes

W. N. McMillan

Maia Carberry and Rudolf Mayer
(*courtesy of Juanita Carberry*)

The wedding of Lord Delamere and Gwladys Markham, 1928
(*courtesy of Kathini Graham*)

John Ainsworth

H. C. E. Barnes

Sir Charles Eliot

Sir Frederick Jackson

Claud Hollis

George Whitehouse

Sir William MacKinnon

Sir Evelyn Baring

Norfolk Hotel, Nairobi,
1928

Nairobi Cathedral, 1930

Torr's Hotel, 1929

Delamere Avenue, Nairobi, 1950s

Railway Workshops, 1952

Kikuyu Land Unit, 1953

Garden party for all races at Government House, early 1960s

Nairobi, 1963 (*courtesy of Dorothy Myers*)

The Second World War was also the occasion for much greater emphasis to be placed upon developing African agriculture. The African Land Development Board (ALDEV) was established in Kenya in 1945, to run parallel with the Board of Agriculture for whites. The following year ALDEV received a £3,000,000 grant from the Colonial Development and Welfare Fund. There was, however, a major problem: the African population had increased but was unable to expand into contiguous areas because whites occupied the land there. One solution was to press Africans to farm communally, as this would allow terracing and crop rotation, but Africans did not like the plan, because it was being imposed by the government and it challenged the traditional way of doing things. Jomo Kenyatta, leader of the Kikuyu Central Association, made public speeches criticising the use of compulsory female labour for the terracing. The scheme abruptly failed.

The white agricultural field staff then turned their attention to devising other methods to develop African farming. There were now a goodly number of such experts, part of the influx of European specialists arriving in Kenya after the war as a result of the Colonial Development and Welfare Act. Under a Ten-Year Development Plan issued in 1946, assistant agricultural officers were posted to new divisional headquarters, thereby increasing the white staff in most districts from one to three or four. By 1952 the total staff involved in agricultural advice in Central Province had grown more than tenfold.[13] These experts, mostly with diplomas and practical experience rather than university degrees, whose holders still tended to be sent to white farming areas, began to press for the spread of cash crops among African farmers. But the European-controlled cash-crop boards resisted this because they feared deteriorating quality and the spread of pests and diseases. Only by promising the highest standards of quality control was white resistance finally overcome. Three cash crops – pyrethrum, coffee and tea – were gradually introduced to African areas. This caused the farming, and therefore social, landscape to change in ways which were to have profound effects on the white presence in Kenya.

The agricultural officers worked closely with the DCs, now ruling their districts with less freedom than before. The new emphasis on African development after the passing of the Colonial Development and Welfare Act meant that officials were kept up to the mark from the centre. Gone were the days when the man on the spot despised the pen-pushers in the Secretariat, for now directions from Nairobi came regularly and had to be obeyed. At the same time, DCs still had to steer a careful course with the settlers. Just as before the war, it was most unwise to cross an influential settler.

After the war the death of an official at the hands of an African caused an apprehensive stir in the white community of Kenya. The victim was Hugh Grant. Tall, fair-haired, blue-eyed and loose-limbed, Grant was a Highlander with a Scottish burr to his voice. Unorthodox in many ways, he indulged a favourite after-dinner pastime of shooting matchboxes off the mantelpiece. He had been in the administrative service in Kenya since 1930, having previously served in the KAR from 1921 to 1925 and then farmed at Limuru. As an official in the Northern Frontier District, he was effective though eccentric, but he was too stubborn, quick-tempered and inflexible to be a success in his posting in March 1946 as DC, Maasai Reserve. 'His inclination', said a colleague, 'was towards bringing about immediate conclusions rather than towards the exercise of tact and patience.'[14]

In order to promote a cattle cull stipulated by the government in 1946, Grant and his livestock officer bought cattle from Maasai chiefs, but on one occasion no cattle were produced voluntarily so the police seized twenty-eight beasts for purchase. The Maasai asked for some of them to be returned and exchanged them for others. Karambu de Sendayo, absent at the time the objections were made, appeared later and made a fuss about his confiscated bullock, wanting to replace it with another. Because matters had already been settled Hugh Grant refused to relent and the young Maasai moran (warrior), frustrated and angry, threw his spear at Grant's back. Maasai spears are seven feet long, with three-foot blades only one and a half inches wide throughout their length.

The spear went right through the DC's body and killed him instantly.

The Governor ordered compensation of 500 bullocks[15] to be paid to Grant's wife and she used the £2,000 they fetched to help pay for the education of her children. Karambu de Sendayu was tried, found guilty and executed. At his trial he said his bullock was like a child to him – he had reared it from a calf, tended it like a mother and loved it dearly. Grant's funeral took place in the Ngong hills, where a pillar of rough-hewn marble was raised above the grave not far from that of Denys Finch Hatton.

The post-war officials still oversaw African justice. One of them remembered an unusual case:

A man was brought before me charged with unnatural inter-course with a cow. The owner of the cow and three witnesses had evidently rehearsed their evidence well, each adding a little more artistic verisimilitude to the story. The accused was naturally distraught and claimed that the whole story was a fabrication. He said that he had actually been making love to the wife of the owner of the cow and when he heard people approaching, he had slipped out and hidden in the cattle *boma* where he had been discovered . . . I therefore found myself in a quandary. However, I remembered that adultery was considered to be a serious offence under the local African law. I therefore convicted him, reminded him that even what he had admitted was a serious offence, and gave him the rather lesser sentence than he would have received for adultery under African law and custom.[16]

Officials struggled to do their work with few funds at their disposal. They certainly received very little money for their own buildings or recreation. None the less, squash and tennis courts, and golf courses were constructed and maintained near the government bomas. At Embu the DC Robin Wainwright built a squash court by selling the army two tons of avocado pears from a tree in his garden. And, with only a tiny entertainment allowance, administrators were hard put to do all the entertaining required of them. Wainwright discovered that from August 1953 to the end of 1958 he gave 1,142 lunches and 932 dinners, and 355 people stayed at his house overnight – all on a minute entertainment allowance.[17] As yet, Africans were almost wholly excluded from the social life of officials.

By the 1950s, though, there were rising numbers of educated Africans enjoying a higher standard of living. When Mitchell first became Governor there were only two African university graduates. His reorganisation of Makerere College in Uganda caused fairly rapid post-war educational advance among Africans. Several Kenya Africans took external London BAs there, and Kenya also had a sizeable number of highly educated Asians. A few whites were prepared to associate with such people in social and educational circumstances, and even to contemplate an erosion of the exclusive white highlands land policy. Bruce Mackenzie, a leading farmer, was the first important European to say that land use should be governed by good agricultural practice, and not by race. The more diehard whites of the Electors' Union and revived Convention of Associations kept an eye on 'subversives' such as him. For example, a report on Graham F. Thomas of Siriba African Teacher Training College noted that Thomas was a supporter of Aneurin Bevan and Fenner Brockway, a personal friend of Eamonn de Valera and the rebel leader in the Sudan, and that Gaitskell was godfather to his only child.[18]

In reality the colour bar in hotels and restaurants, a measure enforced by custom alone rather than by law, was out of date, but social ostracism threatened whites who transgressed the rules. Graham F. Thomas described what happened when a white man attempted to take an African into a bar:

At a meeting Tom Mboya said to me, 'That's the trouble with you bloody liberals, you wouldn't invite me to have a drink with you in the New Stanley bar.' At that time the bar was open to Europeans only, but the gauntlet was down and I had to respond. So a date and time was agreed . . . Until this date no African had been allowed in the New Stanley Hotel except for the employees, so it was a giant step. The bar was extremely long, and about twenty or so Europeans – all armed – were drinking their sundowners. Behind the bar was the Asian barman and a Luo assistant. As we walked in all conversation ceased – the silence was palpable. I asked the bartender for two beers (Tusker), but he was rigid with fright, and totally unable to move. So I asked the Luo, who was grey with apprehension, but when Tom nodded to him he did bring the two pints, and we drank them quite slowly. Not a word was uttered; the atmosphere was electric. Then Tom said, 'Come on, you've made your point.'[19]

Joan Karmali, a European married to the Ismaili photographer John Karmali, recalled,

We rarely encountered overt hostility because John and I took care never to expose ourselves to it. No one was openly impolite – except once. Against our better judgement, we accepted the invitation of some European friends to a New Year's dance. At one point the bandleader came on to the floor and said to our friend, 'If you don't get that Indian out of here, we'll stop playing.'[20]

On one occasion a Goan, John Dias, was shot dead by a white farmer called Potter in the Rift Valley because the latter's daughter was in love with Dias and wanted to marry him. Though charged, the farmer got away scot free, thus causing outrage in the Goan community.[21]

When the customs officer Patrick Sweeney played tennis at Mombasa Sports Club with an Anglo-Indian doctor, he was taken aside later and told he was an embarrassment to the European community by being partnered by a non-white.[22] Not only Africans were barred from clubs – whites of low status or the wrong background suffered too. Alderman Izzie Somen, mayor of Nairobi, was refused membership of the Nairobi Club because he was Jewish, and Hannah Vasey, wife of Ernest, was barred from the same establishment because of her German-Jewish ancestry. Members of the police inspectorate had low social status. Trevor W. Jenkins, an inspector and therefore only a second-class official, was invited by his squash partner, the private secretary to the Governor, to have an after-game drink in the long bar of the Nairobi Club. The following day he was marched before his superior to receive an official rebuke.[23] Settlers tended to treat such white policemen as at their beck and call, for however trivial a matter.

The social separation between the races was partly due to different patterns of living. Africans in villages and the countryside had ways of life and standards of hygiene so at variance with those of whites that the latter would not contemplate social intercourse. The common view of Africans by whites was described by a Medical Officer of Health:

> The African labourer is regarded by the European farmer as being lazy, irresponsible and unreliable and there is certainly some excuse for this opinion as his output of work is low no matter what wages he receives. It is therefore uneconomical to pay good wages. Constant European supervision is required to maintain a reasonable standard of output of work, and so the farmer tends to employ no labour in excess of the number he can personally supervise. Consequently the available land on his farm is not fully developed.[24]

The MOH explained the African output of work as due to sub-normal health and a low standard of living. There was a vicious circle of ill health, poor output of work, low wages and a low standard of living.

The poor standard of African health was partly due to the incidence of malaria; when insecticides were introduced to Ruiru Sisal Estate to control mosquitoes, there was a 50 per cent drop in absenteeism two months later. Other factors lowering individual vitality were scabies, tropical ulcers, dysentery, typhoid fever, venereal disease and the almost universal helminthic infection (from hookworm, tapeworm and other nasty members of the worm family). But after the war a medical innovation appeared which could have been a factor in the accelerated development of Kenya – anti-malarial drugs. At last white people could live in Kenya with no fear of suffering from malaria, and the health of members of other races who took the tablets improved dramatically. In most cases, however, Africans could not afford the prophylactic pills.

Even missionaries, usually the most enlightened of the whites, could be reluctant to invite Africans into their own homes. But there was a realisation that things must change. One missionary, Peter Bostock, wrote in 1945: 'We missionaries have got to get our own attitude right about welcoming the educated African in to our home for meals, and sometimes maybe for sleeping . . . We must be far more ready and generous with our hospitality.'[25] He deplored what he saw of white attitudes and asked, 'Is a real effort being made to bring home to the European community that part of the responsibility at least for the present unrest lies with them, because of their general attitude to and treatment of Africans and their contentment to learn little or no language?'[26] An old African compared whites to jiggers boring into toes beneath the nails, causing considerable irritation and pain.

Paradoxically, whites could be kindly and considerate to individual workers in their houses and on their farms, and loyalty and strong affection developed between many whites and individual Africans, on both sides. For example, two Luo men cared devotedly for the Hon. Frederick Savile in his squalid shack at Maseno village during his final years of senility, and the local Indian shopkeeper kept him supplied with free toothpaste.[27] And this was the period when many Europeans started schools for Africans on their farms, though white interest in African education did not penetrate the reserves. Yet such relationships were intrinsically doomed because they were based on paternalism. The standard of living and privileged position of the whites was bound to engender envy and resentment among Africans in the new, post-war, egalitarian world. And some whites, it has to be said, were unbearably rude to Africans. Many of the newcomers adopted the attitudes of diehard settlers. Their views arose from a fear of being swamped by the huge African majority and what the whites considered was a very inferior, even uncivilised way of life. Cultural relativism, whereby all cultures are thought equally valid, was as yet unheard of. There was a general lack of acceptance of social, educational and medical multi-racialism, and this disrespect to Africans cut them very deep.

Yet there were some tentative beginnings of multi-racialism. Kit Henn,[28] a coffee farmer's wife and writer of 'The Distaff Side' column in the *Kenya Weekly News*, helped to establish the Frangipani Club, a multi-racial group that became the Kenya Women's Society. She further put her beliefs into practice by teaching spinning and weaving to African women in Nairobi prison. It was still only a minority of whites who had any idea of how Africans lived; most did not want to know.

The multi-racial Capricorn Africa Society, begun in Rhodesia and launched in Kenya by the surgeon Peter Wood and his wife Susan, was not a success despite the support of Michael Blundell and Ernest Vasey. It never took off among Africans. There was also the United Kenya Club, an inter-racial organisation which regarded all discriminatory practices as wrong. It had a weekly lunch with a speaker in Nairobi, one of them Jomo Kenyatta, recently returned from Russia. The rule was that its three officers – president, secretary and treasurer – should each be of a different race. The club held its first meetings in 1946 in an old wood and iron building, Nairobi's original school and now the Boy Scouts' hut, with its two rooms, hall and kitchen. Tom Askwith, a DC, its first chairman, helped paint the venue, a small revolution in itself as whites were not supposed to get their hands dirty.[29]

In the early 1950s an annual inter-racial holiday camp was organised, for seventy schoolboys for a fortnight, and it included a climb up Mt Kilimanjaro. Derek Q. Erskine, director of Erskine & Duncan, wholesale grocers, ran this local Outward Bound movement, as well as being influential in the non-racial Amateur Athletics Association. Indeed, the commercial community was in general more enlightened than the white farmers – the City Council was multi-racial long before other bodies.

A little tentative multi-racialism there might be, but as for intermarriage between the races, that was still taboo. Until the mid-1950s, when the law was changed, a white male having sexual intercourse with an African woman suffered no penalty, while an African man having sexual relations with a white female could be hanged.[30] When an African lawyer, Chiedo Argwings-Kodhek, brought his white Irish wife back to Kenya, the train was stopped before it reached Nairobi and she was taken off in order to avoid possible demonstrations on the Nairobi platform. A white resident who took pity on the couple and rented them his guest house was contravening his lease terms (the way segregation was enforced, rather than by law). Another example of a white–black marriage was that of a British Council official, Bernard Coffey, and his Kikuyu wife Dolly.

One of the earliest mixed-race families was that of Ernest Elkington. The brothers Jim and Ernest Elkington, old Etonians, had come to Kenya before 1912 when Jim was sent out as a remittance man because he had already lost two fortunes. Jim became a farmer, while Ernest ran a transport business and married a Kikuyu girl. The union produced four sons and two daughters, who were educated by CMS missionaries. One of the sons married a mixed-race girl, with an Afrikaner father and Nandi mother, and they had four girls. The family lived in Ruaraka and were not accepted in white society. When Stephen North, a member of the Army Air Corps, took one of the girls to a coffee bar as late as 1961 his chair was kicked but he was not refused service.[31] People of mixed race did not consider themselves African and tended to marry among themselves or among visiting whites – for example, three of Elkington's four granddaughters married an Englishman, Swede and German. The Second World War caused a rise in the number of people of mixed race, as white soldiers formed liaisons with African women and then returned home after the war, leaving behind their coloured children. The Roman Catholic Church came to the rescue and educated the children, the girls at a convent in Thika.

Education, that tool of social control, remained segregated. A. L. Ribeiro, son of Dr Rozendo Ayres Ribeiro, of zebra-riding fame, and also a medical doctor, married an Englishwoman but their two flaxen-haired sons were denied admission to white schools. It was not generally known that the younger Dr Ribeiro was the author of 'Miranda's Merrier Moments', the *Sunday Post*'s society column.[32] The Governor Philip Mitchell was more progressive than most and encouraged the Ismaili John Karmali and his white wife Joan to begin the non-racial Hospital Hill School, when they failed to gain admission to white schools for their children.[33] The children of Cyril Price, an Anglo-Indian married to a Spaniard and a teacher at Allidina Visram School in Mombasa, were denied admission to the Roman Catholic convent school, which took Europeans only. Admission to European schools was coveted because spending on education for whites was lavish in comparison with that for other races, particularly Africans. Two grand new secondary schools for European children were opened in Nairobi: the Duke of York (now Lenana) School at Ngong for boys in 1949 and the new Kenya High School at Kileleshwa for girls in 1950.

In the Eldoret region the longstanding tensions between the Afrikaner and British settlers continued in the educational field. By 1945 the Central School in Eldoret had 96 per cent of Afrikaans-speakers. The whites of British origin, particularly those from families of officials in Uganda sending their children to Kenya for their education, put pressure on the government, which had in any case to finance a new school to take the increased number of white children in the area. The Hill School was opened in Eldoret in 1945 in the old RAF camp built from timber from the Elgeyo sawmills, with as headmaster Cyril Redhead, formerly an art master at the Prince of Wales School. It was he who designed the buffalo badge of the Kenya Regiment based on the Selous memorial in Nairobi Club. The Central School was renamed the Highlands School. So the predominance of Afrikaners in the Highlands School continued – in 1951, of its 214 pupils, only thirty-nine were non-Afrikaners. Two years later, all 107 pupils from Uganda went to the Hill School.[34] In 1956 the Highlands and Hill Schools were combined and converted into an all-girls secondary school, with 312 pupils, and a new Hill

School was built to take more primary-age pupils – that year its roll was 524, 347 of them being boarders. The construction of the new school was partly a result of the death the previous year of a pupil, John Latin, in a fire in one of the old wooden RAF sheds used as dormitories.[35] Within the new Hill School differences between Afrikaner and British pupils continued, though the staff tried to counter any bullying. The problem solved itself when all the Afrikaners but a handful left around the time of independence in 1963. Ten years after independence only a dozen families remained. In 1996 none but the Krugers and du Toits in Eldoret, the Steenkamps in Kitale, the Prinsloos in Nakuru and the Retiefs in Malindi were left.[36]

Social and educational segregation was reinforced in hospitals. After the war a novel proposal was put forward by the government: a group hospital for all three races to be built and managed by government. Unable to countenance this, both the European and Asian communities decided to assume responsibility for their own medical services. The government therefore had to introduce a statutory insurance scheme known as the 'Hospital Relief Fund'. A new European hospital was built in Mombasa, on the original beautiful site, and opened in 1950, while the Nairobi whites retained their building near Government House on Nairobi Hill, now increasingly becoming known as 'Hospital Hill', until a new European hospital opened on the old polo ground on the Ngong road in 1954. When the white Joan Karmali was about to have a child, she was booked into the maternity section of the European hospital, but two women doctors objected on the grounds that her baby would be half-Indian.[37] The hospital board refused to accept this and allowed her to have her baby in the European hospital. On another occasion, a longstanding Kenya resident brought into the same hospital at midnight caused an argument about his admission because he was an Armenian, and therefore not quite 'white' enough. He did eventually get a bed.[38]

Sometimes sheer necessity required the admission of a white person to an African hospital. For example, one night a strange white woman dressed in shabby, dirty clothes entered the African hospital at Kisii and took staff outside to a semi-conscious white man lying in a Land Rover, his skin a shade of grey, curled up on old sacks stuffed with hay. He was a lone gold miner living in the bush with his mistress eighty miles to the south, who had had an accident with his dynamite.[39] There were several of these eccentric, always elderly, characters; having come down in the world, they chose to live in isolated places.

In 1949 there were ninety-seven doctors, the majority white, and 112 nursing sisters (also mainly European) in the Kenya Medical Service, among a total staff of over 2,000. Most of them worked in the African hospitals spread around the country, a service augmented by the eight mission hospitals run by Protestant missions only.[40] The selfless work of such medical staff is often overlooked in the present tendency to vilify the British empire. In 1947 a children's hospital was started at Muthaiga by Ewart Grogan and named Gertrude's Garden in memory of his wife. It was for whites only. Not until 1957 did the first multi-racial hospital open: the Aga Khan Memorial Hospital, financed by the Aga Khan.

White society in Kenya was self-assured for a few years after the Second World War. The number of whites had increased sufficiently in the towns to permit literary and cultural activities to expand, and as they did so Western culture became more entrenched – a development watched with dismay by Africans. The English-language press flourished with the Nairobi newspapers *East African Standard* and *Sunday Post*, the *Kenya Weekly News*, edited at Nakuru by Mervyn Hill (its last issue was in 1969), and the Mombasa daily *Mombasa Times*. The weekly *East Africa and Rhodesia*, edited by F. S. Joelson and published in Britain, was widely read in the colony and abroad. One of the best-known journalists of the country was Edward Rodwell, editor of the *Mombasa Times*, writer of the 'Coast Causerie' column printed in that paper and from 1956 in the *Kenya Weekly News* under the pseudonym 'The Watchman'. A compendium of local lore and history, and the activities of local people and his own family, the column captured the imagination of the reader with its gentleness and charm and wit. Rodwell, who lived until

26 March 2002, also gave weekly talks on similar subjects for the Kenya Broadcasting Service. Broadcasting, too, flourished, with compères such as the popular Alan Bobbé, knowledgeable about classical music since his father was a musician in the Royal Philharmonic Orchestra. Bobbé started his renowned Bistro in 1962 in the former premises of Hoppy Marshall's Mascot restaurant.

More serious publications such as the *Uganda Journal* (from 1934) and *Tanganyika Notes and Records* (from 1936) offered a forum for specialist articles on history and culture, though Kenya did not develop a similar magazine at this time. In 1946 the East African Literature Bureau under Charles Granston Richards was inaugurated to publish books and pamphlets in several African languages as well as in English. It brought out many short books on Kenya's history, though these were mainly concerned with the European period. A former missionary, Richards also helped found the Kenya History Society in 1955, a group which ceased to function when those whites interested in the subject left Kenya. Not until after independence did the *Kenya Historical Review* of the Historical Association of Kenya put in its appearance. Meanwhile, James Kirkman, excavating at Gedi near Malindi from 1948, and in Fort Jesus in the 1950s, stimulated interest in coast history, while Louis Leakey and Mary Leakey continued their excavations inland and engendered worldwide interest in the origins of man.

The sense of white history going unrecorded prompted the founding in 1952 of the East African European Pioneers' Society, with Lady McMillan and Lord Cranworth as the patrons and Ewart Grogan as president. Foundation members had to have been in Kenya before 4 August 1914, while associate members were required to have been twenty-five years in the country, and ordinary members needed to be direct descendants of foundation members. The Society planned to build up a collection of valuable books and documents and began research on a 'Who's Who' of early settlers. Neither of these plans came to fruition, though the 'Who's Who' cards were later donated to Rhodes House in Oxford.[41] Under the Society's auspices, in July 1956 H. K. Binks unveiled in Forest Road cemetery in Nairobi a memorial to Mary

Walshe, the formidable 'Pioneer Mary'. The Society's newsletter recorded the deaths of early residents – Lady McMillan died in November 1957, George Langridge and T. J. O'Shea in 1958. The organisation was finally dissolved in December 1964, after Kenya became independent and membership numbers had dropped to 300. It went out with a flourish, with a pageant at the Royal Show in Mitchell Park, consisting of a long procession of wagons representing pioneering days.

The perception that the whites would remain the dominant class in Kenya was reinforced by cultural activities that excluded Africans. Performances of Western music were common in this period. Both the East African Conservatoire of Music and Nairobi Musical Society sponsored concerts of classical music. The former owed its existence to the Revd W. E. D. Knight, a farmer and the vicar of the church of St Cuthbert in Limuru and a keen arranger of musical evenings over many years. For those of scientific interests there was the East African Natural History Society, with its weekend botanical and ornithological expeditions, often led by Peter Bally. He was a curator of the Coryndon Museum and married to Joy, who later found fame with her next husband George Adamson by writing the book *Born Free*, which became a popular film. Late in life Marjorie Tweedie, a farmer in the Mt Elgon region since 1924, started to collect plants with the encouragement of the Coryndon Museum, and had four plants named for her by Kew Gardens. She also became a proficient watercolourist and left her collection of paintings to Kew. Another settler from the same area, T. H. E. ('Pinkie') Jackson, was a renowned lepidopterist who left his vast collection to the British Museum of Natural History. He, too, had plants named for him. He was murdered in 1969.[42]

The Donovan Maule Players, a professional repertory theatre, was established in 1948, and a National Theatre was opened in Nairobi by Ralph Richardson in 1952. Mombasa's Little Theatre Club put on regular plays. It performed *The Boyfriend* in 1953, with the assistance of its author Sandy Wilson, who flew out to Mombasa to audition the cast and help with the choreography.

His sister lived in Mombasa. Jasper Maskelyne, a well-known conjuror, went to live in Kenya after the war and entertained the country's white children with his magic tricks.

White society in Kenya now seemed neat and tidy, with churches everywhere available for rites of passage. Work on the completion of Nairobi's cathedral began in 1949. By then, a strong Moral Rearmament movement had emerged in Kenya. The prime movers were Dr Gerald Anderson and his wife Caroline, the Hopcraft family and Lady Eleanor Cole, the builder of the Church of Goodwill for all denominations on her Rift Valley farm near Lake Elementeita, within sight of the main road to Nairobi. The Christian missionaries were equivocal about Moral Rearmament, not really believing it to be a truly Christian movement, and seeing it as something of a threat.

Kenya's capital, Nairobi, grew in size after the war, with 10,377 whites among its 110,951 inhabitants in 1948. Such was the feeling of confidence that in 1950 Nairobi became a city with a royal charter and its own coat of arms, conferred upon it by the Duke of Gloucester. People could choose to celebrate in the restaurants Chez Gaby, Falstaff, Jack Frost or the Horseshoe, and, if those did not appeal, there were always the Lobster Pot, Mascot or '400'. White residential areas of the city spread out importunately into more suburbs, while multi-storeyed office blocks began to change the centre skyline. Because almost all the white wives of Nairobi went out to work, they needed nannies. Seychelloises nannies were regarded as the best, and a sizeable Seychellois community grew up in the city. An old institution, Torr's Hotel, closed in 1958 when the building was taken over by the Ottoman Bank, but the other clubs and hotels, their floors burnished with red Cardinal polish, continued to do good business despite the mishap to the Muthaiga Club whose ballroom collapsed discreetly after breakfast one morning.

In contrast to Nairobi's Europeans, the white population of Mombasa declined after the war, as army and navy personnel were withdrawn. In 1947 there were 2,375 whites there, and in 1948 2,189. There was a gradual relaxation of wartime controls, until rationing ceased in 1948. Then the British withdrawal from India caused a burst of activity in the Coast Province, when a huge military stores depot, to house equipment removed from India, was established at Mackinnon Road some miles inland. There were 15,000 army personnel stationed there, 4,311 of them whites, as well as 836 Italians, remnants of the prisoners of war taken in the Abyssinian campaign.[43] The place became a town in itself, with the concomitant problems of water supply and sewage. Mombasa now needed a better water supply. The military personnel built two pipelines between the Tsavo river and Mackinnon Road, and a reservoir to hold 500,000 gallons. With the country's economy in so healthy a state, the perennial problem of the restricted size of Mombasa's Kilindini harbour had to be addressed once more. Two more deep-water berths (nos 7 and 8) had been completed in 1943, but still more were required. In 1952 work began on berths 9 and 10, and on Kipevu causeway to provide a new rail outlet to the mainland. Mombasa now had its own local shipping line: the Southern Line, run by Tony Bentley-Buckle. He sent one of his ships to the Seychelles in the early 1960s to pick up a sick Noel Coward, before Seychelles airport was opened. On his return to Mombasa, he introduced Coward to members of the Mombasa Yacht Club, where Bentley-Buckle was a keen competitor. He entered the 1956 Olympics yacht races and did fairly well.[44]

Mombasa became a highly popular holiday resort. It was no longer thought that the sun was a Bad Thing and as yet nothing was known of skin cancer. One of the favourite hotels for a visit was Jadini, on Diani beach twenty miles south of Mombasa. Run by Maxwell Trench and his wife Nellie, with his son Dan and wife Madeline to assist, the hotel acquired its name from the first letters of Maxwell's three children, John Ann and Dan, joined to the Swahili word for 'the place of'. Overlooking a beach of brilliant white sand so fine that it squeaked when walked upon, and a reef offshore that could be reached by dugout canoe, the place was a haven for upcountry holiday-makers. On the north coast, Shanzu Hotel was popular. Run by the McCormick and Blunt families, it catered for families with younger children. There are scores of people today who lovingly remember the sandcastle competitions, dressing-up parties, singsongs provided by Uncle Mac and boat trips up Mtwapa creek with Commander David Blunt in his boat *Felusi*. Gradually many more hotels were built along the coast, all with central bar and eating place and simple, separate banda bedrooms roofed with coconut palm fronds laid on mangrove poles.

Among other leisure activities pursued by whites were hunting, fishing and watching wild game in the national parks. Trout in the streams of the Aberdares and Mt Kenya, initially introduced into the Gura river by Ewart Grogan in 1905, had reached such numbers that trout fishing became a popular pastime. The game-watching post of Treetops outside Nyeri was a favourite place for tourists and residents to spend a night, particularly as the stay was preceded by a nervous walk behind an armed white hunter through the sinister, creeper-draped forest. Game was still fairly common outside the parks. Elephants used to wander around the Isiolo government boma. The PC's wife often asked George Adamson, the local game warden, to shoot them, but he would demur, saying 'Madam, where else in the world can you sit on your verandah and watch elephants eating your cannas?'[45]

Game-watching, rather than hunting, became a favourite occupation, particularly when Nairobi National Park, some forty square miles in extent, formerly the Nairobi commonage off the Langata Road in which animals had been protected, was created in 1946. Tsavo National Park soon followed, and other places, such as Marsabit and Amboseli, were also set aside for parks, under the urging of the National Parks director, Mervyn Cowie. In these areas shooting was absolutely prohibited. By 1956 twelve areas, totalling 20,000 square miles, were given varying degrees of protection. It was Cowie who was instrumental in preserving Mzima Springs in Tsavo Park in the 1950s when it was decided to pipe water to Mombasa from that source. As a result of his intercession with the Governor Sir Evelyn Baring, the tapping of water supplying the springs was shifted in order to conserve the hippo pools, and pipes were concealed. The National Parks department was separated from the Game Department, whose duty was paradoxically both to preserve animals for sport and to control those which became vermin or developed marauding behaviour. In 1954 cheetahs were designated royal game, and as such they could not be hunted. The Game Department was also responsible for the suppression of poaching, a duty which led to a rapid increase in its size – by 1950 there were fourteen wardens, 200 game scouts and a host of clerks dealing with African successors of the white ivory poachers of earlier years.

A new generation of white hunters had arisen to accompany tourists on shooting and photographic safaris, among them Harry Selby, Tony Henley, Tony Dyer, Donald Ker, Sydney Downey, Glen Cottar, Reggie Destro, John Sutton, Eric Rundgren, Frank ('Bunny') Allen and Andrew Holmberg. These men worked for firms such as Safariland (the successor of Newland & Tarlton) and Ker & Downey. Theirs was a hard life – their day began at 4.30 a.m. and ended about 11 p.m. The safari firm Ker & Downey also specialised in film work, and Kenya became a regular venue for film-makers. Among the films made there was *King Solomon's Mines* (filmed in 1949, released in 1950), with its stars Stewart Granger and Deborah Kerr being doubled in difficult and dangerous shots by Syd Downey, Tony Henley and Michaela Denis. In 1950 *Where No Vultures Fly* (starring Anthony Steele and Dinah Sheridan) was filmed, to be followed the next year by *The Snows of Kilimanjaro* with Gregory Peck, Susan Hayward and Ava Gardner. In 1952 *Mogambo* was on location, bringing Clark Gable, Donald Sinden, Grace Kelly and, again, Ava Gardner to Kenya, where they stayed in Nairobi's New Stanley Hotel. The arrival of the stars (including Frank Sinatra, Ava Gardner's husband) was always an exciting event, and they were entertained at Government House and charity balls. One Christmas Eve Sinatra serenaded a sweating audience with 'White Christmas'.

The Mau Mau movement put a stop to filming for several years. It was resumed in the early 1960s with *The Lion* (1960/61), and *Hatari* (1961) during the filming of which Diana Hartley, the wife of a hunter and the step-daughter of Gray Leakey whose son Nigel had earned a posthumous VC in the Second World War, was killed by a lion. Then came *Call Me Bwana* (1961/62) and *Sammy Going South* (1962). Carr Hartley, a huge man rumoured to have fought a full-grown male lion with his bare hands, ran a big-game farm at Rumuruti and supplied the films with animals when required. His farm was also a source of animals for zoos and circuses.

These films introduced a new generation to the delights of Kenyan safari and encouraged tourism, particularly from America, to such an extent that it had a post-war golden age. Celebrities such as Bing Crosby enjoyed their safaris and went home to tell their friends about Kenya. Game was still plentiful in the eighty-eight shooting blocks covering three-quarters of the country, and photographic safaris were likewise popular. Everything was made much easier by the Willys jeeps left behind by the military after the war and by the introduction in 1948 of the Land Rover. An abrupt halt came to this golden age when the Mau Mau rebellion broke out and tourists no longer went to Kenya.

*   *   *

> You would not know him now, so maimed he lies
> Upon his stolen earth;
> For I have thieved his entrails and his eyes.
> I have erased his accident of birth
> And dyed his skin, which he had thought divine,
> Darker than purple wine;
> Darker than the price for which he dies –
> The soil, that now is mine.[46]

The post-war prosperity, the new confidence, the steady immigration – all these were as froth on a dangerous wave. Beneath the foam was seething Kikuyu discontent. The first covert stirrings were ignored by settlers and government both. From 1948 a movement (called Mau Mau from 1951) began to hold oathing ceremonies, a traditional Kikuyu practice, in Central Province. A descendant, if a collateral one, of two proscribed organisations, the Kikuyu Central Association and the Kenya African Union, it was subverted by radicals who began a campaign of violence and intimidation against Kikuyu headmen and chiefs in 1951. Many huts of 'loyalist' Kikuyu, as they became known, were burned down and the first murders of headmen and chiefs began at the end of the year. People who refused to co-operate with the taking of oaths were punished or killed, causing great turmoil in Kikuyu society. In January 1952 the first oaths were administered in Nairobi. Local administrators in the Nyeri area warned the Governor that such was the unrest in Kikuyuland that Princess Elizabeth, due to undertake a royal visit, would not be safe if she stayed at the new royal lodge built for her at Sagana. When their warnings went unheeded in Nairobi they could only conclude that Sir Philip Mitchell so keenly wanted a KCVO that he declined to cancel the royal tour. However, Mitchell's personal secretary maintains that the warnings from Kikuyuland were never passed to the Governor by the Secretariat.[47] The officers in Nairobi thought the people on the spot were exaggerating and issued reprimands.[48]

But when the royal couple arrived, immense pains were taken to keep them safe, and they had to be hurried from the country not by any local difficulty but because the King had died and Elizabeth succeeded to the throne. The circumstances were peculiar. At Sagana lodge, after a night watching wild animals in Treetops, Trevor W. Jenkins, the personal policeman to the Princess, was told by Michael Parker, Prince Philip's aide, that he had heard a rumour from the press of the King's death. Parker and Jenkins listened to the lunchtime news on the radio. What they heard confirmed the rumour and Parker telephoned Buckingham Palace to make absolutely sure. The Palace was shocked to find that the Princess did not already know she was Queen – many hours beforehand it had placed an embargo on the release of the news while Government House in Nairobi was informed of the death. The trouble was that the Palace's telegram was in cipher, and the cipher books had been taken to Mombasa, to the ship *Gothic*, on which the royal couple was about to depart for Australia. No one could decipher the telegram at Government House.[49]

Parker went to inform Prince Philip that the King was dead, and it was left to him to tell his wife the news.[50] The Kikuyu telephonist at Nyeri, through whom all phone calls had to be routed, coped wonderfully with the spate of calls that had to be made. Kathini Graham, the Governor's secretary on the spot, managed to get through to the Princess's dresser in London to arrange for a black hat to be ready at London airport, to be taken on to the couple's plane upon its arrival. A black dress, intended for Anzac Day in Australia, was fortunately found in the royal luggage.[51] Passengers on a BOAC plane were happy to disembark and allow their aircraft to fly the royal couple to England. A car took the royals to Nanyuki airstrip some forty miles from Sagana, past local farmers standing silently at the roadside. As dusk fell, a small DC3 bearing the couple took off for Entebbe airport in Uganda, where the BOAC plane was waiting to fly them to England.

Only five months later, on 3 October 1952, the colony's Europeans were thrown into consternation by the murder of one of their number, a woman stabbed to death by Mau Mau on a farm off the Thika road, ten miles from Nairobi. The situation continued to deteriorate and on 21 October a state of emergency was declared. On the same day Jomo Kenyatta, the Kikuyu political leader suspected of being behind Mau Mau, was arrested. Four weeks later his trial began at Kapenguria. It lasted until the following April, when he was sentenced to seven years' hard labour for managing Mau Mau. Meanwhile the reign of terror spread. Senior Kikuyu chiefs continued to be murdered, as were two African members of Nairobi City Council. Still in their desert fatigues, the Lancashire Fusiliers were hastily deployed from Egypt to Kenya. On 24 January 1953 the colony was shocked by the brutal murder of Roger Ruck and his family at their home in north Kinangop; Esmé Ruck died as her unborn child was ripped from her womb. Photographs of the bodies were widely available to settlers. Feeling that the government was doing too little to counter Mau Mau ran so high that 1,000 whites demonstrated outside Government House in Nairobi. They broke through a police cordon and clustered at the main entrance threatening to enter the building until Michael Blundell, leader of the European elected members, came out with some of his colleagues and

addressed them. He gave assurances on the conduct of the
campaign against Mau Mau and the demonstrators dispersed.

The settlers' wrath was directed at Sir Evelyn Baring, Mitchell's
successor as Governor, whom they regarded as incapable of making
up his mind and taking a decisive lead against Mau Mau. Baring had
not wanted the job as Governor of such a troublesome colony but
was persuaded to take it by Sir Winston Churchill. A patrician and
a diplomat, he was a cautious man and did not rush into things –
often to the dismay of his civil service and elected ministers who
deplored what they saw as procrastination and inability to come to
a decision. In reality he was trying to get as many points of view as
he could before making a judgement. Sometimes he seemed
strangely detached, almost as if he was keeping problems at arm's
length in order to see them more clearly. One disadvantage was
that he was not physically fit, having suffered from liver problems in
India, and could not touch alcohol or eat food other than that of his
strict diet.

The terror in the Kikuyu reserve came to a head on 25 March
1953, at the little African village of Lari near Kiambu. Mau Mau
surrounded some of the villagers' huts at night and set fire to them.
As the people tried to get out ninety-seven of them were butchered
or burnt alive. It was difficult to apprehend the real perpetrators of
atrocities like this, for the radical Mau Mau had taken to the forests
of Mt Kenya and the Aberdares where they were most effectively
concealed, and it was only their local collaborators who were
arrested. At night the forest gangs entered white farms to steal food
and attack the farmers, their families and their animals. In an attempt
to capture the rebels, the Aberdare mountains were surrounded by a
complete circle of police outposts, and every day white and black
policemen made forays from them into the forests. Troops poured in
from Britain – the Lancashire Fusiliers were joined by the Devons,
Royal Inniskilling Fusiliers, Gloucesters, Royal Irish Fusiliers, Black
Watch, Rifle Brigade and Royal Air Force. The last of these bombed
the forests of Mt Kenya and the Aberdares with aircraft whose
drone became a familiar sound to settlers, though the strategy was
more comforting than effective.

In contrast to the attitude of the people of Britain towards conscription, the white settlers of Kenya fully approved of the conscription of their young men into the local force, the Kenya Regiment, for they considered it to be a stronghold against black revolution. The young men of the Kenya Regiment were attached to every British battalion and to the King's African Rifles as teachers, guides, interpreters and intelligence advisers. They also took the initiative to capture Mau Mau in the forests by infiltrating the gangs with pseudo-Mau Mau, ex-rebels who had been 'turned' and trained by the Regiment.

For many months the battle against Mau Mau seemed to be making no headway. Cattle thefts and maiming were a daily occurrence, and there was a steady trickle of white murders on lonely farms on the Kinangop, near Thomson's Falls, at Ol Kalou and in many other places. The white population was small and everyone knew someone who had been murdered. Various methods of keeping Europeans safe were tried. Farmers had to put on their lawn a large T visible by aircraft, and if they were in need of assistance the T had to be changed to an X – impractical when under fire. Everyone was armed and strict penalties for loss of firearms imposed so that guns did not fall into Mau Mau hands. Whites carried their guns in holsters strapped to their hips, though some men had shoulder-holsters instead. On the farms everyone slept with guns, kept guns on the table while they ate, had guns beside them as they took baths. Strenuous efforts were made to provide farmers with distress rockets, telephones, guards and wire netting, and to provide watches at police posts throughout the night. Houses without telephones on the Kinangop erected high posts with searchlights to be turned on in case of attack, so that they could be seen by police posts. Farmers were required to collect their labour into one wired-in village and to lock all house servants out of their farmhouses before sunset. Crops had to be carefully guarded to prevent theft for food by Mau Mau members, and all potatoes were dug up and disposed of. Occasional farmers would not co-operate, and these were watched by the CID.

At Naivasha the farmer R. E. V. Denning refused to believe

that his headman was a Mau Mau treasurer, although the man confessed later. Denning petitioned the Colonial Office, appealed to the attorney-general, brought a civil suit for libel against Mervyn Hill, the editor of the *Kenya Weekly News*, and gave the administration much extra work that it could have done without. In the end he had to be protected from other farmers who tried to get hold of him to tar and feather him.[52] Mau Mau members usually went for soft targets and good employers, whose work-forces were reluctant to co-operate with Mau Mau; they left alone the tough and bad employers. For example, they murdered while in his bath Eric Bowyer, an old man rather deaf and almost blind without his glasses, who lived alone. They also brutally killed two boys, C. R. Twohey and Geoffrey Danby, while the lads were out shooting birds with an air rifle at a farm on the Nairobi–Thika road.

It was the good employers, such as Gray Leakey, who were reluctant to accept that their trusted employees could be impli-cated in Mau Mau (most of them were, such was the intimidation), and they would fight hard to stop them being removed and detained. Leakey paid the price for his naïveté, or charity, according to which way you look at it. He and his second wife Mary Littleton were attacked in their farm at Kiganjo, outside Nyeri, while Mary's adult daughter Diana Hartley was visiting. Leakey was carried by ten men to 'a place of sacrifice' in the forest five miles from his farm, where they placed him face downwards in a shallow grave and buried him alive. Mary managed to push her daughter into the loft before being strangled in the farmhouse.[53] Diana Hartley escaped after the raiders had gone, only to die later during the making of a film in Kenya.

So many people had taken Mau Mau oaths that sweeps were made to arrest Kikuyu people on farms and in towns. The range of capital offences was extended – Africans could now be hanged for taking oaths or being members of Mau Mau gangs, or for having arms or ammunition in their possession, or even for being in the company of someone with arms. Those detained were taken to screening camps and if found to be implicated were moved to detention camps. At one time there were 80,000 detainees. The men in charge of the camps tried to persuade people to renounce the oaths they had taken. More than occasionally brutality was used and many confessions were made under duress. One official who opposed this, T. G. Askwith, was sacked.[54]

The system unhappily led to abuses. Bodies of Mau Mau members were put on display from time to time outside Karatina police station; one of its policemen said he never managed to get used to the smell of rotting human flesh.[55] The rumours of irregularities by the security forces were mainly directed at mem- b   e   r   s of the Kenya Regiment and the Kenya Police Reserve, a body of civilians called up on a part-time basis, mainly for night patrols. Too many Africans were being beaten or 'shot while attempting to escape' or 'shot while resisting arrest'. One white man poured paraffin over a suspect and pretended to light it; two others held a man over a fire, and there were cases of torture.[56] There were also incidents connected with white personnel of the King's African Rifles. Usually their defence was that African soldiers had perpetrated the abuse in the absence of white officers. Although the authorities brought such matters to court, this course of action was heavily criticised as tending to lower the morale of troops fighting Mau Mau. One of the cases of abuse prompted the British Parliament to send a delegation to examine the matter in February 1954. The investigation discovered there had been 130 prosecutions for brutality among the police forces, and it was perturbed to find that the European public had started a fund to pay the legal expenses of white members of the security forces accused of committing offences in the course of their duty. The view of many whites was that the Africans had got what they deserved.

Summary and collective punishments were occasionally officially imposed on Africans, a practice frowned upon by the Attorney-General, the highly unpopular John Whyatt. He was severely critical of the government's behaviour – 'If Governors shall not observe the law,' he asked, 'who shall endure it?'[57] Whyatt was a complex character, devoid of any personal charm. A foundling child, brought up by Jesuit priests, he was defensive, aggressive and at times very unpleasant. But he was a good lawyer and refused to countenance rough justice for Mau Mau personnel or to show partiality to members of the security forces, and he faced much local unpopularity in consequence. Eventually he was prevented from returning from leave by being appointed Chief Justice of Singapore in 1955, after his entire staff threatened to resign if he went back to Kenya.

Baring understood that when 'extreme violence is used on the one side, it is human nature to answer with extreme violence on the other side'.[58] With considerable wisdom he decided the only sensible way forward was an amnesty scheme, and further concentration of staff and resources on African agriculture and education. On 18 January 1955 the Mau Mau were invited to surrender, without punishment. This was vigorously opposed by the settlers. A leaflet, signed 'We are European Settlers', and typewritten in the Kikuyu language, was distributed where it could be found by Mau Mau: 'We ourselves know that many of you have killed or helped to kill. And we shall try with all our effort and power to see that all murderers and their helpers who might be captured or surrender get their just deserts for their crimes, and the reward is written in Regulations and it is death by hanging.'[59] This did great damage to the settlers' cause when it was reported in world newspapers. Few Mau Mau took advantage of the lenient government terms to surrender, thus retarding the advance towards African rule – Baring thought that if Africans had indulged in passive resistance rather than the Mau Mau movement they would have achieved political power far sooner than they actually did.[60]

During the Emergency, 63 white, 3 Asian and 525 African members of the security forces were killed. Between 1953 and 1957, 1,048 Africans were hanged. Civilian deaths numbered 32 whites, 26 Asians and 1,832 Africans. Mau Mau casualties from 1952 to the end of August 1955 were 13,320, with 9,514 killed. At the beginning of 1956 it was estimated that there were 2,000 Mau Mau still at large, and 400 at the close of that year. Military forces were withdrawn from operations against the Mau Mau in November 1958 and the police assumed full responsibility for all security measures. The Emergency officially ended in January 1960.

The Mau Mau movement was the direct cause of proposals for African land development. From a farming background himself, Baring pushed through the radical reforms of African agriculture proposed by Roger Swynnerton in 1954. These overthrew the previous view of the African farmer as primarily a subsistence producer to whom anti-erosion methods had to be applied, consolidated scattered African holdings and changed traditional habits of land tenure. There was a complete agrarian revolution during the Mau Mau rebellion, with Africans in the Kikuyu reserve being gathered into villages where hygiene, welfare and educational reforms were implemented. Five million pounds for these developments was allocated by the British Government and they were put into effect by administrative and agricultural officers. There began to be regular meetings of district teams consisting of administrative, medical, veterinary and agricultural officers. The active interventionism of Baring's government extended into industry and offered opportunities for whites, too. An oil refinery, tobacco factory, second cement factory and metal window business were among the new industries established, and Baring also drummed up help from American AID and the World Bank.

The Mau Mau rebellion confused the settlers about what the future held for them. By 1957, settler ministers such as Ernest Vasey and Michael Blundell, and many civil servants, could see that the future of East Africa was bound to be an African one. Developments such as universal franchise and an enormous increase in African representation in the Legislative Council were inevitable, but many, if not most, settlers refused to believe this, despite the evidence that other British African colonies were moving towards independence. Ewart Grogan rousingly addressed a revived Convention of Associations in 1957, 'I am going to suggest it should be the motto of the Convention of Associations that when any question arises of yielding or having stolen from us the ultimate yea or nay of the affairs of this country, that our answer is going to be "Never!"[61] And yet the Lyttelton constitution of 1954, introducing a ministerial type of government instead of a crown colony one, meant there was no turning back. Africans and Asians now participated in government, and continued to press for further access to power and for the abolition of the colour bar. Under Baring's governorship there were some attempts to allow Africans into formerly forbidden fields. The Kenya Regiment, previously regarded as a necessarily all-white body intended to counter black unrest, was ordered to become a multi-racial force. Only the Afrikaners put up much opposition and the first multi-racial course, with fifteen Africans and Asians among the 100 recruits, was a great success militarily and socially.[62] The Kenya Police Force, having grown in size and influence during the Mau Mau movement, began to train large numbers of African officers towards the end of the 1950s. Many white officers left Kenya to seek their fortunes elsewhere, secure for the time being with lump-sum compensation payments (known as 'lumpers' by all government servants who left). One of the leavers penned these lines for those he left behind:

> Farewell and adieu to you, Kenya coppers,
> Farewell and adieu to you lads left behind,
> For we've opted to go, under 'limited lumpers',
> And we praise the day that we opted and signed . . .
> So think of us kindly, and look us up please,
> We'll be standing in line, at the Crown Agents Office
> Searching for jobs, in what's left – 'overseas'.[63]

Other institutions moved more slowly. Education was one of the last citadels to be breached. Even the multi-racial Frangipani Club, in a debate on the issue, thought that 'as yet the African community has little to contribute from its own culture to Kenya'.[64] At the end of the 1950s it was decided to establish boards of governors for the large white secondary schools and to leave to their discretion the admission of children of other races, provided pupils met the required educational standards and could pay the fees. The governing body of Egerton College maintained a rearguard action against the introduction of pupils from races other than white. Eventually it had to capitulate two years before independence was granted to Kenya.

Hotels renounced the colour bar at the end of the 1950s. At the final white bastion, the Muthaiga Club, in a special meeting on 2 February 1962 members by an overwhelming majority made it clear they wished membership to continue on a European basis only. Other races could only be guests of members of the committee – for example, officers at regimental dinners.[65]

Even diehard white settlers began to see the writing on the wall, though Alan Lennox-Boyd, the Colonial Secretary, announced to the House of Commons on 2 April 1959 that the responsibility of the British Government was to all inhabitants of Kenya and it would be a betrayal of responsibility if authority were to be abandoned prematurely. But he was succeeded in his post by Iain Macleod, who held very different views. Later Macleod claimed that his mind had been made up to remove British rule in Kenya as soon as possible when he heard about the Hola affair in 1959.[66] To him it was clear that the British could no longer continue with their old methods of government in Africa, and this meant inexorably moving to African independence.

Events at the Mau Mau detention centre at Hola on the Tana river were shocking. When a party of its detainees refused to work, their Nandi warders beat them so severely that some died. The Nandi were in any case contemptuous of the Kikuyu, whom they did not regard as warrior stock like themselves, and this prejudice was confirmed by the detainees' habit of throwing the contents of their latrine buckets over them. The Nandi warders had been given orders in bad Swahili to be tough on detainees if they refused to work, but their enthusiastic punishment went too far and the three white officials on the spot could not control them. The warders then panicked and threw water over the corpses to revive them. They also poured water down the throats of some of the dead and dying detainees. When taken to task for the deaths, they claimed that the men had been thirsty and had drunk so much water that they drowned. The newly appointed and very young doctor at Hola also reckoned that the prisoners had drowned.

The nearest DC, W. H. Thompson, was called in from Kipini on the coast. He immediately doubted the diagnosis when he saw the corpses' gashes and bruises, and flew to see the Governor to make a report. Meanwhile, alas, a prison officer had said over his radio that the deaths were by drowning and this was picked up by the media. It forced the Kenya Government to issue an erroneous statement and resulted in a web of deceit. While the white prison officers closed ranks, the Governor put a call through to the Colonial Secretary in London and told the truth, but he was informed that it was politically unwise to alter the story because it would put the Colonial Secretary in an untenable position in the House of Commons.[67] There was of course a parliamentary inquiry, the truth emerged and the fate of Kenya's whites was sealed.

Their realisation that their position had changed irrevocably was reinforced shortly afterwards when a white man was convicted of murdering an African and hanged. Peter Poole, married with two young children, the son of Norman Poole who owned an electrical shop in Government Road, was an irascible and arrogant young man. Poole had drawn his gun on an Asian duka-keeper refusing to give him a discount on a torch. He had also shot in the leg an African plain-clothes constable being attacked by his dogs, and there were several other violent incidents in which he featured. Finally, on 12 October 1959 Poole was charged with the murder of Kamawe Musunge in Gordon Road, off the Ngong Road outside Nairobi. Two of Poole's dogs had stopped Musunge as he rode his bicycle. Musunge threw stones at them, but Poole came out of his house, drew a Luger pistol from his pocket and shot the African, who died at the scene. Poole was found guilty by the white jury and sentenced to death.

The verdict caused an uproar among settlers, so unusual was it for a white man to be sentenced to death for the murder of an African. But the sentence was duly carried out on 18 August 1960, while an angry crowd of Europeans and Africans assembled outside the prison. The execution indicated that matters had changed for ever in Kenya. One human being would be executed for the murder of another human being, regardless of colour. The Peter Poole affair profoundly shook white opinion. Many Europeans now understood fully that the days of white supremacy in Kenya were over. Then civil war broke out in the Belgian Congo in 1960. Whites from that country abandoned their homes and businesses and poured into Kenya in cars and lorries and trains. Settlers rallied round, sending them on to Nairobi where white schools were evacuated to house the newcomers. This brought home to the settlers of Kenya that nothing was permanent or safe any more.

Baring had been succeeded as Governor by Sir Patrick Renison, a man of immense experience but rather too much of a civil servant to be the right man for the job. The Attorney-General, Eric Griffith-Jones, thought the appointment was disastrous. Renison was awkward with Africans and made no effort to entertain them in Government House. Walter Coutts, his Chief Secretary, believed that having to sign Peter Poole's death warrant 'broke' Renison, who was never the same man again.[68] It was probably unwise of Renison to publish the Corfield report on the origins of Mau Mau when he did in 1961, and it was a fatal mistake of his to describe Jomo Kenyatta as 'a leader to darkness and death' and to refuse to release him, though he was supported in his view by Griffith-Jones and Coutts. He was also influenced by strong representations from settlers who would not countenance the freeing of Kenyatta. Renison's failings caused him to suffer the displeasure of Iain Macleod and it was not long before he was replaced by Malcolm MacDonald.

There had been an abrupt change in British policy towards the colonies when Iain Macleod became Colonial Secretary in 1959. His predecessor Alan Lennox-Boyd had been thinking in terms of independence for Kenya in about fifteen years' time, whereas Macleod wanted the time reduced to three years. He could never have achieved this had he belonged to the Labour Party, because the Conservatives would have opposed it. But, being a Conservative, he had no opposition from the Labour Party. He pulled Harold Macmillan, the Prime Minister, with him, though Macmillan was startled by the speed with which Macleod moved. West African states already had independence, and Macleod refused to deny the same to East Africa just because there was a white settler community there (one of whom was his farmer brother Roddy). His conviction was that 'although it was extremely dangerous to move quickly it would have been far more dangerous to try to hold back the tide of African nationalism'.[69]

Macleod called Kenyan groups to the Lancaster House conferences in London in 1960 and 1962, to thrash out the details of constitutions and the timetable for independence from Britain. He never thought he could carry the right-wing Europeans with him, but his plan was to get politicians such as Michael Blundell on his side, and to get Blundell and the Africans to agree. In this he succeeded and a radical new constitution was formulated for Kenya. The whites were dismayed and the Africans had not expected to get as much as they did. Blundell had thirty pieces of silver thrown at him when he returned to Kenya, and Macleod's mother, then in her eightieth year, was asked in a Nairobi street what it was like to be the mother of a traitor.[70] Macleod later admitted that if Blundell and other whites had said at the time that they would have nothing more to do with African advancement, independence would have been delayed for a considerable time, because he would not have pushed it forward without the support of white delegates at the conferences.

Macleod had ridden roughshod over the settlers' views and many of them felt utterly betrayed by both Britain and their own politicians. One described the reaction in Kenya when the result of the first conference was publicised as 'one of stunned shock that a British Government could act in such an unscrupulous manner towards those whom it had done all in its power to encourage to develop the country in the belief that we and our heirs would be secure under the Union Jack'.[71] Even moderate men who had devoted their lives to African progress, education and welfare had their doubts. Carey Francis, the head of the Alliance High School for Africans, said 'Lancaster House was a disaster and its decisions madness . . . Kenya Africans are at present quite incapable of managing the country . . . At best there will be widespread corruption and incompetence.'[72] He told Sir Armigel Wade, 'I worry . . . about the handing over of this wonderful country to a set of men none of whom has both ability and integrity, and a few of whom have either. People I regard as silly little children shout abuse at the governor and the government, and especially at colonialism and imperialism.'[73]

Carey Francis echoed the consternation among those of the settlers who deplored the abandonment of white rule. George Pile vilified the progressive whites with the verse:

We are the renegade whites, praying 'Forgive us our skin!'
False to our own flesh and blood, wronging our own
                                        kith and kin;
Pedlars of dubious rights, fanning false African pride,
Foam on the ebony flood, wind on the African tide;
Flinging our womenfolk in, leaving our children to drown,
We are the renegade whites . . . drumming up black,
                                        yellow, brown,
Laying the burden aside, bringing the jungle to town.
And the more we lower our sights, abandoning kith
                                        and kin,
The sweeter we'll sleep of nights . . . still hoping to
                                        save our skin.

But Malcolm MacDonald, the new Governor, disliked any form of colonial power and wanted to dismantle it in every country in which he served. He forged ahead rapidly with Africanisation and advanced the pace of the timetable for elections and independence. Kenyatta was released in 1961, an event profoundly shocking to some whites. He became Kenya's first Prime Minister on 1 June 1963, presiding over a country with internal self-government. Overseeing this hectic political activity, MacDonald was hardly surprisingly unpopular among Kenyan whites, who also deplored his open display of a Chinese mistress, Christina Loke, when his wife left the country on a visit to Canada.

The agricultural experts were told to devise a plan for a million acres of the white highlands to be settled by Africans, and £25 million was made available to buy the white farms. Thirty thousand African families, selected by lottery, had to be settled within three years. Some white farmers co-operated and sold their land, but others hung on as long as they could, which was a disaster for them because on one side of the boundary there were plots of an acre or more selling for £150 an acre while on the other white holdings of 1,000 to 1,500 acres were selling for £10 or £15 an acre.[74] The whites could not believe that the government refused to admit liability for their land titles, both leasehold from the Crown and freehold granted by the Crown, which they had believed to be sacrosanct. They felt they had made the highlands what they were, and that the advanced farming practised within them was a result of their investment and hard work, and they found these things very hard to give up. They reckoned they had earned a stake in the country, having put far more into it than they had taken out. They had tied up all their resources in the land, many of them commuting government pensions so to do, and were terrified of the future.

As one farmer said, 'They cleared the bush and built their homes, planted crops, and those who could afford it, imported splendid cattle from which they bred fine herds. They made many mistakes from which late comers learned wisdom, they emerged undefeated from all the plagues of Africa, locusts, drought, and every animal and vegetable disease under the sun.'[75] Many white farmers now lost heart and began to run down their farms. But when pressure increased to a degree that the whites knew they would have to sell their land, they were gracious about it, helping the agricultural officers transfer the land to Africans. A small amount of money, £750,000, was made available to buy out farms of 240 compassionate cases.

The administration was also ordered to move quickly with Africanisation. It was overstaffed in any case because white personnel had been increased during the Mau Mau and not all the extra men had been removed. There had been very little Africanisation up to now. The administrators were ordered to instruct Africans in methods of government and push forward as many of them as possible into positions of responsibility. Iain Macleod later admitted that 'the political decisions were taken so quickly and their consequences snowballed to such an extent . . . that they did to some extent overwhelm the administrative preparations . . . If one had waited until the administrative consequences were fully worked out the momentum of the political advance would . . . unquestionably have been lost.'[76]

Some white administrators viewed with jaundiced eye this order to deprive themselves of a job:

In truth the only possible conclusion is that the policy of the British government is now quite different from that of five years, even two years ago. It no longer wishes to induce its overseas civil servants to build houses in Kenya, it no longer wishes them to seek a career in Kenya, indeed there are reasons for supposing that it does not even want those who are serving in Kenya to stay in Kenya. It certainly is unwilling to retain any responsibility for them after Uhuru [freedom from British rule]. It now lacks either the desire or the ability, or both, to retain control until it can hand over to an administration of comparative ability.[77]

The civil servants were very concerned about what would happen to them, and whether or not there would be compensation. For those white administrators who left, an Overseas Services Resettlement Bureau was set up by the Colonial Office. Moreover, Alan Lennox-Boyd, former Colonial Secretary, was always very helpful in finding positions for administrators who returned to England.

Iain Macleod believed that 'there was a better and surer future for the European communities in African-run countries than in countries which were potentially explosive because the nationalists were being held back.'[78] He knew that an independent Kenya was an omelette he could not make without breaking eggs, and in this case the eggs were the livelihoods and futures of the country's white residents. On 12 December 1963 Kenya gained its independence. With broken hearts, thousands of white settlers decided to leave. Some stayed and took Kenyan nationality, though by 1966 only 750 had done so. Those who stayed and did not take Kenyan nationality were gradually denied work permits over the course of the next fifteen years, and had to leave if they wanted to earn their living.

Australia and South Africa welcomed whites who left Kenya. South Africa allowed them to import furniture, cars, farm machinery and household effects free from customs duties, and advanced money on generous terms to enable them to buy farms. It also gave those who needed them old-age pensions. This softened the blow, but the lowering of the British flag, right and proper though it was, ruined scores of lives. It left whites cynical and disillusioned, saddened and betrayed. Promises made had not been kept, land legally theirs had been compulsorily purchased, work contracts had been abrogated. The dismantlement of the British empire was bound to have its casualties, and Kenya's whites were high on the list of those who lost their livelihoods and hope. Yet they could take comfort in the fact that much of what they had done was good. Kenya under African rule was economically and politically viable in 1964: it was a democracy; the Africans had embraced twentieth-century ambitions and attitudes; and advanced farming methods had been introduced. Africans were no longer fearful of Arab slave-raiders, as they had been only seventy-five years before, and tribes were no longer fighting each other – indeed, the new slogan was 'Harambee!' which means 'Pull together' or 'Pull in unison'. Kenya's Africans were bright with hope for the independent future of their country as a member of the British Commonwealth. The sacrifice of the whites had not been in vain.

Conclusion

In the mid-twentieth century the British empire collapsed, after flourishing for three hundred years. As the colonial African countries achieved independence one after another, so there was a great exodus of whites from the continent. When Kenya raised its own flag at the end of 1963, large numbers of whites left the country. They preferred to do so despite being offered the option of surrendering their (mainly British) passports and adopting Kenyan nationality. Almost all the Afrikaner farmers and most of the civil servants quit. A few white professionals remained in Kenya, though many travelled to South Africa or Australia, to pursue their professions there. White farmers were mostly bought out and their land distributed to Africans; they dispersed to other areas of the world where they could buy agricultural land, or retired to the British Isles if getting on in years.

The new position was that non-farming whites could stay in Kenya, despite retaining their passports from other countries, as long as there were no Africans capable of doing their jobs. Thus some whites managed to stay on for five, ten or even fifteen more years, while sufficient numbers of Africans were trained to take up their positions.

Those whites who stayed were well treated, because the new President Jomo Kenyatta preferred conciliation to confrontation. Under his leadership, Kenya's early post-colonial years were peaceful and prosperous, with no trouble between the Africans and whites. Rather the friction was between black and Asian, and large numbers of the latter left to go to England, where they soon took over corner shops, newsagents and pharmacies. By working extremely long hours, many regained the wealth they had in Kenya, and their interest in their children's education helped the emergence of Asians in British professions.

The peaceful nature of relations between black and white after Kenya's independence was in marked contrast to the previous situation, when the Mau Mau rebellion left the whites with a legacy of fear for the future. This fear, always latent from the beginning of white occupation, contributed to the distancing of white from black inhabitant. This book's scope has precluded doing anything more than touching on the African response to colonialism, a subject too complicated and important for its confines, but there are several excellent studies an interested reader could consult. There were sporadic African uprisings in the early years of colonialism, all suppressed by armed troops and police, and thereafter there grew up, mainly among the Kikuyu people, political groupings aimed at getting more power and influence for Africans.

The white farmers who left Kenya for Britain after independence had considerable problems of adjustment. In their Kenya years they would have required a great deal of vision to break the mould of benevolent imperialism, seemingly permanent and perpetual, practised at the time, and to foresee the events of the 1950s and 1960s. They had trusted too naïvely in the British adage that 'my word is my bond' when governments pronounced that white settlement must be encouraged, that the highlands were to be kept white and that the British would never abandon the colonists. After both world wars more settlers were sent to Kenya from the home country – was this not evidence of good intentions? Upon independence, the whites felt immensely let down. They had failed to appreciate that governments bow to expediency, and after the Second World War it seemed judicious to part with the British empire. A few thousand British settlers in Kenya were now an embarrassment in the new liberal age that succeeded benevolent imperialism. By the 1960s the British public had little sympathy for the white man bearing burdens. A handful of shattered white lives mattered little in the grand scheme of things and personal tragedies could be disregarded.

The white settlers had been proud of developing the land beyond its ability merely to support people at a subsistence level or to provide items of simple barter and exchange. Now they saw many of their Kenyan farms broken up into small holdings. There was a feeling that this was a backward step and not good husbandry. As one settler said,

> I doubt if anyone who did not know the spirit of the old Kenya of the early farms, and the enthusiasm and the spirit of endeavour that pervaded it, and the hard work and the sacrifice of easy things that accompanied it, can ever comprehend our feeling of utter certainty that what we were doing was good and constructive and would last, and then our bitter disillusion when the evil in others broke out and swamped our efforts.[1]

Yet they need not have been so concerned. African farmers had imbibed much of what they had seen under colonialism and agriculture flourished in the new Kenya.

It was particularly difficult for the former settlers who went to Britain to adjust to life there. Whereas previously they had lived comfortably, with spacious houses and personal service, following a tradition of offering gracious hospitality even to complete strangers, now they must do all their chores themselves and practise severe retrenchment. Some of them never adjusted to the loss of a landscape so very dear to their souls. Others were more hardy and better able to survive the psychological trauma.

The ex-civil servants also had a troubled time when they returned to Britain. They wondered whether their lives in Kenya had been wasted. What they had tried to do latterly was to guide the African peoples through the transition from tribalism to nationalism. In the early days they had kept order in a land of ancient tribal enmities, brought peace where once there was war and released Africans from the horrors of Arab slavery. They had built towns where only mud huts had existed before, constructed roads and bridges and hospitals and schools where all had been plain and bush, and had taught farmers how to improve stock and crops and introduce irrigation. Paternalistic though their methods may have been, they believed their purpose was fine and proper. Sometimes they had done things too late. The government had not prosecuted the education of Africans as vigorously as it should have done, and too few Africans had been brought into the administration. Would the civil servants' endeavours all come to nought upon the granting of independence to Kenya? In fact the structure of administration and law they left behind was retained and worked well. The parliamentary two-party system they instituted was less of a success, because it is not entirely suited to peoples with strong tribal allegiances. And the British abhorrence of corruption was forgotten.

The ex-civil servants found a variety of jobs for themselves outside Kenya, but their career trajectories had been curtailed and many were put on the bottom rung of the ladder again. The older ones lived on government pensions, but not in the manner to which they had been accustomed in Kenya. Some of the younger ones were able to join the British Foreign Office, but most left the civil service altogether and found other employment. They still gather together annually in Henley to exchange news and reminisce. (The former members of the Kenya Police and the Kenya Regiment also have annual reunions.)

As for the white missionaries, most of them stayed in Kenya after independence. In the early days they had been convinced that it was right to lead Africans away from what they saw as a primitive, savage darkness into the light of a Western God and Western civilisation, vastly superior in their view to the African way of life. They thought they were releasing Africans from their atavistic fear of malign spirits, fatalism and hopelessness. Their great legacy was to have provided Africans with education (in the case of the Roman Catholics mainly technical), the means to read the Bible, healthcare and lessons in hygiene to counter the high death-rate. Unlike the settlers (though frequently just as paternalistic), they had lived among Africans, and so adjustment to the new Kenya came more easily to them. Those who returned to their mother countries rejoined their orders or were placed in home parishes.

The whites suffering the most trauma after leaving Kenya were those born there, and most particularly their children, who had seen no other country. Perhaps that is why their school websites flourish and their school reunions in Britain, South Africa and Australia are so well attended. Though African independence was inevitable and entirely right, and they could appreciate the justice of it, nevertheless the youngsters sometimes had the unspoken and politically incorrect feeling that they had been discriminated against because of the colour of their skin. They felt they had 'lost' their country. Many of the children would have preferred to stay in Kenya and adopt Kenyan nationality, but their parents removed them.

The Kenya Africans had an inheritance from the whites that no other African state has had. The whites made an enormous contribution to the economic development and wellbeing of Kenya. Unfortunately the manner in which this was done was frequently arrogant, overbearing and insensitive. Eventually the very presence of white people became intolerable to black Kenyans and they expressed their views vociferously with panga,[2] gun and pen. This understandable resort to terror saw independence achieved within ten years, though some thought that Kenya would have been freed from colonial control earlier had there been no violence. Whatever the truth of the matter, the Mau Mau rebellion left whites disillusioned and bitter. The country was fortunate in its first President, Jomo Kenyatta, who worked hard to heal the rift between white and black.

At present Kenya has a small population of whites. Some are Kenyan nationals who work mainly as farmers or in the wildlife industry. Others are on short-term commercial contracts from other countries. A few Europeans winter in Kenya, having bought retirement homes there. There is ostensibly no colour bar, though white children attend private rather than government schools, and some whites have friends only within their own racial group. Prominent among the latter are the 'Kenya cowboys', young men who race around in cars and give the whites a bad name. But most of the whites cause no offence and are well adjusted to their life beside the Africans in a beautiful country edged by the vast inland sea of Lake Victoria Nyanza in one corner and the coral-reefed Indian Ocean in another, by the barren desert in the north and the lofty mountain Kilimanjaro in the south; and rent by the deep fissure of the Great Rift Valley, from whose wall can be seen the jagged snowy peaks of Mount Kenya.

Appendix: The Indigenous Peoples of Kenya

The African inhabitants of Kenya can be divided into groups by language and activity. The Bantu comprise 65 per cent of the population, the Cushites 3–4 per cent and the Nilotes and Paranilotes 30–31 per cent.

THE HUNTER-GATHERERS
Boni, Dahalo, El-Molo, Ndorobo and Sanye

THE BANTU (AGRICULTURALISTS)
Western: Luhya, Kisii, Kuria, Gusii
Central: Kikuyu, Kamba, Meru, Embu, Tharaka, Mbere
Coastal: The Mijikenda, consisting of the Digo, Duruma, Rabai, Ribe, Kambe, Jibana, Chonyi, Giriama and Kauma. Also the Segeju, Taveta, Pokomo and Taita

NILOTES AND PARANILOTES (PASTORALISTS)
Nilotes: Luo
Teso: Iteso, Turkana
Maasai: Maasai, Samburu, Njemps
Kalenjin: Nandi, Kipsigis, Elgeyo, Sabaot, Marakwet, Tugen, Terik, Pokot

CUSHITES (SHEPHERDS)
Somali, Rendille, Galla, Borana, Gabbra, Orma, Sakuye

CWAHILI (FISHERMEN)
Bajun, Pate, Mvita, Vumba, Ozi, Fundi, Siyu, Shela, Amu

Notes

Abbreviations: RH is Rhodes House Library, now the Bodleian Library of Commonwealth and African Studies, Oxford.

CHAPTER 1

1 Sir Frederick Jackson, *Early Days in East Africa*, London, Edward Arnold, 1930, p. 66.
2 After Martin's retirement from government service he became manager of the Mabira forest concession.
3 Francis (Frank) G. Hall tried a different method, with donkeys, but they died one by one. He loaded the donkeys with water, made each man carry three gallons as well as his own load, and walked through the desert for three nights, sleeping during the day. The donkeys had no water for seventy-two hours. Hall to his father, 10 October 1892, Hall papers, RH, Mss Afr.s.56.
4 Loose sheets with names of camps, distances between them and mileage, in Gedge papers, RH, Mss Brit.Emp.s.290/4.
5 Sir Arthur Hardinge, *A Diplomatist in the East*, London, Cape, 1928, p. 195.
6 H. B. Thomas, 'George Wilson and Dagoretti Fort', *Uganda Journal*, vol. 23, no. 2, Sept. 1959.
7 Jackson to Gedge, 28 [illegible, ? September] 1891, Gedge papers, RH, Mss Brit.Emp.s.290.
8 Edward Russell's diary, 1896, RH, Mss Afr.s.119.
9 A. J. Hopkins, *Trail Blazers and Road Makers*, London, Henry Hooks, no date, but 1928, p. 3.
10 Francis Hall to his father, 12 January 1995, Hall papers, RH, Mss Afr.s.56.
11 Hopkins, *Trail Blazers*, p. 96.
12 Hopkins, *Trail Blazers*, p. 72.
13 Willis R. Hotchkiss, *Then and Now in Kenya Colony*, London, Oliphants, 1937, pp. 76–7.
14 Patterson (sometimes spelt Paterson) obtained the seed from Aden. Coffee bushes also grew in an almost wild state on the Sese islands of Lake Victoria. The beans were chewed by the Baganda rather than made into a drink – 'Report on the Mombasa Victoria Lake Railway Survey', *Parliamentary*

Papers, Cmd. 7025, London, HMSO, 1893. From 1895 cultivated coffee was also grown in the Taita hills, on the French mission at Bura. Brother Solanus Zipper had obtained the seed from a mission at Morogoro in German East Africa, whose Father Bauer had got the seed from Aden via Zanzibar in the late 1880s. In 1892 Zipper was posted from the Morogoro mission to Bura, where he found coffee grew readily, and as soon as the Catholics set up St Austin's mission near Nairobi at the turn of the century they planted coffee seedlings. Boedeker (see below) planted some of the Kibwezi seed at his farm at Fort Smith in 1896, but the main plantings near Nairobi were in 1899 or 1900 when the Kibwezi mission moved there and Patterson took some of his plants with him. The early settlers copied the missions and planted coffee in the highlands, where it thrived mightily and became in time the East Africa Protectorate's most profitable crop.

15 Ernest Gedge in *The Times*, 24 February 1893; J. R. L. Macdonald, *Soldiering and Surveying in British East Africa 1891–1894*, London, Edward Arnold, 1897, pp. 120–1; Dorothy Stanley (ed.), *The Autobiography of Henry M. Stanley*, London, Sampson Low, Marston & Co., 1909, pp. 354, 383.

16 Ernest Gedge in *The Times*, 8 December 1892; Gedge notebooks, 1892, Gedge papers, RH, Mss Brit. Emp.s.290/4; and Hall to his father, 20 June 1892, Hall papers, RH, Mss Afr.s.56.

17 John Pringle's diary, 10 March 1892, RH, Mss Afr.s.528.

18 'Report on the Mombasa Victoria Lake Railway Survey', *Parliamentary Papers*, Cmd. 7025, London, HMSO, 1893.

19 Russell's diary, 8 January 1896, RH, Mss Afr.s.119.

20 Russell's diary, 9 January 1895, RH, Mss Afr.s.118.

21 Hall to his father, 3 September 1894, Hall papers, RH, Mss Afr.s.56.

22 Peter Rogers, 'The British and the Kikuyu, 1890–1905: a Reassessment', *Journal of African History*, vol. 20, 1979, p. 258.

23 Hall to his father, 14 January 1894, Hall papers, RH, Mss Afr.s.56.

24 Hall to his father, 22 October 1894, Hall papers, RH, Mss Afr.s.56.

25 Hall to his father, 22 February 1893, Hall papers, RH, Mss Afr.s.56.

26 Macdonald, *Soldiering and Surveying*, pp. 120–1.

27 Hall to his father, 22 October 1892, Hall papers, RH, Mss Afr.s.56.

28 Hall to his father, 24 November 1893, Hall papers, RH, Mss Afr.s.56.

29 Hall to his father, 12 February 1894, Hall papers, RH, Mss Afr.s.56.

30 Thomas P. Ofcansky, 'The 1889–97 Rinderpest Epidemic and the Rise of British and German Colonialism in Eastern and Southern Africa', *Journal of African Studies*, vol. 8, no. 1, spring 1981.

31 Hall to his father, 15 April 1894, Hall papers, RH, Mss Afr.s.56.

32 Russell's diary, 16 May 1895, RH, Mss Afr.s.118.

33 Hall to his father, 22 October 1892, RH, Mss Afr.s.56.

34 Russell's diary, 1 October 1895 and 21 September 1896, RH, Mss Afr.s.118 and 119.

35 Hall to his father, 22 October 1894, Hall papers, RH, Mss Afr.s.56. There is a detailed account of the search for them by Ainsworth's men in John

Ainsworth's autobiography, RH, Mss Afr.s.380. What really happened to them no one knows. See also Victoria T. Coats, *David Charters, Engineer, Doctor and Missionary 1864–1894*, London, A. & C. Black, 1925, and footnote 37 below.

36 Dick's letter, 26 November 1895, stuck in Russell's diary, 1895, RH, Mss Afr.s.118.

37 Hardinge, *A Diplomatist in the East*, pp. 143–6. The group, which had its headquarters in Vienna, was following the precepts of Dr Theodor Hertzka's book *Freiland: Ein Sociales Zukunftsbild*, 1889, translated into English by Arthur Ransom [*sic*] as *Freeland: A Social Anticipation*, London, Chatto & Windus, 1891. Apart from Dugmore, Francis Colquhoun and R. Glucksellij remained in East Africa, Colquhoun disappeared with David Charters in the bush near Kibwezi (see footnote 35 above), and Glucksellij made his way to Fort Smith. He was deported for mutilating corpses but returned to East Africa. In the 1920s he was employed as a surveyor in Kenya's Public Works Department.

38 Russell's diary, 7 September 1896, RH, Mss Afr.s.119.

39 Ainsworth's typewritten autobiography, RH, Mss Afr.s.380.

40 Russell's diary, 20 March 1895, RH, Mss Afr.s.118.

41 Russell's diary, 1895, passim, RH, Mss Afr.s.118, and Hall to his father, 22 December 1894, and 12 January and 24 April 1895, Hall papers, RH, Mss Afr.s.56.

42 J. Forbes Munro, *Colonial Rule and the Kamba, 1889–1939*, Oxford, Clarendon Press, 1975, pp. 32–6. Ainsworth had a long career in Kenya. He was superintendent of Machakos 1892–95, sub-commissioner of Ukamba province, at Machakos 1895–9, and Nairobi 1899–1906; sub-commissioner of Naivasha province 1906–97; provincial commissioner of Nyanza province 1907–17; military commissioner for labour 1917–18; and chief native commissioner 1918–20. He moved to South Africa to be with his son and died on 31 March 1946.

43 A wedding invitation was stuck into Russell's diary on 3 December 1897, RH, Mss Afr.s.120. The Scott parents came out to Kenya in 1896 with their youngest daughter Ina.

44 Ainsworth's typewritten autobiography, RH, Mss Afr.s.380.

45 Lionel Declé, *Three Years in Savage Africa*, London, Methuen, 1898, p. 484.

46 Russell's diary, 12 April 1896, RH, Mss Afr.s.119.

47 Jackson to Gedge 28 [illegible, ? September] 1891, Gedge papers, RH, Mss Brit. Emp.s.290.

CHAPTER 2

1 Hall to his father, 24 June 1893, Hall papers, RH, Mss Afr.s.56.

2 Hall to his father, 15 March 1894, Hall papers, RH, Mss Afr.s.56.

3 Hall to his father, 12 January 1895, Hall papers, RH, Mss Afr.s.56.

4   J. H. Patterson's diary, 8 September 1989, RH, Mss Afr.r.93.
5   Hall to his father, 10 October 1892, Hall papers, RH, Mss Afr.s.56.
6   Hall to his father, 28 October 1893, Hall papers, RH, Mss Afr.s.56.
7   Hall to his father, 12 January 1895, Hall papers, RH, Mss Afr.s.56.
8   Rachel Stuart Watt, *In the Heart of Savagedom*, London, Marshall Bros, 1913, p. 34.
9   Hall to his father, 14 December 1893, Hall papers, RH, Mss Afr.s.56, and J. A. Stuart Watt, 'Recollections of Kenya 1895–1963', RH, Mss Afr.s.391, which contains the CMS letter.
10 Hall to his father, 14 January 1894, Hall papers, RH, Mss Afr.s.56.
11 Ainsworth's typewritten autobiography, RH, Mss Afr.s.380.
12 *Advertiser of East Africa*, 24 April 1908.
13 Russell's diary, 10 November 1895, RH, Mss Afr.s.118.
14 Russell's diary, 25 December 1895, RH, Mss Afr.s.118.
15 Hall to his father, 24 June and 3 October 1893, Hall papers, RH, Mss Afr.s.56.
16 Russell's diary, 20 January, 6, 13 and 24 February and 11 March 1896, RH, Mss Afr.s.119.
17 Russell's diary, 5 July 1896, RH, Mss Afr.s.119.
18 Russell's diary, 18 August 1896, RH, Mss Afr.s.119. Mary Walshe died on 20 June 1922 and was buried in Forest Road cemetery, Nairobi.
19 Russell's diary, 20 and 28 September 1896, RH, Mss Afr.s.119.
20 J. A. Stuart Watt, 'Recollections of Kenya 1895–1963', RH, Mss Afr.s.391.
21 'The Mysterious Doctor' in Cynthia Salvadori, *We Came in Dhows*, 3 vols, Nairobi, Paperchase Kenya Ltd, 1996, vol. 2, pp. 6–7. Born in 1872, Boedeker was the son of Frederik W. Boedeker, manager of a Scottish-based timber and shipping firm in Moulmein, Burma.
22 Cynthia Salvadori could find no record of this marriage in Scottish registry records.
23 Boedeker's evidence to the Kenya Land Commission, *Parliamentary Papers*, Cmd. 4850, London, HMSO, 1932, vol. 1, p. 695.
24 Sir Malcolm Henderson's diary, 4 July 1900, RH, Mss Afr.s.1484. Boedeker at first grew vegetables on a plot near Fort Smith but left the land in 1899 to work as a government doctor in Naivasha.
25 The McQueens first settled near Fort Smith, then moved to Uganda, only to return and settle for good on the banks of the Mbagathi river at Ngong in 1902.
26 Russell's diary, 11 October 1896, RH, Mss Afr.s.119.
27 Russell's diary, 1 January 1897, RH, Mss Afr.s.120.
28 Lane's evidence to the Kenya Land Commission, *Parliamentary Papers*, Cmd. 4850, London, HMSO, 1932, vol. 1, p. 399.
29 Boedeker's evidence to the Kenya Land Commission, vol. 1, p. 695, and Russell's diary, 11 March and 5 July 1896, RH, Mss Afr.s.119.
30 Boedeker's evidence to the Kenya Land Commission, vol. 1, p. 707.
31 Russell's diary, 6 February 1896, RH, Mss Afr.s.119.

32 J. H. Patterson's diary, 16 April 1898, RH, Mss Afr.r.93.

33 'Report on the Mombasa Victoria Lake Railway Survey', *Parliamentary Papers*, Cmd. 7025, London, HMSO, 1893.

34 Hall to his father, 15 August 1899, Hall papers, RH, Mss Afr.s.57.

35 Russell's diary, 26 May 1895, RH, Mss Afr.s.118.

36 Russell's diary, 19 September 1896, RH, Mss Afr.s.119.

37 Ellis was at Hall's birthday celebrations at Fort Smith on 11 October 1896. Russell's diary, 11 October 1896, RH, Mss Afr.s.119.

38 R. O. Preston, 'Descending the Great Rift Valley', *Kenya Graphic*, 1922.

39 Hall to his father, 1 April 1899, Hall papers, RH, Mss Afr.s.57.

40 H. K. Binks, *African Rainbow*, London, Sidgwick & Jackson, 1959, p. 42. Binks dictated this book when he was old. In it he says he came to Kenya in 1900, but the immigration records prove he came in 1902.

41 Richard Meinertzhagen, *Kenya Diary, 1902–1906*, Edinburgh, Oliver & Boyd, 1957.

42 The last trolley ran on 18 August 1921, after which the rails were lifted. See Henry Gunston and Rosemary Macdonald, 'Street Trollies in Mombasa', *Kenya Past and Present*, issue 21, 1989.

43 Reginald Neville Boustead was born on 21 October 1963 at Wimbledon and was educated at Eton. His family had trading interests in Ceylon and branched out into Zanzibar in the 1870s. Rex expanded the firm into Mombasa in 1892. In 1901 Boustead Ridley went into liquidation, to be succeeded by Boustead Brothers, of Zanzibar and Mombasa (in which Rex was joined by his brother John, known as Jack). In 1908 Boustead Brothers became Boustead & Clarke. Jack died in 1920 and Rex in South Kensington on 12 March 1924. Information from Peter Frankl.

44 Hall to his father, 16 March 1900, Hall papers, RH, Mss Afr.s.57.

45 Hall to his father, 12 and 25 April and 17 October 1899, Hall papers, RH, Mss Afr.s.57.

46 Hall to his father, 17 October 1899, Hall papers, RH, Mss Afr.s.57.

47 Hall to his father, 26 November 1899, Hall papers, RH, Mss Afr.s.57.

48 Ibid.

49 Beatrice Hall to Hall's father, 1 April 1901, Hall papers, RH, Mss Afr.s.57.

50 William Radford to Hall's father, 26 March 1901, Hall papers, RH, Mss Afr.s.57.

51 J. H. Patterson, *In the Grip of the Nyika*, London, Macmillan, 1910, pp. 133–4.

52 'Report by H.M. Commissioner on the East Africa Protectorate, June 1903', *Parliamentary Papers*, Cmd. 1626, London, HMSO, 1903.

CHAPTER 3

1 From 'I Remember' in E. C. Adams, *Lyra Nigeriae*, London, T. Fisher Unwin, 1911.

2 To avoid confusion, the post will be described as Governor. In reality the name was Commissioner until the order-in-council of 22 October 1906, when the post became that of Governor.

3 Sir Harold Parlett's introduction to Sir Charles Eliot's *Japanese Buddhism*, London, Edward Arnold, 1935. Eliot died on 16 March 1931 on board the ship *Hakone Maru* and was buried at sea between Penang and Colombo. As there was no Christian priest on board, the service was conducted according to Japanese burial rites.

4 W. Robert Foran, *A Cuckoo in Kenya*, London, Hutchinson, 1936, p. 20.

5 Robert Alan Remole, 'White Settlers or the Foundation of European Agricultural Settlement in Kenya', Ph.D., Harvard University, March 1959.

6 Stephen Salisbury Bagge, who arrived in 1894. He became a sub-commissioner (later called Provincial Commissioner) in 1902.

7 Chamberlain to Viscount Milner, 29 July 1904, Chamberlain papers, RH, Mss Afr.s.589.

8 Percy Bysshe Shelley, 'Julian and Maddalo', l. 14.

9 Introduction by Lord Cranworth to Foran, *A Cuckoo in Kenya*, p. 16.

10 Noel Smith to his mother, 7 February 1919, Noel Smith papers, RH, Micr.Afr.590.

11 Noel Smith to his mother, 31 July 1919, Noel Smith papers, RH, Micr.Afr.590.

12 *East African Standard*, 12 June 1920, and interview with Will Powys at Ngare Ndare, January 1972, tape in private hands.

13 Archie Cooper to Douglas Cooper, 31 October 1903, copy enclosed in J. P. Cooper to Christine Nicholls, 5 April 2002.

14 Dagoretti Political Record Book, 1908–12, vol. iv, 25 May 1908, Kenya Archives, RH, Micr.Afr.516, reel 5.

15 Bertram Francis Gurdon, 2nd Baron Cranworth, KG, MC (1877–1964), educated at Eton and Trinity College, Cambridge. He served in the Boer War and the First World War. He went to the EAP in 1906 to shoot and take up land, and stayed off and on until the end of the First World War.

16 Ronald Douglas Stuart Mar Erskine, Lord Cardross (1878–1960), who had fought in the Boer War and became 15th Earl of Buchan in 1934. Major William John Bates Van de Weyer (1870–1946) who married Olive Wingfield, daughter of Viscount Powerscourt.

17 Eric Dutton, *Kenya Mountain*, London, Jonathan Cape, 1930, p. 14.

18 Eleanor Cole, *Random Recollections of a Kenya Settler*, Woodbridge, Suffolk, Baron Publishing, 1975.

19 W. N. McMillan Scrapbooks, RH, Micr.Afr.641.

20 Photographs of this event exist in R. A. W. Porter, 'Random Reminiscences', RH, Mss Afr.s.702. There was another public hanging in Mombasa, in 1917, of one of the two spies who had told the Germans that the British warship *Pegasus* had put in to Zanzibar, where the Germans sank it – Sir Gordon Covell, 'The Military Campaign in East Africa', RH, Mss Afr.s.385–7.

21 Stephen Seymour Butler journals, RH, Mss Afr.r.195/1.

22 For lists of who came when, see Brian M. du Toit, *The Boers in East Africa*, Westport, Connecticut, Bergin & Garvey, 1998.

23 Papers of Betty Minchin, RH, Micr.Afr.594.

24 Lord (Bertram) Cranworth, *A Colony in the Making*, London, Macmillan, 1912, p. 83.

25 Foreign firms established in Mombasa included the Germans Hansing & Co., H. Robitsek & Reis, Konrad Schauer, W. Oswald & Co. and W. Hintzmann & Co.; the Austrians Otto Markus and Rudolf Loy's East African Trading Co., which had the monopoly of hurricane lanterns; the Italian Societa Coloniale Italiana; the Central African Trading Co. run by the Dutch B. Besseling; the American Harris R. Childs of Childs & Co.; the Italians Arnaldo Parenti and Luigi Frigeria of the German firm Max Klein; and the Greek D. Papadopulo & Co.

26 He married Emily in 1904 and had two sons. He was in the Legislative Council from 1910 to 1924, first as a nominated, and later an elected, member. In 1927–28 he was mayor of Nairobi.

27 George Hutton ('Jack') Riddell, whose mother was the daughter of the Earl of Craven, went to Eton and Sandhurst. He then fought in the Boer War before going in 1906 to East Africa, where he was seconded to the KAR. Hornyold came from two completely Anglicised families and also fought in the Boer War.

28 Born in 1850, the son of a clergyman in Bedfordshire, Neumann was in South Africa from the age of eighteen until he joined IBEAC in 1890.

29 A. Cecil Hoey, who arrived in 1904. He and his brother Alfred E. Hoey, who had arrived in 1901, took up land in Trans-Nzoia in 1912. A. C. Hoey became a member of the Legislative Council. The town Hoey's Bridge (now Moi's Bridge) was named for Alfred Hoey.

30 De Gex, of the Lancashire Fusiliers, died on 11 October 1901. Lucas and his working partner G. H. Goldfinch had a farm on the slopes of Ol Donyo Sabuk. Lucas died in Nairobi hospital after refusing to have a limb amputated.

31 A government official killed by a lion near Rumuruti in 1911.

32 Theodore Roosevelt, *African Game Trails*, London, John Murray, 1910.

33 J. H. Patterson, *The Man Eaters of Tsavo*, London, Macmillan, 1907.

34 Alfred Arkell-Hardwick, *An Ivory Trader in North Kenya*, London, Longmans Green, 1903, p. 65.

35 J. E. Gough, 'Travels in East Africa', RH, Mss Afr.s.2046.

36 W. D. M. Bell, *Karamojo Safari*, Suffolk, Neville Spearman, 1949, p. 39.

37 R. Gorell Barnes, *Babes in the African Wood*, London, Longmans Green, 1911, p. 135.

38 Stewart E. White, *The Land of Footprints*, London, no date but 1913, p. 220.

39 Foran, *A Cuckoo in Kenya*, p. 71.

40 A. C. Hollis, 'Autobiography', vol. 3, RH, Mss Brit.Emp.s.295.

41 Eric Dutton, 'The Night of the Hyena', RH, Micr.Afr.587, p. 42.

42 Autobiography of Sir Percy Girouard, RH, Mss Afr.s.1865.

43 The marriage was dissolved in 1914 and she died in 1916 giving birth to the twins of Robert Oppenheim whom she had married in 1915.

44 An African woman.

45 EAP Audit Office papers, RH, Mss Afr.r.126.

46 Dr Walter Halliburton Babington Macdonald, the first Principal Medical Officer, who arrived in 1895. Macdonald was a huge man who married a nursing sister in Mombasa hospital, another person of impressive size. He died in 1916.

47 Audit Office papers, RH, Mss Afr.r.126. A full version of the poem is printed in *Coast Guardian*, 5 October 1937 and included in the Tana River Political Record Book, Kenya Archives, RH, Micr.Afr.516, reel 15. It appears to have been written by a former habitué of the Alhambra Music Hall in Leicester Square, London, who lost a great deal of money by betting on horse-racing. One of the verses reads:

> I ain't a repentant sinner
> And if I did put back the clock
> It's six to four I'd keep the whore
> Who landed me in the lock.

A lock was a venereal diseases hospital.

48 F. W. Isaac to Captain V. M. Fisher, 2 March 1919 and V. M. Fisher to F. W. Isaac, 2 March 1919, sent to Principal Medical Officer, Nairobi, Kenya Archives, Medical Department, July 1919, no. 21/3018/1. Reference supplied by Stephen North. Duff had fought in the First World War and then been attached to the BEA Forestry Department, from where he had applied locally to join the administration – Sir Edward Northey to Colonial Secretary, 30 June 1919, PRO, CO 533/211.

49 Willoughby Harry Thompson, 'Colonial Memories of Kenya 1944–1963', RH, Mss Brit.Emp.s.519.

50 PRO, RG 36–8/145.

51 W. H. Thompson to Christine Nicholls, 13 September 2002. See also J. S. S. Rowlands, 'Notes on the Tana River', 7 December 1955, RH, Mss Afr.s.2282.

52 The Belazoni Estate was abandoned in 1940 and is now covered in thick bush.

53 See J. S. S. Rowlands, 'Notes on the Tana River', 7 December 1955, RH, Mss.Afr.s.2282, and Henry Wright, 'A Haunted Boma', in John Johnson (ed.), *Colony to Nation*, Banham, Norfolk, Erskine Press, 2002, pp. 126–7. Henry Wright to Peter Fullerton (both former DOs at Kipini), enclosed in Fullerton to Christine Nicholls, 12 July 2002, gives a detailed account of the graves and the ghosts. Pitt had a magnificent marble tombstone provided by his family, Duff a simple wooden cross made by the Mombasa Public Works Department in 1927, with cement surround, and Mitchell a reinforced concrete cross built locally in 1927. In May 1931 a barbed-wire fence with cemented corner posts was erected around the cemetery – Tana

River Political Record Book, Kenya Archives, RH, Micr.Afr.516, reel 15. Henry Wright revisited the graves in 1996, found them completely obliterated by bush, and paid for the site to be cleared. At Liddington church, Wiltshire, where Pitt's father was rector, there is a stained-glass window behind the altar, depicting C. G. Pitt wearing a cloak and holding a spear.

54 Cranworth, *A Colony in the Making*, p. 76.

55 These numbers show the expansion of the administration: PCs: 1897 4; 1903 7; 1918 6. DCs: 1897 7; 1903 19; 1910 30; 1918 44. ADCs (DOs): 1897 11, 1903 20; 1910 45; 1913 51; 1918 91. New stations that were opened were Kitui (1897), Kibwezi (1898), Kisumu in Uganda (1899), Fort Hall (1900), shores of Lake Baringo (1900), Nyeri (1902), Kiambu (1902), Kisumu taken over from Uganda (1902), Kakamega (1903), Kericho (1903), Karungu (1903, transferred to Kisii 1907), Rumuruti (1905), Embu (1906), Moyale (1907), Meru (1908), Kerio Valley (1908, moved in 1910 to Ngabotok), Archer's Post (1909), Marsabit (1909), Mt Kulal (1910), Serenli (1910), Narok (1911), Wajir (1912).

56 See T. R. H. Cashmore, 'Studies in District Administration in the East Africa Protectorate, 1895–1918', Cambridge University Ph.D., 1978.

57 Ibid.

58 Blackwater fever was sometimes thought to be precipitated by an injection, or excessive dose, of quinine. So many doctors of the time observed this, that there may be something in it. Today corticosteroids prevent further haemolysis, while kidney failure is overcome by blood transfusion. After the Second World War regular prophylactic antimalarials made blackwater fever rare.

59 Harold Charles Edward Barnes, who entered Somerset House in 1894, became assistant auditor of Sierra Leone and Gambia in 1895, and in 1897 went to East Africa as assistant auditor of the East Africa Protectorate and Uganda Railway.

60 William John Monson, educated at Eton and Magdalen College, Oxford. He went to East Africa in 1899 and became Secretary to the administration and Registrar-General of the EAP in 1907.

61 Barnes to Monson, 26 January 1914, and Monson to Barnes, 28 January 1914, EAP Audit Office papers, RH, Mss Afr.r.126.

62 Sheelagh Silvester, 'Flashback', *Women in Kenya* (EAWL magazine), Nairobi, March 1971, p. 12.

63 Derek Peterson, 'Colonizing Language? Missionaries and Gikuyu Dictionaries, 1904 and 1914', *History in Africa*, vol. 24, 1997, pp. 257–72.

64 One of the lay brothers was Benedict Falla, who helped write a book about his experiences – Gabriele Soldati (trans. Michael Cunningham), *The Pioneer: The African Adventure of Benedict Falla*, Slough, St Paul's Publications, 1991 (for Istituto Missioni Consolata). See also Madie Cator to Miss Tylden Wright, 2 March 1904, RH, Mss Afr.r.150.

65 C. A. Wiggins, 'Early Days in British East Africa and Uganda', 1960 (cyclostyled), RH.

66 Diary of Sir Malcolm Henderson, 2 July 1900, RH, Mss Afr.s.1484.

67 Richard Gethin papers, RH, Mss Afr.s.1747.

68 It has been suggested that Chamberlain may have realised that the ultimate success of his post-Boer War policies in South Africa would rest on whether he had the support of the Jews, because of the strength of the Jewish mining magnates in the Rand.

69 Hugh Cholmondeley, 3rd Baron Delamere, *The Grant of Land to the Zionist Congress and Land Settlement in British East Africa*, London, Harrison & Sons, 1903.

70 Lord (Charles) Hindlip, *British East Africa, Past, Present and Future*, London, T. Fisher Unwin, 1905.

71 Robert Weisbord, *African Zion*, Philadelphia, Jewish Publication Society of America, 1968, demolishes this supposition, put about in many books. See also *Report on the Work of the Commission Sent out by the Zionist Organization for the Purpose of Jewish Settlement in BEA*, London, Wertheimer, Lea & Co., 1905.

72 The first doctor appointed to IBEAC was Dr Archibald D. Mackinnon. He arrived in 1888, to be joined in 1889 by Dr I. S. Macpherson. In 1891 Dr T. M. Rae (died 1893) was stationed at Malindi and Lamu, and in the same year Dr R. A. Moffat was sent to Kibwezi to the Scottish Mission. Mackinnon, Macpherson and Moffat all went to Uganda in 1895. Another Scottish Mission doctor, David Charters, disappeared in 1895 (see Chapter 1, p. 37). Dr C. S. Edwards arrived as a CMS medical missionary in Mombasa (1890). In 1896 Dr. H. A. Boedeker came as a settler. The Uganda Railway brought its own doctors, under Captain James Will. For Macdonald, see note 46, above.

73 P. A. Clearkin, 'Ramblings and Recollections of a Colonial Doctor, 1913–1958', RH, Mss Brit.Emp.r.4/1.

74 Major Henry Rayne, *The Ivory Raiders*, London, Heinemann, 1923, p. 145.

75 Mavis Birdsey, 'Sigh Softly, African Winds', RH, Mss Afr.s.1794.

CHAPTER 4

1 Brian Brooks [Korongo], 'The Missing Something', *Poems of Brian Brooks*, London, John Lane, no date but 1917. Brooks settled in BEA, joined the East African Mounted Rifles, went to France and was killed at the battle of Mametz in 1916.

2 Ukamba Annual Reports, 1906–07, Kenya Archives, RH, Micr.Afr.515/1.

3 Ukamba Annual Reports, 1909–15, Kenya Archives, RH, Micr.Afr.515/1.

4 Donald Garvie was born in Edinburgh and emigrated to South Africa with his parents in 1881. There he married a Boer girl, Cornelia Steyn. In 1903 they went to the EAP and settled among the Nandi. Donald Garvie died in 1912. See Brian M. du Toit, *The Boers in East Africa*, Westport, Connecticut, Bergin & Garvey, 1998, pp. 57–8.

5 Registration Department to Mr Croall, 18 May 1909, Audit Office papers, RH, Mss Afr.r.126.

6 Ukamba Annual Reports, Kenya Archives, RH, Micr.Afr.515/1.

7 B. L. Bremner to his sister, 3 February 1915, Bremner papers, RH, Mss Afr.s.1372.

8 David Round-Turner (compiler), *Nairobi Club: The Story of 100 Years*, Nairobi, Nairobi Club, 2001, passim.

9 Queenie Sandbach Baker and her husband (a former cotton merchant in Manchester) had arrived in the EAP in 1901 and acquired 1,600 acres at Muthaiga, where they built 'The Homestead' and established a farm to supply Nairobi with meat and dairy products. In 1933 H. F. Ward claimed in an interview with Elspeth Huxley (Huxley papers, RH, Mss Afr.s.782/ 1/5) that Mrs Sandbach Baker sold the land on her husband's death, but there is a picture of him very much alive accompanying A. B. Crooks's interview with him in *The African World* magazine of 1912.

10 T. R. L. Nestor, 'Reminiscences 1912–1949', RH, Mss Afr.s.1086. Nestor's sister Vivian, who went to join him in the EAP, married Hugh Stutchbury, the secretary of the Muthaiga Club. I am grateful to Neil McCormick (email 10 August 2003) for some of this information.

11 Lord Cranworth, *A Colony in the Making*, London, Macmillan, 1912, p. 325.

12 See Emilie Delap-Hilton, *Snips without Snaps of Kenya*, London, Arthur H. Stockwell, no date but c. 1927. Although lightly fictionalised, this book gives a good account of life in the camp.

13 Elspeth Huxley's interview with Blancke, RH, Mss Afr.s.782/1/5.

14 C. A. Wiggins, 'Early Days in British East Africa and Uganda', 1960 (cyclostyled), RH.

15 R. Gorell Barnes, *Babes in the African Wood*, London, Longmans Green, 1911, pp. 207–8.

16 From 'The Mosquito Theory' by E. C. Adams in *Lyra Nigeriae*, 1911.

17 C. A. Wiggins, 'Early Days in East Africa and Uganda', 1960 (cyclostyled), RH.

18 These remedies are mentioned by Mavis Birdsey in her 'Sigh Softly African Winds', RH, Mss Afr.s.1794.

19 These figures are taken from the PMO's reports in the Ukamba Annual Reports of 1906 to 1919, Kenya Archives, RH, Micr.Afr.515/1.

20 From 'The Story of David' in E. C. Adams, *Lyra Nigeriae*, 1911.

21 Cynthia Salvadori, 'Doctor on a Zebra', *We Came in Dhows*, 3 vols, Nairobi, Paperchase Kenya Ltd, 1996, vol. 2, pp. 22–3.

22 Registers of European School, Nairobi, RH, Mss Afr.s.828.

23 Edith Klaprott, 'Woodsmoke', RH, Micr.Afr.591.

24 Matthew Hall Kell (1875–1930) had been tutor to the son of a rajah, but took up land in the EAP, on which he planted coffee, and built a house at Kiambu in 1907.

25 Ukamba Annual Report, 1908–09, Kenya Archives, RH, Micr.Afr.515/1.

26 Nairobi Chamber of Commerce minutes, 7 February and 26 September 1918, RH, Mss Afr.s.1467.

27 Nairobi School roll, RH, Mss Afr.s.829.

28 This information is from Edith Klaprott, 'Woodsmoke', RH, Micr. Afr.591; Gerrit D. Groen, 'The Afrikaners in Kenya, 1903–1969', Michigan State University Ph.D., 1974; Brian M. du Toit, *The Boers in East Africa*, Westport, Connecticut, Bergin & Garvey, 1998; and Mavis Birdsey, 'Sigh Softly African Winds', RH, Mss Afr.s.1794.

29 Peel died in Mombasa on 15 April 1916. He was succeeded by Richard Stanley Heywood, who transferred his seat to Nairobi and was in his turn succeeded in 1936 by Reginald Percy Crabbe. In 1953 Leonard Beecher became bishop.

30 McGregor Ross joined the Uganda Railway in April 1900 as a junior assistant engineer. He was director of public works from 6 April 1905 until 1923, when he was removed. In 1911 he was appointed an extraordinary member of the Legislative Council by Girouard. He was very opposed to having a settler majority in the Legislative Council and lost no opportunity to criticise the settlers in print.

31 Hilda Macnaghten, 'Happy Days in East Africa', RH, Mss Afr.s.1217.

32 Figures taken from Mombasa Annual Reports, Kenya Archives, RH, Micr.Afr.515/56.

33 Hobley was born on 1 June 1867 in Nuneaton and educated in Birmingham. He went to East Africa in March 1890, as geologist to IBEAC. He joined the civil service in Uganda in 1894, and was transferred to the EAP in 1902.

34 John Ainsworth's autobiography, RH, Mss Afr.s.380, p.85.

35 Marion W. Dobbs, 'Recollections of Kenya 1906–1931', RH, Mss Afr.s.504.

36 George Archibald Swinton Home, born in Berwickshire in 1875. He hunted on the Uasin Gishu in 1906 and settled on a large estate at Soy in 1912.

37 Edward P. H. Pardoe, born in Graveley, Hertfordshire in 1881, and his wife P. A. Lee. He served in the Royal Marine Light Infantry and with the 3rd KAR in the First World War. He farmed at Kampi ya Simba near Eldoret.

38 See Chapter 2, and for a full list of the Boers see du Toit, *The Boers in East Africa*.

39 R. W. Ball to Secretary of Pioneers' Society, 6 March 1958, East African European Pioneers' Society papers, RH, Mss Afr.s.1456/4.

40 Edith Klaprott, 'Woodsmoke', RH, Micr.Afr.591, and Gerrit Groen, 'The Afrikaners in Kenya, 1903–1969'.

41 Groen, op. cit.

42 Robert Craig Muirhead, who had gone to Nairobi in 1903. He was so very tall that when he died Wreford Smith had to get into his grave at Kitale and lengthen it to enable the coffin to reach the bottom. See Betty Minchin papers, RH, Micr.Afr.594.

43 Mavis Birdsey, 'Sigh Softly, African Winds', RH, Mss Afr.s.1794.
44 Known as Henry Mitford Barber until 1916, when he changed his name to Mitford-Barberton because he had helped found the town of Barberton in the De Kaap goldfield of the Transvaal. Barberton daisies were named after the family.
45 Mitford-Barberton letters, RH, Mss Afr.1166.
46 Rudyard Kipling, 'The Lost Legion', *Collected Verse of Rudyard Kipling*, London, Hodder & Stoughton, 1912.
47 Journals of Stephen Seymour Butler, RH, Mss Afr.r.195/1.
48 Diary of Madeleine de la Vie Platts, RH, Mss Afr.s.1058.
49 Cherry Kearton and James Barnes, *Through Central Africa from East to West*, London, Cassell, 1915, p. 13. This was probably W. G. Bailey of the Veterinary Department, who went to East Africa in 1909 and later farmed at Solai.
50 Cottar had had a commission in the Royal Irish Rifles and served in the Boer War and India. He had arrived in Mombasa broke in 1911. When asked to produce £36 as security before being allowed to land, he drew himself up, said the demand was an insult to an officer in the British army and signed a note confirming he had the money in his possession. He was allowed in. He inaugurated Cottar's Safari Service and was killed by a rhino in 1941.
51 Richard Gethin, 'An Old Settler Remembers', RH, Mss Afr.s.1277.
52 From 'Juggernaut' in E. C. Adams, *Lyra Nigeriae*, London, T. Fisher Unwin, 1911. Brian Brooks [Korongo], 'The Missing Something', *Poems of Brian Brooks*, London, John Lane, no date but 1917.

CHAPTER 5

1 Sung by Charles Udall at a citizens' meeting at the Theatre Royal, Nairobi, in September 1915.
2 Brian Havelock Potts papers, RH, Micr.Afr.596.
3 Otto Markus papers, RH, Micr.Afr.593.
4 Nairobi Chamber of Commerce minutes, 8 July and 1 October 1915, RH, Mss Afr.s.1467.
5 Ibid., 16 February 1919. Fluent in German, Mayer had served in intelligence throughout the war, moving to GHQ in GEA in 1916 – memo by R. Meinertzhagen, Dar-es-Salaam, 23 November 1916, PRO, CO 533/212. Mayer applied to become a British subject after the war.
6 Peggy Forrester papers, RH, Micr.Afr.586.
7 The others killed were A. C. Burridge, Alan Impey, W. F. Somerville, J. L. Elliot, F. E. Buller, S. F. Edmonds and J. D. Burgess.
8 The others killed were H. M. Furley, E. W. Kay-Mouat, L. J. Moon, F. G. Drummond, W. G. Bellasis, W. A. Smith and T. H. Drake. F. Thompson died later from his wounds.

9   B. L. Bremner to his mother, 7, 20 and 26 August and 18 September 1914, RH, Mss Afr.s.1372.
10 Sir Gordon Covell, 'The Military Campaign in East Africa', RH, Mss Afr.s.385–7.
11 Bulpett to McMillan, 8 January 1917, W. N. McMillan Scrapbooks, RH, Micr.Afr.641.
12 W. N. McMillan Scrapbooks, RH, Micr.Afr.641.
13 Cara Buxton to her nephew Desmond Buxton, 2 June 1917, RH, Micr.Afr.585.
14 Many of the intercepted German messages are in the R. K. Rice papers, RH, Mss Afr.s.1386.
15 Jack Wall arrived in East Africa in 1902 and became a prominent worker for African education. He opened the Nyabururu mission in 1911.
16 Richard Gethin's account of the incident, RH, Mss Afr.s.1747.
17 Noel Smith to his mother, 21 July 1916, Noel Smith papers, RH, Micr.Afr.590.
18 Sir Gordon Covell, 'The Military Campaign in East Africa', RH, Mss Afr.s.385–7.
19 Brian Havelock Potts papers, RH, Micr.Afr.596.

CHAPTER 6

1   Colonial Office Annual Reports, East Africa Protectorate, and Census of the European Population, 1911 and 1921.
2   C. T. Todd, 'Kenya's Red Sunset', RH, Mss Afr.s.917.
3   T. R. L. Nestor, 'Reminiscences', RH, Mss Afr.s.1086.
4   C. J. D. Duder, 'The Soldier Settlement Scheme of 1919 in Kenya', University of Aberdeen Ph.D., 1978.
5   M. W. Dobbs, 'Recollections of Kenya, 1906–1931', RH, Mss Afr.s.504.
6   Milner to Governor of Kenya, 21 May 1920, C. Kenneth Archer papers, RH, Mss Afr.s.2304, Box 2.
7   The Convention of Associations was a body formed in 1910. It consisted of delegates from about twenty-seven local European associations, such as the Donyo Sabuk Association, the Sergoit Farmers' Association and the Kikuyu District Settlers' Association, and met twice yearly. It had a permanently elected executive which met once a month and referred its decisions to the government.
8   C. Kenneth Archer papers, RH, Mss Afr.s.2304, Box 4.
9   Wheatley to his father, 16 January 1923, Wheatley papers, RH, Mss Afr.s.799.
10 Noel Smith to his mother, 24 January 1923, Noel Smith papers, RH, Micr.Afr.590.
11 Wheatley to his father, 22 January 1923, Wheatley papers, RH, Mss Afr.s.799.

12 Wheatley to his father, 8 September 1922, Wheatley papers, RH, Mss Afr.s.799.
13 Illegible to C. K. Archer, 26 May 1923, C. Kenneth Archer papers, RH, Mss Afr.s.2304, Box 4.
14 Coryndon's secret despatch to the Duke of Devonshire, 15 January 1923, Coryndon papers, RH, Mss Afr.s.633, Box 3.
15 Felling had come from South Africa in 1922 to put Kenya's chaotic railway affairs in order. He did this very effectively, but died suddenly of malaria in August 1928, a great blow to the colony.
16 Memo by Eric Dutton, Coryndon papers, RH, Mss Afr.s.633, Box 3.
17 Newspaper cutting in Coryndon papers, RH, Mss Afr.s.633, Box 3.
18 C. J. D. Duder, 'The Soldier Settlement Scheme of 1919 in Kenya'.
19 The acreage of each crop rose thus: 32,109 acres of maize in 1920 to 200,926 in 1930; 4,613 acres of wheat to 68,852; 27,813 of coffee to 96,689; and 30,698 of sisal to 137,299. Kenya Agricultural Census annual reports, 1920–30.
20 T. R. L. Nestor, 'Reminiscences', RH, Mss Afr.s.1086.
21 John Evans-Freke, who became tenth Baron Carbery (*sic*) but did not use his title and altered the spelling to Carberry. He made a fortune bootlegging in America during Prohibition, and bought a coffee farm at Nyeri. He married the aviator Maia, daughter of A. G. W. Anderson, Rudolf Mayer's partner – though, according to her daughter Juanita Carberry, actually the daughter of Rudolf Mayer.
22 The daughter of Charles Clutterbuck of Njoro, she was to achieve fame as the first person to fly the Atlantic from east to west and as the author of *West with the Night*, London, Harrap, 1942, and London, Penguin, 1988.
23 Florence Kerr Fernie was born in Liverpool in 1879. She married Herbert Wilson in 1902 and emigrated to Kenya after the First World War.
24 Brian Brooks [Korongo], 'Magadi', *Poems of Brian Brooks*, London, John Lane, no date but 1917.
25 Northey to Coryndon, 31 December 1923 and 26 March 1924, Coryndon papers, Box 12, RH, Mss Afr.s.633.
26 Coryndon was born and brought up in South Africa, the son of a solicitor in Kimberley.
27 Eric Dutton, 'The Night of the Hyena', RH, Micr.Afr.587.
28 P. A. Clearkin, 'Ramblings and Recollections of a Colonial Doctor 1913–1958', RH, Mss Brit.Emp.r.4/1. When W. Ormsby-Gore was Colonial Secretary in 1936 he told Sir Robert Brooke-Popham, the new Governor of Kenya, that the doctor who operated on Coryndon blamed his death on heart failure under the anaesthetic due to Nairobi's altitude. The doctor maintained, erroneously of course, that if he had been operated on at sea level in Mombasa, he could have been saved – Ormsby-Gore to Brooke-Popham, 5 November 1936, RH, Mss Afr.s.1120.
29 The building of this stone Government House began on 27 June 1905.
30 Delamere to Gwladys Delamere, 10 April and 31 May 1930, Delamere papers, RH, Mss Afr.s.1424.

31 Grigg to Sir William Gowers, 26 January 1927, Coryndon papers [*sic*], Box 16, RH, Mss Afr.s.633.

32 Conversation between Sir George Schuster and Margery Perham, 1967, RH, Mss Afr.s.1795.

33 Colonial Office Annual Reports, East Africa Protectorate (after 1920 Colony and Protectorate of Kenya).

34 Mahoney to his father, 1 February 1922, Mahoney papers, RH, Mss Afr.s.487.

35 R. A. W. Proctor, 'Random Reminiscences', RH, Mss Afr.s.702.

36 P. A. Clearkin, 'Ramblings and Recollections of a Colonial Doctor, 1913–1958', RH, Mss Brit.Emp.r.4/1.

37 Lady Antrobus to L. B. Freeston of the Colonial Service, 9 March 1928, Overseas Nursing Association papers, RH, Mss Brit.Emp.s.400, Box 136/1.

38 Burns died on 1 August 1944.

39 Walter was born on 14 July 1877, the son of a stationer on Blackheath hill, London. He went to Nairobi as head of the Statistical Department, one of the functions of which was to provide statistics for the East African Governors' conferences. He created censuses, including the agricultural census; migration, crime, bank and price statistics; and statistics of births and deaths. When air services started he had to furnish them with meteorological information, and as a result became director of meteorological services.

40 A. Walter papers, RH, Mss Brit.Emp.s.391.

41 Elspeth Huxley and Arnold Curtis (eds), *Pioneers' Scrapbook*, London, Evans Bros, 1980, p. 104.

42 Dr P. A. Clearkin saw the whole affair from the window of his office on Government Road. He thought the officer was manhandled to the ground. P. A. Clearkin, 'Ramblings and Recollections of a Colonial Doctor, 1913–1958', RH, Mss Brit.Emp.r.4/1.

43 McGregor Ross, 'The Missionary Situation in the Kikuyu Country, 1929–30', McGregor Ross papers, RH, Mss Afr.s.1178/4/2.

44 C. M. Dobbs, 'Kenya 1906–1931', RH, Mss Afr.s.665.

45 Robert H. Rockwell, *My Way of Hunting: The Adventurous Life of a Taxidermist*, London, Robert Hale, 1956.

46 Osa Johnson, *I Married Adventure*, London, Hutchinson, 1940, p. 247.

47 Robert Ruark, *Use Enough Gun*, London, Hamish Hamilton, 1967, p. 75.

48 Ibid., pp. 75–6.

49 Coryndon papers, RH, Mss Afr.s.633, Box 12.

50 Cherry Kearton, *In the Land of the Lion*, London, Arrowsmith, 1929, pp. 17, 18.

51 A. Radclyffe Dugmore wrote such books as *Camera Adventures in the African Wilds*, New York, Doubleday, 1910.

52 Osa Johnson, *I Married Adventure*, p. 202.

53 Elspeth Huxley, *Love Among the Daughters*, London, Chatto & Windus, 1968, pp. 195–6.

CHAPTER 7

1   The white population in the five main towns rose thus: Nairobi 2,339 (1921), 4,813 (1926), 7,164 (1931); Mombasa 656 (1921), 869 (1926), 1,121 (1931); Nakuru, Kisumu and Eldoret together 571 (1921), 790 (1926), 1,546 (1931). Totals: 4,156 in 1921 (43 per cent of total white population), 6,472 in 1926 (51 per cent), and 9,925 in 1931 (59 per cent).

2   For commerce the figures are 937 in 1921 and 1,290 in 1926, an increase of 38 per cent; for domestic service 182 in 1921 and 310 in 1926, an increase of 70 per cent; for government 1,082 in 1921 and 1,294 in 1926, an increase of 20 per cent; for the railway 789 in 1921 and 876 in 1926, an increase of 107 per cent; for industry (carpenters, mechanics, bakers) 559 in 1921 and 607 in 1926 (an increase of 9 per cent); for professions excluding government servants 22 in 1921 and 164 in 1926 (an increase of 645 per cent); and for professions including government servants 48 in 1921 and 255 in 1926, an increase of 431 per cent). Figures taken from government censuses.

3   For the three years of 1921, 1926 and 1931, the figures are 1,878 (20 per cent); 2,804 (17 per cent) and 2,475 (14 per cent) from South Africa: 305, 477 and 561 from India; 157, 188 and 230 from Australia; 53, 69, and 113 from New Zealand; and 196, 386 and 593 from elsewhere in the British empire.

4   *Mombasa Times* editorial, 7 July 1928.

5   Minutes of meeting of 12 May 1921, Lumbwa Farmers' Association papers, RH, Mss Afr.s.613.

6   T. R. L. Nestor, 'Reminiscences', RH, Mss Afr.s.1086.

7   Ronald Storrs Fox to his father, 29 July 1920, Storrs Fox letters, RH, Mss Afr.s.1029.

8   Aubrey Charles M. Mullins's diary, May 1928, RH, Mss Afr.s.760.

9   Roger Noel Money, *Ginia, My Kenya Coffee Shamba, 1918–1939*, Perth, Western Australia, privately printed, 2000, p. 64.

10 Delamere to Glady Delamere, 21 April 1930, Delamere papers, RH, Mss Afr.s.1424.

11 D. F. Smith to J. J. Tawney, 15 October 1966, RH, Mss Afr.s.1053.

12 J. H. Clive, 'A Cure for Insomnia, Reminiscences of Administration in Kenya, 1920–1947', RH, Mss Afr.s.678.

13 His subordinate was K. L. Hunter – K. L. Hunter, 'Memoirs of an Administrative Officer', RH, Mss Afr.s.1942.

14 161 (1921) 152 (1926) and 173 (1931) from USA; 140 (1921) 146 (1926) and 214 (1931) from Italy; 18 (1921) 105 (1926) and 304 (1931) from Germany, 89 (1921) 85 (1926) and 113 (1931) from France; and 338 (1921) 439 (1926) and 653 (1931) others, a total of 746 people.

15 Daphne Moore's diary, 23 May 1929, RH, Mss Brit.Emp.s.466.

16 Report of the Local Government Commission, 1927. There is a copy of this in RH, Buxton papers, Mss Brit.Emp.s.390, Box 7.

17 Built in 1919 and owned and run by Eva Maud Noon, whose husband was in the Transport Deptartment of the Public Works Department.

18 See Chapter 4, note 30.

19 McGregor Ross to J. K. Robertson, 28 October 1920, McGregor Ross papers, RH, Mss Afr.s.1178.

20 *East African Standard*, 12 May 1921.

21 H. E. Fitzgibbon papers, RH, Mss Afr.s.1231, Box 1.

22 The *Clan Mackenzie* was the first to berth, on 28 July, before thousands of spectators.

23 Mombasa District Annual Report, April–December 1921, Kenya Archives, RH, Micr.Afr.515, reel 50.

24 Mombasa District Annual Report, 1922, ibid.

25 This fell to 676 in 1926, but rose to 885 in 1927.

26 *Mombasa Times* editorial, 29 May 1928.

27 There was a 315-foot gap in the causeway, which was closed by a bridge. In the Second World War this bridge was regarded as vulnerable to air attack and was replaced in 1940 by a stone and earth embankment, so that the causeway ran all the way from the island to the mainland.

28 Information from Mombasa District Annual Reports, 1925–30, Kenya Archives, RH, Micr.Afr.515, reel 50.

29 Mrs R. Gascoigne, 'Nanyuki 34 Years Ago', East Africa European Pioneers' Society papers, RH, Mss Afr.s 1456, Box 6.

30 Philip Wheatley to his father, 31 July 1922, Wheatley papers, RH, Mss Afr.s.799.

31 M. H. Hamilton, *Turn the Hour*, Lewes, Sussex, Book Guild, 1991, p. 105.

32 Daphne Moore's diary, 26 June 1929, RH, Mss Brit.Emp.s.466.

33 Ibid., 15 August 1929.

34 Julian Huxley, *Africa View*, London, Chatto & Windus, 1931, p. 166.

35 Before 1910 there were at various times, apart from the *East African Standard* (which began in Mombasa under the editorship of W. H. Tiller as the *African Standard* on 15 November 1902 before changing its name in 1905 and moving to Nairobi in 1910); the *Globetrotter* (a weekly begun in 1906 by David Garrick Longworth); the *Advertiser of East Africa*; the *Daily Leader* with H. F. Ward as a director (absorbed into the *East African Standard* in 1921); the *East African Quarterly*, concentrating on agricultural matters; *The Times of East Africa* edited by Ernest Low; and the *East Africa and Uganda Mail* begun by Olive Grey in Mombasa in 1899 but discontinued in 1904. Olive Grey had been Major Grey of the Salvation Army in India, where she wore Indian dress, and then she moved to Australia where she was known as 'Guanapoo'. She lived with a Eurasian, Charles Palmer. In the First World War *Reveille*, published by the Swift Press, was a flourishing newspaper, and in the 1920s the *East Africa Chronicle* and the *Kenya Graphic* had brief existences. The *Coast Guardian* was published in the 1930s.

36 Julian Huxley, *Africa View*, p. 213.

37 Mrs E. C. R. Le Breton, 'Grim's Tale', RH, Mss Afr.s.1978.

38 Ibid.

39 M. G. Redley, 'The Politics of a Predicament: The White Community in Kenya, 1918–1932', Cambridge University Ph.D., 1976.

40 Wotton, who started teaching at the school in November 1914, became headmaster on 1 January 1931.

41 Governor's minute, 6 July 1925, misc. papers on Nairobi School, RH, Mss Afr.s.899.

42 J. P. Cooper to Christine Nicholls, 16 April 2002.

43 The book was published in New York by H. Holt & Co. in 1924 and in London by T. Butterworth in 1927.

44 Lord Francis Scott's diary, October 1920, RH, Mss Brit.Emp.s.349. Williams, of the Knightwick estate in the Kedong Valley, died in 1934 – see PRO, CO 533/450/9.

45 Delamere to Glady Delamere, 12 April 1930, Delamere papers, RH, Mss Afr.s.1424.

46 Delamere to Glady Delamere, 27 March 1930, ibid.

47 Lord Francis Scott's diary, 21 January 1920, RH, Mss Brit.Emp.s.349.

48 Daphne Moore's diary, 26 May 1929, RH, Mss Brit.Emp.s.466.

49 Correspondence of January 1924 in Coryndon papers, RH, Mss Afr.s.633, Box 10/5.

50 George Nightingale's memoirs, RH, Mss Afr.s.1951.

51 M. H. Hamilton, *Turn the Hour*, pp. 151–2.

52 *Mombasa Times*, 16 August 1928.

53 Daphne Moore's diary, 16 July 1929, RH, Mss Brit.Emp.s.466.

54 *East African Standard*, 22 May 1926.

55 J. H. Clive, 'A Cure for Insomnia, Reminiscences of Administration in Kenya, 1920–1947', RH, Mss Afr.s.678.

56 Daphne Moore's diary, 29 June 1929, RH, Mss Brit.Emp.s.466.

57 Torr's was financed by Ewart Grogan and designed by the architect of the Muthaiga Club, Harold Henderson, who took his inspiration from Stockholm town hall. It was built of brick in 1928, and let to Joe and Lilly Torr, owners of a bakery and confectioner's in Government Road. The Hotel Avenue, of reinforced concrete, was begun in 1927 and completed at the beginning of 1929.

CHAPTER 8

1 The Countess of Cromer, *Lamuriac and Other Sketches*, London, Methuen, 1927, p. 108.

2 M. H. Hamilton, *Turn the Hour*, Lewes, Sussex, Book Guild, 1991, p. 204.

3 Christopher T. Todd, 'Kenya's Red Sunset', RH, Mss Afr.s.917.

4 Roger Noel Money, *Ginia, My Kenya Coffee Shamba, 1918–1939*, Perth, Western Australia, privately printed, 2000, pp. 156–7.

5 'Cases dealt with by the Salvation Army', Rosalie Trembeth papers, RH, Mss Afr.s.1154.

6 *East African Standard*, 1 December 1934.

7 All sorts of similar practical hints were gathered together and published – see G. St. Orde Browne, *Here's How*, London, East Africa Ltd, 1937.

8 Brian Brooks [Korongo], 'Nature', *Poems by Brian Brooks*, London, John Lane, no date but 1917.

9 Eric Dutton to Sir Sydney Henn, 12 March 1930, Henn papers, RH, Mss Afr.s.715/1/10.

10 C. Kenneth Archer papers, Box 5/2, RH, Mss Afr.s.2304.

11 Ibid.

12 Dutton to Henn, 30 December 1935, Henn papers, RH, Mss Afr.s.715/1/10.

13 F. Lodge to J. M. Silvester, 28 September 1935, Kenya Association papers, RH, Mss Afr.s.595.

14 J. M. Silvester to F. Lodge, 2 October 1935, Kenya Association papers, RH, Mss Afr.s.595.

15 Lists in Kenya Association papers, RH, Mss Afr.s.595.

16 Anna Ortlepp to Kenya Association, 17 July 1936, Kenya Association papers, RH, Mss Afr.s.595.

17 Brooke-Popham to Colonial Secretary Malcolm Macdonald, 9 June 1939, RH, Brooke-Popham papers, Mss Afr.s.1120/1/4.

18 Tommy Joseph, *Why There were Jews in Nakuru: Their Story*, privately printed in Haifa, Israel, 1998, pp. 28–9.

19 Dutton to Henn, 22 February 1932, Henn papers, RH, Mss Afr.s.715/1/10.

20 Dutton to Henn, 2 September 1935, Henn papers, RH, Mss Afr.s.715/1/10.

21 Cavendish-Bentinck had originally landed in East Africa in 1912. He was allocated a soldier-settler farm in 1919 but did not take it up. He returned to East Africa in 1925 as private secretary to Sir Ernest Gowers, Governor of Uganda, and then went to Kenya in 1927 to work in Equator Sawmills. A founder of the Kenya Association in 1932, he became the member of the Legislative Council for Nairobi North in 1934. In 1977 he inherited the dukedom of Portland from a cousin.

22 Grigg to Henn, 19 June 1933, Henn papers, RH, Mss Afr.s.714/2/2.

23 C. Kenneth Archer to Henn, 17 March 1935, Henn papers, RH, Mss Afr.s.715/1/2.

24 Mrs Sheelagh Silvester (wife of J. M. Silvester), 'Flashback', *Women in Kenya* [EAWL magazine], Nairobi, March 1971, p. 4.

25 Robin Wainwright, 'Memoirs', RH, Mss Brit.Emp.s.524.

26 W. Ormsby-Gore to Brooke-Popham, 21 October 1936, RH, Brooke-Popham papers, Mss Afr.s.1120/1/2.

27 Evan E. Biss to his children, Biss papers, 19 May 1935, RH, Mss Afr.s.1069.

28 E. C. Palmes, 'The Scene Changes, 1931–53', RH, Mss Afr.s.946.

29 Nora K. Strange, *Kenya To-Day*, London, Stanley Paul, 1934, pp. 39–40.

30 M. Aline Buxton, *Kenya Days*, London, Edward Arnold, 1927, pp. 174–5.

31 Llewelyn Powys to John Cowper Powys, 25 January 1915, in Louis Wilkinson (ed.), *The Letters of Llewelyn Powys*, London, John Lane, 1943, p. 72.

32 Ibid., 28 July 1915, p. 76. '[Cole] has more intelligence than anybody else in East Africa and more distinction of mind' – p. 86.

33 *East African Standard*, 1 December 1934.

34 This is not to be confused with the East African European Pioneers' Society, inaugurated in 1952 – see Chapter 10.

35 R. R. Kuczynski, *Demographic Survey of the British Colonial Empire*, London, OUP, 1949, vol. 2 (of 3), p. 158.

36 George Nightingale, 'Memoirs', RH, Mss Afr.s.1951.

37 Llewelyn Powys to John Cowper Powys, 14 November 1915, in Louis Wilkinson (ed.), *The Letters of Llewelyn Powys*, p. 81.

38 Derek Franklin, *A Pied Cloak*, London, Janus Publishing, 1996, p. 121.

39 *East African Standard*, 1 December 1934.

40 The Manor Hotel was demolished in the late 1990s in an act of historical vandalism.

41 Diary of M. McHardy, 20 January 1938, RH, Mss Afr.r.76.

42 Peter de Polnay, *My Road: An Autobiography*, London, W. H. Allen, 1978, p. 78.

43 M. H. Hamilton, *Turn the Hour*, p. 221.

44 De Ganahl was the brother-in-law of Arthur Harris, better known later as Bomber Harris.

45 Presented to the House of Commons on 9 May 1933 by Sir Robert Hamilton, formerly Chief Justice of Kenya. A copy is in the McGregor Ross papers, RH, Mss Afr.s.1178/4.

46 Eve Bache, *The Youngest Lion*, London, Hutchinson, 1934, p. 239.

47 J. H. Clive, 'A Cure for Insomnia, Reminiscences of Administration in Kenya, 1920–1947', RH, Mss Afr.s.678.

48 C. R. V. Bell to his fiancée, 9 April 1935, Bell papers, RH, Mss Afr.s.1113.

49 Frederick J. Wright, 'A Tenth Child's Family History', in private hands. For Hugh Grant, see Chapter 10.

50 J. H. Clive, 'A Cure for Insomnia, Reminiscences of Administration in Kenya, 1920–1947', RH, Mss Afr.s.678.

51 Brian Brooks [Korongo], 'Nature', *Poems by Brian Brooks*.

52 Mervyn Cowie, *Fly, Vulture*, London, Harrap, 1961, p. 78.

53 Interview of Sir Anthony Swann by Dr William Beaver, 6 November 1979, RH, Mss Afr.s.1715/268.

54 Eve Bache, *The Youngest Lion*, p. 247.

55 An interesting account of the affair is given in L. S. B. Leakey, *By the Evidence, Memoirs 1932–1951*, New York, Harcourt Brace Jovanovich, 1974. Leakey was part of the investigating team.

56 Margaret Gillon, 'The Wagon and the Star', RH, Mss Afr.s.568.

CHAPTER 9

1 *East African Standard*, 8 September 1939.
2 Figures from Brooke-Popham papers, Box 1/10, RH, Mss Afr.s.1120.
3 James P. Cooper, 'The Making of an African Soldier' in Kenya Regiment Association UK branch Newsletter, May 1988.
4 Because it was so unhealthy in Uganda, the Kenya Regiment moved to the race course at Eldoret, the horse stables becoming its barracks.
5 There was no census taken after 1931, and official estimates of population were inaccurate. See R. R. Kuczynski, *Demographic Survey of the British Colonial Empire*, London, OUP, 1949, vol. 2 (of 3), p. 159. The number of Africans was generally estimated as about 3 million.
6 Mrs E. C. R. Le Breton, 'Grim's Tale', RH, Mss Afr.s.1978.
7 M. F. Hill, *Permanent Way*, Nairobi, East African Railways and Harbours, 1949, pp. 534–5.
8 Kenneth Gandar Dower, *Abyssinian Patchwork*, London, Frederick Muller, 1949, pp. 123–4.
9 John Seymour, *One Man's Africa*, London, Eyre & Spottiswoode, 1955, p. 221.
10 Brian James Crabb, *Passage to Destiny: The Sinking of the Khedive Ismail in the Sea War Against Japan*, Stamford, Lincolnshire, Paul Watkins, 1997.
11 K. L. Hunter, 'Memoirs of an Administrative Officer', RH, Mss Afr.s.1942.
12 Account by Hazel Macgregor, of Mombasa in wartime, sent to Christine Nicholls 23 August 2002.
13 Ibid.
14 Francis Gerard Finch, 'The Role of British Forces in Africa', RH, Mss Afr.s.1715/90.
15 Interview with Kathy Cuthbert, 28 June 2002.
16 Daphne Moore to her mother, 24 March 1940 and 20 December 1943, RH, Mss Brit.Emp.s.466/2.
17 J. H. Clive, 'A Cure for Insomnia, Reminiscences of Administration in Kenya, 1920–47', RH, Mss Afr.s.678.
18 The murder and trial are considered in detail in Errol Trzebinski, *The Life and Death of Lord Erroll*, London, Fourth Estate, 2000, and Rupert Furneaux, *The Murder of Lord Erroll*, London, Stevens, 1961. See also James Fox, *White Mischief*, London, Jonathan Cape, 1982, passim.
19 Frederick Alfred Smith, *White Roots in Africa*, London, Janus Publishing Co., 1997, p. 91.
20 *Daily Telegraph*, 22 August 2002, p. 13.
21 *K.W.E.O., 1938–1946*, no author, printed pamphlet issued by the Kenyan Printing Press, Portal St, Nairobi, 1946.
22 In 1942 the acreages of white farmers' crops were: sisal 185,430; wheat 131,075; maize 83,750; coffee 74,850; pyrethrum 36,930; flax 31,870; tea 13,950. There were also large stock-breeding and dairying industries

(Liebig's meat factory had opened in 1938) and a considerable market-garden trade, while the wattle-bark and timber industries also flourished.

23 Figures from Brooke-Popham papers, Box 1/10, RH, Mss Afr.s.1120.

24 Jean Crosskill, 'A Countrywoman in Kenya', *East African Annual*, Nairobi, 1958–59, pp. 119–23.

25 Nellie Grant to Elspeth Huxley, 13 May 1944, Elspeth Huxley papers, RH, Mss Afr.s.2154.

26 Ian Spencer, 'Settler Dominance, Agricultural Production and the Second World War in Kenya', *Journal of African History*, vol. 21, 1980, pp. 497–514.

27 R. R. Kuczynski, *Demographic Survey of the British Colonial Empire*, vol. 2, p. 149.

28 Edith Klaprott, 'Woodsmoke', RH, Micr.Afr.591.

29 L. S. B. Leakey, *By the Evidence: Memoirs, 1932–1951*, New York, Harcourt Brace Jovanovich, 1974, p. 185.

30 Interview on tape with Anna Czyzewska, 15 September 2001. Formerly a Warsaw journalist, Anna Czyzewska worked in Nairobi on the Polish newspaper, *The Pole in Africa*, and at the Polish radio station, also at Nairobi. For a description of the Polish settlement at Masindi, see Elspeth Huxley, *The Sorcerer's Apprentice*, London, Chatto & Windus, 1956, p. 238.

31 Allen Leeds, *Long Ago and Far Away*, Upton-on-Severn, Square One Publications, 1998, p. 42.

32 Robin Wainwright, 'Memoirs', RH, Mss Brit.Emp.s.524.

33 Ibid.

34 Brooke-Popham to Moore, 25 October 1939, Brooke-Popham papers, Box 2/9, RH, Mss Afr.s.1120.

35 Daphne Moore to her mother, 15 January 1940, RH, Mss Brit. Emp.s.466/2.

36 Ibid.

37 Lorna Bell to Nesta, 27 October ?1944, C. R. V. Bell papers, RH, Mss Afr.s.1113.

38 Nellie Grant to Elspeth Huxley, 7 October 1943, Elspeth Huxley papers, RH, Mss Afr.s.2154

39 Governor to Secretary of State, 19 March 1945, Public Record Office, CO822/114/46523/1945.

CHAPTER 10

1 Llewelyn Powys, 'Black Gods', in *Ebony and Ivory*, London, Grant Richards, 1923, pp. 26–7.

2 Elspeth Huxley, *Out in the Midday Sun*, London, Chatto & Windus, 1985, p. 86.

3 *East Africa Statistical Department Annual Reports*, 1948–56. The estimates rose thus: 1949 33,800, 1950 36,200, 1951 38,600, 1952 40,700, 1953 42,200, 1954 46,500, 1955 52,400, 1956 57,700.

4 A. Gordon-Brown (ed.), *Year Book and Guide to East Africa*, London, Sampson, Low & Marston, 1950, p. 29.

5 Ibid., p. 60.

6 Kenya Sessional Paper no. 8 of 1945 on *Land Utilization and Settlement*, November 1945.

7 *Hansard*, 7 March 1946, p. 129.

8 F. A. Levy, 'The Snows of Yesteryear', RH, Micr.Afr.576.

9 Between the end of the war and December 1947, 669 white settlers took up land in Kenya. Of these, 481 were Kenya nationals, and of the 188 who came from outside 147 were ex-servicemen. In addition to these farm settlers, there were 259 residential settlers, of whom 166 were Kenya nationals – *Journal of the Fabian Colonial Bureau*, vol. 10, no. 12, June 1948.

10 *Daily Herald*, 15 January 1953.

11 J. F. Lipscomb (chairman of the Board), *We Built a Country*, London, Faber & Faber, 1956, pp. 96–7.

12 Papers of Henry Izard, of the Settlement Board, RH, Mss Afr.s.1257.

13 D. W. Throup, 'The Governorship of Sir Philip Mitchell in Kenya, 1944–1952', Cambridge University Ph.D., 1983.

14 Sir John Thorp, 'The Glittering Lake', RH, Mss Afr.s.973, p. 186. See also Anne Goldsmith (ed.), *Gentle Warrior, A Life of Hugh Grant*, Bodmin, MPG Books, 2001.

15 Elizabeth Watkins, *Jomo's Jailor*, Watlington, Britwell Books, 1993, pp. 120–1.

16 Philip Jones in Sir John Johnson (ed.), *Colony to Nation*, Banham, Norfolk, Erskine Press, 2002, pp. 49–50.

17 Robin Wainwright, 'Memoirs', RH, Mss Brit.Emp.s.524.

18 Cedric Owen Oates papers, RH, Mss Afr.s.1950.

19 Graham F. Thomas, *Far from the Valleys*, Lewes, Sussex, Book Guild, 1995, p. 140.

20 Joan Karmali quoted in Cynthia Salvadori, *We Came in Dhows*, Nairobi, Paperchase Kenya Ltd., 1996, 3 vols., vol. 3, pp. 178–9.

21 Examples of European–Asian marriages are those between Mayo-Smith and Krishna Sondhi, and Bentley and Dias. For this and other information about Goans and Asians I am indebted to Mervyn Maciel.

22 Patrick Brian Sweeney, 'A Game Warden's Permit for a Corpse', RH, Mss Brit. Emp.s.518.

23 Trevor W. Jenkins's report on his police service in Kenya, RH, Mss Afr.s.1784/23.

24 C. S. Pitt , 'Malaria Control and its Relationship to other Environmental Work in a European Settled Area, Kenya Colony', April 1955.

25 Peter Bostock's annual letter, 1945, Bostock papers, RH, Micr.Afr.642, reel 6.

26 Peter Bostock to Leonard Beecher, Bishop of Mombasa, 4 March 1953, Bostock papers, RH, Micr.Afr.642, reel 6.

27 Graham F. Thomas, *Far from the Valleys*, pp. 135–6.

28 Hester Katharine ('Kit') Henn went to Kenya in 1928 when she married John Frederic Henn, son of Sir Sydney Henn.

29 T. G. Askwith, 'Memoirs', RH, Mss Afr.s.1770.

30 For the repeal of the law, and the debate it engendered, see Richard Frost, *Enigmatic Proconsul: Sir Philip Mitchell and the Twilight of Empire*, London, Radcliffe Press, 1992, p. 213.

31 Stephen North interview, 15 April 2002.

32 Vivien Schapira Prince, *Kenya: The Years of Change*, New York, Carlton Press, 1987, p. 41.

33 Joan Karmali, *A School in Kenya: Hospital Hill 1949–1973*, Upton-on-Severn, Square One, 2002, p. 58.

34 Gerrit D. Groen, 'The Afrikaners in Kenya, 1903–1969', Michigan State University Ph.D., 1974.

35 C. S. Pitt, *Annual Report on Medical Services, Eldoret*, 1955, RH, Mss Afr.s.1194.

36 Brian M. du Toit, *The Boers in East Africa*, Westport, Connecticut, Bergin & Garvey, 1998, p. 172.

37 Joan Karmali, *A School in Kenya*, pp. 72–3.

38 Graham Thomas, *Far from the Valleys*, pp. 146–7.

39 Bridget M. Robertson, 'African Mosaic', RH, Mss Afr.s.1972/128.

40 The information in this paragraph is from the Director of Medical Services in Kenya 1949–56, T. Farnworth Anderson, 'Reminiscences', RH, Mss Afr.s.1653.

41 Joan Considine edited Mary Gillett's work on these cards and brought out *Tribute to Pioneers* (privately printed, Oxford, 1986). There are nine boxes of the Society's records in Rhodes House – Mss Afr.s.1456.

42 Email from Neil McCormick, 10 August 2003.

43 Annual reports of the PC of the Coast Province, Eric Davies, 1947 and 1948, copies of which are in the Eric Davies papers, RH, Mss Afr.s.513.

44 Email from Neil McCormick, 10 August 2003.

45 Percy Turner Wild, *Bwana Polisi*, Braunton, Devon, Merlin Books, 1993, p. 48.

46 Barbara Rochford, 'The Oath Taker', *The Month*, vol. 2, no. 1, January 1954.

47 Interview with Kathini Graham, 7 September 2002.

48 Sir Anthony Swann, 'The Rise of Mau Mau', RH, Mss Afr.s.1915.

49 Interview with Kathini Graham, 7 September 2002.

50 Trevor W. Jenkins's report on his police service in Kenya, RH, Mss Afr.s.1784/23.

51 Interview with Kathini Graham, 7 September 2002.

52 D. G. Christie-Miller papers, RH, Mss Afr.s.1676/1 and 2.

53 *East African Standard*, 16 October 1954.

54 T. G. Askwith, 'Memoirs', RH, Mss Afr.s.1770.

55 Percy Turner Wild, *Bwana Polisi*, p. 10.

56 Peter Evans, *Law and Disorder*, London, Secker & Warburg, 1956, pp. 260–72.

57 John Whyatt to Sir Evelyn Baring, 19 August 1954, Whyatt papers, RH, Mss Afr.s.1694.

58 Interview of Lord Howick (Baring) by Margery Perham, 24 November 1971, RH, Mss Afr.s.1575.

59 *East African Standard* leader, 18 February 1955.

60 Interview of Lord Howick (Baring) by Margery Perham, 24 November 1971, RH, Mss Afr.s.1575.

61 Speech at the inaugural meeting of the new Convention of Associations, 8 May 1958, Cedric Oates papers, RH, Mss Afr.s.1950/3.

62 Report by the commanding officer, Brigadier H. R. W. Vernon, RH, Mss Afr.s.1715/283.

63 *Kenya Police Review*, December 1961.

64 H. K. Henn papers, RH, Micr.Afr.589.

65 D. G. Christie-Miller papers, RH, Mss Afr.s.1676/2.

66 Transcript of interview of Iain Macleod by W. P. Kirkman, 29 December 1967, RH, Mss Afr.s.2179.

67 W. H. Thompson was in the room when Baring made the call – W. H. Thompson, 'Colonial Memories of Kenya 1944–1963', RH, Mss Brit. Emp.s.519.

68 Transcript of interview of Sir Walter Coutts by George Bennett, 1 December 1967, RH, Mss Afr.s.1621.

69 Transcript of interview of Iain Macleod by W. P. Kirkman, 29 December 1967, RH, Mss Afr.s.2179.

70 Ibid.

71 Christopher T. Todd, 'Kenya's Red Sunset', RH, Mss Afr.s.917.

72 Edward Carey Francis to D. G. C. Symonds, 19 December 1960, D. G. C. Symonds papers, RH, Mss Afr.s.573.

73 Carey Francis to Sir Armigel Wade, 9 August 1961, RH, Mss Afr.s.1637.

74 Interview of Alexander Storrar by William Beaver and Gowher Rizvi, 23 May 1979, RH, Mss Afr.s.1717/149.

75 E. C. Palmes, 'The Scene Changes, 1931–1953', RH, Mss Afr.s.946.

76 Transcript of interview of Iain Macleod by W. P. Kirkman, 29 December 1967, RH, Mss Afr.s.2179.

77 A. Bateson, 'To Go or Not to Go', August 1962, RH, Mss Afr.s.1083.

78 Transcript of interview of Iain Macleod by W. P. Kirkman, 29 December 1967, RH, Mss Afr.s.2179.

CONCLUSION

1 J. F. Lipscomb, *We Built a Country*, London, Faber & Faber, 1986.
2 A machete-like knife.

Bibliography

Aaronovitch, S. and K., *Crisis in Kenya*, London, Lawrence & Wishart, 1947

Adams, E. C., *Lyra Nigeriae*, London, T. Fisher Unwin, 1911

Altrincham, Lord (Edward Grigg), *Kenya's Opportunity: Memories, Hopes and Ideas*, London, Faber & Faber, 1955

Ambler, Charles H., *Kenya Communities in the Age of Imperialism*, New Haven, Connecticut and London, Yale University Press, 1988

Anderson, A. G., *Our Newest Colony*, Nairobi, East African Standard Press, 1910

Anderson, David, *Histories of the Hanged*, London, Weidenfeld & Nicolson, 2005

Anderson, Jean *et al.*, *They Made It Their Home*, Nairobi, East Africa Women's League, 1962

Anderson, John, *The Struggle for the School*, London, Longman, 1970

Archer, Sir Geoffrey, *Personal and Historical Memoirs of an African Administrator*, London, Oliver & Boyd, 1963

Arkell-Hardwick, Alfred, *An Ivory Trader in North Kenya*, London, Longmans Green, 1903

Aschan, Ulf, *The Man Whom Women Loved*, New York, St Martin's Press, 1987

Bache, Eve, *The Youngest Lion: Early Farming Days in Kenya*, London, Hutchinson, 1934

Barnes, R. Gorell, *Babes in the African Wood*, London, Longmans Green, 1911

Beard, Peter Hill, *The End of the Game*, New York, Viking, 1965

Beachey, R. W., *A History of East Africa, 1592–1902*, London, Taurus Academic, 1996

Beck, Ann, *A History of the British Medical Administration of East Africa, 1900–1950*, Cambridge, Massachusetts, Harvard University Press, 1970

Bell, W. D. M., *The Wanderings of an Elephant Hunter*, London, C. Scribner's Sons, 1923

—— *Karamojo Safari*, Suffolk, Neville Spearman, 1949

Bennett, George, *Kenya: A Political History*, London, Oxford University Press, 1963

Berman, Bruce, *Control and Crisis in Colonial Kenya*, London, James Currey, 1990

Best, Nicholas, *Happy Valley: The Story of the English in Kenya*, London, Secker and Warburg, 1979

Binks, H. K., *African Rainbow*, London, Sidgwick & Jackson, 1959

Blundell, Michael, *So Rough a Wind*, London, Weidenfeld & Nicolson, 1964

—— *A Love Affair with the Sun*, Nairobi, Kenway Publications, 1994

Boyes, John, *King of the Wa-Kikuyu*, London, Methuen, 1911

Brander, Michael, *The Big Game Hunters*, London, Sportsman's Press, 1988

Brett, F. A., *Colonialism and Underdevelopment in East Africa: The Politics of Economic Change 1919–1939*, New York, NOK, 1973

Brockway, Fenner, *African Journeys*, London, Gollancz, 1955

Brodhurst-Hill, Evelyn, *So This is Kenya!*, London and Glasgow, Blackie & Son, 1936

Brooks, Brian [Korongo], *Poems of Brian Brooks*, London, John Lane, no date but 1917

Brown, Monty, *Where Giants Trod*, London, Quiller Press, 1989

Bull, Bartle, *Safari: A Chronicle of Adventure*, London, Viking, 1988

Buxton, M. Aline, *Kenya Days*, London, Edward Arnold, 1927

Cameron, Roderick, *Equator Farm*, London, William Heinemann, 1955

Campbell, Guy, *The Charging Buffalo: A History of the Kenya Regiment 1937–1963*, London, Leo Cooper, 1986

Carlebach, Julius, *The Jews of Nairobi 1903–1962*, Nairobi, Nairobi Hebrew Congregation, 1962

Carman, John A., *A Medical History of the Colony and Protectorate of Kenya: A Personal Memoir*, London, Rex Collings, 1976

Carnegie, V. A., *A Kenya Farm Diary*, Edinburgh and London, William Blackwood & Sons, 1930

Carson, J. B., *Sun, Sand and Safari*, London, Robert Hale, 1957

—— *Pages from the Past – Kenya*, Braunton, Merlin Books, 1990

Cashmore, T. H. R., 'Studies in District Administration in the East Africa Protectorate, 1895–1918', Cambridge University Ph.D., 1965

Cell, John W. (ed.), *By Kenya Possessed: The Correspondence of Norman Leys and J. H. Oldham 1918–1926*, Chicago, Illinois, University of Chicago Press, 1976

Churchill, Winston S., *My African Journey*, London, Hodder & Stoughton, 1908

Clayton, Anthony and Donald Savage, *Government and Labour in Kenya, 1895–1963*, London, Frank Cass, 1974

Clough, Marshall S., *Fighting Two Sides, Kenyan Chiefs and Politicians, 1918–1940*, Niwot, University Press of Colorado, 1990

Coats, Victoria T., *David Charters, Engineer, Doctor and Missionary 1864–1894*, London, A. & C. Black, 1925

Cobbold, Lady Evelyn, *Kenya: The Land of Illusion*, London, John Murray, 1935

Cole, Eleanor, *Random Recollections of a Pioneer Kenya Settler*, Woodbridge, Suffolk, Baron Publishing, 1975

Colvile, Sir Henry, *The Land of the Nile Springs*, London, Edward Arnold, 1895

Coupland, Sir Reginald, *The Exploitation of East Africa*, London, Faber & Faber, 1939

Cowie, Mervyn, *Fly, Vulture*, London, Harrap, 1961

Crabb, Brian James, *Passage to Destiny: The Sinking of the Khedive Ismail in the Sea War Against Japan*, Stamford, Lincolnshire, Paul Watkins, 1997

Cranworth, Lord (Bertram), *A Colony in the Making, or Sport and Profit in British East Africa*, London, Macmillan, 1912

—— *Kenya Chronicles*, London, Macmillan, 1939

Crawford, E. May, *By the Equator's Snowy Peak*, London, Church Missionary Society, 1913

Cromer, Countess of, *Lamuriac and Other Sketches*, London, Methuen, 1927

Curtis, Arnold (ed.), *Memories of Kenya*, Nairobi, Evans Bros, 1986

Davis, Alexander, *A Microcosm of Empire (British East Africa)*, Nairobi, Caxton (BEA) Printing and Publishing, *c.*1918

Davis, A. and H. J. Robertson, *Chronicles of Kenya*, Cecil Palmer, 1928

Davis, Cecil (compiler), *The Kenya Annual and Directory, 1922*, Nairobi, Caxton Printing and Publishing, 1922

Davis, Peter J., *East African, an Airline Story*, Egham, Runnymede Malthouse Publishing, 1993

Declé, Lionel, *Three Years in Savage Africa*, London, Methuen, 1898

Delamere, Hugh Cholmondeley, 3rd Baron, *The Grant of Land to the Zionist Congress and Land Settlement in British East Africa*, London, Harrison & Sons, 1903

Delap-Hilton, Emilie, *Snips without Snaps of Kenya*, London, Arthur H. Stockwell, no date but *c.*1927

Dilley, Marjorie Ruth, *British Policy in Kenya Colony*, New York, Thomas Nelson & Sons, 1937

Dinesen, Isak, *Out of Africa*, New York, Random House, 1937

—— *Shadows on the Grass*, New York, Random House, 1961

—— *Letters from Africa 1914–1931*, London, Weidenfeld & Nicolson, 1982

Douglas-Home, Charles, *Evelyn Baring: The Last Proconsul*, London, Collins, 1978

Dower, Kenneth Gandar, *Abyssinian Patchwork: An Anthology*, London, Frederick Muller, 1949

Duder, C. J. D., 'The Soldier Settlement Scheme of 1919 in Kenya', Aberdeen University Ph.D., 1978

Dugmore, A. Radcliffe, *Camera Adventures in the African Wilds*, New York, Doubleday, 1910

Du Toit, Brian M., *The Boers in East Africa*, Westport, Connecticut, Bergin & Garvey, 1998

Dutton, Eric, *Kenya Mountain*, London, Jonathan Cape, 1930

East African Annual, Nairobi, published annually from the 1930s onwards by the *East African Standard*, Nairobi

East African Red Book, The, Nairobi, *East African Standard*, published annually. This began in 1903 as *Handbook for East Africa, Uganda and Zanzibar* (published in Mombasa, compiled by J. W. Tritton, S. C. E. Baty and Henry Fitzgerald-Bell). By 1912 it was called *Directory of B. East Africa, Uganda and Zanzibar* (compiled by the Standard Printing and Publishing Works)

Eliot, Sir Charles, *The East Africa Protectorate*, London, Edward Arnold, 1905

Elkins, Caroline, *Britain's Gulag*, London, Jonathan Cape, 2005

Evans, Peter, *Law and Disorder*, London, Secker & Warburg, 1956

Farrant, Leda, *The Legendary Grogan*, London, Hamish Hamilton, 1981

—— *Diana, Lady Delamere and the Lord Erroll Murder*, Nairobi, privately published, 1997

Farson, Negley, *Last Chance in Africa*, London, Gollancz, 1949

Fey, Venn, *Cloud Over Kenya*, London, Collins, 1964

Fitzgerald, W. W. A., *Travels in British East Africa, Zanzibar and Pemba*, London, Chapman & Hall, 1898

Foran, W. Robert, *A Cuckoo in Kenya: The Reminiscences of a Pioneer Police Officer in British East Africa*, London, Hutchinson, 1936

—— *The Kenya Police*, London, Robert Hale, 1962

Fox, James, *White Mischief*, London, Jonathan Cape, 1982

Franklin, Derek, *A Pied Cloak*, London, Janus Publishing, 1996

Frost, Richard, *Enigmatic Proconsul: Sir Philip Mitchell and the Twilight of Empire*, London, Radcliffe Press, 1992

Furneaux, Rupert, *The Murder of Lord Erroll*, London, Stevens, 1961

—— *Famous Criminal Cases 7*, London, Odhams, 1962

Furse, Ralph, *Aucuparius: Recollections of a Recruiting Officer*, London, Oxford University Press, 1962

Galbraith, John S., *Mackinnon and East Africa, 1878–1895*, Cambridge, Cambridge University Press, 1972

Gann, L. H. and Duignan, Peter, *The Rulers of British Africa, 1870–1914*, London, Croom Helm, 1978

—— *White Settlers in Tropical Africa, 1962*, Harmondsworth, Penguin Books, 1982

Gavaghan, Terence, *Of Lions and Dungbeetles*, Ilfracombe, Arthur H. Stockwell, 1999

Gillett, Mary, *Tribute to Pioneers*, Oxford, privately published, 1986

Goldsmith, Anne (ed.), *Gentle Warrior: A Life of Hugh Grant, Soldier, Farmer and Kenya Administrator*, Bodmin, MPG Books, 2001

Goldsmith, F. H., *John Ainsworth, Pioneer Kenya Administrator, 1864–1946*, London, Macmillan, 1955

Gordon-Brown, A. (ed.), *Year Book and Guide to East Africa*, London, Sampson, Low & Marston, 1950

Graham, A. D., *The Gardeners of Eden*, London, Allen & Unwin, 1973

Grant, Lavinia, *On a Kenya Ranch*, Camserney, Perthshire, Pioneer Associates, 2001

Greaves, L. B., *Carey Francis of Kenya*, London, Rex Collins, 1969

Gregory, J. R., *Under the Sun: A Memoir of Dr R. W. Burkitt, of Kenya*, Nairobi, English Press, 1951

Gregory, J. W., *The Great Rift Valley*, London, John Murray, 1896

Groen, Gerrit, 'The Afrikaners in Kenya 1903–1969', Michigan State University Ph.D., 1974

Hamilton, Genesta, *A Stone's Throw: Travels from Africa in Six Decades*, London, Hutchinson, 1986

Hamilton, M. H., *Turn the Hour*, Lewes, Sussex, Book Guild, 1991

Hardinge, Sir Arthur, *A Diplomatist in the East*, London, Cape, 1928

Hardy, Ronald, *The Iron Snake*, London, Collins, 1965

Harlow, Vincent, and E. M. Chilver, *History of East Africa*, vol. 2, Oxford, Clarendon Press, 1965

Hemsing, Jan, *Old Nairobi and the New Stanley Hotel*, Nairobi, Church Raitt & Associates, 1974

—— *Naivasha and the Lake Hotel*, Nairobi, Sealpoint, 1987

—— *Then and Now: Nairobi's Norfolk Hotel*, Nairobi, Sealpoint, 1975

—— *Treetops Outspan Paxtu*, Nairobi, Church Raitt & Associates, 1974

Hill, Mervyn, *Planters' Progress: The Story of Coffee in Kenya*, Nairobi, East African Standard, 1956

—— *Permanent Way*, Nairobi, East African Railways and Harbours, 1949

—— *Magadi, the Story of the Magadi Soda Company*, Birmingham, Kynoch Press for Magadi Soda Co., 1964

Hinde, Hildegarde Beatrice, *Some Problems of East Africa*, London, Williams & Norgate, 1926

Hindlip, Lord (Charles), *British East Africa: Past, Present and Future*, London, T. Fisher Unwin, 1905

Hobley, C. W., *Kenya, from Chartered Company to Crown Colony*, London, H., F. & G. Witherby, 1929

Hook, Hilary, *Home from the Hill*, Harmondsworth, Penguin, 1988

Hopkins, A. J., *Trail Blazers and Road Makers*, London, Henry Hooks, no date but 1928

Hotchkiss, Willis R., *Then and Now in Kenya Colony*, London, Oliphants, 1937

Howe, Stephen, *Anticolonialism in British Politics*, Oxford, Clarendon Press, 1993

Hunter, J. A. and Daniel Mannix, *African Bush Adventures*, Hamish Hamilton, 1954

Huxley, Elspeth, *White Man's Country: Lord Delamere and the Making of Kenya*, 2 vols., London, Macmillan, 1935

—— *Red Strangers*, London, Chatto & Windus, 1939

—— *Race and Politics in Kenya* (with Margery Perham), London, Faber & Faber, 1944

—— *Settlers of Kenya*, London, Longmans Green, 1948

—— *The Sorcerer's Apprentice*, London, Chatto & Windus, 1948

—— *No Easy Way: A History of the Kenya Farmers' Association and Unga Ltd.*, Nairobi, East African Standard, 1957

—— *The Flame Trees of Thika: Memories of an African Childhood*, London, Chatto & Windus, 1959

—— *A New Earth*, London, Chatto & Windus, 1960

—— *The Mottled Lizard*, London, Chatto & Windus, 1962

—— *Forks and Hope*, London, Chatto & Windus, 1964

—— *Nellie: Letters from Africa*, London, Weidenfeld & Nicolson, 1980

—— *Out in the Midday Sun*, London, Chatto & Windus, 1985

—— *Nine Faces of Kenya*, London, Harvill Press, 1990

—— and Arnold Curtis (eds), *Pioneers' Scrapbook: Reminiscences of Kenya 1890 to 1968*, London, Evans Bros, 1980

Huxley, Julian, *Africa View*, London, Chatto & Windus, 1931

Ingham, Kenneth, *A History of East Africa*, London, Longmans, 1962

Jackson, Sir Frederick, *Early Days in East Africa*, London, E. Arnold, 1930

Jewell, John H. A., *Mombasa, the Friendly Town*, Nairobi, East African Publishing House, 1976

Joelson, F. S., *Rhodesia and East Africa*, London, East Africa & Rhodesia, 1958

Johnson, John, (ed.), *Colony to Nation*, Banham, Norfolk, Erskine Press, 2002

Johnson, Osa, *I Married Adventure*, London, Hutchinson, 1940

Joseph, Tommy, *Why There were Jews in Nakuru: Their Story*, Haifa, Israel, privately published, 1998

Kanogo, Tabitha, *Squatters and the Roots of Mau Mau*, London, James Currey, 1987

Karmali, Joan, *A School in Kenya: Hospital Hill 1949–1973*, Upton-on-Severn, Square One, 2002

Kearton, Cherry, *In the Land of the Lion*, London, Arrowsmith, 1929

—— and James Barnes, *Through Central Africa from East to West*, London, Cassell, 1915

Kenyatta, Jomo, *Facing Mt Kenya*, London, Secker & Warburg, 1938

Kuczynski, R. R., *Demographic Survey of the British Colonial Empire*, vol. 2, London, Oxford University Press, 1949,

Leakey, L. S. B., *By the Evidence, Memoirs, 1932–1951*, New York and London, Harcourt Brace Jovanovich, 1974

—— *White African*, London, Hodder & Stoughton, 1937

Leys, Norman M., *Kenya*, London, Hogarth Press, 1924

—— *A Last Chance in Kenya*, London, Hogarth Press, 1931

—— *The Colour Bar in East Africa*, London, Hogarth Press, 1941

Lipscomb, J. E., *White Africans*, London, Faber & Faber, 1955

—— *We Built a Country*, London, Faber & Faber, 1956

Lonsdale, John, *Politics in Kenya*, Edinburgh, Edinburgh University Centre for African Studies, 1992

—— 'The Politics of Conquest: The British in Western Kenya, 1894–1908', *Historical Journal*, vol. 20, no. 4, 1977

Lovell, Mary S., *Straight on Till Morning: The Life of Beryl Markham*, London, Hutchinson, 1987

Low, D. A. and Alison Smith (eds) *History of East Africa*, vol. 3, Oxford, Clarendon Press, 1976

Lugard, F. D., *The Rise of Our East African Empire*, 2 vols, London, William Blackwood & Son, 1893

Lyell, Denis D., *The African Elephant and Its Hunters*, London, Heath Cranton, 1924

Lytton, Earl of (Noel), *The Desert and the Green*, London, Macdonald, 1957

McDermott, P. L., *British East Africa, or IBEA*, London, Chapman & Hall, 1893

Macdonald, J. R. L., *Soldiering and Surveying in British East Africa*, London, Edward Arnold, 1897

Maciel, Mervyn, *Bwana Karani*, Braunton, Merlin Books, 1985

Macmillan, Allister (compiler), *Eastern Africa and Rhodesia*, London, W. H. and L. Collingridge, 1930

Mangat, J. S., *A History of the Asians in East Africa c.1886 to 1945*, Oxford, Clarendon Press, 1969

Markham, Beryl, *West with the Night*, London, Harrap, 1942

Maxon, R. M., *John Ainsworth and the Making of Kenya*, Lanham, Maryland, University Press of America, 1980

Meinertzhagen, Richard, *Kenya Diary*, Edinburgh and London, Oliver & Boyd, 1957

Miller, Charles, *The Lunatic Express*, London, Macdonald, 1971

—— *Battle for the Bundu: The First World War in East Africa*, New York, Macmillan, 1974

Mitchell, Sir Philip, *African Afterthoughts*, London, Hutchinson, 1954

Money, Roger Noel, *Ginia, My Kenya Coffee Shamba 1918–1939*, Perth, privately published, 2000

Morell, Virginia, *Ancestral Passions: The Leakey Family*, Simon & Schuster, 1995

Moyse-Bartlett, H., *The King's African Rifles*, Aldershot, Gale & Polden, 1956

Mungeam, G. H., *British Rule in Kenya 1895–1912*, Oxford, Clarendon Press, 1966

Munro, J. Forbes, *Colonial Rule and the Kamba*, Oxford, Clarendon Press, 1975

Ogot, Bethwell, *Historical Dictionary of Kenya*, Metuchen, N.J., Scarecrow Press, 1981

Oliver, Roland, *The Missionary Factor in East Africa*, London, Longmans, 1954

—— and Gervase Mathew (eds), *History of East Africa*, vol. 1, Oxford, Clarendon Press, 1963

O'Shea, T. J., *Farming and Planting in British East Africa*, Nairobi, Newland & Tarlton, 1917

Oswald, Felix, *Alone in the Sleeping-Sickness Country*, London, Kegan Paul, Trench, Trübner & Co., 1915

Paice, Edward, *Lost Lion of Empire: The Life of 'Cape to Cairo' Grogan*, London, HarperCollins, 2001

Patience, Kevin, *Steam in East Africa*, Nairobi, privately published, printed by Kenya Litho Ltd, 1976

Patterson, J. H., *The Man Eaters of Tsavo*, London, Macmillan, 1907

—— *In the Grip of the Nyika*, London, Macmillan, 1910

Percival, A. Blayney, *A Game Ranger's Note Book*, London, Nisbet, 1924

—— *A Game Ranger on Safari*, London, Nisbet, 1928

Perham, Margery, *East African Journey: Kenya and Tanganyika 1929–30*, London, Faber & Faber, 1976

—— *Lugard: The Years of Adventure*, London, Collins, 1956

Peters, Carl, *New Light on Dark Africa*, London, Ward, Lock, 1891

Playne, Somerset (ed. F. Holderness Gale), *East Africa (British): Its History, People, Commerce, Industries and Resources*, London, Foreign & Colonial Compiling and Publishing Co., 1908–09

Pollard, John, *African Zoo Man: The Life Story of Raymond Hook*, London, Robert Hale, 1963

Polnay, Peter de, *My Road: An Autobiography*, London, W. H. Allen, 1978

Powys, Llewelyn, *Black Laughter*, London, Macdonald, 1953

—— *Ebony and Ivory*, London, Grant Richards, 1923

—— *The Letters of Llewelyn Powys*, ed. Louis Willkinson, London, John Lane, 1943

Preston, R. O., *Descending the Great Rift Valley*, Nairobi, Colonial Printing Works, no date

—— *The Genesis of Kenya Colony*, Nairobi, Colonial Printing Works, no date

—— *Oriental Nairobi*, Nairobi, Colonial Printing Works, 1938

Prince, Vivien Schapira, *Kenya: The Years of Change*, New York, Carlton Press, 1987

Rayne, Henry, *The Ivory Raiders*, London, Heinemann, 1923

Redley, Michael Gordon, 'The Politics of a Predicament: The White Community in Kenya 1918–32', Cambridge University Ph.D., 1976

Reece, Alys, *To My Wife – 50 Camels*, London, Harvill, 1963

Remole, Robert Alan, 'White Settlers, or the Foundation of European Agricultural Settlement in Kenya', Harvard University Ph.D., 1959

Riddell, Florence, *Kenya Mist*, London, Thornton Butterworth, 1924

Rockwell, Robert H., *My Way of Hunting: The Adventurous Life of a Taxidermist*, London, Robert Hale, 1956

Rodwell, Edward, *The Mombasa Club*, Mombasa, Mombasa Club, 1988

Rogers, Peter, 'The British and the Kikuyu 1890–1905: A Reassessment', *Journal of African History*, vol. 20, no. 2, 1979, pp. 255–69

Roosevelt, Theodore, *African Game Trails*, London, John Murray, 1910

Rosberg, Carl G. and John Nottingham, *The Myth of 'Mau Mau', Nationalism in Kenya*, New York, Hoover Institution, 1966

Ross, W. McGregor, *Kenya from Within: A Short Political History*, London, Allen & Unwin, 1927

Rotberg, Robert, *Joseph Thomson and the Exploration of Africa*, London, Chatto & Windus, 1971

Round-Turner, David (compiler), *Nairobi Club: A Centenary Celebration*, Nairobi, Nairobi Club, 2001

Routledge, W. S. and K. Routledge, *The Akikuyu of British East Africa*, London, Edward Arnold, 1910

Ruark, Robert, *Use Enough Gun*, London, Hamish Hamilton, 1967

Salvadori, Cynthia, *We Came in Dhows*, 3 vols, Nairobi, Paperchase Kenya Ltd, 1996

Salvadori, Max, *La Colonisation européenne au Kenya*, Paris, Larose Editeurs, 1938

Sanger, Clyde, *Malcolm MacDonald, Bringing an End to Empire*, Liverpool, Liverpool University Press, 1995

Scott, Pamela, *A Nice Place to Live*, Wilton, Michael Russell, 1991

Seaton, Henry, *Lion in the Morning*, London, John Murray, 1963

Seymour, John, *One Man's Africa*, London, Eyre & Spottiswoode, 1955

Simpson, Alyse, *The Land that Never was*, London, Selwyn & Blount, 1937

Smith, Frederick Alfred, *White Roots in Africa*, London, Janus Publishing, 1997

Soldati, Gabriele (trans. Michael Cunningham), *The Pioneer: The African Adventure of Benedict Falla*, Slough, St Paul's Publications, 1991 (for Istituto Missioni Consolata)

Sorrenson, M. P. K., *Origins of European Settlement in Kenya*, Nairobi, Oxford University Press, 1968

Spencer, Ian, 'Settler Dominance, Agricultural Production and the Second World War in Kenya', *Journal of African History*, vol. 21, no. 4, 1980, pp. 497–514

Stapleton, James W., *The Gate Hangs Well*, Hammond, Hammond & Co., 1956

Stoneham, C. T., *Big Stuff: African Big Game and Its Hunters*, London, Jenkins, 1954

Strange, Nora K., *A Wife in Kenya*, London, Stanley Paul, 1925

—— *Kenya To-Day*, London, Stanley Paul, 1934

Strayer, Robert W., *The Making of Mission Communities in East Africa: Anglicans and Africans in Colonial Kenya, 1875–1935*, London, Heinemann, 1978

Thomas, Graham F., *Far from the Valleys*, Lewes, Sussex, Book Guild, 1995

Thomas, H. B., 'George Wilson and Dagoretti Fort', *Uganda Journal*, vol. 23, no. 2, September 1959

Thomson, Joseph, *Through Masai Land*, London, Sampson, Low & Marston, 1885

Throup, David, *Economic and Social Origins of Mau Mau*, London, James Currey, 1988

Thurman, Judith, *Isak Dinesen: The Life of Karen Blixen*, London, Weidenfeld & Nicolson, 1982

Thurston, Anne, 'The Intensification of Smallholder Agriculture in Kenya' (cyclostyled), Oxford, Rhodes House Library, Oxford Development Records Project, Report 6, 1984

Tidrick, Kathryn, *Empire and the English Character*, London, I.B. Tauris, 1990

Tignor, Robert L., *The Colonial Transformation of Kenya: The Kamba, Kikuyu and Maasai from 1900 to 1939*, Princeton, N.J., Princeton University Press, 1976

Trench, Charles Chenevix, *Men Who Ruled Kenya*, London, Radcliffe Press, 1993

—— *The Desert's Dusty Face*, London, William Blackwood & Sons, 1964

Trzebinski, Errol, *The Kenya Pioneers*, London, Heinemann, 1985

—— *Silence Will Speak: A Study of the Life of Denys Finch Hatton and his Relationship with Karen Blixen*, London, Heinemann, 1977

—— *The Lives of Beryl Markham*, London, Heinemann, 1993

—— *The Life and Death of Lord Erroll*, London, Fourth Estate, 2000

Van Zwanenberg, R. M. A., *Colonial Capitalism and Labour in Kenya, 1919–1939*, Nairobi, East African Literature Bureau, 1975

Vere-Hodge, E. R., *Imperial British East Africa Company*, London, Macmillan, 1960

Ward, H. F. and J. W. Milligan (compilers), *Handbook of British East Africa 1912–13*, London and Nairobi, 1913

Wasserman, Gary, *The Politics of Decolonization: Kenya Europeans and the Land Issue*, Cambridge, Cambridge University Press, 1976

Watkins, Elizabeth, *Jomo's Jailor*, Watlington, Britwell Books, 1993

Watt, Rachel Stuart, *In the Heart of Savagedom*, London, Marshall Bros, 1913

Watteville, Vivienne de, *Out in the Blue*, London, Methuen, 1927

Waugh, Evelyn, *A Tourist in Africa*, London, Chapman & Hall, 1960

—— (ed. Michael Davie), *The Diaries of Evelyn Waugh*, London, Weidenfeld & Nicolson, 1976

Weisbord, Robert G., *African Zion: The Attempt to Establish a Jewish Colony in the East Africa Protectorate 1903–1905*, Philadelphia, Pennsylvania, Jewish Publication Society of America, 1968

Weller, Henry Owen, *Kenya without Prejudice*, London, East Africa, 1931

White, Stewart E., *The Land of Footprints*, London, Nelson, 1913

—— *The Rediscovered Country*, London, Hodder & Stoughton, no date but 1915

Wild, Percy Turner, *Bwana Polisi*, Braunton, Devon, Merlin Books, 1993

Wilson, C. J., *The Story of the East African Mounted Rifles*, Nairobi, East African Standard, no date

Wolff, Richard D., *The Economics of Colonialism: Britain and Kenya, 1870–1930*, New Haven, Connecticut, Yale University Press, 1974

Wymer, Norman, *The Man from the Cape*, London, Evans Bros, 1959

Youé, Christopher P., *Robert Thorne Coryndon*, Gerrards Cross, Colin Smythe, 1986

Young, Francis Brett, *Marching on Tanga*, London, Heinemann, 1917

Index